Essentials of Testing and Assessment

A Practical Guide for Counselors, Social Workers, and Psychologists

Edward S. Neukrug
Old Dominion University

R. Charles Fawcett
Old Dominion University

BROOKS/COLE
CENGAGE Learning™

Australia • Brazil • Japan • Korea • Mexico • Singapore • Spain • United Kingdom • United States

BROOKS/COLE
CENGAGE Learning

**Essentials of Testing and Assessment:
A Practical Guide for Counselors, Social
Workers, and Psychologists**
Edward S. Neukrug, R. Charles Fawcett

Executive Editor: Lisa Gebo

Senior Acquisitions Editor: Marquita
Flemming

Assistant Editor: Monica Arvin

Editorial Assistant: Christine Northup

Executive Marketing Manager: Caroline
Concilla

Marketing Assistant: Rebecca Weisman

Senior Marketing Communications
Manager: Tami Strang

Project Manager, Editorial Production:
Christine Sosa

Creative Director: Rob Hugel

Art Director: Vernon Boes

Print Buyer: Barbara Britton

Permissions Editor: Sarah Harkrader

Production Service: Matrix Productions

Text Designer: John Edeen

Photo Researcher: Sue Howard

Copy Editor: Janet Tilden

Illustrator: Scientific Illustrators

Cover Designer: William Stanton

Cover Image: Getty Images

Compositor: Cadmus Professional
Communications

For product information and technology assistance, contact us at
Cengage Learning Customer & Sales Support, 1-800-354-9706

For permission to use material from this text or product,
submit all requests online at **www.cengage.com/permissions**
Further permissions questions can be emailed to
permissionrequest@cengage.com

Library of Congress Control Number: 2005924444

ISBN-13: 978-0-534-63320-2

ISBN-10: 0-534-63320-X

Brooks/Cole
10 Davis Drive
Belmont, CA 94002
USA

Cengage Learning is a leading provider of customized learning solutions with
office locations around the globe, including Singapore, the United Kingdom,
Australia, Mexico, Brazil, and Japan. Locate your local office at
international.cengage.com/region

Cengage Learning products are represented in Canada by
Nelson Education, Ltd.

To learn more about Brooks/Cole, visit **www.cengage.com/brookscole**

Purchase any of our products at your local college store or at our preferred
online store **www.ichapters.com**

Printed in the United States of America
5 6 7 11 10 09

To my father and my brother, the real math experts in the family.
—Ed Neukrug

To my mother and father who always support and believe in me.
—Charlie Fawcett

Brief Contents

Contents

SECTION TWO

Test Worthiness and Test Statistics   41

CHAPTER 3

Test Worthiness: Validity, Reliability, Practicality, and Cross-Cultural Fairness   43

C H A P T E R   4

Statistical Concepts: Making Meaning Out of Raw Scores   65

C H A P T E R   5

Statistical Concepts: Creating New Scores to Interpret Test Data   81

SECTION THREE

Commonly Used Assessment Techniques   103

CHAPTER 6

Assessment of Educational Ability: Survey Battery, Diagnostic, Readiness, and Cognitive Ability Tests   106

C H A P T E R   7

Assessment of Intelligence   128

C H A P T E R   8

Career and Occupational Assessment: Interest Inventories, Multiple Aptitude, and Special Aptitude Tests   147

C H A P T E R   9

Clinical Assessment: Objective and Projective Personality Tests   168

C H A P T E R   1 0

Informal Assessment: Observation, Rating Scales, Classification Methods, and Records and Personal Documents   195

SECTION FOUR

Diagnosis and Writing the Assessment Report   215

CHAPTER 11

Diagnosis in the Assessment Process   217

CHAPTER 12

The Assessment Report Process: The Interview, Assessment Techniques, Environmental Assessment, and the Report   233

A P P E N D I X   A

Websites of Codes of Ethics of Select Mental Health Professional Associations

A P P E N D I X   B

Code of Fair Testing Practices in Education

A P P E N D I X   C

Supplemental Statistical Equations

A P P E N D I X   D

Converting Percentiles from z Scores

A P P E N D I X   E

Assessment Report

Preface

I was talking with one of my graduate students after he had finished taking my course on testing and assessment when he told me, "You should write a book on this course like the way you teach it." I replied, "You know, I've always thought that those traditional books just cover too much stuff, and it's all I can do to get through the basics during the semester. From the moment I walk into class until the end of the semester, I'm working non-stop on completing all of the information necessary to give the student a broad understanding of testing and assessment." I added, "I don't know why those books have all that additional stuff in them—there's no way you can cover it all." Next thing I knew, he was on the phone talking to publishers. Soon, after a discussion with my own publisher, *we* had a contract. Yes, that graduate student is now my colleague, Charlie Fawcett, who is also the co-author of this text. Charlie has come far since that initial conversation, and he is now on faculty with us here at Old Dominion University. It has been a pleasure writing with him, and we have really developed as a team. As for the book—it is what we first planned. It covers the essentials of testing and assessment, nothing more. However, don't let that fool you. The essentials include quite a bit of information! The book is written in a down-to-earth fashion with stories and vignettes that highlight the learning. We are confident the text will offer you all that is needed in an overview course on testing and assessment.

The text is divided into four sections: Section One, History and Current Professional Issues; Section Two, Test Worthiness and Test Statistics; Section Three, Commonly Used Assessment Techniques; and Section Four, Diagnosis and Writing the Assessment Report. Brief definitions of major concepts are provided in the margins, and a glossary highlighting major terms and concepts is included at the end of the book. The following is a brief overview of the four sections of the text. In addition, a short introduction is provided at the beginning of each section.

Section One includes two chapters: Chapter 1, History of Testing and Assessment and Chapter 2, Ethical, Legal, and Professional Issues in Assessment. These chapters offer an overview of the field of testing and assessment and provide a link between the history of assessment and issues that affect us today.

Chapter 1 begins by discussing the differences between testing and assessment and points out how their current definitions are directly related to their history. We then trace the history of assessment from ancient history to the development of modern-day assessment instruments. Along the way, we highlight some of the people who were critical to the development of assessment measures and discuss some of the many controversial issues that arose. The chapter nears its conclusion by examining the current categories of assessment instruments, including ability testing (achievement and aptitude testing), personality assessment, and informal assessment. We finish by raising a number of concerns that continue to face us today as we administer assessment instruments.

Chapter 2 is about the complex ethical, legal, and professional issues that are faced frequently by individuals who are assessing others. We begin by recognizing the complexity of ethical decision-making and then identify some important ethical issues, including identifying codes and standards critical to testing and assessment. We go on to discuss the importance of wise and ethical decision-making, and we identify a number of laws that have been passed and lawsuits resolved that impinge on the use of tests and the assessment process. The chapter concludes with a discussion of some important professional issues, including professional associations that address assessment, accreditation standards of professional associations, assessment as a holistic process, how assessment can be an aid to the counseling process, and concerns about cross-cultural issues in assessment.

Section Two of the text addresses test worthiness and test statistics. The three chapters that make up this section examine how tests are created, scored, and interpreted. These chapters all use test statistics in some manner to explain the concepts being presented. In this section we demonstrate how collecting and interpreting test data is a deliberate and planned process that involves a scientific approach to the understanding of differences among people.

Chapter 3, on test worthiness, looks at four critical areas in test development and test usage: (1) *validity:* whether a test measures what it is supposed to measure; (2) *reliability:* whether the score an individual received on a test is an accurate measure of his or her true score; (3) *cross-cultural fairness:* whether the score the individual has obtained is a true reflection of the individual, and not a function of cultural bias inherent in the test, and (4) *practicality:* whether it makes sense to use a test in a particular situation. After examining these four factors, we conclude with a discussion of five steps to use in order to assure test worthiness when selecting a test to administer. The chapter also provides an explanation of the statistic called "correlation coefficient," as it is core to understanding much of what is presented in this chapter.

Chapter 4 starts with the basics: an examination of raw scores. In this chapter we note that raw scores generally provide little meaningful information about a set of scores, and we provide ways that we can manipulate those scores to make sense out of a set of data. Thus, in this chapter we examine how the following concepts are used to help us understand raw scores: frequency distributions; histograms and frequency polygons; the normal curve; skewed curves; measures of central tendency such as the mean, median and mode; and measures of variability, such as the range, semi-interquartile range, and standard deviation.

Chapter 5, on creating new scores to interpret test data, examines how raw scores are converted to what are called "derived" scores so that individuals can have an easier understanding of what raw scores mean. We start by distinguishing between norm-referenced testing and criterion-referenced testing because these two ways of understanding test scores are quite different, and derived scores are mostly associated with norm-referenced testing. Next, we discuss specific types of derived scores, such as (1) percentiles; (2) standard scores, including: z scores, T scores, Deviation IQs, stanines, sten scores, NCE scores, college and graduate school entrance exam scores (e.g., SATs, GREs, and ACTs) and publisher-type scores; and (3) developmental norms, such as age comparisons and grade equivalents. The chapter nears its conclusion with a discussion of standard error of measurement, which is a mechanism for estimating how close an individual's obtained score is to his or her true score. The chapter ends with a brief discussion of nominal, ordinal, interval, and ratio scales of measurement, in which we explore how each type of scale has unique attributes that may limit the statistical calculations we can perform, and we note that different kinds of assessment instruments use different kinds of scales.

Section Three examines some of the commonly used assessment techniques in the realms of educational ability, intelligence testing, career and occupational assessment, clinical assessment, and conducting an informal assessment. Five chapters make up this section: Chapter 6: Assessment of Educational Ability, Chapter 7: Assessment of Intelligence, Chapter 8: Career and Occupational Assessment, Chapter 9: Clinical Assessment, and Chapter 10: Informal Assessment.

Chapter 6 examines tests typically given in schools to measure what students have learned and what they are capable of learning. First we define the purposes of tests of educational ability and then identify the various categories of educational ability tests, including survey battery achievement tests, diagnostic tests, readiness tests, and cognitive ability tests. Next, we examine some of the more popular tests in each category.

Chapter 7 examines our understanding of intellectual ability and how it has been used in the development of standardized tests of intelligence. Thus, in this chapter we offer a brief definition of intelligence testing and then provide an overview of some models of intelligence. This is followed by an examination of some of the better-known individual intelligence tests.

Chapter 8 examines the kinds of tests that can help an individual make a decision about his or her occupational or career path. Thus, in this chapter we examine tests that are helpful in occupational and career counseling, including interest inventories, which are a type of personality assessment, and special aptitude and multiple aptitude tests, which help an individual identify what he or she is good at doing.

Chapter 9 examines the process of using tests for clinical assessment. We start by underscoring the fact that such assessment has a wide variety of applications and can be an important tool for the clinician or researcher. The chapter then defines clinical assessment and examines some of the major objective and projective tests used in the clinical assessment process.

Chapter 10 covers informal assessment procedures. We start by defining informal assessment and then identify a number of different kinds of informal assessment techniques, including observation, rating scales, classification schemes, and records and personal documents. As the chapter continues we discuss the test worthiness of informal assessment, and this is followed by some final thoughts regarding informal assessment.

The last section of the text, Section Four examines how to make a diagnosis (Chapter 11), which is a type of an assessment of an individual, and then looks at the process of writing a comprehensive test report, which partly involves the use of diagnosis (Chapter 12).

Chapter 11 starts by discussing the importance of making a diagnosis and then describes the *Diagnostic and Statistical Manual, Fourth Edition–Text Revision* (DSM-IV-TR). We offer a brief history of the DSM-IV-TR and discuss its five axes that are used in making a diagnosis. We also show how a five-axes diagnosis is made and present some case studies for additional practice. We conclude the chapter with a discussion of the importance of diagnosis in the total assessment process.

Chapter 12 takes a look at the process of gathering information about clients and writing an effective assessment report. We discuss the purpose of the assessment report and then examine how to conduct the clinical interview, choose appropriate assessment techniques, and conduct an environmental assessment. The second part of the chapter offers ways of writing an assessment report based on the information one has gathered. How a diagnosis is integrated into the report is also shown in this part of the chapter. We use information from a fictitious client to show how each section of the assessment report would be written. The resulting five-page assessment report can be found in Appendix D of the text. We think you will find this example helpful in writing your own assessment reports.

We believe this book is comprehensive without being overbearing. The text provides an overview of testing and assessment in a readable and sometimes even enjoyable fashion, and we hope that after reading it, you come away with a new appreciation of testing and assessment.

Acknowledgments

We would like to give a special thanks to Patrizia Zorzoli for her translation of segments of Jean Esquirol's 1838 book *Des maladies mentales considerees sous les rapports medical, hygienique, et medico-legal*, and Dr. Frederick Lubich for his translation of Carl Jung's 1904 article, Untersuchungen über assoziationen gesunder. We would also like to extend our gratitude to Dr. John Nunnery for his technical review of the statistical portions of the book. The assistance given from Brooks/Cole publishing was critical, and we would particularly like to thank the following people: Marquita Flemming, Senior Acquisitions Editor, for her ongoing support and willingness to publish this text; Christine Sosa, Associate Production Project Manager, for overseeing the production of the text; Christine Northup, Editorial Assistant, for her ongoing support with the project; Monica Arvin, Assistant Editor, for her help in the development of the instructor's manual; and Sarah Harkrader, Permissions Editor, for her assistance with copyright permissions. Finally, a special thanks to Merrill Peterson from Matrix Productions who coordinated the production of the text, as well as Janet Tilden who did the copy editing.

History and Current Professional Issues

This first section of *Essentials of Testing and Assessment* includes two chapters: Chapter 1: History of Testing and Assessment, and Chapter 2: Ethical, Legal, and Professional Issues in Assessment. These chapters offer an overview of the field of testing and assessment and provide a link between the history of assessment and issues that continue to affect us today.

In the first chapter we examine the history of testing and assessment and see how the past has shaped current methods of assessment. We begin this chapter by discussing the differences between testing and assessment and pointing out how their current definitions are directly related to their history. Then we trace the history of assessment, starting with ancient history and working our way to the development of modern-day assessment instruments. Along the way, we highlight some of the people whose contributions were critical to the development of assessment measures, and we discuss some of the many controversial issues that arose.

Near the end of the chapter we examine the current categories of assessment instruments, including ability testing (testing in the cognitive realm); personality assessment (testing in the affective realm); and informal assessment techniques. We also describe how the book is configured around the various kinds of assessment categories we just noted. The chapter concludes by raising a number of concerns that continue to face us today as we administer assessment instruments.

In Chapter 2 we examine the many complex ethical, legal, and professional issues that confront individuals who are assessing others. We start by identifying a number of ethical codes that help guide the practice of mental health professionals, paying special attention to the codes of the American Counseling Association and the American Psychological Association because of their greater emphasis on assessment. This part of the chapter offers a brief overview of the assessment aspects of these important guidelines. Next, we explore three standards that are also used to help guide the practitioner: Standards for Qualifications of Test Users, the Code of Fair Testing Practices in Education, and Responsibilities of Users of Standardized Tests (RUST). This part of the chapter concludes with a discussion of ethical decision-making.

As the chapter continues, we examine a number of laws that have been passed and lawsuits resolved that impinge on the use of tests. Most of these legal constraints involve issues of confidentiality, fairness, and test worthiness (reliability, validity, practicality, and cross-cultural fairness). The last section of the chapter first highlights two professional associations in the field of assessment: The Association for Assessment in Counseling and Education (AACE) and Division 5 of the American Psychological Association: Evaluation, Measurement, and Statistics. Next, we identify three organizations that address curriculum standards in the area of assessment, including the American Psychological Association (APA), the National Association of School Psychologists (NASP), and the Council for the Accreditation of Counseling and Related Educational Programs (CACREP). We discuss the importance of recognizing that assessment works best when it is a holistic process. Next, we explore the ways in which the use of assessment techniques can enhance the counseling process. The chapter concludes with a discussion of cross-cultural issues related to bias in testing.

History of Testing and Assessment

"Pens and pencils down!" Those words still send chills down my spine. With millions of children and adults frightened by the thought of taking a test, this is not a pretty picture. But is there value in this sometimes-terrifying experience? We'll let you answer that question after you have finished reading this book. But how did test-taking start? That question will be answered in this chapter. (Ed Neukrug)

In this chapter we will examine the history of testing and assessment. First, we'll explore the differences between testing and assessment and point out how their current definitions are directly related to their history. We will then take a ride through the history of assessment, starting with ancient history and working our way to the development of modern-day assessment instruments. Along the way, we will highlight some of the people who were critical to the development of assessment measures and discuss some of the controversial issues that arose. As the chapter nears its conclusion, we will examine the current categories of assessment instruments, and we will finish by raising a number of ongoing concerns surrounding the use of assessment instruments.

Distinguishing Between Testing and Assessment

Assessment
A broad array of evaluative procedures

Today, the term *assessment* includes a broad array of evaluative procedures that yield information about a person. Assessment procedures include the clinical interview; informal assessment techniques such as observation, rating scales, classification techniques, and records and personal documents; personality tests such as objective tests, projective tests, and interest inventories; and ability tests, such as achievement tests and aptitude tests (see Figure 1.1).

Tests are a subset of assessment techniques that yield scores based on the gathering of collective data (e.g., adding a number of correct answers on a

3

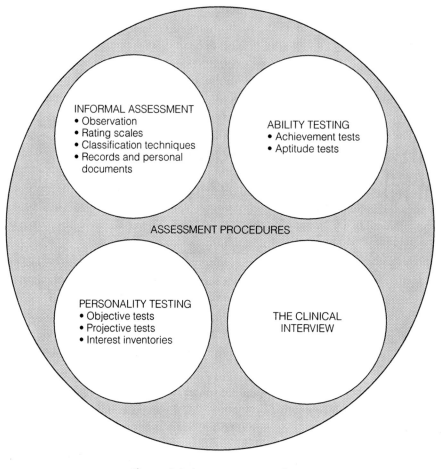

INFORMAL ASSESSMENT
- Observation
- Rating scales
- Classification techniques
- Records and personal documents

ABILITY TESTING
- Achievement tests
- Aptitude tests

ASSESSMENT PROCEDURES

PERSONALITY TESTING
- Objective tests
- Projective tests
- Interest inventories

THE CLINICAL INTERVIEW

Figure 1.1 Assessment procedures

Tests
Instruments
that yield scores
based on col-
lected data—
a subset of
assessment

multiple-choice exam). Assessment procedures can be formal, where the procedure is scientifically shown to be sound, or valid and reliable; or informal, which
implies that such rigor has not been demonstrated, although the procedure might
still yield valuable information.

Generally, the greater the number of procedures used in assessing an individual, the greater the likelihood that they will yield a clearer snapshot of the
client. Thus, using multiple assessment procedures should *always* be considered

*Multiple assess-
ment procedures
should always
be considered.*

when making important decisions about a client's life. In this text we will examine a broad array of formal and informal assessment procedures, all of which can
be used in the decision-making process (Halperin & McKay, 1998; Meyers et al.,
2001). But let's start at the beginning and see how events of the past have moved
us toward our current use of assessment instruments.

The History of Assessment

The history of assessment goes back to ancient times, but it was not until the early part of the twentieth century that the modern era of assessment began. Let's examine some of the changes in assessment that have taken place over the centuries.

Ancient History

How long has assessment been around? We might say that Abraham's loyalty was assessed when God asked him to kill his son Isaac, and no doubt informal assessment procedures were around long before Abraham. The Chinese government is often given credit for developing one of the first widely used tests when it began to test individuals for fitness to work in government positions in approximately 2200 B.C.E. (DuBois, 1970). The selection process was grueling, with testing done in hundreds of small cubicles or huts. Under the intense strain of the examinations, some examinees would die (Cohen & Swerdlik, 1999). The testing was finally abolished in 1905 (DuBois, 1970). Another ancient example of assessment is found in passages from Plato's (428–327 B.C.E.) writing that indicate the Greeks assessed both the intellectual and physical ability of men when screening for state service (Doyle, 1974).

Precursors to Modern-Day Test Development

As the concepts of experimentation and controlled research spread throughout the scientific community during the 1800s, physicians and philosophers began to apply these research principles to the understanding of people, particularly the human psyche. One of the first individuals to put these concepts into action was a physician named Jean Esquirol (1772–1840). Working in the French mental asylums, he began to use language to identify varying levels of intelligence of his patients (Zusne, 1984; Drummond, 2004). Some consider this the forerunner of verbal IQ. Esquirol began to realize that mental retardation or "idiocy" was not an illness, but rather a developmental deficiency as compared to similar-aged peers (Esquirol, 1838, p. 76). At around the same time, another Frenchman, Edouard Sequin (1812–1880), who worked with the mentally retarded, developed the form board to increase his patients' motor control and sensory discrimination. (Some consider this the forerunner of IQ based on performance measures.) Versions of the form board, which is similar to the toy in which children place shapes in their respective grooves, are still used today in some performance-oriented IQ tests (DuBois, 1970).

Meanwhile, during the mid-1800s, Charles Darwin (1809–1882) developed his theory of evolution. Intrigued by Darwin's theory, scientists soon became engrossed in trying to understand the development of the human species (Watson, 1968). For instance, Sir Francis Galton (1822–1911), Darwin's cousin, became fascinated by the differences among people (Flugel, 1941; Gillham, 2001). Galton hypothesized that individuals who had a quicker reaction time and

Jean Esquirol Used language to identify intelligence—forerunner of verbal IQ

Edouard Sequin Developed the form board to increase motor control—forerunner of performance IQ

Sir Francis Galton Examined relationship of sensory motor responses to intelligence

stronger grip strength might be superior intellectually. His curiosity led him to examine the relationship among such characteristics, and his research spurred others to develop the statistical concept of correlation coefficient, which describes the strength of the relationship among variables (Dubois, 1970). Calculating the correlation coefficient has become an important tool in the development and refinement of tests.

Wilhelm Wundt
Developed one of the first psychological laboratories

James Cattell
Brought statistics to mental testing—coined term *mental test*

Wilhelm Wundt (1832–1920) set out to create "a new domain of science" that he called physiological psychology, which later became known as psychology. Around 1875, at the University of Leipzig, Wundt developed one of the first psychological laboratories that used experimental research. Many of the experiments in Wundt's laboratory studied reaction time of hearing, sight, and other senses in response to stimuli (Watson, 1968). James McKeen Cattell (1860–1944), a doctoral student under Wundt who later was greatly inspired by Galton, became one of the earliest psychologists to use statistical concepts in understanding the person (Roback, 1961). Cattell's main emphasis became testing mental functions, and he is known for coining the term *mental test* (Watson, 1968).

The Emergence of Ability Tests (Testing in the Cognitive Domain)

Influenced by the new scientific approach to understanding human nature, researchers at the beginning of the twentieth century began to develop instruments that could scientifically measure an individual's abilities. This era saw the emergence of ability tests, including individual intelligence tests and group tests of ability.

Individual Intelligence Testing

Alfred Binet
Created first modern intelligence test

Lewis Terman
Enhanced Binet's work to create Stanford-Binet intelligence test

Intelligence quotient
Chronological age divided by mental age

Commissioned in 1904 by the Ministry of Public Education in Paris, Alfred Binet (1857–1911) was eager to develop an intelligence test to assist in the integration of "sub-normal" children into the schools. Highly critical of the processes used for diagnosing mental deficiency, Binet and his colleague Theophile Simon studied the ability level of healthy children between the ages of 3 and 12 years. The information gained from their observations was then used to develop the first modern-day intelligence test (Watson, 1968). A relatively short time later, Lewis Terman (1877–1956), from Stanford University, began analyzing and methodically gathering extensive normative data on Binet and Simon's scale from hundreds of children in the Stanford area (Minton, 1988). Based on these data, Terman made a number of revisions to the original scale. Originally called the Stanford Revision of the Binet and Simon scale, the test later took on the name Stanford-Binet, which it continues to use today (Minton, 1988). Terman was the first to incorporate in his test the ratio of chronological age and mental age, calling it the "intelligence quotient" or "IQ" (Minton, 1988) (see Box 1.1).

BOX 1.1
Developing the Notion of "IQ"

Lewis Terman wanted to develop a logical and relatively easy way of expressing an individual's intelligence. Using the data from his research, he quickly realized that he could compute a ratio score for each child by dividing a child's mental score (the age score at which the child performed) by the child's actual age. Thus, if a child was performing at the level of the average 12-year-old but was actually 9 years old, the ratio would be 12/9 or 1.33. Multiplying this number by 100 to eliminate the decimal point, would yield 133 as the intelligence quotient ("IQ")*. Use this method to determine the IQs of the children below, based on their mental age scores and their actual ages.

Child 1: mental age of 6 and chronological age of 8

Child 2: mental age of 16 and chronological age of 16.

Child 3: mental age of 10 and chronological age of 9.

Answer: Child 1: 75 (6/8 x 100), Child 2: 100 (16/16 x 100), Child 3: 111 (10/9 x 100).

---

* Note: IQ is no longer determined in this manner, and the current method of calculation will be discussed later in the text.

Group Tests of Ability (Group Testing in the Cognitive Domain)

Realizing the importance of obtaining accurate information from examinees, Terman and others developed standardized directions to use in testing and stressed the importance of having trained examiners administer tests individually (Geisinger, 1994; Thorndike & Lohman, 1990). However, it soon became clear that individual testing took an inordinate amount of time and was costly. During World War I, these practical concerns became paramount when it became critical to quickly administer tests of cognitive ability to large groups of recruits in order to place them in the military. Robert Yerkes, the president of the American Psychological Association, chaired a special committee that was appointed to create a screening test for these new recruits. The committee, composed of many well-known psychologists including Terman, was able to prepare a draft of the test in only four months (Geisinger, 2000). The original test the committee developed was known as the Army Alpha (see Box 1.2).

Robert Yerkes
Chairman of the committee that developed the Army Alpha

Army Alpha
First modern group test— used during WWI

Even though the instrument was far from perfect, it was a large step forward. The Army Alpha was administered to more than 1.7 million recruits in less than 2 years (Haney, 1981). Since there were many foreign-born recruits and large numbers of people who could not read, a second language-free version of the test, known as the Army Beta, was created. The Army Beta applied the use of form boards and mazes, and directions were given by pantomime so recruits could take the entire test without reading (Thorndike & Lohman, 1990). Although crude by today's standards, the Army Alpha and Army Beta ushered in the era of group tests of ability.

BOX 1.2
The Army Alpha Test

The Army Alpha test was created to place recruits in the military. Based on this test, it was found that the average mental age of the recruit was 13 (Thorndike & Lohman, 1990). Take the test below in the 3-minute time allotment given. After taking it, consider potential issues of bias and cultural fairness of the questions on the test.

The Army Alpha was used to determine placement in the armed forces during WWI. Below is an adaptation of the test, as printed in *Discover* magazine. Take the test and discuss your thoughts about it.

The average mental age of the recruits who took the Army Alpha test during WWI was approximately 13. Could you do better? You have three minutes to complete these sample questions, drawn verbatim from the original exam. (McKean, 1985)

The following sentences have been disarranged but can be unscrambled to make sense. Rearrange them and then answer whether each is true or false.

1. Bible earth the says inherit the the shall meek.   true   false
2. a battle in racket very tennis useful is   true   false

Answer the following questions:

3. If a train goes 200 yards in a sixth of a minute, how many feet does it go in a fifth of a second?
4. A U-boat makes 8 miles an hour under water and 15 miles on the surface. How long will it take to cross a 100-mile channel if it has to go two-fifths of the way under water?
5. The spark plug in a gas engine is found in the: crank case   manifold   cylinder   carburetor
6. The Brooklyn Nationals are called the: Giants   Orioles   Superbas   Indians
7. The product advertised as 99.44 per cent pure is:
   Arm & Hammer Baking Soda   Crisco   Ivory Soap   Toledo
8. The Pierce-Arrow is made in: Flint   Buffalo   Detroit   Toledo
9. The number of Zulu legs is: two   four   six   eight

Are the following words the same or opposite in meaning?

10.   vesper–matin   same   opposite
11.   aphorism–maxim   same   opposite

Find the next number in the series:

12.   74,   71,   65,   56,   44,   Answer:
13.   3,   6,   8,   16,   18,   Answer:

14. Select the image that belongs in the mirror: 15. & 16. What's missing in these pictures?

15.   16.

Answers: 1. true, 2. false, 3. twelve feet, 4. nine hours, 5. cylinder, 6. superbas, 7. Ivory Soap, 8. Buffalo, 9. two, 10. opposite, 11. same, 12. 29, 13. 36, 14. A, 15, spoon, 16. gramophone horn
Scoring: All items except 3, 4, 10, and 11 = 1.25 points. Items 3 and 4 = 1.875 points, Items 10 & 11 = .625 points. Add them all up, they equal your mental age. What is wrong with this test? Examine it for problems with content, history, cross-cultural contamination, and so forth.

Source: McKean, K. (1985). Intelligence: New ways to measure the wisdom of man. *Discover Magazine* 6(10), 28. Reprinted by permission of Disney Publications.

Recruits taking the Army Alpha at Camp Lee, 1917

U.S. Signal Corps photo number 11-SC-386 in the National Archives.

In contrast with individual intelligence tests, group tests of cognitive ability tend to be paper-and-pencil measures to assess the academic promise of an individual. Probably the most well known of these has been the Scholastic Aptitude Test (now the SAT Reasoning Test, or SAT). Developed by the Educational Testing Service after World War II, the test in many ways was the brain child of James Bryant Conant, president of Harvard. Believing in a democratic, classless society, Conant thought that such tests could identify the ability of individuals and ultimately help to equalize educational opportunities. Unfortunately, many have argued that instead of fostering equality, the SATs have been used to separate the social classes (Frontline, 1999).

James Bryant Conant Developed SAT to equalize educational opportunities

Paralleling the rise of group tests of cognitive ability was the administration of group tests of achievement in the schools. Traditionally, such tests had been given orally, and later in essay fashion, but the practicality of administering objective tests of academic performance to large groups of students was obvious. And, with the new scientific approach to testing, many people, such as Edward Thorndike, thought that such tests could be given in a format that was more reliable than the previous tests. This move toward group testing culminated with the

Edward Thorndike Developer of the Stanford Achievement Test

BOX 1.3
Eugenics and the Testing Movement:
A Devastating Example of the Misuse of Tests

As the new scientific approach to knowledge increasingly began to examine differences among people, a number of scientists began attributing these differences to genetics. This information was used to bolster support for the emerging Eugenics Movement, whose adherents believed in improving the human race through selective breeding.

Individuals such as Galton, Terman, and Yerkes believed that the data retrieved from tests could help distinguish those who were naturally bright from those who, they argued, were less fortunate. The information derived from tests was used to advocate for providing incentives for the upper class to procreate and finding methods to prevent the lower classes from having children (Gillham, 2001). Based on flimsy evidence and misguided thinking, this movement is seen today as having racist undertones.

Believing that the Army Alpha and Army Beta measured innate ability, Terman, Yerkes, and oth-

ers used the results of these tests to support the Eugenics Movement. However, the tests were a far cry from measuring intelligence, as they were saturated with cultural bias and were largely based on achievement, or what has been learned, as opposed to some kind of raw, inherent intelligence. Unfortunately, their beliefs about the test and what should be done as a result of the test data led the U.S. government to manipulate whom it would allow to immigrate to the United States. As a result, thousands—perhaps millions—of individuals were unable to emigrate from tyrannical governments in Europe and other parts of the world (Gould, 1996).

Question to Ponder: If a test could definitively identify those who were brighter than the rest of the population, would you support some kind of modified Eugenics Movement, such as encouraging individuals to mate only with individuals from a brighter gene pool?

---

development of the Stanford Achievement Test in 1923 (Kaplan & Saccuzzo, 2001). Today, these tests are commonplace and are given to students en masse in school systems throughout America.

Frank Parsons
Leader in vocational counseling

The first half of the twentieth century saw the spread of vocational counseling. Led by Frank Parsons (1909, 1989) and others, vocational counseling was seen as a process of "True Reasoning," whereby individuals would acquire self-knowledge, learn about the world of work, and through the "true reasoning" process, find a suitable occupational match. It was soon evident that to assist an individual with this process, tests to measure likes and dislikes, as well as abilities, would need to be used to assist the individual in understanding self. Thus, during the middle of the twentieth century "multiple aptitude" tests began to be used. For example, the General Aptitude Test Battery (GATB) was developed by the United States Employment Service to measure abilities in a number of specific areas. These areas of ability could be directly matched with job characteristics to identify appropriate occupational choices.

GATB
Developed by U.S. Employment Service to measure multiple aptitudes

The Emergence of Personality Tests
(Testing in the Affective Realm)

Paralleling the rise of tests in the cognitive domain, personality tests (or tests in the affective realm) began to be devised. Thus, around the turn of the twentieth century three types of personality assessment instruments were developed: interest inventories, objective personality tests, and projective personality tests. Let's take a brief look at each of these areas.

Interest Inventories and Vocational Assessment

One of the first researchers in the field of vocational assessment was Edward Thorndike (1874–1949). In 1912 Thorndike published the results of a study that examined the interests of 100 students as they progressed from elementary school through college (DuBois, 1970). However, it wasn't until 1922 that J. B. Miner developed one of the first formal interest blanks that was used to assist large groups of high school students in selecting occupations. Miner (1922) understood that his test was only part of the total assessment process, and he explained that the "blank becomes the basis for individual interviews with vocational counselors" (p. 312).

On the heels of Miner's interest blank, in the mid-1920s Edward Strong (1884–1963) teamed up with a number of other researchers to develop what was to become the most well-known interest inventory (Cowdery, 1926; DuBois, 1970; Strong, 1926). Known as the Strong Vocational Interest Blank, the original inventory consisted of 420 items. Strong spent the rest of his life perfecting his vocational interest inventory. Having undergone numerous revisions over the years, this inventory continues to be one of the most widely used instruments in career counseling. Today, interest inventories like the Strong are often used in conjunction with multiple aptitude tests as part of the career counseling process.

Objective Personality Assessment

Although Emil Kraeplin developed a crude word association test to study schizophrenia in the 1880s, Woodworth's Personal Data Sheet is considered to be the ancestor of all modern-day personality inventories. Woodworth's instrument, which was developed to screen WWI recruits for their susceptibility to mental health problems (DuBois, 1970), had 116 items to which individuals were asked to respond by underlining "yes" or "no" to indicate whether or not the statement represented them (see Box 1.4). These rather obvious questions were then related to certain types of neuroses and pathologies. Although the test had questionable validity compared to today's instruments, it became an early model for a number of other, better refined instruments including the Minnesota Multiphasic Personality Inventory (MMPI) (DuBois, 1970).

J. B. Miner Developed one of the first group interest inventories

Edward Strong Founder of the Strong Vocational Interest Blank—derivative still used today

Emil Kraeplin Developed early word association test

Objective personality assessment Paper-and-pencil tests to measure personality

Woodworth's Personal Data Sheet First modern personality inventory—used during WWI

BOX 1.4
Items from Woodworth's Personal Data Sheet

Although crude by today's standards, Wood-worth's Personal Data Sheet was one of the first instruments that attempted to assess one's personality. Below are some of original 116 items.

    Answer the questions by underlining "Yes" when you mean yes, and by underlining "No" when you mean no. Try to answer every question.

1. Do you usually feel well and strong?   YES   NO

3. Are you often frightened in the middle of the night?   YES   NO

27. Have you ever been blind, half-blind, deaf or dumb for a time?   YES   NO

51. Have you hurt yourself by masturbation (self abuse)?   YES   NO

80. At night are you troubled by the idea that somebody is following you?   YES   NO

88. Did you ever have the habit of wetting the bed?   YES   NO

112. Has any of your family been a drunkard?   YES   NO

Source: Adapted from *A History of Psychological Testing* (pp. 160–163), by P. DuBois, 1970, Boston: Allyn and Bacon.

Projective Testing

Clearing his mind and recording his associations to a number of stimulus words, Galton wrote:

> *Experiments such as these allow an unexpected amount of illumination to enter into the deepest recess of the character, which are opened and bared by them like the anatomy of an animal under the scalpel of a dissector in broad daylight* (Galton, 1879, p. 431).

These words of Galton speak to the premise of projective testing: present a stimulus to an individual in an attempt to tap into the unconscious mind and discover the inner world of that person. Recognizing the importance of Galton's work, Cattell examined the kinds of associations that mentally healthy individuals made to a standard list of words (DuBois, 1970).

Carl Jung
Used word associations to identify mental illness

Herman Rorschach
Developed famous Rorschach Inkblot test

    By 1904, Carl Jung (1875–1961) had developed a list of 100 words that subjects were to respond to as quickly as possible. Depending on the response and the answer time, Jung believed he could identify mental illness (Jung & Riklin, 1904). However, it was Herman Rorschach (1884–1922), a student of Jung, who developed the most well known projective test—the Rorschach Inkblot test. Rorschach created this test by selecting ten ink blots "thrown on a piece of paper, the paper folded, and the ink spread between the two halves of the sheet" (Rorschach, 1942, p. 1). Rorschach believed the interpretation of an individual's reactions to these forms could tell volumes about the individual's unconscious life. This test was the precursor to many other kinds of projective tests, such as

Henry Murray
Developed
Thematic
Apperception
Test (TAT)
Henry Murray's Thematic Apperception Test, or TAT, which asks a subject to view a number of standard pictures and create a story to explain the situation.

The Emergence of Informal Assessment Procedures

*Informal
assessment
procedures*
User-created
and situational
The twentieth century saw the increased use of informal assessment procedures, which are assessment instruments that are often developed by the user and are specific to the testing situation. For instance, as business and industry expanded during the 1930s, the situational test became more prevalent. In these tests, businesses took individuals who were potential hires or candidates for promotion and placed them into "contrived naturalistic situations" to assess their ability to respond to real-life situations. Meanwhile, as treatment of mental health clients improved, the importance of the clinical interview became obvious. The clinical interview became especially important as clients were increasingly being assessed for a diagnosis through the use of the *Diagnostic and Statistical Manual*, first developed by the American Psychiatric Association in 1952 (Neukrug & Schwitzer, 2006).

During the 1960s and 1970s the use of tests in the schools greatly increased and laws were passed that called for the assessment of students with disabilities. Schools began to use observation, rating scales, classification techniques, and the review of records and personal documents to assess learning problems of children. Informal assessment techniques such as these are used today in a variety of settings to assess individuals for myriad reasons.

Modern-Day Use of Assessment Procedures

As complex statistical analyses became possible through the use of computers, the quality of assessment instruments advanced rapidly. Today, assessment instruments can be found in every aspect of society and their uses have been vastly expanded. Although one can categorize such instruments in many ways, we have found it helpful to classify them into the following groups: (1) ability tests, or testing in the cognitive domain; (2) personality tests, or testing in the affective domain; and (3) informal assessment procedures. Figure 1.2 is a graphic display of these instruments, and this is followed in Box 1.5 by short definitions of the various categories.

In Section Two of the text, we will demonstrate how all of the assessment categories noted in Figure 1.2 and Box 1.5 are used today in a variety of ways. Below, you can see how the chapters in Section Three of the text correspond to the categories:

Chapter 6: Assessment of Educational Ability: Survey Battery, Diagnostic, Readiness, and Cognitive Ability Tests

Chapter 7: Assessment of Intelligence (Individual Intelligence Tests)

Chapter 8: Career and Occupational Assessment: Interest Inventories, Multiple Aptitude, and Special Aptitude Tests

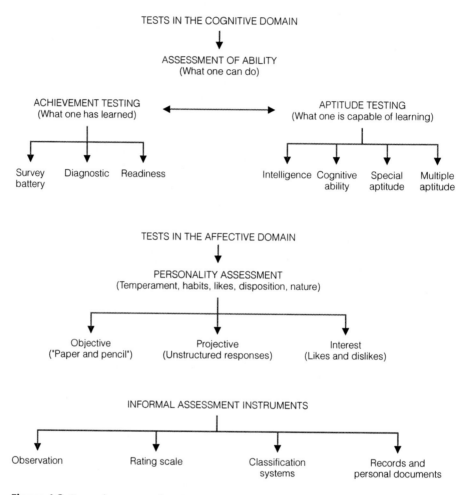

Figure 1.2 Types of assessment instruments

Questions to Consider When Assessing Individuals

It is clear that today's assessment instruments have widespread applications. With the knowledge that many individuals have used assessment instruments for less than honorable reasons (e.g., Eugenics Movement), it is critical that we remain

BOX 1.5
Brief Definitions of Assessment Categories

ASSESSMENT OF ABILITY

Tests that measure what a person can do in the cognitive realm.

Achievement Testing

Tests that measure what one has learned.

Survey Battery Tests: Paper and pencil tests, usually given in school settings, which measure broad content areas. Often used to assess progress in school.

Diagnostic Tests: Tests that assess problem areas of learning. Often used to assess learning disabilities.

Readiness Tests: Tests that measure one's readiness for moving ahead in school. Often used to assess readiness to enter first grade.

Aptitude Testing

Tests that measure what one is capable of learning.

Individual Intelligence Testing: Tests that measure a broad range of cognitive functioning and generally result in one "IQ" score. Often used to identify mental retardation, giftedness, and general cognitive functioning.

Cognitive Ability Tests: Often based on what one has learned in school, these instruments measure a broad range of cognitive ability and are useful in making predictions about the future (e.g., whether an individual might succeed in college).

Special Aptitude Tests: Tests that measure one aspect of ability. Often useful in determining the likelihood of success in a vocation (e.g., a mechanical aptitude test to determine potential success as a mechanic).

Multiple Aptitude Tests: Tests that measure many aspects of ability. Often useful in determining the likelihood of success in a number of vocations.

PERSONALITY ASSESSMENT

Tests in the affective realm used to assess habits, temperament, likes and dislikes, character, and similar behaviors.

Objective Personality Testing: Paper-and-pencil tests, often in multiple-choice or true/false formats, that assess various aspects of personality. Often used to increase client insight, to identify psychopathology, and to assist in treatment planning.

Projective Personality Tests: Tests that present a stimulus to which individuals can respond. Personality factors are interpreted based on the individual's response. Often used to identify psychopathology and to assist in treatment planning.

Interest Inventories: Tests that measure likes and dislikes as well as one's personality orientation toward the world of work. Generally used in career counseling.

INFORMAL ASSESSMENT INSTRUMENTS

Assessment instruments, often developed by the user, that are specific to the testing situation. All of these instruments can be used to assess broad areas of ability and personality attributes in a variety of settings.

Observation: Observing an individual in order to develop a deeper understanding of one or more specific behaviors (e.g., observing a student's acting-out behavior in class or assessing a client's ability to perform eye-hand coordination tasks as a means of determining potential vocational placement).

Rating Scales: Scales developed to assess any of a number of attributes of the examinee. Can be rated by the examinee or someone who knows the examinee well (rating a faculty member's teaching ability or a student's ability to make empathic responses).

continued

BOX 1.5
Continued

Classification Systems: A mechanism whereby information is provided about whether or not an individual has, or does not have, certain attributes or characteristics (asking a person to check off those adjectives that seem to be most like him or her).

Records and Personal Documents: Items such as diaries, personal journals, genograms, school records, and so forth, that are examined to gain a broader understanding of one individual.

---

vigilant about the use of such instruments. Keeping this in mind, we should continually be asking ourselves some important questions regarding the use of assessment instruments, including the following:

1. How valid is the information gained from assessment instruments, and how should that information be applied?
2. How do assessment instruments invade one's privacy, and does the government have, at times, the right to insist that an individual be assessed?
3. Can the use of some assessment instruments lead to labeling, and what are the implications for individuals who are "labeled"?
4. Are assessment procedures used to foster equality for *all* people, or do they tend to reinforce existing societal divisions based on class?

Summary

We began this chapter by defining assessment and pointing out that assessment encompasses a broad range of techniques, including testing. We noted that modern-day assessment has been greatly influenced by the long history of assessment. Going back to 2200 B.C.E., we pointed out that the Chinese developed one of the first widely used tests and that at around the same time the Greeks assessed intellectual and physical ability of men for state service.

As we neared the modern era of testing, we pointed out that individuals such as Esquirol examined the relationship between language ability and intelligence, while others, such as Sequin, looked at the relationship between motor control and intelligence. We noted that Darwin's evolutionary theories spurred others such as Galton, Wundt, and Cattell to examine individual differences, a focus that would be critical to the nature of assessment.

Moving forward in time, we noted that the late 1800s saw Alfred Binet develop the first intelligence test. Later revised by Terman, the Stanford-Binet compared an individual's chronological age to his or her mental age. We noted that the early 1900s saw the development of group tests of ability, including the Army Alpha and Army Beta, achievement tests in the schools, and multiple aptitude tests. We then noted that during the 1900s individuals such as Galton, Yerkes, and Terman were influential in the Eugenics Movement. This misguided venture attempted to use test data to show intellectual differences among cultural groups and ended up influencing government policy, including laws regarding who would be allowed to immigrate to this country.

We pointed out that many of the first personality tests paralleled the development of ability tests. For instance, the early 1900s saw Thorndike, Miner, and Strong research the area of vocational assessment and develop some of the first interest inventories. Kraeplin developed a crude word association test, and Woodworth developed his "personal data sheet," which many consider the precursor of modern-day personality inventories. Word association experiments by individuals such as Galton, Wundt, and Cattell were soon followed by the development of a word association test by Carl Jung. Other early projective tests included Rorschach's Inkblot Test and Murray's Thematic Apperception Test. As the twentieth century continued, a number of informal assessment instruments were developed, including observational techniques, rating scales, classification schemes, and records and personal documents.

Near the end of the chapter, we highlighted various assessment categories including ability testing (achievement and aptitude), personality testing, and informal assessment instruments. The chapter concluded by highlighting a number of important issues in assessment, including test validity, invasions of privacy, caution regarding labeling, and the importance of assuring that assessment procedures foster equality.

Chapter Review

1. Identify some of the ancient precursors to assessment.

2. Identify some of the precursors to modern-day assessment during the 1800s.

3. Discuss how the work of Darwin, Galton, Wundt, and Cattell has influenced the development of modern-day testing.

4. Identify some of the individuals involved and describe the precursors to modern-day intelligence testing.

5. What was the Eugenics Movement, and how did it influence government policy in the United States?

6. Identify some of the early group tests of ability, the main players in their development, and their uses.

7. Identify some of the early personality tests and the main players involved in their development.

8. Describe the contributions of some of the early developers of projective testing.

9. Draw four diagrams (see Figure 1.2) that list the various kinds of achievement testing, aptitude testing, personality assessment, and informal assessment. Define each type of assessment category on your diagrams.

10. Make a list of every historical figure discussed in this chapter, and define each person's contribution to testing and assessment.

CHAPTER 2

Ethical, Legal, and Professional Issues in Assessment

A psychologist who is a friend of mine believed that a colleague was not writing up adequate test reports. After witnessing a series of what she thought were incompetent test reports, my friend reported her colleague to the ethics committee of the American Psychological Association. She reported her colleague under the area of "competence," which includes the following statements:

> *Psychologists provide services, teach, and conduct research with populations and in areas only within the boundaries of their competence, based on their education, training, supervised experience, consultation, study, or professional experience.* (APA, 2003, Section 2.01a)

and

> *Psychologists undertake ongoing efforts to develop and maintain their competence.* (APA, 2003, Section 2.03)

My friend felt a sense of self-righteousness for having reported this psychologist. Much to her surprise, her colleague turned around and reported her, stating that she had not first gone directly to her colleague and tried to work out the situation informally.

> *When psychologists believe that there may have been an ethical violation by another psychologist, they attempt to resolve the issue by bringing it to the attention of that individual, if an informal resolution appears appropriate and the intervention does not violate any confidentiality rights that may be involved.* (APA, 2003, Section 1.04)

Ultimately, it was my friend who was sanctioned, and her colleague was found not to have committed an ethical violation. (Ed Neukrug)

In this chapter we will look at the complex ethical, legal, and professional issues that confront individuals who are assessing others. Sometimes what is perceived to be a clear ethical violation by one person is actually much more complex. In this chapter we will begin by identifying some important ethical issues, go on to highlight a number of legal matters, and finish by discussing some important professional concerns.

Ethical Issues in Assessment

Today, a number of ethical codes are available to guide the practice of mental health professionals, including ethical guidelines for counselors, psychologists, social workers, marriage and family therapists, psychiatrists, human service professionals, and others. Although these codes have much in common, differences do exist. For instance, some of these codes place more emphasis on assessment than others do (e.g., ACA, APA). This section will offer a brief overview of some of the important ethical codes relative to assessment as highlighted by the American Counseling Association (ACA) and the American Psychological Association (APA). In addition, we will offer a brief overview of three standards that are also used to help guide the practitioner: The Standards for the Qualifications of Test Users (ACA, 2003), Responsibilities of Users of Standardized Tests (RUST) (AACE, 2003), and the Code of Fair Testing Practices in Education (JCTP, 2002). Finally, we will discuss the process of making ethical decisions.

Ethical Codes

Ethical codes Professional guidelines for appropriate behavior

The ethical codes of our professional associations provide us with guidelines about how to respond under certain situations. Some codes, like those of the ACA (1995) and APA (2003), include standards that specifically address issues of testing and assessment. The following discussion summarizes some points in the codes that are of particular importance, such as choosing appropriate assessment instruments, competence in the use of assessment instruments, confidentiality, cross-cultural sensitivity, informed consent, invasion of privacy, proper diagnosis, release of test data, test administration, test security, and test scoring and interpretation. Please review the ethical guidelines of the professional associations, the websites of which can be found in Appendix A, as well as the actual assessment guidelines of ACA and APA, which can be found in Box 2.1 and Box 2.2, respectively.

Choosing Appropriate Assessment Instruments

Attend to test worthiness in choosing assessment instruments.

Attention to test worthiness, which has to do with the reliability, validity, cross-cultural fairness, and practicality of a test, is an important aspect of the ethical codes and will be examined in detail in Chapter 3. The ethical codes assert that professionals should choose assessment instruments that show test worthiness for the assessment procedure at hand. When issues of test worthiness arise, professionals should make such notations in any results reported.

Competence in the Use of Tests

Competence in using tests
Requires adequate knowledge and training in administering an instrument

Competence to use tests accurately is another aspect that is stressed in the codes. The codes declare that professionals should have adequate knowledge about testing and familiarity with any test they may use. To establish who is qualified to give specific tests, the American Psychological Association (APA) in 1950 adopted a three-tier system for establishing test user qualifications. Although the APA is currently reevaluating this system (Bartram, 2001), many test publishers continue to use it or similar variations. The original system labeled some tests according to the following three levels:

- Level A tests are those that can be administered, scored, and interpreted by responsible nonpsychologists who have carefully read the test manual and are familiar with the overall purpose of testing. Educational achievement tests fall into this category.
- Level B tests require technical knowledge of test construction and use and appropriate advanced coursework in psychology and related courses (e.g., statistics, individual differences, and counseling).
- Level C tests require an advanced degree in psychology or licensure as a psychologist and advanced training/supervised experience in the particular test. (APA, 1954, pp. 146–148)

More specifically, an individual with a bachelor's degree who has some knowledge of assessment and is thoroughly versed with the test manual can give a Level A test and, under some limited circumstances, a Level B test. For example, teachers can administer most survey battery achievement tests. The master's level counselor or other helping professional who has taken a basic course in tests and measurement can administer Level B tests. For example, counselors can administer a wide range of personality tests, including most interest inventories and many objective personality tests. However, they cannot administer tests that require additional training, such as most individual tests of intelligence, most projective tests, and many diagnostic tests. These Level C tests are reserved for those who have a minimum of a master's degree, a basic testing course, and advanced training in the specialized test (e.g., school psychologists, learning disabilities specialists, clinical and counseling psychologists, and master's-level therapists who have gained additional training).

Confidentiality

Confidentiality
Ethical guideline to protect client information

Whether testing takes place within a long-term therapeutic encounter or a one-time meeting for ability or personality assessment, issues related to confidentiality are critical to the effective helping relationship and are addressed in all ethical codes. Although ethical guidelines differ slightly on when one can reveal confidential information, generally, it is considered permissible to do so under the following conditions:

1. If a client is in danger of harming himself or herself or someone else;
2. If a child is a minor and the law states that parents have a right to information about their child;

3. If a client asks you to break confidentiality (for example, your testimony is needed in court);
4. If you are bound by the law to break confidentiality (for example, you are hired by the courts to assess an individual's capacity to stand trial);
5. To reveal information about your client to your supervisor in order to benefit the client;
6. When you have a written agreement from your client to reveal information to specified sources (for example, the court has asked you to send a test report to them).

Confidentiality is an ethical guideline, not a legal right. The legal term that ensures the right of professionals not to reveal information about their clients is *privileged communication* (Glosoff, Herlihy, & Spense, 2000) and this topic will be discussed in the section on legal issues later in this chapter.

Cross-Cultural Sensitivity

Cross-cultural sensitivity
Ethical guideline to protect clients from discrimination and bias in testing

In reference to cross-cultural sensitivity, the codes tend to focus on the potential biases of assessment procedures when selecting, administering, and interpreting such procedures. In addition, they stress the importance of professionals being aware of and attending to the effects of age, color, cultural identity, disability, ethnicity, gender, religion, sexual orientation, and socioeconomic status on test administration and test interpretation. Later in this chapter, and in Chapter 3, we will discuss this important topic in greater detail.

Informed Consent

Informed consent
Permission given by client after assessment process is explained

Obtaining informed consent to be assessed is another guideline highlighted in the codes. This means that individuals being assessed should give their permission for the assessment after they have received information concerning the nature and purposes of the assessment, fees, involvement by others in the assessment process (e.g., teachers, therapists), and the limits of confidentiality.

Invasion of Privacy

Invasion of privacy
Testing is an invasion of a person's privacy

The codes generally acknowledge that to some degree, all tests invade one's privacy. However, concerns about invasion of privacy are lessened if the client has given informed consent, has some real choice to accept or refuse testing, and knows the limits of confidentiality, as noted earlier.

Proper Diagnosis

Proper diagnosis
Choose appropriate assessment techniques for accurate diagnosis

Due to the delicate nature of diagnoses, the codes emphasize that professionals should be particularly careful when deciding which assessment techniques to use in forming a diagnosis for a mental disorder.

Release of Test Data

Release of test data
Test data are protected—client release required

Test data can be, and have been, misused. Thus, the codes assert that data should only be released to others if the client has signed a release form. The release of such data is generally only given to individuals who can adequately interpret the test data, and professionals should assure that those who receive such data do not misuse the information.

Test Administration

Test administration Use established and standardized methods

As you might guess, the codes reinforce the notion that tests should be administered appropriately as defined by the way they were established and standardized. Alterations to this process should be noted and interpretations of test data adjusted if testing conditions were not ideal.

Test Security

Test security Ensure integrity of test content and test itself

The codes remind professionals that it is their responsibility to make reasonable efforts to assure the integrity of test content and the security of the test itself. Professionals should not duplicate tests or change test material without the permission of the publisher.

Test Scoring and Interpretation

Test scoring and interpretation Take into consideration problems with tests

Finally, the codes highlight the fact that when scoring tests and interpreting their results, professionals should reflect on how issues of test worthiness, including the reliability, validity, cross-cultural fairness, and practicality of the test, might affect the results. Results should always be couched in terms that reflect potential problems with test interpretation.

Clay Bennett, The Christian Science Monitor.

BOX 2.1
American Counseling Association's Ethical Code

Section E: Evaluation, Assessment, and Interpretation

E.1. GENERAL

Appraisal Techniques. The primary purpose of educational and psychological assessment is to provide measures that are objective and interpretable in either comparative or absolute terms. Counselors recognize the need to interpret the statements in this section as applying to the whole range of appraisal techniques, including test and nontest data.

Client Welfare. Counselors promote the welfare and best interests of the client in the development, publication, and utilization of educational and psychological assessment techniques. They do not misuse assessment results and interpretations and take reasonable steps to prevent others from misusing the information these techniques provide. They respect the client's right to know the results, the interpretations made, and the bases for their conclusions and recommendations.

E.2. COMPETENCE TO USE AND INTERPRET TESTS

Limits of Competence. Counselors recognize the limits of their competence and perform only those testing and assessment services for which they have been trained. They are familiar with reliability, validity, related standardization, error of measurement, and proper application of any technique utilized. Counselors using computer-based test interpretations are trained in the construct being measured and the specific instrument being used prior to using this type of computer application. Counselors take reasonable measures to ensure the proper use of psychological assessment techniques by persons under their supervision.

Appropriate Use. Counselors are responsible for the appropriate application, scoring, interpretation, and use of assessment instruments, whether they score and interpret such tests themselves or use computerized or other services.

Decisions Based on Results. Counselors responsible for decisions involving individuals or policies that are based on assessment results have a thorough understanding of educational and psychological measurement, including validation criteria, test research, and guidelines for test development and use.

Accurate Information. Counselors provide accurate information and avoid false claims or misconceptions when making statements about assessment instruments or techniques. Special efforts are made to avoid unwarranted connotations of such terms as IQ and grade equivalent scores. (See C.5.c.)

E.3. INFORMED CONSENT

Explanation to Clients. Prior to assessment, counselors explain the nature and purposes of assessment and the specific use of results in language the client (or other legally authorized person on behalf of the client) can understand, unless an explicit exception to this right has been agreed upon in advance. Regardless of whether scoring and interpretation are completed by counselors, by assistants, or by computer or other outside services, counselors take reasonable steps to ensure that appropriate explanations are given to the client.

Recipients of Results. The examinee's welfare, explicit understanding, and prior agreement determine the recipients of test results. Counselors include accurate and appropriate interpretations with any release of individual or group test results. (See B.1.a. and C.5.c.)

E.4. RELEASE OF INFORMATION TO COMPETENT PROFESSIONALS

Misuse of Results. Counselors do not misuse assessment results, including test results, and

BOX 2.1
Continued

interpretations, and take reasonable steps to prevent the misuse of such by others. (See C.5.c.)

Release of Raw Data. Counselors ordinarily release data (e.g., protocols, counseling or interview notes, or questionnaires) in which the client is identified only with the consent of the client or the client's legal representative. Such data are usually released only to persons recognized by counselors as competent to interpret the data. (See B.1.a.)

E.5. PROPER DIAGNOSIS OF MENTAL DISORDERS

Proper Diagnosis. Counselors take special care to provide proper diagnosis of mental disorders. Assessment techniques (including personal interview) used to determine client care (e.g., locus of treatment, type of treatment, or recommended follow-up) are carefully selected and appropriately used. (See A.3.a. and C.5.c.)

Cultural Sensitivity. Counselors recognize that culture affects the manner in which clients' problems are defined. Clients' socioeconomic and cultural experience is considered when diagnosing mental disorders.

E.6. TEST SELECTION

Appropriateness of Instruments. Counselors carefully consider the validity, reliability, psychometric limitations, and appropriateness of instruments when selecting tests for use in a given situation or with a particular client.

Culturally Diverse Populations. Counselors are cautious when selecting tests for culturally diverse populations to avoid inappropriateness of testing that may be outside of socialized behavioral or cognitive patterns.

E.7. CONDITIONS OF TEST ADMINISTRATION

Administration Conditions. Counselors administer tests under the same conditions that were

established in their standardization. When tests are not administered under standard conditions or when unusual behavior or irregularities occur during the testing session, those conditions are noted in interpretation, and the results may be designated as invalid or of questionable validity.

Computer Administration. Counselors are responsible for ensuring that administration programs function properly to provide clients with accurate results when a computer or other electronic methods are used for test administration. (See A.12.b.)

Unsupervised Test Taking. Counselors do not permit unsupervised or inadequately supervised use of tests or assessments unless the tests or assessments are designed, intended, and validated for self-administration and/or scoring.

Disclosure of Favorable Conditions. Prior to test administration, conditions that produce most favorable test results are made known to the examinee.

E.8. DIVERSITY IN TESTING

Counselors are cautious in using assessment techniques, making evaluations, and interpreting the performance of populations not represented in the norm group on which an instrument was standardized. They recognize the effects of age, color, culture, disability, ethnic group, gender, race, religion, sexual orientation, and socioeconomic status on test administration and interpretation and place test results in proper perspective with other relevant factors. (See A.2.a.)

E.9. TEST SCORING AND INTERPRETATION

Reporting Reservations. In reporting assessment results, counselors indicate any reservations that exist regarding validity or reliability because of the circumstances of the assessment or the inappropriateness of the norms for the person tested.

continued

BOX 2.1
Continued

Research Instruments. Counselors exercise caution when interpreting the results of research instruments possessing insufficient technical data to support respondent results. The specific purposes for the use of such instruments are stated explicitly to the examinee.

Testing Services. Counselors who provide test scoring and test interpretation services to support the assessment process confirm the validity of such interpretations. They accurately describe the purpose, norms, validity, reliability, and applications of the procedures and any special qualifications applicable to their use. The public offering of an automated test interpretations service is considered a professional-to-professional consultation. The formal responsibility of the consultant is to the consultee, but the ultimate and overriding responsibility is to the client.

E.10. TEST SECURITY

Counselors maintain the integrity and security of tests and other assessment techniques consistent with legal and contractual obligations. Counselors do not appropriate, reproduce, or modify published tests or parts thereof without acknowledgment and permission from the publisher.

E.11. OBSOLETE TESTS AND OUTDATED TEST RESULTS

Counselors do not use data or test results that are obsolete or outdated for the current purpose. Counselors make every effort to prevent the misuse of obsolete measures and test data by others.

E.12. TEST CONSTRUCTION

Counselors use established scientific procedures, relevant standards, and current professional knowledge for test design in the development, publication, and utilization of educational and psychological assessment techniques.

Standards for Responsible Testing Practices

A number of standards exist that expand upon the ethical codes and address the responsible use of tests. They include The Standards for the Qualifications of Test Users (ACA, 2003), Responsibilities of Users of Standardized Tests (RUST) (AACE, 2003), and the Code of Fair Testing Practices in Education (JCTP, 2002).

The Standards for the Qualifications of Test Users

The Standards for the Qualifications of Test Users notes that professionals should have knowledge and skills in the following areas (ACA, 2003, headings in document):

1. Skill in the practice and knowledge of theory relevant to the testing context and type of counseling specialty.
2. A thorough understanding of testing theory, techniques of test construction, and test reliability and validity.
3. A working knowledge of sampling techniques, norms, and descriptive, correlational and predictive statistics.

BOX 2.2
American Psychological Association Ethical Code

Section 9: Assessment

9.01 BASES FOR ASSESSMENTS

(a) Psychologists base the opinions contained in their recommendations, reports, and diagnostic or evaluative statements, including forensic testimony, on information and techniques sufficient to substantiate their findings. (See also Standard 2.04, Bases for Scientific and Professional Judgments.)

(b) Except as noted in 9.01c, psychologists provide opinions of the psychological characteristics of individuals only after they have conducted an examination of the individuals adequate to support their statements or conclusions. When, despite reasonable efforts, such an examination is not practical, psychologists document the efforts they made and the result of those efforts, clarify the probable impact of their limited information on the reliability and validity of their opinions, and appropriately limit the nature and extent of their conclusions or recommendations. (See also Standards 2.01, Boundaries of Competence, and 9.06, Interpreting Assessment Results.)

(c) When psychologists conduct a record review or provide consultation or supervision and an individual examination is not warranted or necessary for the opinion, psychologists explain this and the sources of information on which they based their conclusions and recommendations.

9.02 USE OF ASSESSMENTS

(a) Psychologists administer, adapt, score, interpret, or use assessment techniques, interviews, tests, or instruments in a manner and for purposes that are appropriate in light of the research on or evidence of the usefulness and proper application of the techniques.

(b) Psychologists use assessment instruments whose validity and reliability have been established for use with members of the population tested. When such validity or reliability has not been established, psychologists describe the strengths and limitations of test results and interpretation.

(c) Psychologists use assessment methods that are appropriate to an individual's language preference and competence, unless the use of an alternative language is relevant to the assessment issues.

9.03 INFORMED CONSENT IN ASSESSMENTS

(a) Psychologists obtain informed consent for assessments, evaluations, or diagnostic services, as described in Standard 3.10, Informed Consent, except when (1) testing is mandated by law or governmental regulations; (2) informed consent is implied because testing is conducted as a routine educational, institutional, or organizational activity (e.g., when participants voluntarily agree to assessment when applying for a job); or (3) one purpose of the testing is to evaluate decisional capacity. Informed consent includes an explanation of the nature and purpose of the assessment, fees, involvement of third parties, and limits of confidentiality and sufficient opportunity for the client/patient to ask questions and receive answers.

(b) Psychologists inform persons with questionable capacity to consent or for whom testing is mandated by law or governmental regulations about the nature and purpose of the proposed assessment services, using language that is reasonably understandable to the person being assessed.

(c) Psychologists using the services of an interpreter obtain informed consent from the client/patient to use that interpreter, ensure that confidentiality of test results and test security are maintained, and include in their

continued

BOX 2.2
Continued

recommendations, reports, and diagnostic or evaluative statements, including forensic testimony, discussion of any limitations on the data obtained. (See also Standards 2.05, Delegation of Work to Others; 4.01, Maintaining Confidentiality; 9.01, Bases for Assessments; 9.06, Interpreting Assessment Results; and 9.07, Assessment by Unqualified Persons.)

9.04 RELEASE OF TEST DATA

(a) The term *test data* refers to raw and scaled scores, client/patient responses to test questions or stimuli, and psychologists' notes and recordings concerning client/patient statements and behavior during an examination. Those portions of test materials that include client/patient responses are included in the definition of *test data*. Pursuant to a client/patient release, psychologists provide test data to the client/patient or other persons identified in the release. Psychologists may refrain from releasing test data to protect a client/patient or others from substantial harm or misuse or misrepresentation of the data or the test, recognizing that in many instances release of confidential information under these circumstances is regulated by law. (See also Standard 9.11, Maintaining Test Security.)

(b) In the absence of a client/patient release, psychologists provide test data only as required by law or court order.

9.05 TEST CONSTRUCTION

Psychologists who develop tests and other assessment techniques use appropriate psychometric procedures and current scientific or professional knowledge for test design, standardization, validation, reduction or elimination of bias, and recommendations for use.

9.06 INTERPRETING ASSESSMENT RESULTS

When interpreting assessment results, including automated interpretations, psychologists take into account the purpose of the assessment as well as the various test factors, test-taking abilities, and other characteristics of the person being assessed, such as situational, personal, linguistic, and cultural differences, that might affect psychologists' judgments or reduce the accuracy of their interpretations. They indicate any significant limitations of their interpretations. (See also Standards 2.01b and c, Boundaries of Competence, and 3.01, Unfair Discrimination.)

9.07 ASSESSMENT BY UNQUALIFIED PERSONS

Psychologists do not promote the use of psychological assessment techniques by unqualified persons, except when such use is conducted for training purposes with appropriate supervision. (See also Standard 2.05, Delegation of Work to Others.)

9.08 OBSOLETE TESTS AND OUTDATED TEST RESULTS

(a) Psychologists do not base their assessment or intervention decisions or recommendations on data or test results that are outdated for the current purpose.

(b) Psychologists do not base such decisions or recommendations on tests and measures that are obsolete and not useful for the current purpose.

9.09 TEST SCORING AND INTERPRETATION SERVICES

(a) Psychologists who offer assessment or scoring services to other professionals accurately describe the purpose, norms, validity, reliability, and applications of the procedures and any special qualifications applicable to their use.

(b) Psychologists select scoring and interpretation services (including automated services) on the basis of evidence of the validity of the program and procedures as well as on other

---

BOX 2.2
Continued

---

appropriate considerations. (See also Standard 2.01b and c, Boundaries of Competence.)

(c) Psychologists retain responsibility for the appropriate application, interpretation, and use of assessment instruments, whether they score and interpret such tests themselves or use automated or other services.

9.10 EXPLAINING ASSESSMENT RESULTS

Regardless of whether the scoring and interpretation are done by psychologists, by employees or assistants, or by automated or other outside services, psychologists take reasonable steps to ensure that explanations of results are given to the individual or designated representative unless the nature of the relationship precludes provision of an explanation of results (such as in some organizational consulting, preemployment or security screenings, and forensic evaluations), and this fact has been clearly explained to the person being assessed in advance.

9.11. MAINTAINING TEST SECURITY

The term *test materials* refers to manuals, instruments, protocols, and test questions or stimuli and does not include *test data* as defined in Standard 9.04, Release of Test Data. Psychologists make reasonable efforts to maintain the integrity and security of test materials and other assessment techniques consistent with law and contractual obligations, and in a manner that permits adherence to this Ethics Code.

From *American Psychologist* 57, p. 1060–1073. Copyright © 2002 by the American Psychological Association. Reprinted with permission.

---

4. Ability to review, select, and administer tests appropriate for the clients or students and the context of the counseling practice.

5. Skill in administration of tests and interpretation of test scores.

6. Knowledge of the impact of diversity on testing accuracy, including age, gender, ethnicity, race, disability, and linguistic differences.

7. Knowledge and skill in the professionally responsible use of assessment and evaluation practice.

Code of Fair Testing Practices in Education

This code was developed specifically for testing in education in the following areas: admissions, educational assessment, educational diagnosis, and student placement. It is intended to assure that testing is "fair to all test takers regardless of age, gender, disability, race, ethnicity, national origin, religion, sexual orientation, linguistic background, or other personal characteristics" (JCTP, 2002, p. 1). The Code provides guidance for test developers and test users in four areas: developing and selecting appropriate tests, administering and scoring tests, reporting and interpreting test results, and informing test takers (see Appendix B).

Responsibilities of Users of Standardized Tests (RUST)

The Responsibilities of Users of Standardized Tests (RUST) is intended to expand on the ACA's Code of Ethics (1995) and on the Code of Fair Testing Practices in

Education (JCTP, 2002). This document speaks to the qualifications of the individual giving tests in the following areas: qualifications needed, technical knowledge, test selection, test administration, test scoring, interpreting test results, and communicating test results.

Making Ethical Decisions

Kitchener
Developed a
moral model for
ethical decision
making

Because ethical codes are just guidelines, it is important that practitioners rely on more than the codes when making ethical decisions. Some have suggested a moral model of decision-making. For instance, Kitchener (1984, 1986) lists five moral values involved in ethical decision-making: *autonomy* of the client (e.g., independence, self-determination, freedom of choice); *beneficence* of society (promoting the well-being of others); *nonmaleficence* (not causing harm to others); *justice* or fairness to all (providing equal and fair treatment to all people); and *fidelity* of the counseling relationship (loyalty, commitment, and faithfulness). The clinician who employs this model will not reject the use of codes but will refer to them while using these moral principles in his or her decision-making process.

Corey, Corey,
and Callanan
Recommend an
eight-step
decision-making
model

A more hands-on, practical, problem-solving model espoused by Corey, Corey, and Callanan (2003) suggests that the practitioner go through eight steps when making complex ethical decisions:

1. identifying the problem,
2. identifying the potential issues involved,
3. reviewing the relevant ethical guidelines,
4. knowing relevant laws and regulations,
5. obtaining consultation,
6. considering possible and probable courses of action,
7. listing the consequences of various decisions, and
8. deciding on what appears to be the best course of action.

Wise ethical
decisions reflect
higher cognitive
development.

Some suggest that regardless of the approach one takes in ethical decision-making, the ability to make wise ethical decisions may well be influenced by the clinician's level of ethical, moral, and cognitive development (Neukrug, Lovell, & Parker, 1996) (see Box 2.3). Those who are at higher levels of cognitive development, they state, view ethical decision making in more complex ways than others (McAuliffe, Eriksen, & Associates, 2000). Certainly, this has broad implications for the training that takes place in clinical programs, as it would be hoped that students are challenged to make decisions that are comprehensive and thoughtful.

Legal Issues in Assessment

A number of laws have been passed and lawsuits resolved that impinge on the use of tests. Most of these legal decisions speak to issues of confidentiality, fairness, and test worthiness (reliability, validity, practicality, and cross-cultural

---

BOX 2.3
Making Ethical Decisions

After reading this section, in small groups in class or as a homework assignment, use Kitchener's and Corey's models of ethical decision making to decide on your course of action in the following situation. Share your answers in class. You will have the opportunity to respond to additional vignettes in Box 2.5.

Situation: You have been asked to provide a broad personality assessment of a 17-year-old high school student who has been truant from school and has a history of acting-out behaviors. After meeting with her, conducting a clinical interview, and administering

a number of projective tests and an MMPI-II, you find evidence that an uncle who is five years older than the client had sexually molested her when she was 12 years old. In addition, you believe that the young woman has been involved in some petty crimes, such as shoplifting and stealing audio equipment from the school. You are writing a test report for the school. What should you include in the report regarding her being molested and the crimes she has allegedly committed? Are you obligated to report this case to Child Protective Services? Do you have any obligation to contact the police? What are your obligations to this young person's parents, to the school, and to society?

Laws about testing
Created to protect the client or examinee

fairness) (Swenson, 1997). We will summarize some of the more important laws that have been passed and legal cases resolved over the years, including the Americans with Disabilities Act (PL 101-336); The Buckley Amendment, otherwise known as FERPA; the Carl Perkins Act (PL 98-24); various Civil Rights Acts (1964 and amendments); the Freedom of Information Act; the Health Insurance Portability and Accountability Act (HIPAA); the Individuals with Disabilities Education Improvement Act, which was an expansion of PL94-142; privileged communication laws; and Section 504 of the Rehabilitation Act.

Americans with Disabilities Act (PL 101-336)

ADA
Accommodations for testing must be made

Passed in 1990, this law states that to assure proper test administration, accommodations must be made for individuals with disabilities who are taking tests for employment and that testing must be shown to be relevant to the job in question.

The Buckley Amendment (FERPA)

FERPA
Affirms right to access test records in the school

Also known as the Family Educational Rights and Privacy Act of 1974, this law affirms the right of all individuals to their school records, including test records.

Carl Perkins Act (PL 98-524)

Carl Perkins Act
Ensures access to vocational assessment, counseling, and placement

Passed in 1984, this law assures that the following individuals have access to vocational assessment, counseling, and placement:

- the economically and academically disadvantaged
- those with physical disabilities
- men and women entering nontraditional occupations

- adults in need of job training
- single parents or homemakers
- individuals with limited English proficiency
- incarcerated individuals

Civil Rights Acts (1964 and Amendments)

Civil Rights Act
Test must be
valid for job in
question

This series of laws asserts that any test used for employment or promotion must be shown to be suitable and valid for the job in question. If not, alternative means of assessment must be provided. Differential test cutoffs are not allowed.

The Freedom of Information Act

*Freedom of
Information Act*
Affirms right
to access fed-
eral and state
records

This law assures the right of individuals to access their federal records, including test records. Most states have similar laws that assure the right to access state records.

The Health Insurance Portability and Accountability Act (HIPAA)

HIPAA
Ensures privacy
of medical and
counseling
records

The recent passage of the Health Insurance Portability and Accountability Act (HIPAA) assures the privacy of client records, including testing records, and the sharing of such information (Zuckerman, 2003). In general, HIPAA restricts the amount of information that can be shared without client consent and allows clients to have access to their records, except for process notes used in counseling (U.S. Department of Health and Human Services, 2003). In fact, HIPAA requires agencies to show how they have complied with this act. As a result of HIPAA, mental health professionals will generally have to do the following (APA Practice Organization, 2002, p. 2):

- Provide information to patients about their privacy rights and how that information can be used.
- Adopt clear privacy procedures for their practices.
- Train employees so that they understand the privacy procedures.
- Designate an individual to be responsible for seeing that privacy procedures are adopted and followed.
- Secure patient records.

Individuals with Disabilities Education Improvement Act (IDEIA) (Expansion of PL 94-142)

IDEIA
Assures right to
be tested for
learning disabili-
ties in schools

Relative to assessment, this legislative act assures the right of students to be tested, at the school system's expense, if they are suspected of having a disability that interferes with learning. The law, which applies to those from age 3 through age 21, asserts that if a student is found to have a disability, schools must assure that the student is given accommodations for his or her disability and taught within the "least restrictive environment," which often is a regular classroom.

Students who are suspected of having a disability are referred for medical, psychological, communication, and/or vision and hearing evaluations. Any assessment that is conducted should be cross-culturally appropriate, and parents should be informed of the kinds of tests being used and give permission for the child to be tested. If the assessment indicates that a student is eligible for services, an IEP team must develop an Individualized Education Plan (IEP) within 120 days of the evaluation. The plan should address what services are needed and how they can be provided within the least restrictive environment. The IEP team often includes the parent(s), the child's teacher(s), a district representative who is able to provide or oversee the delivery of special education services, the child (when appropriate), representatives from the evaluation team, possible service providers, and other relevant people chosen by the parent or school.

Privileged Communication

Privileged communication Legal right to maintain privacy of conversation

Privileged communication is a conversation conducted with someone that state or federal law identifies as a person with whom conversations may legally be kept confidential (i.e., attorney-client, doctor-patient, therapist-patient, clergy-penitent, husband-wife, etc.). In the case of clinicians, the goal of the law is to encourage the client to engage in conversations without fear that the clinician will reveal the contents of the conversation (e.g., in a court of law), thus ensuring the privacy and efficacy of the counseling relationship. The privilege belongs to the client, and only the client can waive that privilege (Attorney C. Borstein, personal communication, November 11, 2004; Swenson, 1997, p. 464). Privileged communication should not be confused with confidentiality, which is the *ethical* (not legal) obligation of the counselor to keep conversations confidential (Glosoff, Herlihy, & Spence, 2000).

Jaffee v. Redmond Affirms privileged communication laws

A 1996 ruling upheld the right to privileged communication (*Jaffee v. Redmond*, 1996; see Box 2.4). In this case, the Supreme Court upheld the right of a licensed social worker to keep her case records confidential. Describing the social worker as a "therapist" and "psychotherapist," the ruling will likely protect all licensed therapists in federal courts and may affect all licensed therapists who have privileged communication (Remley, Herlihy, & Herlihy, 1997).

Section 504 of the Rehabilitation Act

Section 504 Assessment for programs must measure ability— not disability

This act applies to all federally funded programs receiving financial assistance and was established to create a "level playing field" and prevent discrimination based on disability. Based on this law (U.S. Department of Health and Human Services, n.d., "Prohibited Discriminatory Acts"), employers and organizations cannot:

- Deny qualified individuals the opportunity to participate in or benefit from federally funded programs, services, or other benefits.
- Deny access to programs, services, benefits or opportunities to participate as a result of physical barriers.

BOX 2.4
Jaffee v. Redmond

Mary Lu Redmond, a police officer in a village near Chicago, responded to a 'fight in progress' call at an apartment complex on June 27, 1991. At the scene, she shot and killed a man she believed was about to stab another man he was chasing. The family of the man she had killed sued Redmond, the police department, and the village, alleging that Officer Redmond had used excessive force in violation of the deceased's civil rights.

When the plaintiff's lawyers learned that Redmond had sought and received counseling from a licensed social worker employed by the village, they sought to compel the social worker to turn over her case notes and records and testify at the trial. Redmond and the social worker claimed that their communications were privileged under an Illinois statute. They both refused to reveal the substance of their counseling sessions even though the trial judge rejected their argument that the communications were privileged. The judge then instructed jurors that they could assume that the information withheld would have been unfavorable to the policewoman, and the jury awarded the plaintiffs $545,000.
–Remley et al., 1997, p. 214

After a series of appeals, the Supreme Court heard the case on February 26, 1996. The Court decided that the licensed therapist did indeed hold privilege and that the judge's instruction to the jury was therefore unwarranted.

- Deny employment opportunities, including hiring, promotion, training, and fringe benefits, for which they are otherwise entitled or qualified.

Relative to assessment, any instrument used to measure appropriateness for a program or service must measure the individual's ability, not be a reflection of his or her disability.

Professional Issues

Major professional associations
AACE for ACA and Division 5 for APA

We will begin this section by highlighting two professional associations in the field of assessment: The Association for Assessment in Counseling and Education (AACE) and Division 5 of the American Psychological Association: Evaluation, Measurement, and Statistics. Next, we will discuss the importance of recognizing that assessment works best when it is a holistic process: that is, when formal and informal assessment techniques are combined with a clinical interview. Next, we will explore how the use of assessment techniques can enhance the counseling process. The section will conclude with a discussion of cross-cultural issues.

Professional Associations

Although there are literally dozens of professional associations in the field that might pique your interest (see Appendix A), few specifically focus on assessment. Although we encourage you to join the professional association with which you feel the closest affinity, if you have a strong interest in assessment you might want to consider joining the following two associations.

The Association for Assessment in Counseling and Education (AACE), a division of ACA, "is an organization of counselors, educators, and other professionals that advocates [for] the counseling profession by providing leadership, training, and research in the creation, development, production, and use of assessment and diagnostic techniques" (AACE, 2004a). Consider joining AACE if you are interested in testing, diagnosis, and the training and supervision of those who do assessment, and/or if you are interested in developing and validating assessment products and procedures. AACE publishes a journal entitled *Measurement and Evaluation in Counseling and Development.*

Division 5 of the American Psychological Association: Evaluation, Measurement, and Statistics, is devoted to "promoting high standards in both research and practical application of psychological assessment, evaluation, measurement, and statistics" (Division 5, 2004, para. 1). Division 5 publishes two journals, *Psychological Assessment,* which is geared toward assessment, and *Psychological Methods,* which is research-oriented. Division 5 also publishes a quarterly newsletter, *The Scope,* which focuses on business issues of the association as well as new issues in the field.

Accreditation Standards of Professional Associations

A number of the professional associations have accreditation standards that specifically speak to curriculum issues in the area of assessment. Such standards help to establish a common core of experience for students who enter their programs, regardless of the institution in which the program is housed. Thus, we find organizations such as the American Psychological Association (APA, 2000), the National Association of School Psychologists (NASP, 2000), and the Council for the Accreditation of Counseling and Related Educational Programs (CACREP, 2001), setting standards that drive the curriculum for their graduate programs. In fact, much of what is covered in this text is a result of the authors examining these curriculum standards and trying to assure that we cover them as fully as possible. If you get a chance, you may want to visit the websites listed in the references and examine the standards for each of these organizations.

Testing as a Holistic Process

As we will stress throughout this text, assessment of clients is much broader than simply giving an individual a test. A good assessment involves a number of different kinds of instruments, including formal tests, informal assessment instruments, and a clinical interview. This holistic process helps us obtain a broader and more accurate view of the client than if we were to rely on just one test (Juhnke, 1995; Harrington, 1995). In addition, assessment is not a static process; instead, it should be seen as continuous and ongoing (Vacc, 1982). The assessment of a client occurs at a specific point in time; however, if we believe that a person can change, that point represents only a small sample of an individual's total functioning. Viewing assessment in this way allows us to understand that an

Assessment is a snapshot; clients continually change.

BOX 2.5
Making Ethical Decisions

After reading this chapter, in small groups in class or as a homework assignment, review the situations below, and use Kitchener's and Corey's models of ethical decision making, as well as your knowledge of legal and professional issues, to decide on your courses of action. Share your answers with the rest of the class.

Situation 1: A graduate-level mental health professional with no training in career development is giving interest inventories as she counsels individuals for career issues. Can she do this? Is this ethical? Professional? Legal? If this professional happened to be a colleague of yours, what, if anything, would you do?

Situation 2: During the taking of some routine tests for promotion, a company learns that there is a high probability that one of the employees is abusing drugs and is a pathological liar. The firm decides not to promote him and instead fires him. He comes to see you for counseling because he is depressed. Has the company acted ethically? Legally? What responsibility do you have toward this client?

Situation 3: An African-American mother is concerned that her child may have an attention deficit problem. She goes to the teacher who supports her concerns, and they go to the assistant principal requesting testing for a possible learning disorder. The mother asks if the child could be given an individual intelligence test that

can screen for such problems, and the assistant principal states, "Those tests have been banned for minority students because of concerns about cross-cultural bias." The mother states that she will give her permission for such testing, but the assistant principal says, "I'm sorry, we'll have to make do with some other tests and observation." Is this ethical? Professional? Legal? If you were a school counselor or school psychologist and this mother came to see you, what would you tell her?

Situation 4: A test that has not been researched to show that it is predictive of success for all potential graduate students in social work is used as part of the program's admission process. When challenged on this by a potential student, the head of the program states that the test has not been shown to be biased and the program uses other, additional criteria for admission. You are a member of the faculty at this program. Is this ethical? Professional? Legal? What is your responsibility in this situation?

Situation 5: An individual who is physically challenged and wheelchair bound applies for a job at a national fast food chain. When he goes in to take the test for a mid-level job at this company, he is told that he cannot be given this test because it has not been assessed for its predictive ability for individuals with his disability. You are hired by the company to do the testing. What is your responsibility, if any, to this individual and to the company?

---

individual's cognitive functioning and personality may, and probably will, change significantly throughout the lifespan. Seeing a client in this manner helps us develop treatment plans for the client in the here and now, while reminding us not to be held hostage to labels and diagnoses—for the individual may, and probably will, change.

Using Tests Wisely: The Marriage Between Counseling and Assessment

Use assessment instruments! They allow clients better understanding of self.

Tests are sometimes used as an aid to the counseling process, as they can help clients gain a greater understanding of themselves and can assist them in making smart decisions. However, some clinicians who are primarily trained to do counseling and psychotherapy have an aversion to doing testing, despite the fact that they are also trained in this area (Bradley, 1994a, 1994b; Goldman, 1994). If clients are to get the most out of therapy, all avenues to increased self-knowledge should be made available to them, including the use of tests and other assessment instruments. Thus, clinicians should embrace the appropriate use of tests as an adjunct to the counseling process. Not to do so will prevent the client from learning as much as possible about himself or herself. Freud was known to say that the goal of therapy is to make a little more of the unconscious conscious. Thus, it makes sense to use every available and reasonable means to this goal, with testing being one.

Cross-Cultural Issues in Assessment

All testing should be considered within a framework of cultural diversity.
(Anastasi, 1985, p. xxix)

In recent years there has been an increasing awareness of test bias in the assessment of minorities (Watkins & Campbell, 1990). Lawsuits have questioned the accuracy of some tests, laws have been passed preventing the use of other tests, and research has been conducted that demonstrates the negative impact of tests. In response to these problems, as you saw earlier in this chapter, ethical codes and standards that address assessment almost always include statements concerning how to choose, administer, and interpret tests and assessment instruments for clients of color. Such codes and standards help clinicians and others (1) understand the cultural bias inherent in tests, (2) know when a test should not be used because of bias, and (3) know what to do with test results when a test does *not* predict well for minorities.

In Chapter 3 we will discuss a number of issues related to cross-cultural issues and test worthiness. We will highlight the fact that a test should accurately measure a construct regardless of one's membership in a class, race, religion, or gender. We will discuss how the U.S. court system, public law, federal acts, and constitutional amendments have all supported the notion that testing must be fair for all groups of people and free from bias. We will note how tests cannot be used to track students and that as a result of the Supreme Court case of *Griggs v. Duke Power Company*, tests used for hiring and advancement at work must show that they can predict job performance for all groups. Also, as we highlighted in this chapter and will discuss in Chapter 3, a number of laws have been passed that impinge on the use of tests and assert the rights of all individuals to be tested fairly. In the future, we are likely to see an increased emphasis on understanding the inherent bias in tests, the creation of new tests that are less biased, and new efforts to properly administer, score, and interpret tests with the understanding that they will, to some degree, have bias.

Summary

This chapter began by highlighting significant assessment issues in the ethical codes of the ACA and APA, including (1) choosing assessment procedures based on test worthiness, (2) assuring competence, (3) keeping information confidential, (4) attending to cross-cultural issues, (5) obtaining informed consent,

(6) invasion of privacy issues and understanding limits of test confidentiality, (7) being cautious when diagnosing mental disorders, (8) releasing information properly and carefully, (9) administering tests based on how they were established and standardized, (10) assuring the integrity of test content and test security; and (11) properly scoring and interpreting tests.

We next briefly described three standards that have expanded upon the ethical codes. First, we noted seven areas of knowledge and skills as identified by the Standards for the Qualifications of Test Users. We then discussed the fact that the Code of Fair Testing Practices in Education was developed to provide guidance in developing and selecting appropriate tests, administering and scoring tests, reporting and interpreting test results, and informing test takers. Finally, we noted that the Responsibilities of Users of Standardized Tests (RUST) speaks to the qualifications of individuals giving tests in the following areas: qualifications needed, technical knowledge, test selection, test administration, test scoring, interpreting test results, and communicating test results.

As the section on ethical issues continued, we discussed the fact that good ethical decision making is more than just relying on a code of ethics. We presented Kitchener's moral model of ethical decision making, which examines the autonomy of the client, beneficence of society, nonmaleficence of people, justice to all, and the fidelity of the counseling relationship. We then presented Corey's eight-step model, which includes identifying the problem, identifying the potential issues involved, reviewing the relevant ethical guidelines, knowing relevant laws and regulations, obtaining consultation, considering possible and probable courses of action, listing the consequences of various decisions, and deciding on what appears to be the best course of action. We suggested that the ability to make wise ethical decisions might well be influenced by the counselor's level of ethical, moral, and cognitive development.

The next part of the chapter examined some legal issues involving the use of tests, including the Americans with Disabilities Act (PL 101-336); The Buckley Amendment, otherwise known as FERPA; the Carl Perkins Act (PL 98-524), Civil Rights Acts (1964 and amendments); the Freedom of Information Act; the Health Insurance Portability and Accountability Act (HIPAA); the Individuals with Disabilities Education Improvement Act, which was an expansion of PL94-142; privileged communication laws; and Section 504 of the Rehabilitation Act. We noted that most of this legislation speaks to issues of confidentiality, fairness, and test worthiness.

In this chapter we examined a number of professional issues. First, we highlighted two professional associations in the field of assessment: the Association for Assessment in Counseling and Education (AACE), which is a division of ACA; and Division 5 of the American Psychological Association. We next highlighted three of the accrediting bodies in the helping professionals that address curriculum standards in assessment. Then we spoke of the importance of viewing assessment as a holistic process that should involve assessing the client in multiple ways, including the use of formal tests, informal assessment instruments, and the clinical interview. We pointed out that assessment should be viewed as an ongoing process because people change as they live and learn, and we suggested that clinicians should remain open to using assessment instruments as part of their counseling process.

Finally, we highlighted the fact that in recent years there has been an increasing awareness of bias when assessing clients of color. We noted that our ethical codes have increasingly spoken to this problem and that they accentuate the importance of test worthiness for all groups of individuals in a norm group. We stated that a number of federal laws have supported the notion that testing must be fair for all groups of people. We noted that Chapter 3 would expand on the discussion of cross-cultural issues in assessment.

Chapter Review

1. Relative to testing and assessment, identify and discuss some of the major themes addressed in ethical codes.
2. In addition to the ethical codes, other standards have been developed to guide individuals in test selection, administration, and interpretation. Describe some of these standards.
3. Describe APA's levels of test user competence.
4. Describe Kitchener's moral model and Corey's problem-solving model of ethical decision-making.
5. Compare and contrast how individuals at different cognitive developmental levels would go about making ethical decisions.
6. Identify some of the major legal issues that have affected the selection, administration, and interpretation of assessment instruments.
7. List two professional associations that specifically address assessment issues.
8. What is the role of accreditation in the delivery of curriculum content in the area of assessment?
9. What is needed for a good assessment of an individual?
10. Why should assessment procedures often be considered when working with clients?
11. Describe the importance of having an understanding of cross-cultural issues when using assessment procedures.

Test Worthiness
and Test Statistics

In Section Two we will examine how tests are created, scored, and interpreted. Chapters 3, 4, and 5 use test statistics to explain the concepts being presented. Being able to understand these statistics and how they are applied to the assessment process is crucial if one is to interpret test data appropriately. As you read these chapters, we will show you that the development of tests and the interpretation of test data is a deliberate and planned process that involves a scientific approach to the understanding of differences among people. We try to present this information in a down-to-earth and comprehensible fashion.

Chapter 3 describes test worthiness and defines it as an involved, objective analysis of a test. To do this objective analysis, however, we must first understand a basic statistic called the correlation coefficient. Thus, the correlation coefficient is defined early in this chapter, and we subsequently show how this important statistic is used to conduct an analysis of four factors in test construction and test use: (1) *validity:* whether the test measures what it's supposed to measure; (2) *reliability:* whether the score an individual has received on a test is an accurate measure of his or her true score; (3) *cross-cultural fairness:* whether the score the individual has obtained is a true reflection of the individual, and not a function of cultural bias inherent in the test, and (4) *practicality:* whether it makes sense to use a test in a particular situation. The chapter concludes with a list of five steps to use in test selection to assure test worthiness.

Chapter 4 starts with the basics: an examination of raw scores. We first show that raw scores generally provide little meaningful information about a set of scores, and then we look at various ways that we can manipulate raw scores to make sense out of a set of data. Thus, in this chapter we examine how a variety of basic statistics and graphs can help us understand raw scores. Some of these include frequency distributions; histograms and frequency polygons; the normal curve; skewed distributions; measures of central tendency such as the mean, median, and mode; and measures of variability such as the range, semi-interquartile range, and standard deviation.

Chapter 5 is a natural extension of Chapter 4, and in it we examine derived scores and explore how they are used to help us understand raw scores. We start by distinguishing norm-referenced testing and criterion-referenced testing because these two ways of understanding test scores are quite different, and derived scores are mostly associated with norm-referenced testing. Next, we discuss specific types of derived scores: percentiles; standard scores, including z scores, T scores, Deviation IQs, stanines, sten scores, college and graduate school entrance exam scores (e.g., SATs, GREs, and ACTs), NCE scores, and publisher-type scores; and developmental norms such as age comparisons and grade equivalents. The chapter nears its conclusion with a discussion of standard error of measurement, which is a mechanism for estimating how closely an individual's obtained score approximates his or her true score. The chapter ends with a brief discussion of nominal, ordinal, interval, and ratio scales of measurement. We describe how each type of scale has unique attributes that may limit the statistical calculations we can perform, and we mention that different kinds of assessment instruments use different kinds of scales.

Test Worthiness: Validity, Reliability, Practicality, and Cross-Cultural Fairness

I'm walking down a Cincinnati street, and a man walks up to me and asks, "Want to take a test?" "Sure," I reply. He takes me to a storefront, gives me a test, and then goes to a back room to score it. A few minutes later he reappears and tells me, "Well, you're pretty bright and have a fairly good personality, but if you take Ron Hubbard's course in Scientology, you will be brighter and have a better personality." I tell him, "No thanks." A few years later, I'm walking down a street in Minneapolis and a man comes up to me and inquires, "Want to take a test?" This time I say, "If you can show me that this test is a good test—that is, it has good reliability and validity—I'll take it." He says, "I'm sure it has good reliability and validity." I say, "Show me." He says, "Well, I know our New York office must have that information." I say, "Well, I tell you what, I'll buy Ron Hubbard's book, Dianetics, *and if and when you can get me the information from the New York office, I'll read the book." I gave him my name and address. I never heard from him again.* (Ed Neukrug)

Test worthiness
Based on validity, reliability, cross-cultural fairness, and practicality

As you might expect from the above example, this chapter is about test worthiness, or how good a test actually is. Demonstrating test worthiness requires an involved, objective analysis of a test in four critical areas: (1) *validity:* whether it measures what it's supposed to measure; (2) *reliability:* whether the score an individual receives on a test is an accurate measure of his or her true score; (3) *cross-cultural fairness:* whether a person's score is a true reflection of the individual and not a function of cultural bias inherent in the test; and (4) *practicality:* whether it makes sense to use a test in a particular situation. After examining these four factors, we will conclude the chapter with a discussion of five steps to use in test selection to assure test worthiness. However, prior to examining the four critical factors of validity, reliability, cross-cultural fairness, and practicality, and before discussing test selection, we will examine the concept of correlation coefficient because it is central to understanding much of what will be presented in this chapter.

Correlation Coefficient

Correlation coefficient
Relationship between two sets of test scores

Correlation coefficient, which shows the relationship between two sets of scores, is a statistical concept frequently used in discussions of the critical factors listed above. Correlation coefficients range from 1.00 to –1.00 and generally are reported in decimals of one-hundredths (see Figure 3.1). A positive correlation shows a tendency for scores to be related in the same direction. For instance, if a group of individuals took two tests, a positive correlation would show a tendency for those who obtained high scores on the first test to obtain high scores on the second test, for those who obtained low scores on the first test to obtain low scores on the second test, and so forth. On the other hand, a negative correlation shows an inverse relationship between sets of scores; for instance, individuals who obtain high scores on the first test would be likely to obtain low scores on the second test.

A correlation that approaches +1 or –1 demonstrates a strong relationship, while a correlation that approaches 0 shows little or no relationship between two measures or variables (see Figure 3.1). For instance, if I wanted to show that SAT scores predict college performance, I would have to show that the correlation coefficient does not approach zero and is significant enough to warrant its use (House & Johnson, 1993a, b). Similarly, if I wanted to show that my newly made test of depression was worthwhile, I could correlate scores on my new test with an established test of depression. In this case I would expect to find a relatively high correlation coefficient as evidenced by the fact that individuals who scored high on my test would have a tendency to score high on the established test,

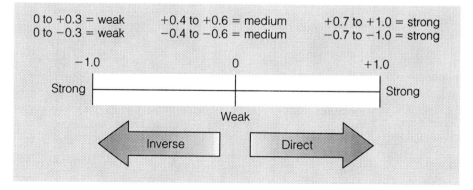

Figure 3.1 Correlation coefficient

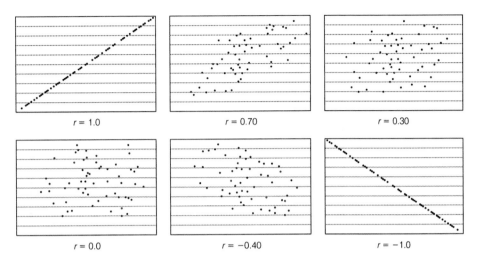

r = 1.0   r = 0.70   r = 0.30

r = 0.0   r = −0.40   r = −1.0

Figure 3.2 Scatterplot charts and correlational estimates

individuals who scored low on my test would have a tendency to score low on the established test, and so forth. As we discuss the four critical factors of validity, reliability, cross-cultural fairness, and practicality, you will see that correlation coefficient often plays an important role in many of them. If you would like to find out how to calculate a correlation coefficient, see Appendix C.

Scatterplot
Graph showing two or more sets of test scores

A correlation between two sets of variables, or test scores, can also be plotted on a graph. By placing an individual's first score on the horizontal (*x*) axis and second score on the vertical (*y*) axis, you can plot this person's scores on the graph. If you continue doing this for the remaining members of a group of people, each of whom has two sets of scores, you will end up with what's called a scatterplot (see Figure 3.2).

As illustrated in Figure 3.2, as the dots come close to forming a diagonal line, the scores on the *x*-axis are more closely related to scores on the *y*-axis, or the correlation becomes closer to plus or minus 1.0. As the dots become more random (little relationship between scores on the two tests), the correlation approaches zero. Additionally, it is called a positive correlation if the general slope of the dots rises from left to right and a negative correlation if it rises from the right to the left.

Coefficient of Determination (Shared Variance)

Squaring the correlation coefficient gives you the coefficient of determination, or shared variance between two variables. This variance is a statement about underlying factors that account for the relationship between two variables. Thus, if the correlation is .70, the square is .49, which represents a percentage of shared variance—in this case, 49 percent. For instance, in one study, a correlation of .85

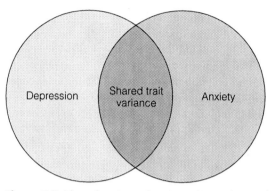

Figure 3.3 Shared variance between depression and anxiety (r = .85, r² = .72)

Coefficient of determination
Common factors that account for a relationship; square of the correlation coefficient

was found between scores on a test of depression and scores on a test that measured anxiety (Cole, Truglio, & Peeke, 1997). Therefore, in this case it can be said that 72% of the variance is shared variance (.85 squared), or, in other words, a large percentage of similar factors underlie feelings of depression and anxiety as measured by these tests (see Figure 3.3). What might some of these factors be? An educated guess might lead us to think that they could be environmental stressors (e.g., job loss, relationship problems, etc.), cognitive schemata (ways of understanding the world), chemical imbalance, and so forth. All of these factors could trigger feelings of depression and of anxiety. Of course, we need to keep in mind that 28% of the variance is not shared, which means that other factors differentially affect whether one feels depressed or anxious. Keep the concept of coefficient of determination in mind when you read the next section on validity.

Validity

> *Validity is a unitary concept. It is the degree to which all of the accumulated evidence supports the intended interpretation of test scores for the intended purpose (AERA, APA, & NCME, 1999, p. 11).*

Validity
Evidence supporting the use of test scores

How well does a test measure what it's supposed to measure? That is the primary question that validity attempts to answer. Over the years a number of methods have been developed to determine the validity of a test. Logically, it makes sense that the more methods one can use to provide evidence that a test is valid, the stronger the case one can make that the interpretation of test scores is accurate for the manner in which the test is being used (AERA, APA, & NCME, 1999). Various types of validity that help to provide the evidence needed to demonstrate the worthiness of a test include content validity; criterion-related validity, which includes concurrent validity and predictive validity; and construct validity, which includes methods of experimental design, factor analysis, discriminant validity, and convergent validity.

Content Validity

Content validity
Evidence that
test items repre-
sent the proper
domain

Probably the most basic form of validity is content validity. As with all types of validity, its name is reflective of what it attempts to show: Is the content of the test valid for the kind of test it is? In assuring content validity, a process is used to develop items for a test, such as examining established books in the field, gathering information from experts, and examining curriculum guides. In demonstrating content validity, test publishers need to do the following (see Figure 3.4):

Step 1: Show that the test developer adequately surveyed the domain through the processes noted above.

Step 2: Show that the content of the test matches what was found in the survey of the domain.

Step 3: Show that test items accurately reflect the content.

Step 4: Show that the number of items for each content area matches the relative importance of these items as reflected in the survey of the domain.

To illustrate this process, let's look at the creation of a fourth-grade math achievement test to be used nationally. In demonstrating content validity, the test developer should do the following:

Step 1: Show that information for the test was gathered from places such as fourth-grade math books, teachers of fourth-grade math, curriculum specialists in the schools, professors at colleges who are training fourth-grade math teachers, and so forth (Grant & Davis, 1997).

Step 2: Show that the content was chosen based on the information that was gathered (e.g., addition, subtraction, multiplication, division, decimals, fractions).

Step 3: Show that the items reflect the content chosen.

Step 4: Show that the number of items for each content area reflects the relative importance of that area (e.g., multiplication and division might be emphasized more than the other items) (see Figure 3.4).

Despite one's painstaking attempts to assure content validity, not all fourth-grade teachers would be teaching the same math content, so the test might hold more validity for some fourth-grade classes than for others. Thus, content validity is somewhat contextual and depends on who is taking the test (Goodwin, 2002a, 2002b).

Face validity
Superficial
appearance of a
test—not true
validity

Face validity, which is not considered an actual type of validity, is sometimes confused with content validity. Face validity has to do with how the test superficially looks. If you were examining the test, would it appear to be measuring what it is supposed to measure? Although most tests should have face validity, some tests could be valid yet not have it. For instance, there might be some items on a personality test that, on the surface, do not seem to be measuring a quality

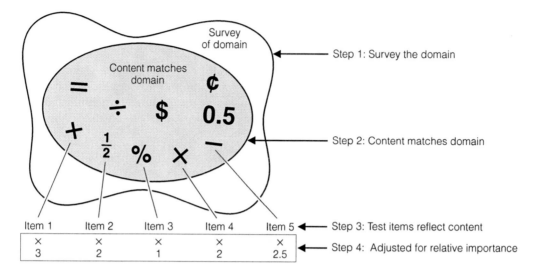

Figure 3.4 Establishing content validity

that the test is attempting to assess. Look, for example, at the hypothetical item below that is assessing whether or not an individual may have a panic disorder.

In the past week, check the following symptoms that you have experienced:

_____ *a. chills*   _____ *c. hot flashes*   _____ *e. depersonalization*

_____ *b. choking*   _____ *d. abdominal distress*   _____ *f. unsteady feelings*

Even though the symptoms listed above might not seem obvious to a person unfamiliar with panic disorder, they are often associated with the disorder, as noted in the *Diagnostic and Statistical Manual-IV-TR* (APA, 2000). On the surface, this item might not seem to be measuring the construct, but individuals with panic disorder often have some or all of these symptoms, and thus such a question is conceivable and might be important to ask. Therefore, the item might be important to the content validity of the test.

Criterion-Related Validity

Criterion-related validity
Relationship between test scores and another standard

What is the relationship between a test and a criterion (external source) that the test should be related to? That is the essence of criterion-related validity. Two types of criterion-related validity generally described are concurrent validity and predictive validity.

Concurrent, or "here and now," validity occurs when a test is shown to be related to an external source that can be measured at around the same time the test is being given. For instance, suppose I develop a test to measure the tendency toward alcohol abuse. I might give this test to 500 individuals and then have significant people in each examinee's life rank order the examinee's use of

---

EXERCISE 3.1 Demonstrating Content Validity

In small groups, discuss how you might show content validity for a test that measures depression. Share your ideas in class.

Concurrent validity
Relationship between test scores and another currently obtainable benchmark

Predictive validity
Relationship between test scores and a future standard

alcohol to see if there is a correlation between alcohol abuse and use of alcohol (e.g., number of drinks per day). Clearly, I would suspect a high correlation (the higher the score, the more one drank), and if I did not find one, my test would be suspect.

Whereas concurrent validity relates a test to a "here and now" measure, predictive validity relates a test to a criterion in the future. This kind of validity is clearly important if a test should be predicting something about an individual. For instance, the GREs should have predictive validity for GPA in graduate school; otherwise they would not be valuable and should not be used. In actuality, the correlation between the GREs and GPA in graduate school is about .34, which is not very high (see Table 3.1). However, when placed in the context of other possible predictors of college success (e.g., undergraduate GPA, extracurricular activities, and interviews), it's not so bad. And, if we combine the use of predictors of graduate school GPA, we increase our ability to make a prediction about students' success. For instance, the correlation between undergraduate GPA and grades in graduate school is .37, and when we combine the GRE scores and GPA in undergraduate school we find a correlation of .46 with grades in graduate school (see Table 3.1).

EXERCISE 3.2 Demonstrating Criterion-Related Validity

In class, form small groups, some of which will examine concurrent validity while others will examine predictive validity. In your groups, choose a test from the list below or come up with another test. Next, discuss criteria with which you might compare your test.

POSSIBLE TESTS:

High school achievement test	Depression test	Clerical aptitude test
SATs, GREs, MATs	Test of anxiety	First-grade reading test
Intelligence test	Test of hypochondriasis	

Construct Validity

What is intelligence? When teaching an assessment class, we have found that this often becomes a "hot" topic for discussion, with students arguing over what they believe actually makes up this construct. Construct validity is the scientific basis for showing that a construct (idea, concept, or model) such as intelligence is being measured by a test. Showing evidence of construct validity is particularly

TABLE 3.1

Average Estimated Correlations of GRE General Test (Verbal, Quantitative, and Analytical) Scores and Undergraduate Grade Point Average with Graduate First-Year Grade Point Average by Department Type

TYPE OF DEPARTMENT	NUMBER OF DEPARTMENTS	NUMBER OF EXAMINEES	PREDICTORS					
			V	Q	A	U	VQA*	VQAU*
All departments	1,038	12,013	.30	.29	.28	.37	.34	.46
Natural sciences	384	4,420	.28	.27	.26	.36	.31	.44
Engineering	87	1,066	.27	.22	.24	.38	.30	.44
Social sciences	352	4,211	.33	.32	.30	.38	.37	.48
Humanities & arts	115	1,219	.30	.33	.27	.37	.34	.46
Education	86	901	.31	.30	.29	.35	.36	.47
Business	14	196	.28	.28	.25	.39	.31	.47

V = GRE Verbal, Q = GRE Quantitative, A = GRE Analytical, U = Undergraduate grade point average
* Combination of individual predictors

Source: Graduate Record Examinations, 2004–2005. GRE materials selected from 2004–2005 Guide to the Use of Scores, p. 22. Reprinted by permission of Educational Testing Service, the copyright owner.

Construct validity
Evidence that an idea or concept is being measured by a test

important when developing tests that measure abstract domains, such as intelligence, self-concept, depression, anxiety, empathy, and many other personality characteristics. On the other hand, construct validity becomes much less of an issue when one is measuring well-defined areas, such as achievement in geometry.

To demonstrate construct validity it is often useful to provide multiple sources of evidence that the construct we are measuring is indeed being exposed. Although some have argued that almost any kind of validity is evidence that the construct being measured exists (Goodwin, 2002a), a more restrictive definition of construct validity includes an analysis of a test through one or more of the following methods: (1) experimental design, (2) factor analysis, (3) convergence with other instruments, and/or (4) discrimination with other measures.

Experimental Design Validity

Experimental design validity
Using experimentation to show that a test measures a concept

You've just developed your new test of depression, and you're very proud of it. Of course, you want to show that it is indeed valid. You already have shown that it has content validity by developing items through an examination of DSM-IV-TR, scholarly journal articles, and consultation with experts. However, now you want to show that the test indeed works—that it measures your construct. So you approach a number of expert clinicians who work with depressed clients and ask them to identify new clients on their caseloads who are depressed. You then request that they administer your depression test prior to and at the end of six months of treatment. What should you expect to find? Clearly, if the test is good and does measure the construct depression, it should be able to accurately reflect the change in these clients—in this case, a significant decrease in depression. If not, you need to go back to the drawing board. Experimentally based construct validity thus confirms the hypothesis you developed to scientifically show that your construct exists. Sometimes, when a number of studies are completed, you will find authors conducting a "meta-analysis," which statistically analyzes all of these studies in an effort to offer broader evidence of the existence of the construct being examined.

Factor Analysis

Factor analysis
Statistically examining the relationship between subscales and the larger construct

Factor analysis, another method to show construct validity, demonstrates the statistical relationship among subscales or items of a test. Suppose, for instance, that your depression test has subscales that measure hopelessness, suicidal ideation, and self-esteem. Theoretically, you would expect them all to be related to your larger test score that measures depression. In addition, you would expect them to be somewhat related, but not largely related, to one another. After all, they are measuring something different from one another (although they all make up the larger test "depression"). If your factor analysis upholds these expectations, you have shown construct validity of your test.

Convergence with Other Instruments (Convergent Validity)

Convergent validity
Relationship between a test and other similar tests

Believing strongly that your test does indeed measure depression, you would, of course, expect your test to be related to other existing well-known valid measures of depression (e.g., clinicians' ratings of clients or another test of depression). Thus, you decide to correlate your test with the Beck Depression Inventory II (BDI-II) (Beck, Steer, & Brown, 2004), a well-known, accepted test of depression. You give the BDI-II to 500 subjects and you find a high correlation between the two scores, perhaps .75. You're satisfied, perhaps even glad you didn't get a higher correlation. After all, isn't your test different (and a little better!) than the well-known existing test? Thus, you expect your correlation to be less than perfect. Thus, convergent validity occurs when you find a significant positive correlation between your test and other existing measures of a similar nature. Sometimes this relationship involves very similar kinds of instruments, but other times you would be looking for correlations between your test and variables that may seem only somewhat related. For instance, if you correlate your test with a test to measure despair, you would expect a positive correlation. However, because despair is theoretically different from depression, you would expect a lower correlation—maybe .4.

Discrimination with Other Measures (Discriminant Validity)

With convergent validity you're expecting to find a relationship between your test and other variables of a similar nature. Discriminant validity, in a sense, is the opposite in that you're looking to find little or no relationship between your

Discriminant validity
Showing a lack of relationship between a test and other dissimilar tests

test and measures of constructs that are not theoretically related to your test. For instance, with your test of depression, you might want to compare your test scores with an existing test that measures anxiety. In this case, you give 500 subjects your test of depression as well as a valid test to measure anxiety, looking to find little or no relationship. Consider how important discriminant validity might be in this case if you're working with clients. Clients who are dealing with high amounts of anxiety will often present with depressive features. If you were able to give your client a test that could discriminate depression from anxiety, you would get a better picture of your client. Making a more accurate diagnosis could dramatically affect your treatment plan, as approaches to working with depressed clients will vary dramatically from approaches to working with anxious clients.

EXERCISE 3.3 **Demonstrating Construct Validity**

In small groups, show how you would develop the construct validity of a test that measures self-actualizing values (e.g., being in touch with feelings, being spontaneous, being accepting and nonjudgmental, showing empathy). Try to touch on many of the methods noted in this text, including experimental design, factor analysis, convergent validity, and discriminant validity. Present your group's proposal to the class.

Reliability

Reliability
Degree of freedom from measurement error—consistency of test scores

Test reliability can be compared to eating at the same restaurant over and over again. If it's a highly reliable restaurant, the meals always taste great. On the other hand, a restaurant that has poor reliability can't be trusted. Too many bad ingredients are used and mistakes are made in putting the meals together. And, maybe the restaurant has an atmosphere that turns you off and makes you not enjoy your meal.

Similarly, a test with high reliability is put together well—it has the right ingredients. And when you take the test, it's in an environment that is conducive to you producing your best results. The test is made well and the environment is optimal for the test-taking situation. You can trust that if, hypothetically, you were the same person who had walked in the first time you took this test, and you were to take this test over and over again, you would score about the same each time (e.g., if it were an achievement test, you didn't look up the answers or study the content prior to taking the test again). On the other hand, if you were to take a test with poor reliability over and over again your scores would fluctuate—be higher or lower each time you took it. There are so many problems with the test and with the environment that you would answer items in a different manner every time you take it.

Reliability can be defined as "the degree to which test scores are free from errors of measurement" (AERA et al., 1999, p. 180). Hypothetically, if we had a perfect test and the perfect environment, and a person who remained exactly the same each time he or she took the test, this individual would always score the same on the test, even if he or she took it one thousand times. As we all know, there are no perfect tests or environments, so we always end up with measurement error—or factors that affect one's score on a test (Thompson, 1999; Gronlund & Linn, 1990; Rowley, 1976). Clearly, the more we can reduce error on tests, the more accurate will be the examinee's score.

Have you ever taken a test and received a score that you felt didn't reflect how you actually performed on the test? Some of that difference may be attributed to measurement error. Many factors can cause such error, including poorly worded questions, poor test-taking instructions, test-taker anxiety or fatigue, and distractions in the testing room, to name just a few. On the other hand, part of the discrepancy may be due to lack of knowledge of the subject or lack of awareness of self, and sometimes it's easier to blame a test than ourselves for scores that we did not expect. If we know the amount of error on a test, as measured by reliability estimates, then we should be able to determine, to some degree, whether our unexpected score was due to error or to performance issues.

Test creators will evaluate their new instrument to determine if the scores it produces are reliable (consistent and dependable) and publish this information in the test manual, usually reported in the form of a reliability (correlation) coefficient. The closer the reliability estimate is to 1.0, the less error there is on the test. A good reliability estimate is sometimes a function of the kind of measurement being assessed, although there is no magic cut-off point for what makes a good reliability estimate (Goodwin & Goodwin, 1999; Knapp & Brown, 1995). For instance, teacher-made tests generally will have lower reliability estimates, perhaps around .7, because they do not go through the same type of scrutiny as some other kinds of tests, such as national achievement tests that often have reliability estimates in the .90s. Also, personality tests generally have lower reliability estimates than ability tests because the construct being measured is more abstract and because personality tends to fluctuate and thus is more difficult to define and measure. Some ways of measuring reliability include test-retest, alternative forms, and internal consistency.

Test-Retest Reliability

Test-retest reliability Relationship between scores from one test given at two different administrations

A relatively simple way to determine whether an instrument is reliable is to give the test twice to the same group of people. For example, imagine you have 500 people who come in to take a test. A day later they take the same test at the same place. You would then correlate the scores from the first test with those from the second test. The closer the two sets of scores, the more reliable the test. Although reliability coefficients provide individual test-takers with estimates about the stability of their individual scores, the actual process of gathering reliability information has to do with average fluctuation of many people's scores.

Thus, although one person's score might fluctuate a lot, an instrument can still have high reliability if most scores have little fluctuation.

Accuracy of the test-retest method can be affected by several factors. For instance, depending on the time between test administrations, people may forget information. On the other hand, sometimes people might learn more about a specific subject by reading a book, listening to the radio, searching on the computer, and so on. Also, some people might score higher on a second test because they are more familiar with the test format. As you might expect, test-retest reliability tends to be more effective in areas that are less likely to change over time, such as intelligence.

Alternate, Parallel, or Equivalent Forms Reliability

Alternate forms reliability Relationship between scores from two similar versions of the same test

Another method for determining reliability is to make two or more *alternate, parallel,* or *equivalent* forms of the same test. These alternate forms are created to mimic one another, yet are different enough to eliminate some of the problems found in test-retest reliability (e.g., looking up an answer). In this case, rather than giving the same test twice, the examiner gives the alternate form the second time. Clearly, a challenge involved in this kind of reliability is to assure that both forms of the test use the same or very similar directions, format, and number of questions, and are equal in difficulty and content. Although creating alternate forms eliminates some of the problems found in test-retest reliability, difficulty can arise in ensuring that the two forms are truly parallel. Also, because creating a parallel form is labor intensive and costly, it is often not a practical kind of reliability to implement. If this kind of reliability is used, the burden is on the test creator to prove that both tests are truly equal.

Internal Consistency

Internal consistency Reliability measured statistically by going "within" the test

A third type of reliability is called internal consistency. In this case, a determination is made as to how scores on individual items relate to each other or to the test as a whole. For instance, it would make sense that individuals who score high on a test of depression should, on average, respond to all the items on the test in a manner that indicates depressive ideation. If not, one might wonder why a particular item is not assessing depression. This kind of reliability is called internal consistency because you are looking within the test itself, or not going "outside of the test" to determine reliability estimates as you would be with test-retest or parallel forms reliability. Some types of internal consistency reliability include split-half (or odd-even), Cronbach's Coefficient Alpha, and Kuder-Richardson.

Split-Half or Odd-Even Reliability

Split-half reliability Correlating one half of a test against the other half

The most basic form of internal consistency reliability is called split-half or odd-even reliability. This method, which requires only one form and one administration of the test, splits the test in half and correlates the scores of one half of the test with the other half. Again, imagine 500 individuals who come in to take a test. After they have finished, we gather their responses, split each of their tests in half, and score each half, almost as if each individual had taken two different tests. The scores on the two halves are then correlated with one another. Obviously, advantages of this kind of reliability include only having to give the test once and not having to create a separate alternate form. One potential pitfall of this form of reliability would arise if the two halves of the test were not parallel or equivalent, such as when a test gets progressively more difficult. In that case, you might end up correlating the first half of the test with the second nonequivalent half, which can give you an inaccurately low estimate of your reliability. One common method to alleviate this potential error is to split the test into odd-numbered items and even-numbered items, although even this method runs the risk of not producing parallel halves.

Another disadvantage of this kind of reliability is that by turning one test into two, you have made it half as long. Generally speaking, one obtains a more accurate reading of the reliability of a test the longer it is; consequently, shortening the test may decrease its reliability. One common method to mathematically compensate for shortening the number of correlations is to use the Spearman-Brown equation (Brown, 1910, Spearman, 1910). The generally used Spearman-Brown formula is

$$\text{Spearman-Brown reliability} = \frac{2r_{hh}}{1 + r_{hh}}$$

where r_{hh} is the split-half or odd-even reliability estimate. For example, if the reliability is .70, you would multiply .70 by 2, and then divide by the sum of 1 + .70. This would be 1.40 divided by 1.70, which gives you a reliability estimate of .82 for the whole test. So if a test manual states that split-half reliability was used, check to see if the Spearman-Brown formula was applied. If it was not, the test might be somewhat more reliable than actually noted.

Cronbach's Coefficient Alpha and Kuder-Richardson

Coefficient Alpha or Kuder-Richardson Reliability based on a mathematical comparison of individual items with one another and total score

Although used for different kinds of tests, Coefficient Alpha and Kuder-Richardson forms of reliability are also considered internal consistency methods that attempt to estimate the reliability of all the possible split-half combinations (Cronbach, 1951). In brief, they do this by correlating the scores for each item on the test with the total score on the test and finding the average correlation for all of the items (Salkind, 2004). Clearly, individuals who are producing depressed scores should be responding to test items in a manner that indicates depression, and individuals who are producing scores that indicate they are not depressed should be responding to test items in a manner that does indicate depression. If particular items are not able to discriminate between depressed and non-depressed individuals, there are likely some problems with those items and this will be reflected in an overall lower internal consistency estimate. Obtaining the correlation between each item and the whole test score for each person, and then finding the average of all those correlations, used to be a tedious process. However, with computers, such reliability estimates can now be configured in a millisecond and therefore have become very popular. The difference between these two formulas is that Kuder-Richardson can be used only with tests that have right and wrong answers, such as achievement tests, whereas Coefficient Alpha can be

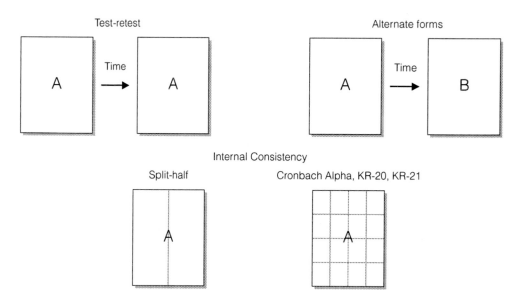

Figure 3.5 Visual representation of types of reliability

applied to assessment instruments that result in varied types of responses, such as rating scales. If you are interested in the actual formulas for Kuder-Richardson and Coefficient Alpha, you can find them in Appendix C.

Visual Representation of Types of Reliability

Figure 3.5 is a visual representation of the three types of reliability. Notice that test-retest is represented by the same test being given again with a time difference, alternative forms is represented by two similar forms that are not affected by time, and two types of internal consistency are shown: split-half, which is represented by a test being split, and Coefficient Alpha and Kuder-Richardson being shown as a grid which represents each item being related to the whole test. These visual representations can help you remember each form.

Cross-Cultural Fairness

> . . . tests must be used in ways that, as far as possible, take advantage of the tremendous utility of test and other assessment data, while also facilitating optimal understanding and nurturance of a wide range of individual and cultural differences (Walsh & Betz, 2001, p. 424).

Another quality important in determining whether a test is worthwhile is whether it is cross-culturally fair. Although inextricably related to the validity and reliability of a test, cross-cultural fairness deserves a separate section due to the

Cross-cultural fairness
Degree to which cultural background, class, disability, and gender do not affect test results

Many laws have affirmed the rights of minorities and others to fairness in testing.

importance we as a nation place on issues of fairness, especially with regard to diversity. Thus, any test should accurately measure the construct that is being assessed, and one's cultural background, class, disability, and gender should not be significant factors in determining test results (AERA, APA, & NCME, 1999).

Although much emphasis is placed on cross-cultural fairness today, this has not always been the case (recall the cultural bias of the Army Alpha described in Chapter 1). In fact, issues of bias in testing did not garner much attention until the civil rights movement of the 1960s when there was concern that African Americans and Hispanics were being compared unfairly against the White majority. In a series of court decisions, it was decided that some tests, such as IQ and achievement tests, could not be used to track students because minority students were being disproportionately placed in lower-achieving classrooms as the result of tests that may not have been accurately assessing their ability (see *Hobsen v. Hansen* and *Moses v. Washington Parish School Board*). And in 1971, the U.S. Supreme Court case of *Griggs v. Duke Power Company* asserted that tests used for hiring and advancement at work must show that they can predict job performance for all groups. Over the years, a number of laws have been passed that impinge on the use of tests and assert the rights of all individuals to be tested fairly (see Chapter 2 for expanded definitions of some of these laws). These laws, and their relationship to assessment, are briefly described below.

Americans with Disabilities Act. *This law states that accommodations must be made for individuals who are taking tests for employment and that testing must be shown to be relevant to the job in question.*

The Buckley Amendment. *Also known as the Family Educational Rights and Privacy Act (FERPA) of 1974, this law affirms the right of all individuals to review their school records, including test records.*

Carl Perkins Act (PL 98-524). *This law assures that individuals who have disabilities or who are disadvantaged have access to vocational assessment, counseling, and placement.*

Civil Rights Acts (1964 and Amendments). *This series of laws asserts that any test used for employment or promotion must be shown to be suitable and valid for the job in question. If not, alternative means of assessment must be provided. Differential test cutoffs are not allowed.*

The Freedom of Information Act. *This law assures the right of individuals to access their federal records, including test records. Most states have expanded this law so that it also applies to state records.*

PL 94-142 and the Individuals with Disabilities Education Improvement Act (IDEIA). *These legislative acts assure the right of students to be tested, at a school system's expense, if they are suspected of having a disability that interferes with learning. The law asserts that schools must make accommodations, within the least restrictive environment, for students with learning disabilities.*

Section 504 of the Rehabilitation Act. *Relative to assessment, any instrument used to measure appropriateness for a program or service must be measuring the individual's ability, not be a reflection of his or her disability.*

BOX 3.1
The Use of Intelligence Tests with Minorities: Confusion and Bedlam

The use of intelligence tests with culturally diverse populations has long been an area of controversy. Some states have found intelligence tests biased and have banned their use in certain circumstances with some groups (Swenson, 1997). Other states have not found widespread evidence of bias. If intelligence tests are used, the examiner needs to be astute to the proper way of administering and scoring the test with all clients.

The concern for bias in testing has gone so far in some circles that if the situation wasn't so serious, it would almost be comical. Take the case in California of Ms. Mary Amaya who was con-

cerned that her son was being recommended for remedial courses he did not need. Having had an older son who was found to *not* need such assistance only *after* he was tested, Ms. Amaya requested testing with an intelligence test for her other son. However, since the incident with her first son, the state of California had decided that intelligence tests were culturally biased and thus banned their use for members of certain groups. Despite the fact that Ms. Amaya was requesting the use of an intelligence test, it was found that she had no legislative right to have the test given to her son.

Today, it is critical that cognitive differences among groups of individuals represent differences in ability, not differences that result from cultural identification, gender, age, or so forth, and that tests used for predictive purposes show that their predictions hold true for all groups of people (e.g., the SATs, MATs, GREs) (Hartman, McDaniel, & Whetzel, 2004; Neisser et al., 1996; Roth, Bevier, Bobko, Switzer, & Tyler, 2001). However, it should also be stressed that such differences do exist, and one of the greatest challenges today is to understand why they exist in order to develop ways to eliminate such differences (Hartman, McDaniel, & Whetzel, 2004). These days, cognitive differences are generally traced to environmental factors, as is evidenced by the No Child Left Behind Act which assumes that all children can succeed in school and demands that school systems show that all children pass minimal competencies, regardless of their gender, culture, or disability (U.S. Department of Education, n.d.a).

EXERCISE 3.4 Differences in Ability Scores as a Function of Culture

In small groups, discuss why there might be differences among cultural groups on their ability scores. Then discuss ways in which such differences could be ameliorated. Discuss your reasons and solutions in class.

Practicality

Although tests should have good validity and reliability, as well as cross-cultural fairness, it is also important for the test to be practical. For instance, would it make sense to give a two-hour exam to first- or second-graders, or might a shorter test that has lower reliability do nearly as well? Or, is it feasible to use a

Practicality
Feasibility considerations in test selection and administration

Wechsler Scale of Intelligence as pre-screening for learning disabilities to hundreds of possible learning disabled students in a school system? Such a test is given individually, takes 1 to 2 hours to administer, and requires another 1 to 2 hours to write up. Decisions about test selection should be made carefully because they have an impact on the person being tested, the examiner, and at times, the institutions that are requiring testing. Examples of practical concerns include time, cost, format, readability, and ease of administration, scoring, and interpretation.

Time

As just noted, the amount of time it takes to administer a test can clearly affect whether or not it is used. Time factors tend to be related to the attention span of the client you are testing, to the amount of time allotted for testing in a particular setting, and to the final cost of testing (time is money!).

Cost

With increasingly limited insurance reimbursements as well as funding cutbacks, counselors and therapists in private practice, public and private agencies, and school systems are forced to hold down expenses. Thus, the cost of testing is an important factor in making a decision about which test to use. For instance, it would be nice to have all high school seniors take an interest inventory to help them in their career decision-making process; however, given that this might cost about $10 per student, it may not be a wise economic decision for many school systems. And what decision would you make if you were working with a person who had just lost his or her job, was short on finances, and needed to take a battery of tests that might cost $500 when other tests, perhaps somewhat less valid and reliable, might cost $100?

Format

The format of a test should also be considered when deciding which test to use. Some format issues include clarity of the print, print size, sequencing of questions, and the type of questions being used. Crocker and Schmitt (1987) found that for many individuals, multiple-choice questions tend to lessen test anxiety while tests requiring constructive responses (i.e., open-ended, essay questions) generally increased test-taker anxiety, anxiety that could reduce cognitive clarity (Powers, 1988). Also, the format of a test could affect scores differentially as a function of culture. In fact, one study across three different types of tests found that test-takers who are male or white tend to do better on multiple-choice tests than members of other groups (Bridgeman & Morgan, 1996). The format of a test should always be considered when choosing which test to use.

Readability

Readability, or the ability of the examinee to comprehend what he or she is reading, is of course critical for all tests other than vocabulary or reading level tests

(Hewitt & Homan, 1991; Homan, Hewitt, & Linder, 1994). No one should be surprised that the validity and reliability of test scores are reduced when readability is not controlled for. Thus, it has been suggested that each item on a test be scrutinized for readability (Homan & Hewitt, 1983; Homan, Hewitt, & Linder, 1994).

Ease of Administration, Scoring, and Interpretation

In deciding how practical a test is to use, the ease of test administration, scoring, and interpretation should always be considered. This dimension involves a number of factors, including the following:

1. The ease of understanding and using test manuals and related information.
2. The number of individuals taking the test and whether or not their numbers affect the ease of administering the instrument.
3. The kind of training and education needed to administer the test, score the test, and interpret test results.
4. The "turnaround time" in scoring the test and obtaining the results.
5. The amount of time needed to explain test results to examinees.
6. Associated materials that may be helpful in explaining test scores to examinees (e.g., printed sheets generated by the publisher).

Selecting and Administering a Good Test

Now you know that a test should be valid, reliable, practical, and cross-culturally fair. But, with more than 3000 tests to choose from (Thorndike, 1997), how exactly does one find a test that meets the specific needs of the testing situation? A number of steps will assist you in the process, as described below.

Step 1: Determine the Goals of Your Client

The information-gathering process, which will be discussed in detail in Chapter 12, is critical to one's ability to determine what is happening with a client. As information is gathered from a client, client goals will become clearer and these goals will help you determine what assessment instruments might be valuable in helping to reach client goals.

Step 2: Choose Instruments to Reach Client Goals

Choosing the right instrument is not always an easy process. However, as soon as you have identified client goals, you have gained a sense of the kinds of instruments that may be helpful. For instance, if a client's goals include developing a career path and making a decision about a job, we might want to consider administering an interest inventory and a multiple aptitude test.

Step 3: Access Information
About Possible Instruments

A number of sources exist today to help you choose possible assessment instruments. Some of these are described below.

a. *Source books on testing.* Source books on testing provide important information about tests, such as the names of the author(s); the publication date; the purpose of the test; bibliographical information; information on test construction; the name and address of the publisher; the costs of the test; information on validity, reliability, cross-cultural issues, and practicality; reviews of the test (see Box 3.2); information on scoring; and other basic information about the test.

*Mental
Measurements
Yearbook*
A tremendous
resource in finding and selecting tests

Two of the most important source books are the *Buros Mental Measurements Yearbook* (MMY) and its companion volume *Tests in Print* (Claiborn, 1991; Plake & Conoley, 1995; Plake, Conoley, Kramer, & Murphy, 1991). The MMY, which is in its sixteenth edition, offers reviews of more than 2000 tests, instruments, and screening devices. Because of the size of this collection of data, not all tests are included in any one edition; consequently, it is often necessary to go back to previous editions to find a specific test that you might be looking for. Most large universities carry hardcover editions of these volumes, and the information is also available online. The MMY test reviews are classified into 18 major categories: achievement, behavior, developmental, education, English and language, fine arts, foreign language, intelligence and general aptitude, mathematics, miscellaneous, neuropsychological, personality, reading, science, sensory-motor, social studies, speech and hearing, and vocations. Online searches of the MMY offer a quick mechanism for obtaining information about assessment instruments. For example, a quick search from the ninth to the sixteenth editions uncovered 457 tests under the subject of intelligence, 249 instruments under career, 115 related to alcohol, and 33 for love.

b. *Publisher resource catalogs.* Test publishing companies freely distribute catalogs that describe the tests they sell. Additional information about the tests usually can be purchased from the publisher (e.g., sample kits, technical manuals, and so on).

c. *Journals in the field.* Professional journals, especially those associated with measurement, will often describe tests used in research or give reviews of new tests in the field.

d. *Books on testing.* Textbooks that present an overview of testing are usually fairly good at highlighting a number of the better-known tests that are in use today.

e. *Experts.* School psychologists, learning disability specialists, experts at a school system's central testing office, psychologists at agencies, and

---

BOX 3.2
Mental Measurement Review of the WAIS-III

The following is part of the summary provided by the second reviewer of the Wechsler Adult Intelligence Scale-III (WAIS-III), as found in the Mental Measurement Yearbook. The actual two reviews run about 10 pages, single-spaced.

The WAIS-III is the oldest and most frequently used intelligence scale for individual administration to adults. It is composed of a set of 14 subtests that have been improved with extensive research while maintaining the historical continuity. Reviewers of the two previous editions have made criticisms and suggestions that have been addressed by the authors, and the changes appear to result in improvements for those practitioners and researchers who use the test. The scores from the test are reliable enough to be used in all of the desig-

nated age ranges and the validity evidence gives confidence that the test scores measure those intellectual constructs that it purports to measure. Psychologists in educational institutions will find it to be a useful tool for assessing those persons who are not adequately evaluated with group intelligence tests. Clinicians and clinical researchers will probably continue to employ the test as their primary instrument for assessing adult intelligence. The manuals are written in a clear, readable manner for those with proper training. Although there are areas in which the manuals can be improved, they provide more information than the manuals of most other tests. The WAIS-III gives promise of continuing the evolutionary trend toward improved measurement. . . .

–Rogers, 2001, p. 1340

---

professors are some of the many experts that can be called upon as providers of testing information.

f. *The Internet.* Today, publishing companies have home pages that offer information about tests they sell. In addition, the Internet has become an increasingly important place in which to search for information about testing. Of course, one needs to assure that any information from the Internet is accurate.

Step 4: Examine Validity, Reliability, Cross-Cultural Fairness, and Practicality of the Possible Instruments

As you gather information about tests you might use, you may also have the opportunity to examine the validity, reliability, cross-cultural fairness, and practicality of possible instruments. However, if the sources do not offer this information, you can do a search of journal articles that may have examined these tests and you can contact the publisher to purchase a copy of the technical manual for the test. This manual should offer you all of the necessary information to make an informed judgment concerning whether or not to use the instrument in question.

Step 5: Choose an Instrument Wisely

You've gone through your steps, and ideally you have some good options available to you. Most likely you narrowed your choices down to a few possible instruments. Now, it's time for you to be wise. Examine the technical information, consider the purpose of the testing, reflect on the ease and cost of the instrument, and make a wise choice—a choice that you will feel comfortable with and a choice that is right for your client.

Summary

In this chapter we examined four components of test worthiness: validity, reliability, cross-cultural fairness, and practicality. We began by explaining the concept of correlation coefficient, and we noted that it ranges between -1.0 and $+1.0$ and describes the strength and direction of the relationship between two sets of variables such as test scores. We then noted that the coefficient of determination, or shared variance, is the square of the correlation (r^2), and is a statement about the commonality between variables.

We next examined validity, a broad evidence-based concept that attempts to verify that a test is measuring what it is supposed to measure. Content validity is based on evidence that test items accurately reflect the examinee's knowledge of the domain being measured. Criterion validity has two forms: concurrent, which demonstrates that the instrument is related to some criterion in the "now" (e.g., depression scores with clinical ratings of clients), or predictive, which examines how well the instrument forecasts some future event. Construct validity shows whether the test is properly measuring the correct concept, model, or schematic idea. Evidence for construct validity is often available in the form of research studies, factorial analysis, and convergence and discrimination with other existing tests.

In the next part of the chapter we examined reliability, or the degree to which test scores are free from measurement error (i.e., consistent and dependable). We highlighted three kinds of reliability: test-retest; alternate, parallel, or equivalent forms; and internal consistency, which includes split-half or odd-even reliability, Cronbach's Coefficient Alpha, and Kuder-Richardson. Test-retest reliability is calculated by giving the same instrument twice to the same group of people and correlating the test scores. Alternate form reliability involves administering two equivalent forms of the test to the same group and correlating the scores. One type of internal consistency reliability, called split-half or odd-even reliability, is used when one-half of the test items are correlated with the other half. Other forms of internal consistency, such as Cronbach Alpha and Kuder-Richardson reliability, use more complex statistical calculations to find the average correlation of all test items.

The next area of test worthiness we discussed was cross-cultural fairness. We noted that a test should accurately measure a construct regardless of one's membership in a class, race, disability, religion, or gender. We saw how the legal system has supported the notion that testing must be fair for all groups of people and free from bias. We specifically highlighted the fact that tests that may be biased could not be used to track students and that as a result of the Supreme

Court case of *Griggs v. Duke Power Company*, tests used for hiring and advancement at work must be predictive of job performance for all groups. We also noted that a number of laws have been passed that assert the rights of all individuals to be tested fairly, including The Americans with Disabilities Act, The Buckley Amendment, The Carl Perkins Act (PL 98-524), Civil Rights Acts (1964 and Amendments), The Freedom of Information Act, PL 94-142 and IDEIA, and Section 504 of the Rehabilitation Act.

Our last area of test worthiness was practicality, which includes the amount of time it takes to give the test, the cost of the test, the readability of the instrument, test format, and the ease of administration, scoring, and interpretation. We concluded the chapter by offering five steps for selecting a good test.

Chapter Review

1. What are the four cornerstones of test worthiness? Briefly define each of the four types of test worthiness.

2. Explain what is meant by a correlation coefficient and describe how it is applied to the understanding of test validity and test reliability.

3. Describe the three main types and the various subtypes of validity.

4. Why is validity known as a "unitary concept"?

5. Why is "face validity" not considered a type of validity?

6. Describe the three main types and various subtypes of reliability.

7. Why have cross-cultural issues taken on such importance in the realm of tests and assessment?

8. Relative to cross-cultural issues and assessment, provide a brief explanation for each of the following:
   a. *Griggs v. Duke Power Company*
   b. Americans with Disabilities Act
   c. The Buckley Amendment (FERPA)
   d. Carl Perkins Act (PL 98-524)
   e. Civil Rights Acts (1964) and Amendments
   f. The Freedom of Information Act
   g. PL 94-142 and the IDEIA
   h. Section 504 of the Rehabilitation Act

9. Describe the main issues involved in assessing the practicality of an assessment instrument.

10. Describe the five steps critical to the selection of a good assessment instrument.

Statistical Concepts: Making Meaning Out of Raw Scores

My wife and I and our two daughters, Hannah (9) and Emma (4), have some pretty interesting conversations around the dinner table. One night we were talking about testing, and I was sharing the difficulty I sometimes have explaining the value of testing. Suddenly, Hannah said, "Testing is good because teachers know what level you are at and then know what to teach you." I looked at her and said, "That's right." Then Emma chimed in, "[Test scores are important because] when somebody is sad, you should help them." They made it so simple! (Ed Neukrug)

This chapter will help us understand how numbers are used to determine, as Hannah noted, what "level" individuals are at. Understanding this concept will enable us to do our job: help others. Whether it be an achievement test score that shows deficiencies in reading, or a personality test that indicates clinical depression (or as Emma noted, sadness), test scores can help us identify problem areas in a person's life.

To understand the importance of test scores, we will start with the basics: an examination of raw scores. After concluding that raw scores generally provide little meaningful information, we will look at various ways that we can manipulate those scores to make sense out of a set of data. Thus, in this chapter we will examine how the following are used to help us understand raw scores: frequency distributions; histograms and frequency polygons; the normal curve; skewed curves; measures of central tendency such as the mean, median and mode; and measures of variability, such as the range, interquartile range, and standard deviation. In Chapter 5, which is a natural extension of this chapter, we will examine derived scores and see how they too are used to help us understand raw scores. But let's start with the basics: raw scores.

Raw Scores

Let's say Jeremiah receives a score of 47 on a test, and Elise receives a score of 95 on a different test. How have they done? If Jeremiah's score was 47 out of 52, one might assume he had done fairly well. But if 1000 people had taken this test and all others had received a higher score than Jeremiah, we might view his score somewhat differently. And to make things even more complicated, what if a high score represents an undesirable trait (e.g., cynicism, depression, schizophrenia)? Then clearly, the lower he scores compared to his norm (peer) group, the better he has done, and vice versa.

Raw score
Untreated score before manipulation or processing

What about Elise's score? Is a score of 95 good? What if it is out of a possible score of 200, or 550, or 992? If 1000 people take the test and Elise's score is the highest and a higher score is desirable, we might say that she did well, at least compared with her norm group. But if her score is on the lower end of the group of scores, then comparatively she did not do well.

RULE NUMBER 1:   **Raw Scores Are Meaningless**

Raw scores alone tell us little, if anything, about how a person has done on a test. We must take an individual's raw score and do something to it to give it meaning.

Because raw scores provide little information, we need to do something to make them meaningful. One simple procedure is to add up the various types of responses an individual makes (e.g., number of right or wrong items on an achievement test, number of different kinds of personality traits chosen). Although this can provide us with a general idea of the types of responses the person has made, comparing an individual's responses to those of his or her norm group can usually give us more in-depth information. Norm group comparisons are helpful for the following reasons:

- *They tell us the relative position, within the norm group, of a person's score.* For instance, Jeremiah and Elise, or others interested in Jeremiah's or Elise's scores (e.g., teachers, counselors), can compare their scores with those of people who took the same test and are like them in some important way (e.g., similar age, same grade in school).
- *They allow us to compare the results among test-takers who took the same test but are in different norm groups.* For instance, a parent who has two children, two grades apart, could determine which one is doing better in reading relative to his or her norm group (e.g., one child might score at the 50th percentile, the other at the 76th, relative to their respective norm groups). Or a school counselor might be interested in the self-esteem scores of all the fifth-graders as compared to all the third-graders.
- *They allow us to compare test results on two or more different tests taken by the same individual.* For instance, it is sometimes valuable for a

TABLE 4.1
Frequency Distribution

SCORE	FREQUENCY	SCORE	FREQUENCY	SCORE	FREQUENCY
66	1	53	3	43	4
63	1	51	5	42	1
60	1	50	5	40	2
58	2	49	7	38	2
57	3	48	6	37	1
55	2	47	4	35	1
54	5	45	5	32	1

teacher to know an individual's score on an achievement test and on an aptitude test because a discrepancy between the two tests might indicate the presence of a learning disability. Or, when conducting a personality assessment, it is not unusual to give a number of different tests with an effort made to find similar themes running through the various tests (e.g., high indications of anxiety on a number of different tests).

To help us make some sense out of raw scores, a number of procedures have been developed to allow normative comparisons. In the rest of this chapter we will look at some of these procedures.

Frequency Distributions

Frequency distribution
List of scores and number of times the score occurred

One method of understanding test scores is to develop a frequency distribution. Such distributions order a set of scores from highest to lowest and list the corresponding frequency of each score (see Table 4.1). A frequency distribution allows one to easily identify the most frequent scores and is helpful in identifying where an individual's score falls relative to the rest of the group. For instance, by examining Table 4.1, we can easily see that most of the scores occurred around the 50 range, with fewer occurring as we move to the higher or lower ends. If an individual scored a 60, he or she can quickly see that such a score is higher than most.

Histograms and Frequency Polygons

Once a frequency distribution has been developed, it is relatively easy to convert it to either a histogram (similar to a bar graph) or to a frequency polygon. These visual representations of the frequency distribution are often easier for individuals to understand. In order to develop a histogram or frequency polygon,

TABLE 4.2
Scores Arranged with a Class Interval of 5

CLASS INTERVAL	FREQUENCY
62–66	2
57–61	6
52–56	10
47–51	27
42–46	9
37–41	5
32–36	2

BOX 4.1
Configuring the Number of Intervals You Want for Your Graph

To determine how many numbers should be in your class interval, follow these instructions (*Note:* calculations are based on the data in Table 4.1)*:

1. Subtract the lowest number in the series of scores from the highest number:
   66 – 32 = 34
2. Divide this number by the number of class intervals you want to end up with:
   34/7 = 4.86
3. Round off the number you obtained in step 2:
   4.86 is rounded off to 5

4. Starting with the lowest number in your series of scores, use the number obtained in step 3 (the number 5 in this case) as the number of scores you should place in each interval:
   32–36, 37–41, 42–46, 47–51, 52–56, 57–61, 62–66

---

* Please note that this is a crude method of configuring the number of intervals you want and sometimes can be off by 1 interval.

Class interval
Grouping scores by a predetermined range

Histogram
Bar graph of class interval and frequency of a set of scores

one has to first determine what *class intervals* are to be used. Class intervals are derived from your frequency distribution and are groupings of scores that have a predetermined range. For example, we could take the frequency distribution from Table 4.1 and rearrange or group the scores by fives (the predetermined range), starting with the lowest score. The first class of scores would then be 32 to 36 (i.e., 32, 33, 34, 35, or 36). The next interval would be 37 to 41, and so forth. Table 4.2 illustrates the frequency distribution of the class intervals using a range of 5.

Of course, the class interval does not have to be 5. You could arrange the class interval to have any predetermined range, such as 3, 4, 6, 10, or whatever might be useful (see Box 4.1).

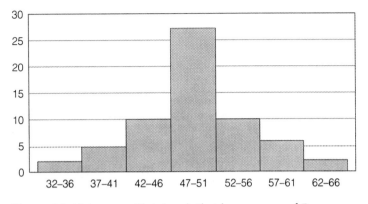

Figure 4.1 Histogram with intervals that have a range of 5 (based on Table 4.2)

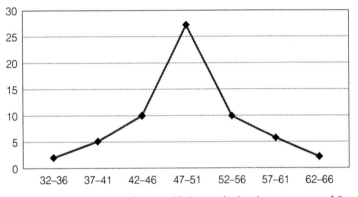

Figure 4.2 Frequency polygon with intervals that have a range of 5 (based on Table 4.2)

Frequency polygon
Line graph of class interval and frequency of a set of scores

After you have constructed your class interval, the scores can be placed onto a graph in the form of a histogram or frequency polygon. To create a histogram, one places the class intervals along the *x*-axis and the frequency of scores along the *y*-axis (see Figure 4.1). In this case, a vertical line is placed at the beginning and end of each class interval and a horizontal line connects these two lines at the height (as measured along the vertical axis). The horizontal line represents the respective frequency of the specific interval being drawn.

To create a frequency polygon of the class interval of scores from Table 4.2, we would simply place a dot at the center of each class interval across from its respective frequency and then connect the dots (see Figure 4.2).

Normal Curves and Skewed Curves

Normal curve
Bell-shaped
distribution that
human traits
tend to fall
along

As we collect data from test scores and create histograms or frequency polygons using class intervals, we will see that our distributions are sometimes skewed (asymmetrical) and other times represent what is called a normal or bell-shaped curve. Each of these types of curves has different implications for how we compare scores. Let's take a look at each of these types of curves and then see how measures of central tendency and measures of variability, two important measurement concepts, are applied to them.

The Normal Curve

Quincunx
Board devel-
oped by Sir
Francis Galton
to demonstrate
bell-shaped
curve

A number of years ago while I was visiting the Boston Museum of Science, I (Ed Neukrug) saw a device called a *quincunx* (also known as *Galton's Board*) through which hundreds of balls would be dropped onto a series of protruding points (see Figure 4.3). Each ball had a 50/50 chance of falling left or right every time it would hit one of the protruding objects. After all the balls were dropped, they would be collected and automatically dropped again. All day long this machine would drop the balls over and over again. Now, this process in and of itself was not so amazing. However, what did seem extraordinary was the fact that each time those balls were dropped, they would distribute themselves in the shape of a *normal curve* (also called the *bell-shaped curve*). Now, mind you,

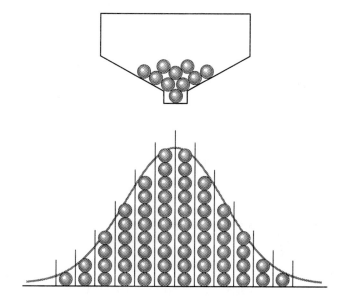

Figure 4.3 A quincunx

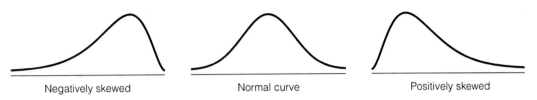

Negatively skewed   Normal curve   Positively skewed

Figure 4.4 Skewed and normal curves

they were not distributing themselves in that manner because they were being sent in that direction (see http://www.stattucino.com/berrie/dsl/Galton.html).

In point of fact, the resulting bell-shaped curve is a product of the natural laws of the universe and is explained through the laws of probability. So perfect are these natural laws that some people have given religious connotations to them. However, no matter how you explain these results, it is amazing that such a predictable pattern occurs over and over again. What does this have to do with testing? Like the balls dropping in this device, when we measure most traits and abilities of people, the scores tend to approximate a bell-shaped distribution. This is very convenient, for the symmetry of this curve allows us to understand measures of variability, particularly standard deviation, an important concept we will examine later in this chapter.

RULE NUMBER 2:   **"God does not play dice with the universe."**
                  (Einstein paraphrased*)

So perfect are the laws of nature that some see this as the creation of a perfect God who has set in motion the wheels of the universe. Whether or not you believe this is a God-inspired phenomenon, it has great implications for testing. Concepts such as the bell-shaped curve are crucial to our understanding of norm-referenced testing and allow us to compare individuals to one another in a large array of physical and personal qualities.

*As reported by Bryson (2003).

Skewed Curves

Skewed curve
Test scores not falling along a normal curve

Negatively skewed curve
Majority of scores at upper end

Positively skewed curve
Majority of scores at lower end

Sometimes a distribution of scores does not fall in a symmetrical shape or a normal curve. When this happens, the curve is called skewed or asymmetrical. If the majority of the scores fall toward the upper end, the curve is called negatively skewed. A positively skewed curve occurs when the majority of scores fall near the lower end (see Figure 4.4). If you split a normal curve in half, you will find the same number of scores in the first half of the curve as in the second half. This is not true of skewed curves. For instance, in a negatively skewed curve, there are more scores toward the high end of the curve as compared to the low end, and in a positively skewed curve, there are more scores at the lower end.

Measures of Central Tendency

Measures of central tendency tell us what is occurring in the midrange or "center" of a group of scores. Thus, if you know a person's score, you can compare that score to one of three scores that represent the middle of the group. Three measures of central tendency are the *mean, median,* and *mode.* Although measures of central tendency tell you little about the range of scores or how much scores vary, they do give you a sense of how close a score is to the middle of the distribution.

Mean

Mean
Arithmetic average of a set of test scores

The most commonly used measure of central tendency is the mean, which is the arithmetic average of a set of scores. The mean is calculated by adding together all of the scores and dividing by the number of scores. (See the formula below, where M is the mean, ΣX is the sum of all the scores, and N is the number of scores.)

$$M = \frac{\Sigma X}{N}$$

The first column of Table 4.3 shows how one determines the mean. By summing all of the scores and dividing by 11, we find the mean to be 85.55 (941/11).

Median

The median is the middle score, or the score at which 50% of scores fall above and 50% fall below. In Table 4.3 we can see that there are 11 total scores, and

TABLE 4.3
Determining Measures of Central Tendency

MEAN	MEDIAN		MODE
97	97		97
94	94		94
92	92		92
89	89	5 ↑	**89**
89	89		**89**
87	**87**	Middle #	87
84	84	5 ↓	84
82	82		82
79	79		79
75	75		75
73	73		73
Sum = 941			
N = 11			
M = 85.55 (Mean)	Median = 87		Mode = 89

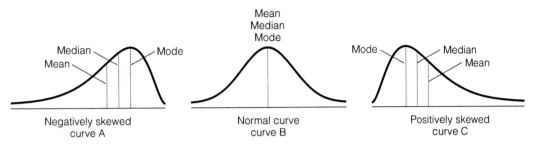

Figure 4.5 Respective positions of measures of central tendency with skewed and normal curves

Median
Score where
50% fall above
and 50% below

*In a skewed
distribution, the
median is a
better measure
of central
tendency.*

the middle score is the one that has 5 scores above it and 5 scores below it; hence, we can see that in this case the middle score, or median, is 87. If there were an even number of scores, we would find not one middle score but two. In the case of an even number of scores we must take the average of the two middle scores and divide by two. In situations involving a skewed set of scores, the median is generally considered a more accurate measure of central tendency because any unusually low or high score does not distort the median as it would with the mean (because all scores are averaged to get the mean). For example, one can use the mean or median when trying to understand "average" salaries. If our community happens to have a relatively small number of individuals who make extremely large incomes, these incomes will be included when computing the mean. On the other hand, extremely large incomes would not affect the resulting median. Which measure of central tendency do you think would be more important if you were considering moving to a community that resembled this example?

Mode

Mode
Most frequently
occurring score

The mode, the final measure of central tendency we will examine, is the score that occurs most often. In Table 4.3 you can quickly see that the mode is 89 because it is the only score that occurs twice. In smaller groups of scores, the mode may be erratic and not very accurate. However, with larger sets of numbers, the mode captures the peak or top of the curve. In addition, sometimes you can have multiple modes, such as when two numbers occur most often and the same number of times.

In examining the mode, consider our earlier example of incomes in a community. One could conceivably have a mean that is higher than the median (due to a few extremely high incomes), and a mode that is lower than the median (because the most commonly found incomes could fall below the median) (see Figure 4.5, curve C). As you review the skewed and normal curves in Figure 4.5, consider the reason why the mean, median, and mode are placed where they are, and then read Box 4.2.

BOX 4.2
Which to Use: Mean or Median?

A school system has asked you to determine the average reading score for its 50,000 fifth-grade students. The assistant superintendent wants to make sure the school system looks "as good as possible" because the press will get hold of the results. On the other hand, you realize that a siz-able population of students read poorly and you want to make sure that their scores are included in your data so that their learning needs are focused upon. Which measure of central tendency do you use? What concerns do you have?

Measures of Variability

Measures of variability tell us how much scores vary in a distribution. Three measures of variability are the *range*, or the number of scores between the highest and lowest scores on a distribution; the *interquartile range*, which measures the range of the middle 50% of a group of scores around the median; and the *standard deviation*, or the manner in which scores deviate around the mean in a standard fashion.

Range

Range
Difference between highest and lowest score plus 1

The simplest measure of variability, called the range, is calculated by subtracting the lowest score from the highest score and adding 1. Although the range tells you the distance from the highest to lowest score, it does little to identify where most of the scores fall. For example, if the highest score on an exam is 98 and the lowest score is 62, the range is 37 (98 – 62 + 1 = 37). However, this range gives no indication where the majority of scores may fall. Thus, the range is limited in function. A more complex and informative measure of variability is the interquartile range.

Interquartile Range

Interquartile range
Middle 50% of scores around the median

The interquartile range provides the range of the middle 50% of scores around the median. Because it eliminates the top and bottom quartiles, the interquartile range is most useful with skewed curves because it offers a more representative picture of where a large percentage of the scores fall (see Figure 4.6).

To calculate the interquartile range, first we subtract the score that is 1/4 of the way from the bottom from the score that is 3/4 of the way from the bottom and divide by 2. Next, we add and subtract this number to the median. For example, Table 4.4 has a set of 12 test scores. Let's find the interquartile range.

Since we have 12 scores, we first find the score that is 1/4 of the way from the bottom (or 1/4 of 12). Since 1/4 of 12 = 3, we find the third score, or 81 (round off if 1/4 of the *N* is not a whole number). Next, we find the score that

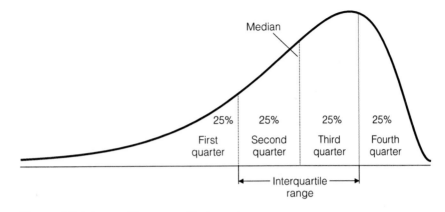

Figure 4.6 Interquartile range with skewed curve

TABLE 4.4
Example of Calculating an Interquartile Range

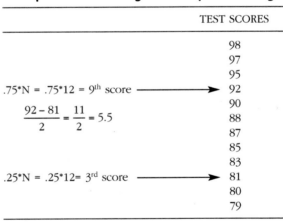

	TEST SCORES
	98
	97
	95
.75*N = .75*12 = 9th score ⟶	92
	90
$\frac{92-81}{2} = \frac{11}{2} = 5.5$	88
	87
	85
	83
.25*N = .25*12= 3rd score ⟶	81
	80
	79

is 3/4 of the way from the bottom (or 3/4 of 12). Since 3/4 of 12 = 9, we find the ninth score, or 92 (round off if 3/4 of the N is not a whole number). Next, we subtract our 1/4 score from our 3/4 score, or 92 − 81 = 11. Finally, we divide 11 by 2 and add this number to the median: 5.5 ± 87.5 (the median). Our interquartile range is 82 through 93. A formula to find the interquartile range is

$$\frac{(1/4)N\,(\text{find that score}) - (3/4)N\,(\text{find that score})}{2} \pm \text{Median}$$

Standard Deviation

Standard deviation
How scores vary from the mean

In contrast to the interquartile range, which examines the spread of scores around the median, the standard deviation is a measure of variability that describes how scores vary around the mean. With normally distributed curves, the standard deviation is a powerful tool in helping us understand test scores. The standard deviation is important because in *all normal curves* the percentage of scores between standard deviation units is the same. For instance, between the mean and +1 standard deviation we find approximately 34% of the scores (see Figure 4.7). Similarly, between the mean and −1 standard deviation we also find 34% of the scores, as each side of the curve is the mirror image of the opposite side. In addition, as you can see in Figure 4.7, approximately 13.5% of the group falls between +1 and +2 standard deviations and another 13.5% between −1 and −2 standard deviations. Most of the rest of the group is between +2 and +3 standard deviations (2.25%), or −2 and −3 standard deviations (another 2.25%). As you can also see, approximately 68% of the group is between −1 and +1 standard deviations, and about 95% of scores will fall between −2 SD and +2 SD (13.5% + 34% + 34% + 13.5% = 95%), and so forth. Although standard deviations continue (e.g., 4 SDs, 5 SDs, and so forth), since 99.5% of people will fall within the first three standard deviations, we tend to focus only on these.

To understand standard deviation, let's suppose for a moment that a test has a mean of 52 and a standard deviation of 20. For this test, most of the scores (about 68%) would range between 32 and 72 (plus and minus one standard deviation; see Figure 4.7). On the other hand, a second test that had a mean of 52

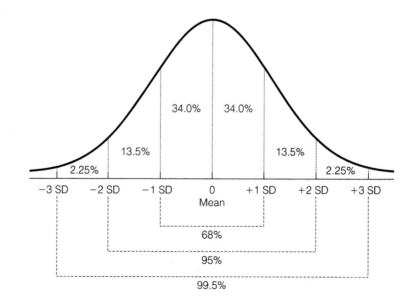

Figure 4.7 Standard deviation and the normal curve

TABLE 4.5
Calculating the Standard Deviation

X (SCORE)	X − M	(X − M)²
10	10 − 7 = 3	3² = 9
8	8 − 7 = 1	1² = 1
7	7 − 7 = 0	0² = 0
7	7 − 7 = 0	0² = 0
6	6 − 7 = −1	−1² = 1
4	4 − 7 = −3	−3² = 9
Σ = 42		
M = 42/6 = 7		Σ = 20

and a standard deviation of 5 would have 68% of its scores between 47 and 57 (again, plus and minus one standard deviation). Clearly, even though the two tests have the same mean, the range of scores around the mean varies considerably. An individual's score of 40 would be in the average range on the first test but well below average on the second test. This example shows why measures of central tendency and measures of variability are both so important in understanding test scores. To actually determine the standard deviation of a group of scores, one uses the following formula (an alternative formula can be found in Appendix C):

$$SD = \sqrt{\frac{\Sigma(X - M)^2}{N}}$$

In this formula, X is each individual test score, M is the mean, and N is the number of scores. For example, let's say we want to find how far one standard deviation is from the mean for a set of test scores in Table 4.5. First we generate a column for the $X - M$ for each score. Next we generate another column to calculate the $(X - M)^2$ for each score. Once this step is complete, we can sum all of the $(X - M)^2$, divide by the number of scores (N), and take the square root.

We calculate the mean (M) of the scores by summing them (42) and dividing by N which is 6, so our $M = 7$. In the next column we subtract the mean from each score to get $X - M$. Now in the third column we square our results from column 2 to get $(X - M)^2$. Next, we sum our $(X - M)^2$ column and get 20. Now, we place the numbers in our equation as follows:

$$SD = \sqrt{\frac{\Sigma(X - M)^2}{N}} = \sqrt{\frac{20}{6}} = \sqrt{3.33} = 1.83$$

This result tells us that each standard deviation is 1.83 from the mean. Applying this to a normal curve would give us Figure 4.8.

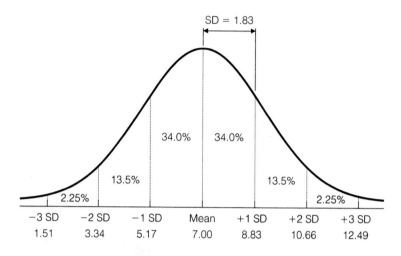

Figure 4.8 A normal distribution (*M* = 7, SD = 1.83)

Consequently, we can see that someone who scored a 5 falls slightly below −1 standard deviation (or at approximately the 15th percentile). Similarly, a person with a score of 11 is slightly above +2 standard deviations (or at approximately the 98th percentile). Standard deviation is a particularly important statistical concept when examining test scores relative to normal curves. In Chapter 5 we will examine how standard deviation is used to help us interpret a wide variety of test score data.

Remembering the Person

It is important to remember that individuals will have their own opinions about their performance. Thus, what is perceived as a high score by one person could be seen as a low score by another. The individual who consistently scores at the highest percentiles on a math test may feel upset about a score that is in the average range, while an individual who consistently scores low may feel good about that same score. Similarly, an individual who has struggled with lifelong depression may feel good about a moderate depression score on the *Beck Depression Inventory*, while another person might be concerned about such a score. As a helper, it is critical to always ask for feedback from the person who was assessed so that you can determine how he or she perceives the score that was received. Similarly, we should be careful to avoid letting our biases about what is a "good" or "bad" score interfere with hearing how an examinee feels about his or her score.

Summary

We began this chapter by examining the usefulness of raw scores. First, we noted that raw scores are not particularly meaningful unless we manipulate them in some fashion, such as by comparing an individual's scores to his or her norm group. Such comparisons (1) tell the relative position, within the norm group, of a person's score, (2) allow for a comparison of the results among test-takers who took the same test but are in different norm groups, and (3) allow for a comparison of test results on two or more different tests taken by the same individual.

Next, we reviewed a series of mechanisms that one could use to make normative comparisons. We first looked at how to create a frequency distribution, because such a distribution can help us understand where most individuals fall. We then showed that data can be placed in class intervals and graphed as a frequency polygon or a histogram, which are visual representations of the norm group.

We next examined the normal curve and distinguished it from skewed curves. We highlighted the amazing fact that due to the natural laws of the universe, many qualities, when measured, approximate the normal curve. We pointed out that the symmetry of the normal curve allows us to apply certain statistical concepts to it, such as measures of central tendency and measures of variability. We noted that in contrast, negatively and positively skewed curves are not symmetrical and have more scores at the higher (negatively skewed) or lower (positively skewed) ends of the distribution.

We went on to define three measures of central tendency: mean, or arithmetic average; median, or middle score; and mode, or most frequent score. We noted that in normal curves the mean, median, and mode are at the midpoint, cutting the curve into two halves. We contrasted this with a skewed curve where the mode is the highest point, the mean is drawn out toward the endpoint, and the median is between the mean and mode. Next we discussed three types of variability: the range, or the difference between the highest and lowest score + 1; the interquartile range, or the middle 50% of scores around the median; and the standard deviation, or how scores deviate around the mean.

Relative to the normal curve, we explained how standard deviation can be used to understand where test scores fall. We noted that the percentage of scores between standard deviation units on a normally distributed curve is constant, with about 34% of scores falling between 0 and +1 standard deviation and another 34% between 0 and −1 standard deviation (68% total), that approximately 13.5% of the scores fall between +1 and +2 and another 13.5% between −1 and −2 standard deviations (27% total), and that approximately 2.5% of the scores fall between +2 and +3 and another 2.5% between −2 and −3 (5% total). Thus, if we know an individual's raw score as well as the mean and standard deviation of a test, we can approximate where on the curve the person's score falls.

As the chapter concluded, we highlighted the importance of always asking the individual who was assessed his or her perception of the score that was received. A high score for one person is a low score for someone else.

Chapter Review

1. Describe how norm group comparisons can make raw scores meaningful.

2. Using the scores below, create a frequency distribution.

1	2	4	6	12	16	14	17
7	21	4	3	11	4	10	
12	7	9	3	2	1	3	
6	1	3	6	5	10	3	

3. Develop a histogram that uses class intervals of 3 and a frequency polygon that uses class intervals of 4 from the numbers in item 2.

4. Describe the relationship between the mean, median, and mode on a negatively skewed curve, a positively skewed curve, and a normal curve.

5. Using the numbers in item 2, determine the mean, median, and mode of this group of scores (measures of central tendency).

6. Using the numbers in item 2, determine the range, interquartile range, and standard deviation of this group of scores (measures of variability).

7. If the scores in item 2 were the scores of a class of graduate students in counseling who took a national test of depression, and if the mean and standard deviation of the test nationally was 14 and 5 respectively for a group of moderately depressed clients, what statement might you be able to make about this group of students?

8. Using the national mean and standard deviation for moderately depressed clients (from item 7), at what approximate percentile has a person scored if he or she obtained a raw score of 9? What if he or she has a raw score of 19?

9. How might you feel if you scored a 19 on this test?

10. Describe the relationship between how a person does on a test, compared to a national mean and standard deviation, and how a person might feel about his or her score. For example, if I had a history of major depression and scored a 15 on the test, how might my interpretation of my score differ from an individual who has never dealt with depression and receives a score of 15?

Statistical Concepts:
Creating New Scores
to Interpret Test Data

I remember taking an organic chemistry test in college and thinking afterwards that there was no doubt I had failed. This would have been the only test I had ever failed, and I was devastated. As I waited for my score, I pondered my future. Suddenly, a friend of mine burst into my dorm room and announced, "You passed. You got a D." I knew that even a score of D would have been impossible, so I asked, "What did I get on the test?" His response was, "You got a 17." By far, this was the lowest grade I had ever received. I responded, "Well, how could I have passed if I received a 17?" My friend explained, "He took the square root of each person's score and multiplied it by 10. Then he applied his usual 'curve,' and your score of 41 was a D." In essence, what had happened was that the professor had "converted" my score. I then understood that things are not always what they appear to be. As it was with my converted organic test score, many raw scores in the world of testing are converted so that they have new meaning. That is the topic of this chapter—varying ways that test publishers and others convert test scores for easier interpretation. (Ed Neukrug)

In this chapter we will examine how raw scores are converted to what are called "derived" scores to make them easier to understand. We will start by distinguishing between norm-referenced testing and criterion-referenced testing, which are two different ways of understanding test scores. As we will see, derived scores are mostly associated with norm-referenced testing. Next, we will discuss specific types of derived scores, such as (1) percentiles; (2) standard scores, including z scores, T scores, Deviation IQs, stanines, sten scores, NCE scores, college and graduate school entrance exam scores (e.g., SATs, GREs, and

ACTs), and publisher-type scores; and (3) developmental norms, such as age comparisons and grade equivalents. As we near the end of the chapter we will discuss standard error of measurement, which is a mechanism for estimating how close an individual's obtained score is to his or her true score. Finally, the chapter concludes with a short discussion of scales of measurement, which allow us to assign numerical values to non-numeric characteristics for purposes of testing.

Norm Referencing Versus Criterion Referencing

Two testing experts pass each other in the hallway, and one turns to the other and says, "How are you doing?" The second expert replies, "Compared to whom?"

Norm referencing Comparison of individual test scores to average score of a group

The terms *norm referencing* and *criterion referencing* are used to describe two different ways of understanding an individual's score. In *norm referencing*, each individual's test score is compared to the average score of a group of individuals, called the norm group or peer group. Thus, one could compare his or her score to the aggregate scores of students who took an organic chemistry test (as in the example at the beginning of the chapter), to the aggregate scores of thousands of individuals who took a national achievement test, or to a representative group of individuals who took a personality test. A large percentage of nationally made standardized tests are norm-referenced.

Criterion referencing Comparison of test scores to a predetermined standard

Criterion referencing, on the other hand, compares test scores to a predetermined value or a set criterion. For example, an instructor may decide that a test score of 90 percent to 100 percent correct is an A, 80 percent correct to 89.9 percent correct is a B, 70 percent correct to 79.9 percent correct is a C, and so forth.

Criterion-referenced testing is generally used by state departments of motor vehicles (DMV), which often require a minimum score of 70 percent correct to pass their written exam. If the DMV used norm-referencing testing and decided that people would pass the test if they received a score above −1 standard deviation, approximately 16% of the individuals taking the test would consistently fail, even if they answered more than 70 percent of the questions correctly. In fact, if suddenly everyone who took this test was studying more diligently and the overall scores were higher, using norm-referenced testing would likely mean that 16% of the group would still fail. So those who fail might have higher scores than those who had previously passed. This could create an administrative mess for many DMVs and also result in a lot of angry people.

Many states have begun using criterion-referenced testing of students as a result of the recent passing of No Child Left Behind legislation. In this case, the federal government has mandated that all students must achieve minimum pre-set scores on statewide exams (e.g., 75 percent correct in reading) (see Box 5.1).

Table 5.1 shows some common tests that are norm-referenced or criterion-referenced. Obviously, the choice to use norm referencing or criterion referencing when considering test results is quite important.

BOX 5.1

**High Stakes Testing: Using Criterion-Referenced Testing
to Assure That All Students Will Achieve**

As you read the following paragraph, substitute the word "criterion" for the italicized word or phrase and you will see why NCLB is based on criterion-referenced testing.

As a result of the federal initiative called "No Child Left Behind" (NCLB), testing has become a critical method of assuring that all students will achieve in schools. In general, NCLB encourages each state to set a *passing score*, known as the "starting point," which is based on the performance of its lowest-achieving demographic group or of the lowest-achieving schools in the state, whichever is higher. The state then sets the *level of student achievement* that a school must attain after two years in order to continue to show "adequate yearly progress." Subsequent *thresholds* must be raised at least once every three years until at the end of 12 years all students in the state are achieving at the proficiency level on state assessments in reading/language arts and math (U.S. Dept. of Education, n.d.b).

Although this is a noble effort, a major criticism of No Child Left Behind is the fact that the federal government has threatened to remove aid to schools if these thresholds are not met, even though little funding has been provided to assist school systems to meet higher standards of achievement (NEA, 2002-2004).

TABLE 5.1

Examples of Norm-Referenced and Criterion-Referenced Tests

NORM-REFERENCED	CRITERION-REFERENCED
GREs, SATs, ACTs, MCATs, etc.	BDI-2 (Beck Depression Inventory)
IQ tests (Wechsler, Stanford-Binet, etc.)	College writing entrance or exit exam
Personality inventories (MBTI, CPI, MMPI-2, etc.)	Driver's licensing exam
Career inventories (Strong Interest Inventory, Self-Directed Search, etc.)	MAST (Michigan Alcohol Screening Test)
College exam scored on a "curve"	College exams scored against a standard (A = 90 percent right, B = 80 percent right, C = 70 percent right, etc.)

Normative Comparisons and Derived Scores

As discussed in Chapter 4, the relative position of an individual in his or her norm group is a reflection of how a person has performed. To review this point, consider the following question:

If John scores a 52 on a test and Mary scores a 98, who has done better?

Reflecting back to Chapter 4, our answer as to who has done better must be based on a number of factors, including the following:

1. The number of items on the test and the highest possible score.
2. The relative positions of a score of 52 and a score of 98 compared with the rest of the group. If out of 1000 examinees, the vast majority scored above 98, then the real difference between a 98 and 52 may be minimal.
3. Whether higher scores are better than lower scores. For instance, on a depression test, lower scores might be better.
4. How an individual feels about his or her score. A low score for some individuals may be a high score for others (e.g., some might be ecstatic with a score at the 80th percentile on a math test, while others might be disappointed).

As you can see from items 1 and 2 above, understanding an individual's relative position in a group is critical if we are to make judgments about that individual's score. Of course, relative position does not tell us whether a lower or higher score is better and does not indicate how a person feels about his or her score (items 3 and 4 above).

To determine an individual's relative position in his or her norm group, raw scores are often converted to frequency distributions, histograms, and polygons to provide a visual representation of what is happening with all the scores. We discussed this process in Chapter 4 and also introduced the concept of measures of central tendency and measures of variability in order to begin to examine how scores are related to the normal curve. In this chapter, we will introduce the concept of *derived* scores, which are conversions of raw scores that allow us to make further comparisons of an individual's score with those of his or her norm group. Derived scores include percentiles; standard scores such as z scores, T scores, Deviation IQs, stanines, sten scores, normal curve equivalents (NCEs), college and graduate school entrance exam scores (e.g., SATs, GREs, and ACTs), and publisher-type scores; and developmental norms, such as age comparisons and grade equivalents.

Derived score
Converted score based against a norm group

Percentiles

Percentile
Percentage of people falling at or below a score

Perhaps the simplest and most common method of comparing raw scores to a norm group is to use *percentile rank*, often just called *percentile*. A percentile represents the percentage of people falling below an obtained score and ranges from 1 to 99, with 50 being the mean. For example, if the median score on a sociology exam was a 45, and an individual scored a 45, his or her *percentile score* would be 50 (p = 50), meaning that 50 percent of the individuals who took the test scored below a 45. If the top score for that exam was 75, then that person would be at the 99th percentile. Be careful not to confuse percentile scores with the term "percentage correct," which refers to the number of correct items. In the example just given, the person with a percentile score of 99 could have answered 75 out of 125 questions correctly, which would have given that person a "percentage correct" score of 60 (75/125). Percentile ranking is considered

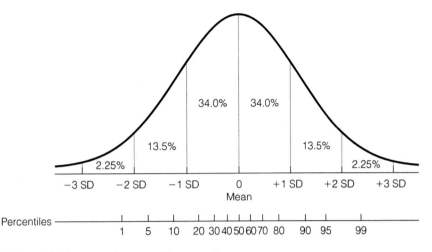

Figure 5.1 The normal curve with percentile scores

norm referencing because it compares an individual's score with the scores of a larger group (the normative group).

By examining Figure 5.1, you can see that on the normal curve percentiles break down in the following approximate manner: –3 SD is a percentile that is less than 1, –2 SD is a percentile that is close to 2, –1 is a percentile of about 16, 0 SD is a percentile of 50, +1 SD is a percentile of about 84, +2 SD is a percentile close to 98 and +3 SD is a percentile that is over 99.

Standard Scores

Standard score
Derived score
based on mean
and standard
deviation

Standard scores represent a number of different kinds of scores that are derived by converting an individual's raw score to a new score that has a new mean and new standard deviation. Standard scores are generally used to make interpretation of test material easier for the examinee. Some of the more common types of standard scores include z scores, T scores, Deviation IQ (DIQ), stanines, sten scores, college and graduate school entrance exam scores (e.g., SATs, GREs, MATs, ACTs), and publisher-type scores.

z Scores

z score
Standard score
with mean of 0
and SD of 1

The most fundamental standard score is called a z score, which is a simple conversion of an individual's raw score to a new score that has a mean of 0 and a standard deviation of 1. Thus, if an individual scored at the mean, the z score would be 0; if an individual scored 1 standard deviation above the mean, the z score would be 1; if an individual scored 1 standard deviation below the mean, the z score would be –1; and so forth. Figure 5.2 demonstrates where z scores lie on the normal curve.

Converting a raw score to a z score is almost always the first step to take when analyzing a raw score. Once the raw score has been converted to a

RULE NUMBER 3: *z* **Scores Are Golden***

z scores are great for helping us see where an individual's raw score falls on a normal curve and are helpful for converting a raw score to other kinds of derived scores. That is why we like to keep in mind that *z scores are golden* and can often be used to help us understand the meaning of scores.

---

* Rules 1 and 2 were introduced in Chapter 4:
Rule 1: Raw scores are meaningless.
Rule 2: God does not play dice with the universe.

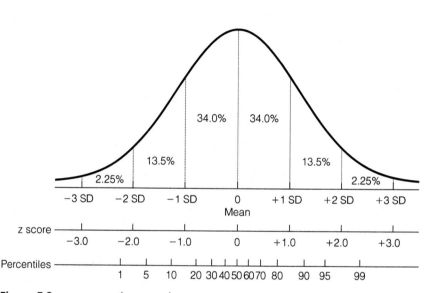

Figure 5.2 *z* scores on the normal curve

z score, almost any other type of derived score can be found, including percentiles, *T* scores, Deviation IQs (DIQ), stanines, and so forth. That is why *z* scores are so critical to our understanding of an individual's raw score (see Rule Number 3).

The formula for converting a raw score to a *z* score is

$$z = \frac{X - M}{SD}$$

where *X* is the raw score, *M* is the mean score, and SD is the standard deviation. For example, let's say an individual takes a psychology exam and the mean turns out to be 45 while the standard deviation is 10. To convert an individual's raw score of 65 on this test to a z score, we would use the conversion formula in the following manner:

$$X = 65 \text{ (raw score)}$$
$$M = 45 \text{ (mean)}$$
$$S = 10 \text{ (standard deviation)}$$

We plug these values into our formula and get

$$z = \frac{X - M}{10} = \frac{65 - 45}{10} = \frac{20}{10} = 2.0$$

From this example we can see that the individual who scored a 65 on the exam has a z score of +2.0. By examining Figure 5.2 you can see that this person has a percentile score of approximately 84.

Using the same formula, see if you can determine what the z score would be for an individual who had a raw score of 30 on this same test. If you followed the formula correctly, you should have had a z score of –1.5. Can you determine the approximate percentile that this person obtained? (All one need do is trace a line from the z score to the percentile rank line on Figure 5.2.) In this case, you can see that the approximate percentile is a 7. If you would like an exact method for determining a percentile from a z score, refer to Appendix D, which offers such a conversion formula. Additionally, Appendix D also includes a look-up table for quicker and easier conversions of z scores to percentiles.

The main value of z scores is to assist the test administrator in understanding where on the curve an individual falls compared with his or her peers, and as noted earlier, as the first step toward configuring other kinds of standard scores that are more readily understandable by clients. Explaining to a client that he or she had a z score of –1.5 might be not only useless but even counterproductive. However, we can convert the z score to other kinds of derived scores (e.g., percentiles, stanines, DIQs, T scores, and others) that are often more palatable for clients.

T Scores

T score
Standard score
with mean of 50
and SD of 10

One type of standard score that can be easily converted from a z score is the T score. T scores have a mean of 50 and a standard deviation of 10 and are generally used with personality tests. Figure 5.3 shows T scores on the normal curve.

To convert a z score to a T score, we use the following formula:

$$\text{Conversion score} = z(\text{SD}) + M$$

where the conversion score is the new standard score to which you are converting (e.g., T score) and one uses the standard deviation and mean of that conversion score (with the T score, the SD = 10 and the M = 50). Continuing with our earlier example, the individual who has received a z score of –1.5 has a T score of 35 (–1.5 * 10 + 50 = 35). What about the person who had a raw score of 65 that converted to a z score of 2.0? What would his or her T score be? If you came up with a T score of 70, you would be correct (2 * 10 + 50 = 70).

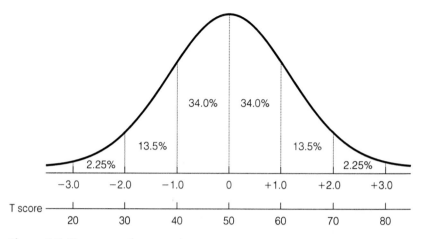

Figure 5.3 *T* scores on the normal curve

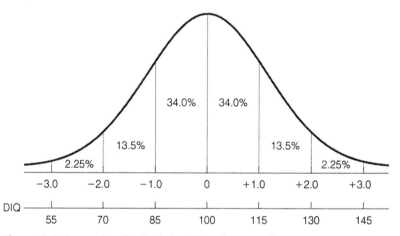

Figure 5.4 Comparing the Deviation IQ to the normal curve

Deviation IQ

Deviation IQ
Standard score
with mean of
100 and SD
of 15

Another commonly used standard score is Deviation IQ. The Deviation IQ has a mean of 100 and a standard deviation of 15. To apply this to the normal curve, see Figure 5.4.

Although most intelligence tests employ this standard of scoring, some caution should be exercised. For example, older versions of the Stanford-Binet Intelligence Test (Fourth Edition) used a mean of 100 and a standard deviation of 16; however, the most recent version (Fifth Edition) uses a mean of 100 and a standard deviation of 15 (Riverside Publishing, 2004a).

To convert a *z* score to a Deviation IQ (DIQ), we utilize the same conversion formula noted earlier [conversion score = *z*(SD) + *M*]. However, in this case

BOX 5.2
IQ, Population, and the Normal Curve

Have you ever heard anyone say he or she knows someone with an IQ of 200?

I have. My grandmother told me that my cousin, Michael, had been tested and found to be brilliant, with an IQ over 200. Using the look-up table for percentiles (see Appendix D), you can see how rare people are at the outer edges of the normal or bell-shaped curve. Looking at the table, you will note that the fourth standard deviation (z = 4.0), which corresponds to an IQ of about 160, is extremely rare; only 3 out of 100,000 people are at this level. An IQ of 175 is found in only 3 out of 10 million people. That would mean there are only 88 people living in the United States with this IQ, assuming a U.S. population of 292 million (U.S.

Census Bureau, n.d.). An IQ of 190 (z = 6.0) is found in only one out of a billion people, which means there are approximately six or seven people in the world with this IQ. As a matter of fact, I was speaking with Senior Project Director of the Stanford-Binet Intelligence Test (personal communication, Dr. Andrew Carson, October 7, 2004), and he said they have failed to ever find a person with an IQ above 160 because it is so rare. So the next time you hear of someone with a 200 IQ, you might want to question them further... apparently they don't know a lot about the normal curve!

–Charlie Fawcett

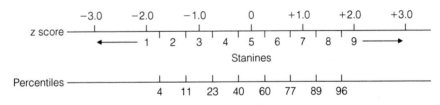

Figure 5.5 Stanines compared to z scores and percentiles

we use the standard deviation of 15 and the mean of 100. Using the example earlier in which an individual obtains a z score of –1.5, we would find a DIQ of 77.5 (DIQ = –1.5 ∗ 15 + 100). What is an individual's DIQ if his or her z score is 2.0? If you came up with a DIQ of 130, you would be correct (2 ∗ 15 + 100 =130). And, finally what would a person's DIQ be if he or she had a z score of 6 (see Box 5.2)?

Stanines

Stanine
Standard score
with mean of 5
and SD of 2

Another standard scoring system frequently used in the schools is stanines, which stands for "standard nines." Often used with achievement tests, stanines have a mean of 5 and a standard deviation of 2, and range from 1 to 9. For example, an individual who scores one standard deviation above the mean would have a stanine of 7 (mean = 5 + 1SD of 2). Similarly, if a student has a z score of –1, his or her stanine would be 5 minus 2, which is 3. Figure 5.5 shows where stanines fall in comparison to z scores and percentiles.

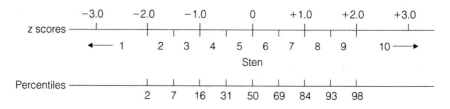

Figure 5.6 Sten scores compared to z scores and percentiles

Unlike other forms of standard scoring we have examined thus far where a score could be identified with a particular z score and percentile (e.g., T score of 60 equals a z score of 1 and percentile of 84), stanines represent a range of z scores and percentiles. For instance, a stanine of 5 runs from a z score of −.25 to +.25 and from the 40th to 60th percentiles (see Figure 5.5). Similarly, a stanine of 6 runs from +.25 to +.75 and from the 60th to 77th percentiles, and a stanine of 7 runs from +.75 to +1.25 and from the 77th to 89th percentiles, and so forth. As you can see from Figure 5.5, any z score that is below −1.75 or above +1.75 is a stanine of 1 or 9, respectively.

Changing z scores to stanines is still done with our conversion formula $z(\text{SD}) + M$. Applying the formula for a z score of −1.5, we would get

$$z = -1.5 \text{ (given)}$$
$$\text{SD} = 2$$
$$M = 5, \text{ so}$$
$$\text{Stanine} = z(\text{SD}) + M = -1.5(2) + 5 = -3 + 5 = 2$$

Consequently, a z score of −1.5 converts to a stanine of 2. Similarly, a z score of 2 converts to a stanine of 9 (stanine = 2 * 2 + 5). Because stanines are reported only as whole numbers, in those cases where the use of the z score in the conversion formula results in a fraction, the fraction should be rounded off to the nearest whole number. For example, a z score of .87 converts to a stanine of 6.74 which is rounded off to 7 (.87 * 2 + 5 = 6.74, or in this case, 7).

As with most forms of standard scoring, stanines are an attempt to explain scoring so that the test-taker, or his or her parents, can easily understand test results. It is usually easier to tell a parent that his or her daughter scored a 7 out of a range from 1 to 9 than to explain that the daughter has a z score of .87.

Sten Scores

Sten score
Standard score
with mean of
5.5 and SD of 2

Sten scores are derived from the name "standard ten" and are commonly used on personality inventories and questionnaires. Stens have a mean of 5.5 and a standard deviation of 2. Stens divide the scale into ten units, each of which is one-half of a z score, except for the first sten, which represents all scores below −2 z scores, and the tenth sten, which represents all scores above +2 z scores. Stens are similar to stanines in that they represent a range of scores rather than an absolute point. Figure 5.6 shows the relationship between stens, z scores, and percentiles.

As you might expect, the conversion formula of z(SD) + M also applies to sten scores. To use our example of a z score of –1.5, we would determine our sten score to be 2.5:

$$z = -1.5 \text{ (given)}$$
$$SD = 2$$
$$M = 5.5, \text{ so}$$
$$\text{Sten} = z(SD) + M = 1.5(2) + 5.5 = -3 + 5.5 = 2.5$$

However, because stens, like stanines, are reported in whole numbers, we would round up a score of 2.5 to a sten of 3. What would be the sten score of an individual who obtained a z score of 2? If you got 10, you would be correct (2 * 2 + 5.5 = 9.5, rounded off to 10).

Normal Curve Equivalents (NCE) Scores

Normal curve equivalent
Standard score with mean of 50 and SD of 21.06

A form of standard scoring frequently used in the educational community is Normal Curve Equivalents or NCE. The NCE has a mean of 50 and a standard deviation of 21.06. These units range from 1 to 99 in equal units along the bell-shaped curve. As can be seen in Figure 5.2, percentile ranks range from 1 to 99 but are not arranged in equal units along the curve. Consequently, the NCE and percentile ranks are the same at 1, 50, and 99 (see Figure 5.7 to compare NCEs with the normal curve). The standard formula for converting scores still applies to NCEs except that the limits are 1 and 99. The formula is NCE = z(21.06) + 50.

College and Graduate School Entrance Exam Scores

SAT/GRE type score
Standard score with mean around 500 and SD of 100

The SATs and GREs use another kind of standard score with which you may be familiar. In this case, the SAT has three sections (critical reading, mathematics, and writing), which use a standard score that has a standard deviation of 100 and a mean of 500. The norm group used in reporting the standard score consists of test results from 1990. However, rather than giving you a percentile as compared with that norm group, they then figure out your percentile score based on students who have taken the test over the past three years. Thus, your standard score is compared to the 1990 norm group, but your percentile is based on a more current norm group. Using the more current norm group for your percentile allows colleges and universities to see where you fall compared to current students who will be going to college and graduate school when you do. Using our conversion formula, see if you can convert z scores of –1.5 and 2 to an SAT-type score. If you got 350 and 700, you would be correct [SAT = –1.5 * 100 + 500 = 350, and 2 * 100 + 500 = 700].

ACT score
Standard score with mean around 21 and SD of 5

The ACT, the most widely used college entrance exam in the United States (ACT Inc., 2004a, 2004b), offers scores in four main subcategories including English, mathematics, reading, and science as well as a combined composite average score. Like the SATs and GREs, the ACTs convert your raw score to a standard score, which in this case uses a mean of 21 and a standard deviation of 5 for college-bound students. Like the SATs and GREs, an individual's raw score is compared to an earlier norm group, in this case 1994, and the percentile is

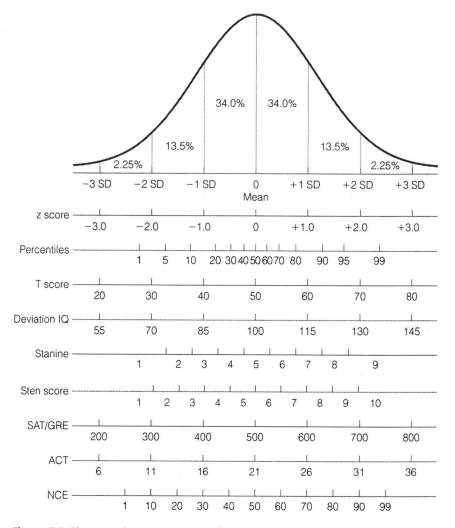

Figure 5.7 The normal curve and types of standard scores

configured from the students who have taken the test over the past three years. Using the conversion formula, see if you can convert z scores of –1.5 and 2 to an ACT-type score. If you got 14 and 31, you would be correct [ACT = –1.5 * 5 + 21 = 13.5 or 14 rounded off, and 2 * 5 + 21 = 31].

Publisher-Type Scores

As you probably have come to realize, the conversion formula can be used to create a standard score with a pre-chosen mean and standard deviation. Consequently, sometimes test developers generate their own standard score. That is why it is common to see standardized achievement tests using unique test

---

BOX 5.3
Mary's Reading Score

	Mary Smartgirl	Grade 5.2	Age: 10.5	
Raw Score*	Percentile		Stanine	Standard Score**
52	93		8	638

* Mean of raw score = 45, Standard deviation of raw score = 4   ** Mean of publisher's standard score = 550, standard deviation = 50

Publisher-type score

Test developer creates own standard score

publisher scores that employ means and standard deviations of the publisher's choice. For instance, if Mary took a standardized reading achievement test and received a raw score of 52, the scores on her actual profile sheet might look something like what you see in Box 5.3.

In the example in Box 5.3, Mary's raw score is equivalent to a percentile score of 93, which is equivalent to a standard score of 638, which is equivalent to a stanine of 8. How did the publisher get these scores? First, they took her raw score and compared it to her norm group's mean and standard deviation to obtain a z score (remember, z scores are golden!). So, hypothetically, we may have seen something like the following: $z = (52 - 45)/4$, which equals a z score of +1.75. By looking at our graph (see Figure 5.2) we can see that a z score of 1.75 is approximately a percentile of 93. Also, by looking at our graph in Figure 5.5, we can see that a z score of 1.75 is equal to a stanine of 8 (but close to 9!). Finally, we can use our conversion formula to determine the publisher's standard score if we know the mean and standard deviation of the publisher's standard score (generally found in the publisher's manual and in this case given in Box 5.3). For instance, with a z score of 1.75 we could determine that the publisher simply plugged the mean and standard deviation into the conversion formula: $1.75 * 50 + 550 = 637.5$ (rounded off to 638).

Unfortunately, test printouts usually only list the publisher's standard score without telling you the mean and standard deviation. This makes it quite difficult to determine what the score actually is based on. We sometimes call these publisher standard scores "magical scores," because they seem to magically appear with little explanation on the part of the publishing company. Thus, we usually suggest using other derived scores, such as percentiles or stanines, when interpreting test data for clients.

Developmental Norms

As opposed to standard scores, which in some manner convert an individual's raw score to a score that has a new mean and standard deviation, developmental norms, such as age comparisons and grade equivalents, directly compare an individual's score to the average scores of others at the same age or grade level.

BOX 5.4

Is Your Head Too Big?

When my older daughter, Hannah, was two months old, the pediatrician measured her head size. He immediately said, "It's at the 98th percentile. Let's measure it again in a month." I asked him if he was concerned, knowing full well that her head size was "outside the norm" or not within the average range for her age group, which could suggest a number of medical problems. Thankfully there were no problems, and it turned out that some members of the family just have "big heads." However, such age norm comparisons can be critical to the identification of possible early developmental problems.

—*Ed Neukrug*

Age Comparisons

Age comparison score Comparison of individual score to average score of others at the same age

Remember when you were a kid and you were always being compared to others of your age on those weight and height charts? The doctor was looking at where your height and weight fell compared to your norm group. Basically, the doctor would compare your height and weight to a bunch of kids who were the same age as you. So, if you were a girl aged nine years and four months, and you were 55 inches tall, and the mean height for girls of your age was 52.5 inches with a standard deviation of 2.4 inches, your z score would be +1.04 [(55 − 52.5)/2.4)]. This z score converts to a percentile of approximately 85. One other way of using age norms is to see how your performance compares to the average performance of individuals at other age levels. Thus, for the 9-year, 4-month-old girl, we could say that she is at the average height for a 10-year, 11-month-old girl. If we were looking at an intelligence test, we might find that a 12-year, 5-month old has the mental age of the average 15-year, 4-month old (see Box 5.4).

Grade Equivalents

Grade equivalent Comparison of individual score to average score of others at the same grade level

Similar to age norms, grade equivalents compare an individual's score to the average score of children at the same grade level. Thus, if a student who was in the second month of the third grade (grade 3.2) took a reading test and scored at the mean, that student's grade equivalent would be 3.2. Unfortunately, this is where the comparison to age norms stops. Rather than actually comparing the raw score of a student to the raw scores of students at differing grade levels (e.g., comparing the raw score of the 3.2 grade student to the raw scores of students in the second grade, fourth grade, fifth grade, and so on), publishing companies usually extrapolate an individual's score. Thus, the student in the 3.2 grade who obtained a score at the 75th percentile when compared to her grade might end up with a grade equivalent of 4.5 despite the fact that she was never actually compared to students in the fourth grade, fifth month.

So, what can be said about a student's grade equivalent when it is either higher or lower than the mean score of students at his or her grade level? The best interpretation would be to state that a student has scored either lower or higher than students in his or her grade. For instance, a student in the 3.2 grade who obtains a grade equivalent of 5.4 has not mastered many of the concepts of the average student in grade 5.4; however, such a student is clearly doing much better than a large percentage of students in the third grade. Thus, it would make sense to say that this student is performing above the average for students at the 3.2 grade and not accurate to state that this student is performing *at* the 5.4 grade level. Similarly, another student in the 3.2 grade who obtains a grade equivalent of 2.2 has mastered many concepts that the average student at the 2.2 grade level has not even examined. Thus, it would make sense to say that this student is performing below the average for students at the 3.2 grade level, and not accurate to state that this student is performing *at* the 2.2 grade level.

You can see why it is important for test interpreters to read and understand how the test developer normed and calculated the grade equivalent score. It should be easy to see why having a strong background in testing and assessment is important in communicating test results.

Putting It All Together

Now that we have learned that norm-referenced scores are based on the normal curve, we can use Figure 5.7 to examine the relationships between most of the various norm-referenced scores that we introduced in the chapter. You are encouraged to become familiar with these scores, as you will come across them often throughout your professional life.

Standard Error of Measurement

As we saw in Chapter 3, all tests have a certain amount of measurement error, which results in an individual's score being an approximation of his or her true score. By using some simple statistics, we can calculate the range or band in which a person's true score might actually lie. Known as the *standard error of measurement*, this range of scores is where we would expect a person's score to fall if he or she took the instrument over and over again (and was the same person each time he or she took it—e.g., no learning had taken place). As you will recall from Chapter 3, reliability is the degree to which a test is free of measurement error. Consequently, we can use the reliability to determine the standard error of measurement if we know the standard deviation of the raw score or of the standard score. The formula for calculating standard error of measurement (SEM) is

Standard error of measurement Range where a "true" score might lie

$$SEM = SD\sqrt{1 - r}$$

where SD is the standard deviation of the raw score or of the standard score and *r* is the reliability coefficient of the test. As an example, let's say Latisha takes a standardized intelligence test and gets a DIQ score of 120. From reading the published data about the instrument, we know that it has a reliability coefficient of

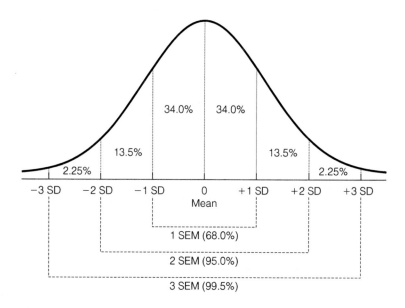

Figure 5.8 Standard error of measurement and the normal curve

.95; we also know that DIQs have a standard deviation of 15. Applying this information to our formula, we get the following result:

$$SEM = SD\sqrt{1-r}$$
$$= 15\sqrt{1-.95}$$
$$= 15\sqrt{.05}$$
$$= 15 \times .22$$
$$= 3.35 \text{ (plus \& minus)}$$

Now we know that if Latisha were to take the intelligence test over and over again, her score would fall plus or minus 3.35 of her score of 120, or between 116.65 to 123.35. As you may recall, the area under the normal curve of plus and minus one standard deviation equals 68 percent of the scores. Hypothetically, then, if Latisha were to take the test 1000 times, 68 percent of the time she would score between 116.65 and 123.35 (see Figure 5.8).

If we wanted greater accuracy, we could use plus or minus two 2 SEMs (two standard deviations around the mean), and that would tell us where her score would fall approximately 95 percent of the time. If we went out to 3 SEMs, we would know where her score would fall 99.5 percent of the time:

$$2 SEM = 2(SD)\sqrt{1-r}$$
$$3 SEM = 3(SD)\sqrt{1-r}$$

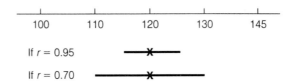

Figure 5.9 Example of SEM on two test reports with different reliabilities

So Latisha's 2 SEM score would be 3.35 times 2 or ± 6.7; that is, 95 percent of the time her score would fall between 113.30 and 126.70, and 99.5 percent of the time her score would fall in the range of 109.95 to 130.05 (3 * 3.35 = ± 10.05).

At this point, you are probably beginning to see that there is an inverse rela-tionship between the reliability coefficient and SEM; that is, as the reliability decreases, the SEM (the range of true scores) increases. Following the example of Latisha, let's say the intelligence test was not very reliable, with r = .70. How would this affect the SEM? Her SEM would increase. Calculating the SEM for the new reliability coefficient of .70, we would find:

Reliability coefficient and SEM have an inverse relationship.

$$SEM = SD\sqrt{1 - r}$$
$$= 15\sqrt{1 - .70}$$
$$= 15\sqrt{.3}$$
$$= 15 \times .55$$
$$= 8.22 \text{ (plus and minus)}$$

So, if Latisha were to take this new intelligence test with a reliability coeffi-cient of .70, 68 percent of the time her true score would fall in the range of 111.78 to 128.22. That range is quite a bit larger than the previous example when we used r = .95 and her SEM was determined to be between 116.35 and 123.35.

If you have observed test reports from the larger test publishers, you may have seen individual test scores with an "X" and with a line on either side of the "X" (see Figure 5.9). This line represents the SEM, or the range in which the true score might fall. Figure 5.9 shows how these bands may look on test reports showing Latisha's score on tests with reliability coefficients of .95 versus .70.

You can see that SEM is particularly important for the interpretation of test scores, because the larger the SEM, the more error and the larger the range where an individual's true score might fall. As we conclude this chapter, do the example in Box 5.5 and then read Rule 4.

Scales of Measurement

Now that we are finished discussing statistical concepts related to interpreting test scores and we are about to discuss commonly used assessment techniques (Section Three), it is important to consider that not all scores are the same. For

---

BOX 5.5
Determining Standard Error of Measurement

Let's say Ed obtained a score on a test of depression that was a *T* score of 60, and the test-retest reliability of the instrument was .75. Assuming that the higher the score, the more depressed a person is, answer the following questions:

1. What is Ed's percentile score on this test?
2. Determine what the SEM is 68 percent and 95 percent of the time.
3. What would be the range of Ed's *T* score and percentile scores 68 percent of the time?
4. What would be the range of Ed's *T* score and percentile scores 95 percent of the time?
5. What implications does the standard error of measurement have for interpreting Ed's score?

ANSWERS:

1. About a percentile of 84.
2. The SEM 68 percent of the time is ± 5, and 95 percent of the time it is ±10: $\left(10\sqrt{1-.75}\right)2$.
3. 68 percent of the time Ed's score would fall between T scores of 55 and 65 (percentiles of 70 to 93). (60 ± 5).
4. 95 percent of the time he would fall between *T* scores of 50 to 70 (percentiles of 50 to 95) (60 ± 10).
5. Error has great implications for the interpretation of Ed's scores. The greater the error, the less we can rely on his score to be an indication of high levels of depression. At first it might seem that he has a fairly high level of depression (*T* score of 60, percentile of 84), but as we consider the error and the range of his "true score," we lower our confidence that the score truly indicates somewhat high levels of depression.

RULE NUMBER 4:   **Don't Mix Apples and Oranges**

As you practice various formulas in class, it is easy to use the wrong score, mean, or standard deviation. For instance, in determining the SEM for Latisha, we used Latisha's DIQ score of 120 and figured out the SEM using the DIQ standard deviation of 15. However, if we had been asked to figure out the SEM of her raw score, we would use her raw score and the standard deviation of raw scores. Whenever you are asked to figure out a problem, remember to use the correct set of numbers (don't mix apples and oranges); otherwise your answer will be incorrect.

---

instance, we can assign people to one of four categories of depression, such as none, low, medium, or high, and give each category a number, such as 0, 1, 2, or 3, respectively. Or we can take the same group of people and have them take a test for depression and examine the group scores, which would fall on a continuum from low to high, based on the number of items on the test. In the first example we can only say that one group is higher or lower than another group. In the second example, however, we can make some judgment about the amount of depression an individual has, relative to another individual, and we can add and subtract the various scores.

To distinguish between different kinds of test scores and subsequently know what kinds of statistics can be applied to them, four kinds of scales of measurement have been identified: nominal scales, ordinal scales, interval scales, and ratio scales. Knowing the scale of measurement to which scores from an instrument belong has profound implications for how the resulting scores can be manipulated statistically, and these implications are particularly important when conducting research. Although the kinds of tests we will examine in Section Three result in scores that are mostly of the interval type, some of the assessment procedures we will examine result in scores that fall into the nominal, ordinal, and ratio scales range. As you read through the text and review the various assessment instruments, you might want to consider the scales of measurement to which the scores from each instrument belong.

Nominal Scale

Nominal scale Numbers arbitrarily assigned to represent categories

The most basic or simple measurement scale is the nominal scale. In this scale numbers are arbitrarily assigned to represent different categories or variables. For example, race might be recorded as 1 = Asian, 2 = Latino, 3 = African American, 4 = Caucasian, etc. The assignment of numbers to these categories does not represent magnitude, so normal statistical calculations cannot be performed. All you can do is count the occurrences or calculate the mode.

Ordinal Scale

Ordinal scale Numbers with rank order but unequal distances between

In the ordinal scale, magnitude or rank order is implied; however, the distance between measurements is unknown. An example of this would be asking someone how much they agree with the statement "The counseling I received was helpful in obtaining the goals I came in for" and then asking them to choose from: 1 = Strongly Disagree, 2 = Somewhat Agree, 3 = Neutral, 4 = Somewhat Agree, 5 = Strongly Agree. These numbers represent rank or magnitude, but it is impossible to know the true distance between "somewhat agree" and "strongly agree."

Interval Scale

Interval scale Numbers with equal distances between but no zero

The interval scale establishes equal distances between measurements but has no absolute zero reference point. The Graduate Record Exam (GRE) you may have taken for admission into school is an interval scale. A score of 530 is 20 equal units above a score of 510; however, there is no true zero point since the minimum possible score is 200. Some basic statistical analysis is appropriate, such as determining how many standard deviations an individual is from the mean, but one cannot say that a student who scores a 700 is twice as likely to succeed in graduate school as a student who scores a 350.

Ratio Scale

Ratio scale Numbers with equal intervals and meaningful zero

The ratio scale has a meaningful zero point and equal intervals; therefore, it can be manipulated by all mathematical principles. Very few behavioral measures fall into this category. Units such as height, weight, and temperature are all ratio scales since they have a true zero reference point. An example of a ratio scale would be the measurement of reaction times. If a researcher is attempting to measure brake response time by individuals with varying blood alcohol content (BAC) levels, both the BAC and the response time would be ratio scales. A BAC level of .00 (sober) might provide an average reaction time of .6 second, while a BAC level of .10 might correspond to an average reaction time of 1.2 seconds. Both the BAC and reaction time have true zero points, and therefore they are considered ratio scales. In other words, a reaction time of .6 second is twice as fast as 1.2 seconds.

Summary

In this chapter we examined how raw scores are converted to what are called "derived" scores so that individuals can more easily understand the meaning of the raw scores. We started the chapter by pointing out that in norm-referenced testing, test scores are compared to a group of individuals called the norm group or peer group, but in criterion-referenced testing, test scores are compared to a predetermined value or a set criterion. We noted that although some tests are criterion-referenced, a large percentage are norm-referenced and employ a range of different kinds of derived scores in an attempt to make sense out of raw scores.

Relative to norm-referenced testing, we noted some factors that can affect our understanding of a raw score, including the number of items on a test and knowledge of what is the highest score possible, the relative position of an individual's score as compared to the scores of others who took the test, whether higher scores are better than lower scores, and how a person feels about his or her score on a test. We next identified a number of derived scores that are used to help us understand an individual's relative position in the norm group, such as (1) percentiles; (2) standard scores, including z scores, T scores, Deviation IQs, stanines, sten scores, NCE scores, college and graduate school entrance exam scores (e.g., SATs, GREs, MATs, and ACTs), and publisher-type scores; and (3) developmental norms, such as age comparisons and grade equivalents.

We defined the derived score known as percentiles, distinguished percentiles from the concept of "percentage correct," and noted that percentiles represent the percentage of people falling below an individual's obtained score and range from 1 to 99.

Next, we examined standard scores, which are obtained by converting a raw score mean and standard deviation to a scale that has a new mean and standard deviation. First we highlighted the z score, which is a standard score that has a mean of 0 and a standard deviation of 1, and offered a formula for obtaining it. We noted that an individual's z score reflects where he or she falls on the normal curve. We pointed out that z scores are so important to our understanding of derived scores that we might say "z scores are golden," meaning that configuring a z score is often the first critical step to finding all other derived scores.

We showed how to convert a z score to a number of standard scores, including T scores (SD = 10, M = 50), DIQs (SD = 15, M = 100), stanines (SD = 2, M = 5), sten scores (SD = 2, M = 55), SATs and GREs (SD = 100, M = 500), ACTs (SD = 21, M = 5), NCEs (SD = 21.06, M = 50), and publisher-type scores, where the standard deviation and mean vary depending on the publisher and the test.

As the chapter continued, we noted that developmental norms are also used to help us understand the relative position of an individual's raw score as compared with his or her norm group. We noted that age norms compare an individual's performance to the average performance of others in his or her age group (e.g., height, weight, mental ability), or to the average performance of individuals in other age groups (e.g., a 12-year-old might have the mental ability of the average 15-year-old). Grade equivalents, we noted, compare an individual's performance to the average performance of other students in his or her grade. We also cautioned that sometimes grade equivalents are misinterpreted because it is falsely assumed that a higher grade equivalent means an individual can perform at that higher grade level or that a lower grade equivalent means that the individual has not learned concepts at his or her own grade level.

Near the end of the chapter, we discussed standard error of measurement, which is a mechanism for estimating how close an individual's obtained score is to his or her true score. We noted that by using the formula to find the standard error of measurement, we can determine the range of scores in which an individual's true score is likely to fall 68 percent of the time (± 1 SEM), 95 percent of the time (± 2 SEM), or 99.5 percent of the time (± 3 SEM). We noted that SEM has great implications for the interpretation of test data, because the higher the error, the less confidence we have about where the individual's true score actually lies. In discussing SEM we highlighted our fourth rule: "Don't Mix Apples and Oranges"; that is, when computing any problem, make sure that you are using the correct scales (e.g., correct mean and standard deviation).

Finally, we had a brief discussion of the four scales of measurement: nominal, ordinal, interval, and ratio. We noted that each type of scale has unique attributes that may limit the statistical and/or mathematical calculations we can perform and that different kinds of assessment instruments use different kinds of scales.

Chapter Review

1. When might a criterion-referenced test be more appropriate to use than a norm-referenced test?

2. Discuss the strengths and weaknesses of using a criterion-referenced test instead of a norm-referenced test to measure progress as defined by No Child Left Behind.

3. Distinguish between the following kinds of derived scores: percentiles, standard scores, and developmental norms.

4. An individual receives a raw score of 62 on a national standardized test. Given that the mean and standard deviation of the test were 58 and 8, respectively, find the individual's z score.

5. Using the z score found in Item 4, find the following derived scores:
   a. percentile (approximate)
   b. T scores

   c. deviation IQ
   d. stanine
   e. sten score
   f. normal curve equivalent (NCE)
   g. SAT-type score
   h. ACT score
   i. a publisher-type score that has a mean of 75 and standard deviation of 15

6. Define the term "developmental norms."

7. Explain what a grade equivalent is. What is a potential major downfall of using a grade equivalent type of score?

8. Find the z score and approximate percentile of a 5.5-year-old child who is 46 inches tall when the mean and standard deviation of height for a 5.5-year-old child are 44 inches and 3 inches, respectively.

9. Referring to Item 5, b through i, find what the standard error of measurement would be 68 percent of the time for each of the scores if the reliability of the test is .84. Also determine what the individual's derived score would be for each of the items (b through i) 95 percent of the time.

10. Identify the four different types of scales of measurement and give examples of situations when some might be more appropriate to use than others.

Commonly Used Assessment Techniques

Section Three examines some of the commonly used techniques for assessing educational ability, intelligence, career and occupational interests and aptitudes, and clinical issues and concerns. In writing these chapters, we did not want to overwhelm the reader with the dozens of assessment techniques that could be identified in each of the above areas. On the other hand, we wanted to present some of the assessment instruments that were most commonly used. We were driven, partly, by a study that identified the eleven tests that were most frequently used (Camara, Nathan, & Puente, 2000) (see Table 1). All of these tests are presented in the following chapters.

TABLE 1

Frequency of Test Use by Clinical Psychologists

TEST	RANK
Wechsler Adult Intelligence Scale – Revised (WAIS-R)	1
Minnesota Multiphasic Personality Inventory (MMPI) I and II	2
Wechsler Intelligence Scale for Children – Revised (WISC-R-III)	3
Rorschach Inkblot Test	4
Bender Visual-Motor Gestalt Test	5
Thematic Apperception Test (TAT)	6
Wide Range Achievement Test – Revised and III (WRAT)	7
House-Tree-Person (H-T-P)	8
Wechsler Memory Scale – Revised	9
Beck Depression Inventory (BDI and BDI-II)	10
Millon Clinical Multiaxial Inventory	10 (tie)

In Chapter 6 we examine tests typically given in schools to measure what students have learned and are capable of learning. First we identify the purpose of the assessment of educational ability. We then define the different kinds of achievement and aptitude tests generally given in the schools, including survey battery achievement tests, diagnostic tests, readiness tests, and cognitive ability tests. Next, we examine some of the more popular tests in these categories (see Table 2).

Chapter 7 defines intelligence testing and presents a number of models that attempt to describe the construct of intelligence, including Spearman's Two-Factor Approach, Thurstone's Multifactor Approach, Vernon's Hierarchical Model of Intelligence, Guilford's Multifactor/Multi-dimensional Model, Cattell's Fluid and Crystal Intelligence, Piaget's Cognitive Development Theory, and Gardner's Theory of Multiple Intelligences. This discussion is followed by an examination of a number of intelligence tests (see Table 2).

In Chapter 8 we look at career and occupational assessment. We first define career and occupational testing and discuss its importance. Next, we look at interest inventories, multiple aptitude tests, and special aptitude tests, all of which are important in career and occupational assessment (see Table 2).

Our focus in Chapter 9 is clinical assessment. We start by defining clinical assessment and identifying its uses. Then we present a number of objective and projective tests used in clinical assessment (see Table 2).

In Chapter 10 we introduce various techniques of informal assessment and identify some positive and negative aspects of their use. We then offer an overview of a number of such instruments, but stress that the ones we demonstrate are by no means an exhaustive list (see Table 2). Near the end of the chapter we discuss how to assess reliability and validity of informal assessment procedures.

In Chapters 6 through 9 we offer a section near the end of the chapter that highlights the role of the helpers in using the assessment procedures being discussed in the particular chapter. Also, each chapter in this section concludes with a section that places the assessment procedures within the context of the whole person and generally stresses the importance of using wisdom and sensitivity when assessing any person.

TABLE 2
Key Assessment Instruments by Category and Chapter

CHAPTER 6: Assessment of Educational Ability	CHAPTER 7: Assessment of Intelligence	CHAPTER 8: Career and Occupational Assessment	CHAPTER 9: Clinical Assessment	CHAPTER 10: Informal Assessment
Survey Achievement Tests	*Individual Intelligence Tests*	*Interest Inventories*	*Objective Personality Tests*	*Informal Assessment Instruments*
• Stanford Achievement Test	• Stanford-Binet	• Strong Vocational Interest Inventory	• Minnesota Multiphasic Personality Inventory (MMPI-2)	• Observation
• Iowa Test of Basic Skills	• Wechsler Scales of Intelligence	• Self-Directed Search	• Millon Clinical Multiaxial Inventory (MCMI-III)	• Rating Scales
• Metropolitan Achievement Test	• Kaufman Assessment Battery for Children	• Career Occupational Preference System	• Beck Depression Inventory (BDI-II)	• Classification Schemes
			• California Psychological Inventory (CPI)	• Records and Personal Documents
Diagnostic Tests		*Special Aptitude Tests*	• Myers-Briggs Type Indicator (MBTI)	
• Wide Range Achievement Test—3		• Clerical Test Battery		
• Key-Math-Revised		• Minnesota Clerical Assessment Battery	*Projective Personality Tests*	
• Peabody Individual Achievement Test		• U.S. Postal Service's 470 Battery Exam	• Thematic Apperception Test (TAT)	
		• Federal Clerical Exam	• Rorschach Inkblot Test	
Readiness Tests		• SkillsProfiler Series	• Bender Visual-Motor Gestalt Test	
• The Metropolitan		• Mechanical Aptitude Test	• House-Tree-Person	
• The Gesell		• Technical Test Battery	• Kinetic-House-Tree-Person Test	
• Kindergarten Readiness Test		• Wiesen Test of Mechanical Aptitude	• Sentence Completion Series	
		• ARCO Mechanical Aptitude & Spatial Relations Tests	• EPS Sentence Completion	
Cognitive Ability Tests		• Bennett Test of Mechanical Comprehension	• Kinetic Family Drawn	
• The Cognitive Ability Test		• Music Aptitude Profile	• Draw-A-Man/Draw-A-Woman	
• The Otis Lennon		• Iowa Test of Music Literacy		
• Higher Ed Admissions Tests: ACTs, SATs, GREs, LSATs, MCATs, MATs		• Group Test of Musical Ability		
		• Advanced Measures of Music Audiation		
		Multiple Aptitude Tests		
		• Armed Services Vocational Aptitude Battery		
		• Differential Aptitude Test		

105

Assessment of Educational Ability: Survey Battery, Diagnostic, Readiness, and Cognitive Ability Tests

It was a dark, dreary day in May, and I wasn't doing very well in my twelfth-grade advanced math class. Suddenly, the teacher placed two Social Security numbers up on the board and said, "These two students will be receiving an 80 in the class unless they can do well on the state achievement test." "Oh my God, I'm one of them," I thought. Even though an 80 might be passable for some students in some classes, in this class it was an embarrassing grade. No one in this advanced math class would be satisfied with such a grade. So I studied, and studied, and studied until the big day—the day of THE TEST. I took it, and I knew I did well. A few weeks later I got my score: "100." Even the brightest kids didn't get "100." I was so proud. I couldn't wait to get my report card, knowing that I would get at least a 90, maybe a 95. Then the big day came, and I got my grade: an 85. She gave me 5 extra points—big deal! After all, didn't I get a 100 on THE TEST? Wasn't it all about THE TEST? After the graduation ceremony I spotted my math teacher, and I bravely went up to her and asked her why I had only received an 85 on my report card. She looked at me and said, "You know why." Well, to this day, I DON'T know why . . . (Ed Neukrug)

National tests of educational ability—we have all taken them, we have all sweated them, and they have affected all of us in some way. That's what this chapter is about—the types of national tests typically given in schools to measure what we have learned and what we are capable of learning. First we will identify and define the different kinds of achievement and aptitude tests generally given in the schools, including survey battery achievement tests, diagnostic, readiness, and cognitive ability tests. Next, we will look at some of the more popular kinds of tests in these categories. As we discuss the various tests, keep in mind that there are literally hundreds of different kinds of achievement tests and cognitive ability tests, many of which assess the same domains. We will then provide an overview of some of the roles played by helpers in the assessment of educational ability and conclude with some thoughts about assessment in this important domain.

Defining Assessment of Educational Ability

Whether it be the "Iowa," the "Stanford," the SAT, or some other national test of educational ability, most students have taken many of these kinds of tests in school. Tests of educational ability have broad applications. For instance, it is not unusual to find these tests being used for the following purposes:

1. As an assessment tool to determine how well a student is learning.
2. To assess how well a class, grade, school, school system, or state is learning content knowledge.
3. To assist in detecting a vast array of learning problems.
4. To assist in identifying giftedness.
5. To help determine if a child is ready to move to the next grade level.
6. To help determine readiness and placement in college and graduate school.

In this chapter we will examine four kinds of educational assessment techniques, including three kinds of achievement tests (survey battery, diagnostic, and readiness) and one kind of aptitude test (cognitive ability tests) (see Figure 6.1). Individual intelligence tests, special aptitude tests, and multiple aptitude

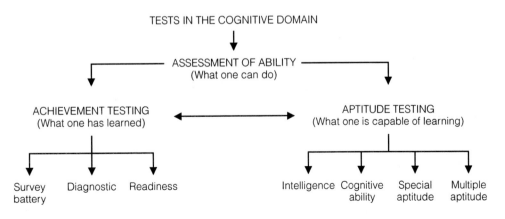

Figure 6.1 Graphic of ability testing

tests, which do not focus on educational ability, are also sometimes used in the schools and have other broad applications. These tests will be covered in Chapter 7 and Chapter 8, respectively.

As you might recall from Chapter 1, we defined survey battery, diagnostic, readiness, and cognitive ability tests in the following ways:

Survey Battery Tests: Paper-and-pencil tests, usually given in school settings, which measure broad content areas. Often used to assess progress in school.

Diagnostic Tests: Tests that assess problem areas of learning. Often used to assess learning disabilities.

Readiness Tests: Tests that measure one's readiness for moving ahead in school. Often used to assess readiness to enter first grade.

Cognitive Abilities Tests: Often based on what one has learned in school, these instruments measure a broad range of cognitive ability and are useful in making predictions about the future (e.g., whether an individual might succeed in school or in college).

You might also remember from Chapter 1 that sometimes the difference between Achievement Testing and Aptitude Testing has more to do with how the test is being used than what the test is actually measuring. For instance, although the SAT seems to be measuring content knowledge or what you have learned in school, it is used to predict success in college and is therefore often listed in the Aptitude Section of Ability Testing. That is why there is a double-headed arrow on Figure 6.1—to remind us that many of these tests share much in common with one another—at least in terms of what they are measuring. In the rest of this chapter we will examine a number of survey battery, diagnostic, readiness, and cognitive ability tests.

Survey Battery Achievement Testing

With literally millions of children taking achievements tests every year, the achievement testing industry is big business. It is therefore no surprise that a number of publishing companies spend a great deal of money on the development and refinement of survey battery achievement tests. Also, with "Standards of Learning" being adopted by many states and the "No Child Left Behind" Act passed at the federal level, achievement testing has become more important than ever before (see Box 6.1).

Survey Battery Achievement Tests can be helpful on a number of levels. For instance, by providing individual profile reports, they can help a student, his or her parents, and his or her teachers identify strengths and weaknesses and develop strategies for working on weak areas. Similarly, profile reports at the classroom, school, or school system level can make it possible for teachers, principals, administrators, and the public to see how students are doing and, when necessary, provide needed resources in areas where a number of students seem

Survey battery tests
Paper-and-pencil tests measuring broad knowledge content

NCLB
Federal law ensuring all children succeed in school

BOX 6.1
Achievement Testing, Standards of Learning, and No Child Left Behind

Many states have developed *standards of learning* to assure that all children are succeeding in school. At the federal level, the No Child Left Behind (NCLB) Act requires that each state have a plan to show how, by the year 2014, *all* students will have obtained proficiency in reading/language arts and math (also see Box 5.1). Not surprisingly, scores on achievement tests are generally used to measure success for both the standards of learning and NCLB. Thus, the development of new achievement tests, or the use of existing achievement tests, has become more important than ever in showing that all children are succeeding.

Test scores not only allow schools to identify students who are not meeting specified levels of achievement but also demonstrate how well the

school, the district, and the state are performing. The No Child Left Behind (NCLB) Act ties federal funding to the success of school districts and defines a number of actions the state must do to show that attempts are being made to increase student scores (U.S. Department of Education, n.d.b). For good or bad, the NCLB puts a lot of pressure on the lower-performing school districts, which tend to be located in poorer neighborhoods (Baker, Robinson, Danner, & Neukrug, 2001; Bond, 1990; Groth-Marnat, 2003). Thus, many school districts in disadvantaged areas will find themselves struggling to focus limited resources on bringing up achievement test scores while also trying to maintain other needed resources.

---

to be struggling (see Figure 6.2). Three of the most frequently used survey battery achievement tests include the Stanford Achievement Test, the Iowa Test of Basic Skills (ITBS), and the Metropolitan Achievement Test.

Stanford Achievement Test

As mentioned in Chapter 1, the Stanford Achievement Test is one of the oldest survey battery achievement tests, having been introduced in 1923. Since that time it has gone through a number of revisions prior to publication of its tenth edition in 2003. The Stanford Achievement Test (SAT10) is given to students in grades K-12 and has been normed against hundreds of thousands of students (Harcourt Assessment, 2004a).

SAT10
Assesses subject areas in school

This latest edition of the Stanford offers many options such as full-length or abbreviated versions as well as content modules, which are tests for specific subjects such as reading, language, spelling, mathematics, science, social studies, and writing. The Stanford Achievement Test also has sections that can be completed in open-ended format, requiring students to fill in the blank, respond with short answers, or write an essay that will be scored by the classroom teacher using criterion grading.

Reliability of the Stanford Achievement Test appears sound, with most subtests scoring in the mid .80s to low .90s using KR-20 internal consistency estimates. However, reliability estimates for the open-ended sections generally fell to the .60s to .80s and in some cases to the mid .50s (Harcourt Assessment, 2004a). The Stanford Achievement Test appears to have sound validity, with content

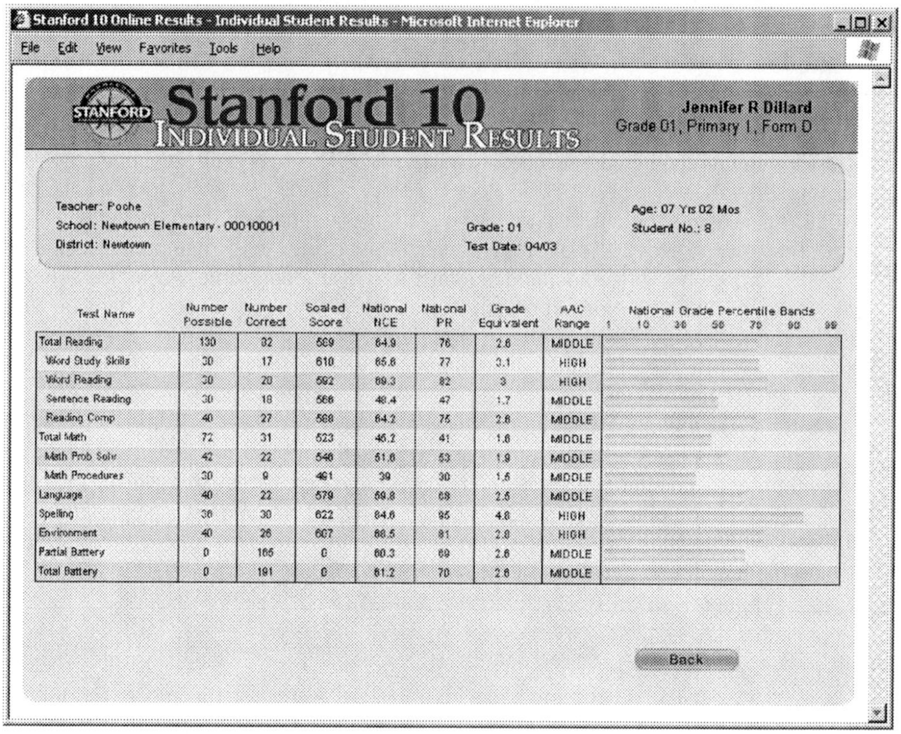

Stanford 10 Online Results - Individual Student Results - Microsoft Internet Explorer

File   Edit   View   Favorites   Tools   Help

Stanford 10
INDIVIDUAL STUDENT RESULTS

Jennifer R Dillard
Grade 01, Primary 1, Form D

Teacher: Poche
School: Newtown Elementary - 00010001
District: Newtown

Grade: 01
Test Date: 04/03

Age: 07 Yrs 02 Mos
Student No.: 8

Test Name	Number Possible	Number Correct	Scaled Score	National NCE	National PR	Grade Equivalent	AAC Range	National Grade Percentile Bands 1 10 30 50 70 90 99
Total Reading	130	82	569	64.9	76	2.6	MIDDLE	
Word Study Skills	30	17	610	65.8	77	3.1	HIGH	
Word Reading	30	20	592	69.3	82	3	HIGH	
Sentence Reading	30	18	566	48.4	47	1.7	MIDDLE	
Reading Comp	40	27	568	64.2	75	2.6	MIDDLE	
Total Math	72	31	523	45.2	41	1.8	MIDDLE	
Math Prob Solv	42	22	546	51.6	53	1.9	MIDDLE	
Math Procedures	30	9	481	39	30	1.5	MIDDLE	
Language	40	22	579	59.8	68	2.5	MIDDLE	
Spelling	36	30	622	84.6	95	4.8	HIGH	
Environment	40	26	607	68.5	81	2.8	HIGH	
Partial Battery	0	165	0	60.3	69	2.6	MIDDLE	
Total Battery	0	191	0	61.2	70	2.6	MIDDLE	

Back

Figure 6.2 Individual profile sheet of the Stanford Achievement Test

Source: Stanford Achievement Test Series, Tenth Edition. Scoring & Reporting Services. Retrieved on August 16, 2004 from http://harcourtassessment.com <http://harcourtassessment.com>. Copyright © 2004 by Harcourt Assessment, Inc. Reproduced with permission. All rights reserved.

validity being established by working with content experts, teachers, editors, and measurement specialists. Evidence for construct validity was established by comparing scores on subtests with the Otis-Lennon School Ability Test, which produced a fairly high correlation. Criterion-related validity was addressed by numerous studies and is thorough and reasonable (Harcourt Assessment, 2004a).

The Stanford Achievement Test, like other nationally made survey battery achievement tests, offers a number of interpretive reports, including Individual Profile Sheets, Class Grouping Sheets, Grade Grouping Sheets, and School System Grouping Sheets. Figure 6.2 shows an example of an Individual Student Profile, and Figure 6.3 shows an example of data from a third-grade class. Examine these profile sheets and based on the information you learned in Chapter 5, see if you can make sense out of the data presented. Take particular note of how the data are broken down into ethnic groups, gender, and disability. This type of information is particularly useful for school systems because it allows them to target groups that are doing poorly.

Stanford 10
SUMMARY RESULTS

Grade: 3 , Primary 3 . Form C , Test Date: 04/03
Students Selected: All

Group	Total Reading									Total Math								
	N	Mean Raw Score	Mean Scale Score	Mean NCE	PR of Mean NCE	% in Quartile				N	Mean Raw Score	Mean Scale Score	Mean NCE	PR of Mean NCE	% in Quartile			
						1	2	3	4						1	2	3	4
Newtown	25	65.4	643.3	61.6	71	8	28	20	44	25	41.4	620.1	56.3	62	16	12	40	32
Male	9	67.6	628.7	54.0	57	22	22	33	22	9	43.3	614.9	53.7	57	22	0	56	22
Female	16	64.2	651.6	65.9	77	0	31	13	56	16	40.3	623.0	57.8	64	13	19	31	38
Asian	2	58.5	654.0	67.2	79	0	0	50	50	2	42.0	648.0	70.2	83	0	0	50	50
Black	1	44.0	605.0	41.3	34	0	100	0	0	1	37.0	620.0	57.0	63	0	0	100	0
Hispanic	2	56.5	657.5	68.7	81	0	50	0	50	2	37.5	635.5	62.4	72	0	50	0	50
White	17	73.1	651.5	66.0	78	6	18	24	53	17	43.4	616.9	54.8	59	24	6	35	35
Other	3	39.3	593.0	35.0	24	33	67	0	0	3	34.0	609.0	51.6	53	0	33	67	0
Low SES	3	70.3	608.3	43.4	36	33	33	33	0	3	36.7	577.7	34.4	23	67	0	33	0
Non Low SES	22	64.7	648.1	64.1	75	5	27	18	50	22	42.0	625.9	59.3	67	9	14	41	36
Non LEP	25	65.4	643.3	61.6	71	8	28	20	44	25	41.4	620.1	56.3	62	16	12	40	32
IEP	2	59.5	590.5	33.9	22	50	50	0	0	2	24.5	549.5	19.8	8	100	0	0	0
Non IEP	23	65.9	647.9	64.0	75	4	26	22	48	23	42.9	626.2	59.5	67	9	13	43	35
Newtown Elementary	25	65.4	643.3	61.6	71	8	28	20	44	25	41.4	620.1	56.3	62	16	12	40	32
Male	9	67.6	628.7	54.0	57	22	22	33	22	9	43.3	614.9	53.7	57	22	0	56	22
Female	16	64.2	651.6	65.9	77	0	31	13	56	16	40.3	623.0	57.8	64	13	19	31	38
Asian	2	58.5	654.0	67.2	79	0	0	50	50	2	42.0	648.0	70.2	83	0	0	50	50
Black	1	44.0	605.0	41.3	34	0	100	0	0	1	37.0	620.0	57.0	63	0	0	100	0
Hispanic	2	56.5	657.5	68.7	81	0	50	0	50	2	37.5	635.5	62.4	72	0	50	0	50
White	17	73.1	651.5	66.0	78	6	18	24	53	17	43.4	616.9	54.8	59	24	6	35	35
Other	3	39.3	593.0	35.0	24	33	67	0	0	3	34.0	609.0	51.6	53	0	33	67	0
Low SES	3	70.3	608.3	43.4	36	33	33	33	0	3	36.7	577.7	34.4	23	67	0	33	0
Non Low SES	22	64.7	648.1	64.1	75	5	27	18	50	22	42.0	625.9	59.3	67	9	14	41	36
Non LEP	25	65.4	643.3	61.6	71	8	28	20	44	25	41.4	620.1	56.3	62	16	12	40	32
IEP	2	59.5	590.5	33.9	22	50	50	0	0	2	24.5	549.5	19.8	8	100	0	0	0
Non IEP	23	65.9	647.9	64.0	75	4	26	22	48	23	42.9	626.2	59.5	67	9	13	43	35

Figure 6.3 Highlight on the Stanford Achievement Test

Iowa Test of Basic Skills

ITBS
Measures skills
to "satisfactorily"
progress
through school

One of the oldest and best-known achievement tests is the Iowa Test of Basic Skills (ITBS). Initially developed in 1935, it has changed greatly from its early inception. Today, the test emphasizes the basic skills necessary to make satisfactory progress through school. The latest "M" version of the test, which is for grades K through 8, has numerous subtests for various grade levels, including language, reading, vocabulary, listening, word analysis, math, social studies, science, and writing assessment.

Although some have criticized the test for not measuring "higher-order thinking" (Brookhart & Cross, 1998), it is still considered one of the better achievement tests with reliability of most subtests in the .80s to .90s and strong content validity established by test developers who took into account curriculum, texts, recommendations of professional organizations, and practices of school districts (Brookhart & Cross, 1998).

Metropolitan Achievement Test

Metropolitan Achievement Test
Assesses subject areas in school —has option for open-ended questions

The Metropolitan Achievement Test is a popular paper-and-pencil test that was first published in the 1930s. The newest version, which is the eighth edition, was published in 1993 (Harwell & Lukin, 2005). It is designed to test students in grades K-12 for knowledge of a broad range of subjects such as reading, language arts, mathematics, science, and social studies. It has 13 subtests and can be given in a short form that takes 90 minutes or the complete form that can take up to five hours. Test items consist of multiple-choice questions, which are graded correct or incorrect, and open-ended items, which are scored as 0 to 3. Although research based on extensive sampling data has been fairly exhaustive, some have suggested that the data might be too heavily weighted for rural classrooms and underrepresent urban classrooms (Harwell & Lukin, 2005). As with the Stanford and ITBS, reliability estimates are quite high, usually between .8 and .9 for most subtests, and content, criterion, and construct validity are sound (Harwell & Lukin, 2005).

Diagnostic Testing

PL 94-142
Asserts right to be tested for learning disabilities

Diagnostic tests
Used to assess learning disabilities or difficulties

With the passage of *Public Law 94-142* (PL94-142) in 1975 (Federal Register, 1977) as well as the more recent Individuals with Disabilities Education Improvement Act (IDEIA), millions of children and young adults between the ages of 3 and 21 who were found to have a learning disability were assured the right to an education within the *least restrictive environment*. These laws also assert that any individual who is suspected of having one of many disabilities that interfere with learning has the right to be tested, at the school system's expense, for the disability. Thus, diagnostic testing, usually administered by the school psychologist or learning disability specialist, has become one of the main ways to determine who might be learning disabled. These laws also state that a school team should review the test results and other assessment information obtained, and that the learning-disabled student would be given an Individualized Education Plan (IEP) describing services that should be offered to assist the student with his or her learning problem.

IEP
Mandatory plan
to accommodate
students with
special needs

Although diagnostic testing was certainly in existence prior to PL94-142, its use, as well as the development of new diagnostic tests, greatly expanded as the result of these laws. In this section we will review three of the more common diagnostic tests of achievement often used to assess learning problems: the WRAT-3, the Key Math Diagnostic Arithmetic Test, and the Peabody Individual Achievement Test. Throughout our discussion, keep in mind that dozens of diagnostic tests are in use today.

The Wide Range Achievement Test

WRAT-3
Assesses funda-
mental learning
problems in
reading, spell-
ing, and arith-
metic

The Wide Range Achievement Test 3 (WRAT-3) was developed to assess basic reading, spelling, and arithmetic skills. It is called "wide-range" because it can be used for populations from age 5 to 75. The test takes about 30 minutes to administer and must be given individually since some sections are read aloud by the examinee. There are two equivalent forms of the exam called "blue" and "tan."

The WRAT-3 attempts to eliminate the effects of comprehension in determining whether the individual has a learning disability. In other words, the publisher is trying to assure that the test is assessing the fundamentals of reading, spelling, and arithmetic, as opposed to comprehension, which is often the case when examinees are asked to read multiple-choice questions or paragraphs. Thus, the test is fairly simple, as the individual is asked by the examiner to "read" (pronounce) words, to spell words, and to figure out a number of math problems. Although percentiles, grade equivalents, and other standard scores can be obtained, often a Deviation IQ (DIQ) is used so that the WRAT-3 can be compared to scores on an intelligence test, such as the Wechsler Intelligence Scale for Children—III (WISC—III) (Ward, 1995). This is important as a significantly lower score on any of the scales of the WRAT-3, as compared to the overall DIQ, could indicate the presence of a learning disability. Generally, more intensive testing for a learning disability would follow such findings.

*Significant
differences
between WRAT-
III and IQ may
indicate learn-
ing disability.*

Internal consistency reliability estimates, as reported in the manual, are impressive and generally run in the .90s (Wilkinson, 1993). The authors provide a rationale for the content of the test and demonstrate evidence of construct and criterion validity, such as moderate correlations with the WISC-III, the Wechsler Adult Intelligence Test–Revised (WAIS-R), and the Stanford Achievement Test. Recently, some have questioned the sample size used for determining the reliability estimates of the WRAT-3, as well as whether it shows sufficient evidence of construct validity (Mabry, 1995; Ward, 1995). In addition, there have been questions concerning whether enough effort was made to detect and eliminate any sociocultural bias that may exist in test items (Mabry, 1995). Thus, as with any test, the WRAT-III should be used selectively and cautiously.

KeyMath
Comprehensive
test to assess for
learning disabili-
ties in math

Key Math Diagnostic Arithmetic Test

The Key Math-Revised has been described as "one of the very best test batteries for assessing a student's knowledge and understanding of basic mathematics and providing useful diagnostic information to teachers" (Wollack, 2001, p. 641). This test is comprehensive and is often used as a follow-up when there is a suspected math learning disability. The test is generally administered and interpreted by a person who has been well versed in the test and in learning disabilities.

The test, which is administered individually and takes between 35 and 50 minutes, assesses three broad mathematical areas: basic concepts, operations, and application. Additionally, there are 13 subtests and 43 specific content domains. The Key Math-R has two forms, each of which has 258 items. The test administrator uses basal and ceiling levels to determine where the testing begins and ends (discussed further in Chapter 7). Several derived scores are often used, including percentile ranks, grade equivalents, and scaled scores.

Reliability ranges from .88 for split-half and alternate forms to the high .90s for the composite score. Reliability scores dropped modestly for the three broad content areas, and content domains' reliability values were quite variable (.07 to .94) (Kingsbury, 2001). The manual notes how content validity was developed with the help of experts and by assessing the content being tested. Correlational studies with previous versions of the Key Math, with the Comprehensive Test of Basic Skills, and with the Iowa Test of Basic Skills (math sections) show evidence of construct validity (Kingsbury, 2001).

Peabody Individual Achievement Test

PIAT
Six content areas for screening K-12 students

The Peabody Individual Achievement Test – Revised – Normative Update (PIAT-R/NU) provides academic screening for children in grades K – 12 and covers six content areas: general information, reading recognition, reading comprehension, mathematics, spelling, and written expression. The test, which updated its normative data in 1995-1996, is individually administered and takes about one hour to give. Multiple derived scores can be obtained, including Deviation IQ, percentile ranks, stanines, and age and grade equivalents (AGS Publishing, 2004a; Markwardt, 1989).

A wide variety of reliability estimates for the revised version show a median of approximately .94 (Benes, 1992), although the written portion subtest, which is hand-graded, had significantly lower interrater reliability (Benes, 1992). Content validity was established by using a number of school curriculum guides, and the manual shows evidence of criterion and construct validity (Rogers, 1992). The new normative data sample of 3,184 students from 40 states mimics the U.S population demographics and includes special education and gifted students (Cross, 2001).

Other Diagnostic Tests

Reviewing the dozens of other diagnostic tests available would exceed the scope of this book. However, two additional diagnostic instruments must be mentioned because of their popularity. The Wechsler Individual Achievement Test – Second Edition (WIAT-II) is an achievement test for ages 4 to adult. It is designed to work well with the other Wechsler intelligence scales (see Chapter 7) to aid in identifying disparities between ability and achievement (Harcourt Assessment, 2005a).

BOX 6.2
Ready or Not?

When my daughter, Hannah, was old enough to enter kindergarten, we asked if she could be assessed for readiness for first grade, since her birthday missed the school system's deadline to enter first grade by only two days and she seemed to have adapted well to preschool. After she took a reading readiness test given by a reading specialist, we were told she would be a star in kindergarten and have some "catching up" to do in first grade. We were also told that it was our decision as to whether or not to move her into first grade. Knowing that such a decision should be based on many factors, not just one test, we took into account that she was socially adept and we felt confident that she would "fit in" nicely in first

grade. However, we were still not convinced this was the correct move. We consulted with her preschool teachers as well as other educational specialists but obtained mixed opinions. Finally, after our daughter had spent two weeks in kindergarten, her teacher looked at us and said, "Get her out of here; she's ready for first grade." Well, that made our decision much easier. We moved her, and as the reading specialist predicted, she did have some catching up to do. However, our decision seems to have been a good one, since she has excelled in school and socially since that time.

—Ed Neukrug

Another complete battery of tests to assess and compare achievement and ability is the Woodcock-Johnson III (WJ III), which contains two instruments: (1) the Woodcock-Johnson Tests of Achievement and (2) the Woodcock-Johnson Tests of Cognitive Abilities. These tests offer standard and extended versions and were recently renormed against a diverse 8,800-subject sample (Riverside Publishing, 2004b).

Readiness Testing

Readiness tests Usually assess readiness for the first grade

Readiness tests measure what a person has learned and then use this information to discern whether he or she is ready to enter the next educational level. Although a readiness test theoretically can be created for any age level, they are used almost exclusively to measure readiness to enter kindergarten or first grade. Because children change so rapidly at these young ages, and because the predictive ability of these tests is minimal at best, their usefulness has been questioned (Kim & Suen, 2000). In addition, because the exams carry cultural and language biases, children from low-income families, minority groups, and homes where English is not the first language will often obtain lower scores, despite the fact that their actual ability level may be the same as other children. Thus, these tests need to be administered with care if they are given at all. Despite the problems with these tests, they can sometimes be helpful in deciding whether a child is "ready" to move to the next level (see Box 6.2) and are used in many preschools and elementary schools. Although many readiness tests exist, we will examine three of the more popular ones: the Metropolitan Readiness Test, the Gesell School Readiness Test, and the Kindergarten Readiness Test.

Metropolitan Readiness Test

MRT6
Assesses literacy development, reading, and mathematics

The Metropolitan Readiness Test, Sixth Edition (MRT6), is designed to assess beginning educational skills in preschoolers, kindergarteners, and first graders. Level 1 of the test is administered individually and assesses literacy development for preschoolers and beginning kindergarteners, while Level 2 assesses reading and mathematics development of kindergarteners through beginning first graders and is usually given in a group setting. The test generally takes between 80 and 100 minutes to administer, and the results are often used as an aid in determining whether a student should be placed in first or second grade. Results of the Metropolitan Readiness Test are reported as raw scores, stanines, or percentiles (Novak, 2001).

Reliability scores for the composite test are strong and hover around the .90s. Individual subtest reliabilities tend to deteriorate, often ranging from .53 to the .80s (Novak, 2001). Some have questioned the validity evidence of the MRT6 and its earlier versions (Mabry & Stoner, 1995; Kamphaus, 2001; Novak, 2001). In fact, Kamphaus (2001) states that the Level 1 test has no evidence of validity and that Level 2 has virtually "none" and is "unacceptable" (p. 748). However, others are more forgiving and find the MRT6 "useful in determining early academic or 'readiness' skills in reading and math" (Novak, 2001, p. 751).

Gesell School Readiness Test

Gesell School Readiness Test
Assesses developmental readiness and adaptive behaviors

The Gesell School Readiness Test, Fifth Edition, was published in 1980 and is designed to assess personal and social skills, neurological and motor growth, language development, and adaptive behavior, or the ability of the child to adapt to new situations. The test is based on the work of Arnold Gesell, who spent years examining the normal development of children (Gesell Institute of Human Development, 2000-2002). The test is administered in a non-threatening and comfortable environment by a highly trained examiner who observes the child and compares that child's developmental patterns to the normal patterns of children of the same age (Bradley & Waters, 1985).

Reliability information on the Gesell Readiness Test is lacking and not sufficiently supplied by the publisher (Bradley & Waters, 1985), and the test has also been criticized for weak evidence of validity. However, the publisher does claim a .74 correlation between test scores and performance of students in the sixth grade. Another criticism of the test is its outdated and minimal normative data (Bradley & Waters, 1985). Although the test manual describes age-appropriate responses, the manual does not clearly specify how placement recommendations are made once an assessment has been completed (Bradley & Waters, 1985, p. 610) (see Box 6.3). Despite these problems, the test is often used because it offers a view of readiness different from those that are based strictly on achievement in a content area. As far as Gesell was concerned, "achievement" involved more than getting high scores on a reading or math test.

BOX 6.3
Challenge to Gesell

A group of parents from the Norwood-Norfolk School District in upstate New York were outraged when they found out that their children would be held back from "regular" kindergarten and placed in a "developmental" kindergarten based on test results from the Gesell Readiness Test. The parents found that 61% of the students were to be held back, which likely meant that the following year those children would be placed in "regular" kindergarten, thus leaving them one year behind their peers. The plaintiffs filed a class-action brief with the New York State Department of Education claiming that state and federal laws had been violated, including their right for their children to enter kindergarten at age 5.

One expert witness stated that it was unsound to hold back a child based on the information from one test. Another witness questioned the validity and reliability of the Gesell test since such a high percentage of children were being held back. As a result of the lawsuit, the school district reached a settlement with the families of all the children who had been placed in developmental kindergarten. The district made drastic changes in its policies regarding parental rights to place their children in regular kindergarten, the use of testing in placement decisions, and parental notification procedures.

—Fairtest, n.d.

Kindergarten Readiness Test

Kindergarten Readiness Test Assesses a broad range of cognitive and sensory motor skills

In 1988 Slosson Educational Publications published the Kindergarten Readiness Test, whose purpose is to determine if a child is ready to begin kindergarten. The test is administered individually, takes about 15 minutes, and covers Reasoning, Language, Auditory and Visual Attention, Numbers, Fine Motor Skills, and several other cognitive and sensory perception areas (SEDL, 2000).

Although administrative procedures and item quality are acceptable, items sometimes seem out of sequence and reliability and validity information is minimal (Beck, 1995; Sutton & Knight, 1995). Also, the sample population is drawn entirely from a four-state region in the Midwestern United States, which is not representative of the nation (Sutton & Knight, 1995). Despite these drawbacks, this instrument may be useful in determining whether a student is ready to begin kindergarten.

Common Cognitive Ability Tests

As noted earlier, cognitive ability tests are aptitude tests that measure what one is capable of doing and are often used to assess a student's potential to succeed in grades K-12, college, or graduate school. In this section we will look at the Cognitive Ability Test, the Otis-Lennon School Ability Test, and a number of college and graduate school admission tests, including the American College Testing

---

BOX 6.4
Identifying Needed Services

When I was in private practice, I worked with a third-grader who, a couple of years prior to my first meeting him, had been identified as having a math learning disability. This disability was first hypothesized after a large discrepancy was found between his cognitive ability score in math and his math achievement in school. Further testing verified the disability, and he was soon given an Individualized Education Plan that included three one-hour sessions of individualized assistance with math each week. After receiving this help, he soon began to do much better in math. However, after he had been getting higher math scores for about a year, the school discontinued tutoring ser-

vices. I met him soon after this, following his parents' divorce, when his math scores had once again dropped. The scores had likely dropped due to the chaos at home as well as the removal of services. I immediately realized that this young man was not being given the extra help he was legally entitled to receive. I contacted the school, which agreed that he should be given assistance in math based on his Individualized Education Plan. Within a few weeks after obtaining this assistance, his math scores once again improved, and he was a noticeably happier child.

—Ed Neukrug

Cognitive ability tests
Measure what one is capable of doing

Assessment (ACT), the SAT Reasoning Test (SAT), the Graduate Record Exam (GRE), the Law School Admission Test (LSAT), and the Medical College Admission Test (MCAT).

The Cognitive Ability Test

CogAT
Assesses verbal, quantitative, and nonverbal reasoning abilities; uses both Vernon's and Cattell's models of abilities

The Cognitive Ability Test (CogAT), Form 6, is designed to assess cognitive skills of children from kindergarten to twelfth grade (Riverside Publishing, 2004c). The CogAT is constructed with two models of intelligence in mind: Vernon's hierarchical abilities and Cattell's fluid and crystallized abilities (Lohman & Hagen, 2002) (see Chapter 7). Thus, there is an attempt to measure some of the same things measured in individual intelligence tests. However, cognitive ability tests should never be viewed as substitutes for individual intelligence tests, as the manner in which they are created and administered is vastly different from intelligence tests and they tend to focus primarily on traditional knowledge as obtained in school, particularly verbal and mathematical ability.

Cognitive ability tests of this kind are particularly important for identifying students who are not succeeding in school because of learning disabilities, motivation, problems at home, problems at school, or self-esteem issues. When students do significantly better on a cognitive ability test than they do on an achievement test or a teacher's assessment, one or more of these issues may be operating and teachers, as well as support staff, should examine the possible reasons for the discrepancy (see Box 6.4).

The CogAT provides scores in three areas: verbal, quantitative, and nonverbal reasoning abilities. An additional composite score is also calculated. Scores can be converted to standard age scores (standard score with a mean of 100 and standard deviation of 16), percentile ranks, and stanines. The entire test takes between two and three hours and is given in multiple administrations, depending on the age range of the student.

In 2000, the CogAT normed its scores against a nationwide sample of more than 180,000 students. The sample was stratified to correctly weigh public, Catholic, and non-Catholic private schools, as well as socioeconomic status, geographic region, and racial/ethnic representation (Lohman & Hagen, 2002). Reliability coefficients, using the KR-20, ranged from .86 to .96 for the verbal, quantitative, and nonverbal sections. Composite scores ranged from .94 to .98, depending on grade level (Lohman & Hagen, 2002).

Because it is difficult to define any theoretical model that can clearly identify a knowledge base that predicts future ability, cognitive ability tests in general have a difficult time establishing content validity. However, the CogAT does offer a rationale by stating that the content domain was defined logically and through the sampling of student textbooks (Lohman & Hagen, 2002). Concurrent validity with the Iowa Test of Basic Skills (ITBS) was .83. Studies are in progress to correlate the CogAT Form 6 with the Woodcock-Johnson III and the Wechsler Intelligence Scale for Children III. In addition, when the CogAT was administered in the fourth grade, it correlated .79 with ninth-grade scores on the ITBS (Lohman & Hagen, 2002).

Otis-Lennon School Ability Test

OLSAT 8
Assesses thinking and reasoning skills via verbal, quantitative, and nonverbal sections

The Otis-Lennon School Ability Test, Eighth Edition (OLSAT 8), is another common cognitive ability test for students. Through assessing students' thinking and reasoning skills via verbal, quantitative, and nonverbal sections, it provides educators with information about what to expect of students and why they may have challenges in certain subject areas. Comparing OLSAT 8 ability scores with other achievement scores, such as the Stanford Achievement Test (SAT 10), can provide important information to determine whether students are reaching their full potential and find ways to enhance their strengths (Harcourt Assessment, 2004b).

The OLSAT 8 has a number of test levels for children from kindergarten to twelfth grade, with testing times varying between 60 and 75 minutes depending on the age of the student. Raw scores can be converted to stanines, percentile rank, a standard score called the school ability index, and normal curve equivalents (NCEs) by age or grade. The norm groups consisted of 275,000 students in the spring of 2002 and an additional 135,000 in the fall of 2002. Internal consistency measures of reliability based on the KR-20 for the composite score ranged from .89 to .94. Reliabilities for individual subtests using the KR-21 ranged from .52 to .82, with most falling in the .60s and .70s (Harcourt Assessment, 2002). Evidence of test content validity is somewhat vague as the publisher notes that each user must determine if the content fits the population they are testing. Correlation coefficients for the OLSAT 8 composite scores with OLSAT 7 scores

THE FAR SIDE®   By GARY LARSON

Before their admission to any canine university, dogs must first do well on the CATs.

demonstrated coefficients in the range of .74 to .85, depending on grade level. Similarly, correlations among different levels of the OLSAT 8 were adequate. Finally, the test also showed reasonable correlations with the SAT10 (Harcourt Assessment, 2002).

College Admission Exams

A number of cognitive ability tests are used to predict achievement in college and graduate school. Some of the ones with which you might be familiar include the American College Testing Assessment (ACT), the SAT Reasoning Test from the College Board, the Graduate Record Exam (GRE) General Test and Subject Tests published by the Educational Testing Service, the Miller Analogies Test (MAT), the Law School Admission Test (LSAT), and the Medical College Admission Test (MCAT).

ACT

ACT
Assesses educational development and ability to complete college work

The ACT Assessment is the most popular college admission exam at the undergraduate level. It is designed to assess educational development and the ability to complete college-level work. The test covers four skill areas, including English, math, reading, and science. The ACT contains 215 multiple-choice questions and takes three and one-half hours to complete. Test scores range from 1 to 36 with a mean of 18 and a standard deviation of 5 for "average" high school students. However, the actual mean for the college-bound students taking the

---

BOX 6.5
Use of College Admission Exams

Students in our testing and assessment classes frequently ask why universities continue to use college admission exams if the predictive validity correlation estimates are sometimes as low as the .30s or .40s (or about the same as correlation with high school GPA). This is a good question. There are many reasons to use these exams, but an important reason that is often overlooked is the fact that it levels the playing field. The range of academic difficulty in high schools varies considerably across the United States; that is, a 3.9 GPA performance in one high school may be equivalent to a 3.2 GPA in another. Perhaps the student

with the 3.2 GPA went to an extraordinarily difficult and rigorous high school and took many advanced classes, whereas the student with the 3.9 GPA might have coasted in relatively easy classes at a school that graded liberally. The college admission exam gives both of these students a fair and equal chance to show what they know. One additional reason for using the ACT or SAT is that predictions of how a student will do in college are more accurate if scores on the tests are used in conjunction with high school GPA.

—Charlie Fawcett

---

exam in 2003 was 20.8 (ACT, Inc., 2004c). The SEM for the composite score is 1. The ACT publishers performed a major norm sampling in 1988 with more than 100,000 high school students and another resampling update in 1995 with 24,000 students stratified against the U.S. Department of Education figures for region, school size, affiliation, and ethnicity (ACT, Inc., 1997). Reliability estimates for the 1995 national sample ranged between .84 and .91 for the four skill areas and .96 for the composite score. Evidence of content validity is shown through the test development process by continually ensuring that test items are "representative of current high school and university curricula" (ACT, Inc., 1997, p. 37). The ACT publishers also performed studies that showed a sound correlation between students' ACT scores and their high school GPAs. Predictive validity studies correlating ACT scores and first-year college GPA had a median of .43. Combining ACT scores with high school GPA increased the predictive validity to a correlation of .53 (ACT, Inc., 1997). Numerous other studies of validity are available in the ACT technical manual.

SAT

SAT
Assesses reading, math, and writing— predicts mildly well for college grades

The other major undergraduate college exam is the SAT Reasoning Test. A new format for the SAT was released in 2005 with sections in critical reading, mathematics, and writing, with an essay required as part of the writing section. On each of the three sections students earn a score that ranges between 200 and 800 as well as a percentile score that compares the test-taker's results to those of students who have taken the test recently. In addition, on the mathematics and critical reading sections, longitudinal comparisons can be made as test scores are compared to earlier norm groups that used a mean of 500 and standard deviation of 100. Thus, if the mean mathematics score of students in 2005 is 580 and the standard deviation is 108, it can be said that this group is doing better than an earlier norm group with a lower mean and similar standard deviation. Such comparisons make it possible to determine whether today's students are doing better or worse in mathematics and reading than students in past years. On the writing section, students also receive a multiple-choice subscore that ranges between 20 and 80, and a writing subscore that ranges between 2 and 12 and is based on an analysis of a written essay evaluated by two or three readers.

The publisher of the SAT hopes the new writing section will increase the predictive validity of this test; however, as of this writing, results are not available. The trade-off of including essay questions on these types of exams is that the reliability decreases with the use of hand graders. The reliability for the essay section will probably fall to the .70s while the rest of the exam is .91 to .93. Predictive validity correlations for the combined math and verbal scores range from .44 to .61 as a predictor of college grades (College Board, 2004).

GRE General Test

GRE
Assesses verbal reasoning, quantitative reasoning, and analytical writing; predicts graduate school success

The GRE General Test is a cognitive ability test frequently used by U.S. graduate schools. The General Test contains three sections: verbal reasoning, quantitative reasoning, and analytical writing. The scoring for the verbal and quantitative reasoning sections is similar to the SAT and ranges from 200 to 800. However, the Educational Testing Service does not "set" the mean or standard deviation and instead uses a scaled score with a mean and standard deviation that floats over time. For instance, the mean on the verbal reasoning section for those who took the test between July 1, 2000 and June 30, 2003 was 470 and the standard deviation was 121, while the mean and standard deviation for quantitative reasoning were 598 and 148, respectively. Thus, it is probably prudent to look at percentile ranks as opposed to scaled scores.

The analytical section is scored by two trained readers, and scores range from 0 to 6 (a third reader is brought in if the two scores are more than 1 point apart). For those who took the test between October 2002 and June 2003 the mean was 4.2 and the standard deviation was 1.0 (Educational Testing Service, 2004). The reliability estimates are in the low .90s for the verbal and quantitative reasoning sections and .72 for the analytical writing section. The predictive validity correlation estimate of the composite score and first-year GPA of graduate school is .34; however, when combined with the undergraduate GPA, the correlation increases to .46 (Educational Testing Service, 2004).

GRE Subject Tests

In addition to the GRE General Test, a number of subject tests are provided for those graduate programs that wish to assess more specific ability. The available subject tests include biochemistry, cell and molecular biology; biology; chemistry; computer science; literature in English; mathematics; physics; and psychology. Like the GRE General Test, the subject tests use a floating mean and standard deviation; however, the Subject Test's scaled score ranges between 200 and 990, as opposed to 200 and 800 on the General Test. Means and standard deviations can vary dramatically among subject tests. For instance, the mean and standard deviation for those examinees who took the biochemistry, cell and molecular biology test between July 2000 and June 2003 were 517 and 100 respectively, while the mean and standard deviation for chemistry during that time were 682 and 125. Subject scores are better predictors of grades in graduate school than the General Test scores, with correlations running between .27 and .51 for the subject scores when used alone and from .43 to .58 when the subject scores were combined with undergraduate grades.

MAT

MAT
Uses analogies to assess analytical abilities; predicts graduate school success

The Miller Analogies Test is intended to measure analytical abilities by assessing one's capability to find analogous relationships based on ideas, general knowledge, and word fluency (Harcourt Assessment, 2005b). The test-taker has one hour to complete 120 partial analogies. The MAT scaled score ranges from 200 to 600 normed against a group of 126,000 subjects. Percentile scores are also available. Internal reliability coefficients range from .91 to .94. Predictive validity studies have had mixed results. One larger study found a correlation between the MAT and graduate school GPA of .23 (Harcourt Assessment, 2004c).

LSAT

LSAT
Assesses acquired reading and verbal reasoning skills; predicts grades in law school

Most law schools require the LSAT, which is a half-day test to assess acquired reading and verbal reasoning skills. The LSAT has a unique scoring method that ranges from 120 to 180 and has a mean of 150 and a standard deviation of 10. Reliability estimates are quite high, ranging from .90 to .95 (LSAC, 2004a). Predictive validity estimates average .39, and when combined with GPA, increase to .50 (LSAC, 2004b). The SEM is 2.6.

MCAT
Assesses knowledge of physical biological sciences, verbal reasoning, and writing skills; predicts grades in medical school

MCAT

Most medical schools use the MCAT as one factor in determining admissions. The test consists of four sections: physical sciences, biological sciences, verbal reasoning, and a writing sample. Means and standard deviations vary with the test and the norm group. As of the time of this writing, the latest scaled scores had a mean of 24.7 with a standard deviation of 6.2 (MCAT, 2003). Predictive validity estimates are quite high, ranging from .62 to .65 for the first two years of medical school. When MCAT scores were combined with GPA, the estimates increased to an amazing .70 to .76 (Koenig & Wiley, 1996).

The Role of Helpers in the Assessment of Educational Ability

In addition to teachers, a variety of helping professionals can play critical roles in assessing educational ability. For instance, school counselors, school psychologists, learning disabilities specialists, and school social workers often work together as members of the school's special education team to assess eligibility

> **BOX 6.6**
> **Assisting Teachers to Interpret Standardized Testing**
>
> A school system once hired me to run a series of workshops for their teachers on how to interpret the results of national standardized testing, such as survey battery achievement test scores. I was quite surprised to learn that few of them had ever taken a course on how to interpret such data and thus had no idea of the important information that could be gained from analyzing these data. I was, however, impressed with the content knowl-
> edge that these teachers possessed. It was almost as though I was teaching them Greek (basic test statistics used in test interpretation) and they were teaching me Latin (the meaning of the content areas that were being reported on the test reports). It was certainly a learning experience for all of us!
>
> —*Ed Neukrug*

for assessment of learning disabilities and to help determine a child's Individualized Education Plan (IEP). School psychologists and learning disability specialists are generally the testing experts who are called upon to do the testing to identify learning problems. Sometimes outside experts in assessment, such as clinical and counseling psychologists, are called upon to do additional assessments or to contribute a second opinion to the school's assessment.

Because school counselors are one of the few experts in assessment who are housed at the school (school psychologists generally float from school to school), they will sometimes assist teachers in understanding and interpreting educational ability tests (see Box 6.6). In addition, by disaggregating the data from achievement tests, school counselors can play an important role in helping to identify students and classrooms that might need additional assistance in learning specific subject areas. Finally, licensed professionals in private practice need to know about the assessment of educational ability when working with children who are having problems at school. In fact, it is often critical that these clinicians consult with professionals in the schools to assure that the child is making adequate progress (see Box 6.4).

Final Thoughts About the Assessment of Educational Ability

As you can see from this chapter, the assessment of educational ability has become an important aspect of testing in the United States. Despite the widespread use of these tests, many criticisms have arisen, including the following:

1. Teachers are increasingly being forced to teach to the test. This prevents them from being creative and limits the kind of learning that takes place in the schools.
2. Testing leads to labeling, which causes peers, teachers, parents, and others to treat the child as the label. For the child, the label sometimes

becomes a self-fulfilling prophecy that prevents him or her from being able to transcend the label.

3. Some tests, particularly readiness tests and cognitive ability tests, are just a mechanism to allow majority children to move ahead and to keep minority children behind.

4. Testing fosters competitiveness and peer pressure, creating a failure identity for a large percentage of students.

On the other hand, many have spoken positively about tests of educational ability and have made the following points:

1. Tests allow us to identify children, classrooms, schools, and school systems that are performing poorly. This, in turn, allows us to address weaknesses in learning. In fact, evidence already exists that as a result of state standards of learning and the achievement testing associated with them, poor children, minority children, and others who traditionally have not done as well in schools have been doing better academically (Achievement Tech., 2002).

2. Without diagnostic testing we could not identify those children who have a learning disability, and we would not be able to offer them services to help them learn.

3. Testing allows a child to be accurately placed in his or her grade level. This ultimately provides a better learning environment for all children.

4. Testing helps children identify what they are good at and pinpoint weak areas that require added attention.

Probably both the criticism and praises of educational ability testing hold some truth. Perhaps as we realize the positive aspects of such testing we should also pay attention to the criticisms and find ways to address them.

Summary

In this chapter we examined the assessment of educational ability. We started by noting that such tests have a variety of purposes, including determining if students are learning; assessing content knowledge of classes, schools, and school systems; identifying learning problems; determining giftedness; deciding whether a child is ready to move to the next grade level; and predicting achievement in college and graduate school.

We identified four kinds of educational ability testing, including three kinds of achievement tests (survey battery, diagnostic, and readiness) and one kind of aptitude test (cognitive ability testing). We defined each of these test categories and noted that often the difference between achievement testing and aptitude testing involves how the test is used as opposed to what it is measuring.

We looked at three types of survey battery achievement tests: the Stanford Achievement Test, Iowa Test of Basic Skills, and the Metropolitan Achievement Test. We noted that these tests tend to have very good validity and reliability and in recent years have become particularly important in measuring progress in meeting states' standards of learning and guidelines as set by No Child Left Behind. These tests are good at identifying the individual strengths and weaknesses of students and how well individual teachers, schools, and school systems are doing at teaching content areas.

Next, we noted that diagnostic testing has become increasingly important in the identification and diagnosis of learning disabilities. This is partly due to the passage of PL94-142 and the Individual with Disabilities Education Improvement Act (IDEIA), which state that all students with a learning disability must be given accommodations for their disability within the least restrictive environment. We noted that Individualized Education Plans address any accommodations that need to be made to help the student learn.

As the chapter continued we focused on three diagnostic achievement tests: the Wide Range Achievement Test—3, which looks at whether an individual has learned the basic codes for reading, spelling, and arithmetic; the Key-Math-Revised, which offers scrutiny of a child's math ability when he or she is suspected of having a math disability; and the Peabody Individual Achievement Test, which provides academic screening for K–12 students in a wide range of content areas. As with the survey battery tests, these tests tend to have good validity and reliability. Additionally, we mentioned some other common diagnostic tests.

The final area of achievement testing we looked at was readiness testing. Although the validity information on readiness testing is weak, these tests are sometimes helpful in determining whether a child is ready to begin kindergarten or first grade. Three readiness tests we examined included the Metropolitan Readiness Test, which measures literacy development for kindergarteners and reading and mathematics for first graders; the Gesell, which assesses personal and social skills, neurological and motor growth, language development, and adaptive behavior; and the Kindergarten Readiness Test, which assesses reasoning, language, auditory and visual attention, numbers, fine motor skills, and several other cognitive and sensory-perception areas.

As the chapter continued, we reviewed a number of cognitive ability tests, starting with the Cognitive Ability Test (CogAT), which measures cognitive skills for children from kindergarten to twelfth grade. Somewhat based on Vernon's and Cattell's theories of intelligence, this test provides scores in three areas: verbal, quantitative, and nonverbal reasoning abilities. We next briefly reviewed the Otis-Lennon, which is similar to the CogAT. We noted that cognitive ability tests such as these are particularly helpful in identifying students who have potential to do well in school but are not succeeding due to such things as learning disabilities, motivation, problems at home, problems at school, or self-esteem issues. We warned that tests such as these should not be confused with individualized intelligence tests.

Next, we went on to examine cognitive ability tests that are used to predict achievement in college and graduate school. For instance, we identified the American College Testing Assessment (ACT) and the SAT Reasoning Test as two tests that predict how well an individual will do in college, with about the same level of predictive accuracy as high school GPA. On the graduate level, we identified the Graduate Record Exam (GRE) General Test and Subject Tests, which predict grades moderately well, and the Miller Analogies Test (MAT). We also noted that the Law School Admission Test (LSAT) and the Medical College Admission Test (MCAT) both are fairly good predictors of achievement in law school or medical school.

As the chapter neared its conclusion, we identified some of the important roles played by school counselors, school social workers, school psychologists, and learning disabilities specialists in the schools relative to the assessment of educational ability. We also highlighted the importance of private practice clinicians knowing about such types of assessment.

The chapter concluded with some final thoughts about the assessment of educational ability. We noted that such tests have been attacked for forcing teachers to teach to the test, labeling children, hindering progress of minority children, and fostering competitiveness and peer pressure. On the other hand, they have been praised because they can identify which children, classrooms, schools, and school systems are performing poorly; signal the presence of learning disabilities; allow children to be accurately placed in their grade levels; and help students identify what areas they need to focus upon. We stressed that probably both the criticism and praises of educational ability testing hold some truth.

Chapter Review

1. Discuss applications of tests for assessing educational ability.

2. Define the following types of tests of educational ability: survey battery tests, readiness tests, diagnostic tests, and cognitive ability tests.

3. From your reading in the chapter, identify two or three survey battery tests and discuss how they might be applied.

4. Relative to survey battery achievement tests, what are some of the uses of classroom, school, and school system profile reports?

5. Discuss the relevance of diagnostic testing to PL94-142 and to the IDEIA.

6. Identify and describe two or three diagnostic tests discussed in this chapter.

7. Compare and contrast a readiness test such as the Metropolitan with one like the Gesell.

8. Identify one or more cognitive ability tests that are typically used in the schools and discuss their applications. In particular, how are they important for the identification of learning problems?

9. Discuss two or more types of cognitive ability tests that are typically used for admission into college or graduate school.

10. Discuss the role of school counselors, school psychologists, learning disability specialists, school social workers, and private practice clinicians in the assessment of educational ability.

Assessment of Intelligence

I was working on my master's degree in counseling and taking a course in the clinical psychology department on the administration and interpretation of intelligence tests. Part of the course involved giving a number of intelligence tests. One day, I was asked to give an intelligence test to a young man who was mentally retarded. To administer a subtest of this assessment instrument, called "block design," I was required to give this young man four blocks with different designs and ask him to replicate a design made from the blocks pieced together like a puzzle. Before giving him the blocks, I was supposed to show him how it was done. Suddenly my mind went blank, and I had difficulty showing him how to put the four blocks together to make this rather simple design. I was feeling anxious about testing this young man, and my anxiety was interfering with my ability to do this simple task. I managed to pull myself together and show him the design. This experience made me realize the significance of the relationship between examiner and examinee when administering an intelligence test. (Ed Neukrug)

The above vignette demonstrates the importance of being able to properly administer a standardized test. When a test is not properly administered, the results may not reflect the individual's best performance. In this chapter we will explore the concept of intellectual ability and how it has been used in the development of standardized tests of intelligence. As in the example above, these types of tests rely on an accurate assessment of the client's best performance and should be given only by individuals who are trained in the administration of intellectual assessment instruments. The chapter will begin with a brief definition of intelligence testing and then provide an overview of some models of intelligence. Next, we will examine some of the better-known individual intelligence tests. We will then look at some of the roles helpers take on in the assessment of intelligence and conclude with some final thoughts about the assessment of this important domain.

Defining Intelligence Testing

As mentioned in Chapter 1, intelligence testing is a type of aptitude testing that measures a broad assessment of one's cognitive capabilities and generally results in an "IQ" score. Like special aptitude testing, multiple aptitude testing, and cognitive ability testing, intelligence testing measures what one is capable of doing (see Figures 1.2 and 6.1). Special and multiple aptitude testing will be examined in Chapter 8 as types of testing for occupational and career counseling. Cognitive ability tests were examined in Chapter 6 as a type of educational ability testing, and although intelligence tests are often used to measure educational ability, they tend to have much broader applications. Intelligence tests are used for a variety of purposes, including the following:

1. To assist in determining giftedness.
2. To assess mental retardation.
3. To identify certain types of learning disabilities.
4. To help understand changes in brain function as a result of accidents, dementia, the aging process, abuse, and disease processes.
5. As part of the admissions process to certain private schools.
6. As part of a personality assessment battery to aid in understanding the whole person.

We will begin this chapter by presenting a number of models of intelligence and this will lead into a discussion of some of the more frequently used types of intelligence tests. As you read the chapter, reflect on how these intelligence tests reflect the models we are about to discuss.

Models of Intelligence

In an attempt to define intelligence, a number of theoretical models have been proposed. These models are sometimes quite involved, and in this text we offer a brief overview of a few of the more prevalent ones, including Spearman's Two-Factor Approach, Thurstone's Multifactor Approach, Vernon's Hierarchical Model of Intelligence, Guilford's Multifactor/Multi-Dimensional Model, Cattell's Fluid and Crystal Intelligence, Piaget's Cognitive Development Theory, and Gardner's Theory of Multiple Intelligences.

Spearman's Two-Factor Approach

When Alfred Binet created the first widely used intelligence test, he developed a number of subtests that assessed a range of what he considered to be intellectual tasks, and then he examined the average scores of individuals belonging to different age groups. Thus, when one took the Binet scale, one could compare his or her score on the test to the average score of individuals of different age

Spearman
Known for his *g*
and *s* factors of
intelligence

groups. Asserting that such a test was a hodgepodge or "promiscuous pooling" of factors, Charles Edward Spearman (1863–1945) was critical of Binet and others (Spearman, 1970, p. 71). Spearman, in other words, felt that Binet lumped a number of different factors together in a spurious fashion.

Spearman (1970) believed in a two-factor approach to intelligence that included a general factor (*g*) and a specific factor (*s*), both of which he considered important in understanding intelligence. He contended that the importance or "weight" of *g* varied as a function of what was being measured. For example, he stated that the "talent for classics" (e.g., understanding the ancient worlds of Rome and Greece) had a ratio of *g* to *s* of 15 to 1; that is, general intelligence is much more significant than the specific ability. However conversely, he purported that the ratio of general intelligence (*g*) to specific talent for music (*s*) was a ratio of 1 to 4 (Spearman, 1970). Although Spearman's theory was one of the earlier models of intelligence, many still adhere to the concept that there is a *g* factor that mediates general intelligence and an *s* factor that speaks to a variety of specific talents.

Thurstone's Multifactor Approach

Thurstone
Believed in
seven different
mental abilities

Using multiple-factor analysis, Thurstone developed a model that included seven primary factors or mental abilities. Although Thurstone's research did not substantiate Spearman's general factor (*g*), he did not rule out the possibility that it existed since there was a large commonality between the seven factors (Thurstone, 1938). The seven primary mental abilities he recognized were verbal meaning, number ability, word fluency, perception speed, spatial ability, reasoning, and memory.

Vernon's Hierarchical Model of Intelligence

Vernon
Developed hier-
archy approach
that is still used
by most tests
today

Perhaps one of the greatest and most widely adopted models of intelligence is Vernon's hierarchical model. Philip Vernon believed that subcomponents of intelligence could be added in a hierarchical manner to get a score for a cumulative (*g*) factor. His hierarchical model comprised four levels, with factors from each lower level contributing to the next level on the hierarchy. Vernon's top level was similar to Spearman's general factor (*g*) and was considered to have the most variance of any of the factors, while the second level had two major factors: *v:ed*, which stands for verbal and educational abilities, and *k:m*, which represents mechanical-spatial-practical abilities. The third level is composed of minor group factors, while the fourth level is made of specific factors (Vernon, 1961), as illustrated in Figure 7.1.

Guilford's Multifactor/Multi-Dimensional Model

Guilford (1967) originally developed a model of intelligence with 120 factors. As if that were not enough, he later expanded it to 180 factors (Guilford, 1988). His

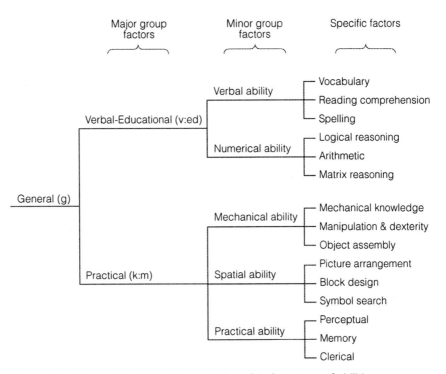

Figure 7.1 Diagram illustrating Vernon's hierarchical structure of abilities

Guilford
Developed 180 factors in his model shaped as a cube

three-dimensional model can be represented as a cube and involves three kinds of cognitive ability: *operations,* or the processes we use in understanding; *content,* or what we use to perform our thinking process; and the *products,* or the end results of our thinking processes (see Figure 7.2). Different mental abilities will require different combinations of processes and contents and will lead to different products. All of the possible combinations are combined to create the (6 * 6 * 5) 180 factors. Guilford's multifactor model provides a broad view of intelligence (Guilford, 1967); however, his model is sometimes considered too unwieldy to implement and has not significantly influenced the testing community.

Cattell's Fluid and Crystal Intelligence

During the 1940s, Cattell forwarded concepts of what he called "fluid" and "crystallized" intelligence, which significantly influenced most of the intelligence tests that are used today. He came up with this idea when, in attempting to remove cultural bias from intelligence tests, he observed marked changes from the

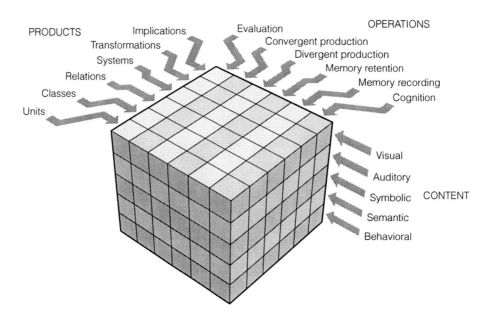

Figure 7.2 Guilford's multifactor model of intelligence

Source: Guilford, J. (1988). Some changes in the structure of the intellect model. *Educational and Psychological Measurement, 48,* 1–4, p. 3. Reprinted by permission of Sage Publications.

Cattell
Differentiated fluid (innate) from crystallized (learned) intelligence

original test scores of individuals (Cattell, 1971). Wondering what could account for this, he realized that as information based on learning was removed from the intelligence test (the portion most affected by cultural influences), the raw or unlearned abilities provided a different score. He then considered the possibility that there were two "general factors" that made up intelligence: fluid (g_f) intelligence, or that culturally free portion of intelligence that is inborn and unaffected by new learning; and crystallized intelligence (g_c), which is acquired as we learn and is affected by our experiences, schooling, culture, and motivation (Cattell, 1979). He eventually estimated that heritability variance within family for fluid intelligence was about .92, which basically means if your parents have it, you are likely to have it (Cattell, 1980). Abilities such as memory and spatial capability are aspects of fluid intelligence.

As one might expect, crystallized intelligence will generally increase with age, while many research studies have found that fluid intelligence tends to decline slightly as we get older (see Box 7.1). Therefore, many theorists believe that overall intelligence (g) is maintained evenly across the lifespan (see Figure 7.3). As we look at specific intelligence tests later in the chapter, see if you can identify how Cattell's ideas have influenced their development.

BOX 7.1
Example of Fluid and Crystallized Intelligence

At our university, we have a good mix of 18- to 22-year-olds as well as older adult (35+) students. It is interesting to observe the behavior of students of different ages when we give exams. The last five or six students left taking an exam will invariably be older adults. Part of the reason may be that they are more careful, but the decrease in fluid intelligence could also be a major factor. Are the older students' scores lower? Absolutely not. As a matter of fact, they are at least equal to the scores of the younger students, if not higher. Why is this so? Perhaps older students may be experiencing a decrease in fluid intelligence, but their crystallized intelligence has increased to make up for the difference.

—Charlie Fawcett

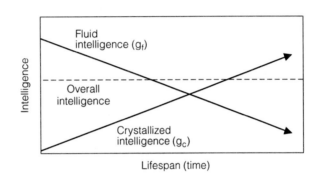

Figure 7.3 Fluid and crystallized intelligence across the lifespan

Piaget's Cognitive Development Theory

Piaget
Cognitive developmental model highlights assimilation and accommodation in learning

Piaget (1950) approached intelligence from a developmental perspective rather than a factors approach. Spending years observing how children's cognitions were shaped as they grew, he developed the now familiar four stages of cognitive development: sensorimotor, preoperational, concrete operational, and formal operational. Piaget (1950) believed that cognitive development is adaptive; that is, as new information from our environment is presented, we are driven to maintain equilibrium.

Piaget believed that we adapt our mental structures to maintain equilibrium through two methods: assimilation and accommodation. *Assimilation* is incorporating new stimuli or information into existing cognitive structures in order to make sense of the world. On the other hand, *accommodation* is creating new cognitive structures and/or behaviors based on new stimuli. For example, a parent might teach a young child that the word "hot" means that one should stay away from certain items (e.g., a stove, iron, etc.) because touching those items can result in something bad happening. The child then learns that stoves are "hot" and should be avoided. In addition, every time the child is near a hot object, he or she knows to avoid it (e.g., match, coal, frying pan, etc.). The new object has been assimilated as something to be avoided.

As the child grows older, he or she comes to realize that not all hot items are hot all the time, and the child accommodates this new information. For instance, as the child comes to understand the stove is not "hot" all the time, he or she creates a new meaning for the concept "stove," which now is seen as an object that can be hot or cold. Consequently, the child's behavior around a stove will change as he or she has accommodated this new meaning into his or her mental framework.

Consider how assimilation and accommodation are also important in the learning of important concepts in school, such as the shift between addition and multiplication (multiplication being a type of advanced addition). Also, consider how you have assimilated or accommodated information from this text into your existing structures of understanding! Although Piaget's understanding of cognitive development does not speak directly to the *amount* of learning taking place, it does highlight the *process* of learning—a critical concept for teachers and helpers to understand.

Gardner's Theory of Multiple Intelligences

Gardner
Theory of multiple intelligences is novel but difficult to apply

Gardner (1983, 1999), who is vehemently opposed to the current construct of intelligence measurement, refers to the predominant notion of intelligence as the "dipstick theory" of the mind; that is, it holds that there is a specific amount or level of intelligence in the brain, and if you could place a dipstick in the brain and pull it out, you should be able to accurately read how smart a person is (Gardner, 1996). In contrast to this approach, he believes that intelligence is much too vast and complex to be measured accurately by our current methods.

Based on his research of brain-damaged individuals, as well as literature in the areas of the brain, evolution, genetics, psychology, and anthropology, Gardner developed his Theory of Multiple Intelligences which asserts there are eight or nine intelligences, and with more research, others might even be found. Below are the nine identified intelligences, although research on the ninth type of intelligence, existential intelligence, has not clearly established its validity at this point (see below) (Gardner, 2003).

1. *Verbal-Linguistic Intelligence:* well-developed verbal skills and sensitivity to the sounds, meanings, and rhythms of words (e.g., poets, writers, journalists, lawyers)
2. *Mathematical-Logical Intelligence:* ability to think conceptually and abstractly, and capacity to discern logical or numerical patterns (e.g., logicians, mathematicians, scientists, computer scientists)
3. *Musical Intelligence:* ability to produce and appreciate rhythm, pitch and timbre (e.g., musicians, composers, directors)

4. *Visual-Spatial Intelligence:* capacity to think in images and pictures, to visualize accurately and abstractly (e.g., pilots, cartographers, architects, geographers)
5. *Bodily-Kinesthetic Intelligence:* ability to control one's body movements and to handle objects skillfully (e.g., dancers, athletes)
6. *Interpersonal Intelligence:* capacity to detect and respond appropriately to the moods, motivations, and desires of others (therapists, sales-people, religious leaders, politicians)
7. *Intrapersonal Intelligence:* capacity to be self-aware and in tune with inner feelings, values, beliefs, and thinking processes (counselors, philosophers)
8. *Naturalist Intelligence:* ability to recognize and categorize plants, ani-mals, and other objects in nature (naturalists, botanists, florists)
9. *Existential Intelligence:* sensitivity and capacity to tackle deep questions about human existence, such as the meaning of life, why do we die, and how did we get here (philosophers, great thinkers) (*Tapping into multiple intelligences*, n.d.)

Gardner's understanding of intelligence is revolutionary and not in the main-stream. Not only are his identified categories novel, but his understanding of how intelligence manifests itself is different, as noted below:

1. All human beings possess a certain amount of all of the intelligences.
2. All humans have different profiles or amounts of the multiple intelli-gences (even identical twins!).
3. Intelligences are manifested by the way a person carries out a task in relationship to his or her goals.
4. Intelligences can work independently or together, and each is located in a distinct part of the brain (Gardner, 1983, 2003).

Theories of Intelligence Summarized

As you can see, the manner in which intelligence is conceptualized varies de-pending on the theory. Thus, how an intelligence test is constructed will reflect the model one believes is most true to the nature of this construct. Table 7.1 sum-marizes some of the major points of each theory discussed in this chapter. Consider what you might measure if you were developing an intelligence test based on one or more of these theories.

Intelligence Testing

It would make sense that to some degree, theories of intelligence are the basis for intelligence tests. So, it is not surprising that over the years a number of intelli-gence tests have been devised to measure such things as general intelligence (g), specific intelligence (s), fluid and crystal intelligence, and factors traditionally seen to be related to intellectual ability. Intelligence tests do not tend to measure

TABLE 7.1
Summary of Models of Intelligence

THEORETICAL MODEL	NUMBER OF FACTORS OR ATTRIBUTES	NATURE OF FACTORS OR ATTRIBUTES
Spearman's Two-Factor Approach	Two: g and s	The g factor mediates general intelligence and the s factor mediates specific abilities. The ratio of g to s varies, depending on ability.
Thurstone's Multifactor Approach	Seven	Research on multiple factor analysis led to Thurstone's belief that there are seven primary factors which may be related to g. They include verbal meaning, number ability, word fluency, perception speed, spatial ability, reasoning, and memory.
Vernon's Hierarchical Model of Intelligence	Four hierarchical levels	The four levels include g, the highest level, with the largest source of variance between individuals; major group factors, including verbal-numerical-educational ($v{:}ed$) and practical-mechanical-spatial-physical ($k{:}m$) ability; minor group factors; and specific factors.
Guilford's Multifactor/ Multi-Dimensional Model	Three-dimensional model with 180 factors	Three kinds of cognitive ability: *operations*, or the six processes we use in understanding; *content*, or the six ways we perform our thinking process; and *products*, or the five possible end results of our thinking processes (6 * 6 * 5 = 180 possible paths).
Cattell's Fluid and Crystal Intelligence	Two: fluid (g_f) and crystallized intelligence (g_c)	Two g factors: fluid g_f intelligence: culturally free intelligence with which we are born; and crystallized intelligence, g_c, which is acquired as we learn, and is affected by our experiences, schooling, culture, and motivation.
Piaget's Cognitive Development Theory	Two: Assimilation and Accommodation	Process model, not a cognitive gain model. Assimilation is adapting new stimuli or information into existing cognitive structures, and accommodation is creating new cognitive structures and/or behaviors from new stimuli. We learn through these processes.
Gardner's Theory of Multiple Intelligences	Eight, maybe nine	Non-traditional model of eight or nine intelligences which all people have at different levels: Verbal-Linguistic, Mathematical-Logical, Musical, Visual-Spatial, Bodily-Kinesthetic, Interpersonal, Intrapersonal, Naturalist, and maybe Existential.

mental ability as defined by Gardner, whose nontraditional concept of intelligence highlights concepts not usually seen as being related to intelligence. Instead, traditional intelligence tests measure intelligence based on traditional constructs. Today, these tests are standardized and administered individually by a highly trained examiner. Although a number of intelligence tests are available today, the Stanford-Binet and the three Wechsler Scales of Intelligence are the most widely used. Thus, we will examine these tests as well as another popular intelligence test known as the Kaufman Assessment Battery for Children.

Stanford-Binet

Probably the most well known intelligence test is the Stanford-Binet, which dates back to the original work of Alfred Binet in 1904. As discussed in Chapter 1, Lewis Terman at Stanford University began improving on Binet's scale in the early 1900s, and since that time, the test has been periodically revised until its most recent fifth edition in 2003.

SB5
Uses routing test, basal and ceiling levels to determine start and stop points; measures verbal and nonverbal intelligence across five factors

The Stanford-Binet Fifth Edition (SB5) takes between 45 and 60 minutes to administer individually and can be given to individuals from 2 to 90+ years old (Riverside Publishing, 2004a). In order to administer the test in a reasonable amount of time to individuals of all ages, the Stanford-Binet uses a vocabulary *routing test,* almost a pretest, to determine where an individual should begin. For example, a 35-year-old engineer does not need to answer all the questions in the mathematics section that would normally apply to an elementary school student. Instead, using the routing test, the examiner determines the age level at which to begin testing. Next, a *basal level* is determined, which is the highest point where the examinee is able to get all the questions right on two consecutive age levels. Testing continues until the *ceiling level* is reached, or the point where the individual misses 75% of the questions on two consecutive age levels. Basal and ceiling levels are important because they help the examinee avoid feeling bored and they lessen the likelihood that the examinee will experience a sense of failure, which could happen if the examinee was asked to respond to all questions on the test. Basal and ceiling levels are also found in other kinds of assessment procedures and are an important concept to understand.

The SB5 measures verbal and nonverbal intelligence across five factors: fluid reasoning, knowledge, quantitative reasoning, visual-spatial processing, and working memory. These divisions create ten subtests (2 domains x 5 factors) (see Table 7.2). Discrepancies between scores on the verbal and nonverbal factors can be an indication of a learning disability.

SB5 recently switched to mean of 100 and SD of 15.

Although previous versions of the Stanford-Binet used a mean of 100 and a standard deviation of 16, the SB5 has now joined most other intelligence tests by using a mean of 100 and a standard deviation of 15. Subtests use a mean of 10 and a SD of 3, and other standardized scoring methods are available such as percentile ranks, grade equivalents, and a descriptive classification (average, low average, etc.). A nice feature of this latest edition of the exam is that the publishers also offer a compatible program called the SB5 Scoring Pro™. This Windows-based software program allows the examiner to enter raw scores which are converted to standard scores, and it provides various profiles related to areas that are assessed. Figure 7.4 provides examples of the Interpretive Worksheet of the Stanford-Binet.

The SB5 norm group was based on a stratified random sample of 4,800 people gathered from the 2000 U.S. Census. Each item was examined for bias in gender, ethnicity, regional, and socioeconomic status. Split-half and test-retest reliabilities for individual subtests by age averaged between .66 and .93, while full-scale IQ reliability was very high and ranged between .97 and .98 for all age

TABLE 7.2
Organization of the Stanford-Binet, Fifth Edition

		Domains	
Factors		**Nonverbal (NV)**	**Verbal (V)**
	Fluid Reasoning (FR)	*Nonverbal Fluid Reasoning** Activities: Object Series/Matrices (Routing)	*Verbal Fluid Reasoning* Activities: Early Reasoning (2–3), Verbal Absurdities (4), Verbal Analogies (5–6)
	Knowledge (KN)	*Nonverbal Knowledge* Activities: Procedural Knowledge (2–3), Picture Absurdities (4–6)	*Verbal Knowledge** Activities: Vocabulary (Routing)
	Quantitative Reasoning (QR)	*Nonverbal Quantitative Reasoning* Activities: Quantitative Reasoning (2–6)	*Verbal Quantitative Reasoning* Activities: Quantitative Reasoning (2–6)
	Visual-Spatial Processing (VS)	*Nonverbal Visual-Spatial Processing* Activities: Form Board (1–2), Form Patterns (3–6)	*Verbal Visual-Spatial Processing* Activities: Position and Direction (2–6)
	Working Memory (WM)	*Nonverbal Working Memory* Activities: Delayed Response (1), Block Span (2–6)	*Verbal Working Memory* Activities: Memory for Sentences (2–3) Last Word (4–6)

Note: Names of the 10 Subtests are in bold italic. Activities are shown with the levels at which they appear. *Routing Subtests

Source: Riverside Publishing (2004a). *The Stanford-Binet Intelligence Scales,* Fifth Edition. Copyright © 2004 by The Riverside Publishing Company. All rights reserved. Chart reproduced from Riverside Publishing's website with permission of the publisher.

groups (Roid, 2003). Content validity included professional judgment of items over a seven-year development process and item analysis using advanced statistical methods. Criterion-related validity showed a "substantial" correlation of .90 with the previous version of the Stanford-Binet (SB IV). Sound predictive validity was also shown with a variety of special groups such as the gifted, mentally retarded, learning disabled, and so on. Correlations with other instruments ranged from .53 to .84 for the SB5 with the Wechsler Scales, Woodcock-Johnson III Tests of Cognitive Abilities, Woodcock-Johnson III Tests of Achievement, and Wechsler Individual Achievement Test (WAIT) (Roid, 2003). Finally, the 217-page technical manual is filled with other advanced statistical analyses that show evidence of reliability and validity.

Wechsler Scales

Although the Stanford-Binet may be the best-known intelligence test, the three Wechsler scales of intelligence are the most widely used intelligence tests today. In contrast to the Stanford-Binet, which assesses intelligence of individuals from

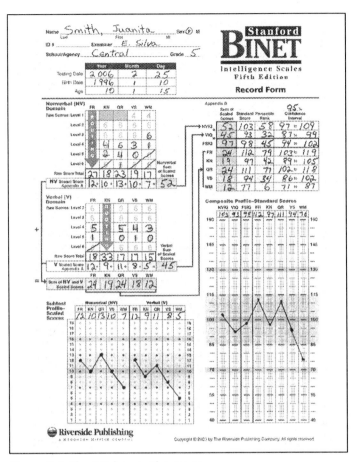

Figure 7.4 The SB5 interpretive report

On the above interpretive report you can see the following (going counter-clockwise): (1) basic demographic information, (2) the routing score to help determine the basal age, (3) verbal and nonverbal subtest raw and scaled scores (M = 10, SD = 3), (4) comparison of verbal IQ, nonverbal IQ, Full-Scale IQ using DIQ, percentile rank, and confidence intervals (range of true scores), (5) comparison of verbal IQ, nonverbal IQ, Full-Scale IQ, and subtest scores using DIQ.

Source: Riverside Publishing (2004a). *The Stanford-Binet Intelligence Scales*, Fifth Edition. Copyright © 2004 by The Riverside Publishing Company. All rights reserved. Chart reproduced from Riverside Publishing's website with permission of the publisher.

Wechsler scales
Three different tests for three different age groups

a broad spectrum of ages, each Wechsler test measures a select age group, with the WPPSI-III (Wechsler Preschool and Primary Scale of Intelligence –Third Edition) assessing children from 2 years, 6 months to 7 years, 3 months; the WISC-IV (Wechsler Intelligence Scale for Children – Fourth Edition) assessing children age 6 through 16; and the WAIS-III (Wechsler Adult Intelligence Scale –

Third Edition) assessing adults from 16 through 89. The WISC-IV is a downward extension of the WAIS-III, and the WPPSI-III is a downward extension of the WISC-IV. Thus, many of the subtests among the three tests are similar, except that they are geared toward their specific age group. All three tests are useful in assessing general cognitive functioning, in helping to determine mental retardation and giftedness, and in assessing probable learning problems. Because the tests are similar in nature, to give you a sense of what these tests are like, we will offer a brief overview of the WISC-IV.

WISC-IV
Subtests measure broad range of cognitive ability; ten subtests combine for a composite score (*g*)

The WISC-IV contains 15 subtests, many of which are similar to those in the WPPSI and WAIS (Wecshler, 2003a). Each subtest measures a different aspect of cognitive functioning, although there is some overlap among certain subtests (see Table 7.3).

The WISC-IV provides a Full-Scale IQ as well as four additional composite score indexes in areas called Verbal Comprehension Index (VCI), Perceptual Reasoning Index (PRI), Working Memory Index (WMI), and Processing Speed Index (PSI). The subtests that are associated with each of their respective composite score indexes are listed in Table 7.4. The ten subtests not italicized in Table 7.4 are used to find the Full-Scale IQ, while each of the five italicized subtests can be used if a subtest is invalidated for some reason (e.g., given incorrectly, not appropriate for a child due to his or her specific disability) or if additional information is warranted.

The four composite score indexes provide important information concerning the child being tested, including identifying strengths and weaknesses of a child as well as helping to identify a possible learning disability. Subtest scores use scaled scores (standard scores) that have a mean of 10 and a standard deviation of 3, while the Full-Scale IQ is reported with a mean of 100 and standard deviation of 15. The front page of the WISC-IV Record Form offers a summary of the child's test scores. Figure 7.5 shows the form, which offers six parts, A–F.

Part A presents the child's age at testing and the date of testing. Part B presents the raw score of each of the subtests given as well as the scaled (standard) scores. In this case, you can see that although two additional subtests were used to gather more information (cancellation and arithmetic), they are not included when deriving the Full-Scale IQ. Part C offers the sum of the scaled scores. Part D offers a summary of the four composite indexes as well as the Full-Scale IQ. Here, the sums of all of the scaled scores are offered as well as converted scores using a mean of 100 and standard deviation of 15. Corresponding percentiles are also presented, and confidence intervals (standard error of measurement) show the probability that 95 percent of the time the score is likely to fall within the range given. Part E shows the breakdown of the specific subtests grouped by composite index. This visual representation allows one to readily see an individual's strengths and weaknesses as based on the composite indexes. Part F shows a visual representation of the composite indexes and the Full-Scale IQ using a mean of 100 and standard deviation of 15. Thus, comparisons can be made to each of the composite indexes with the Full-Scale IQ.

TABLE 7.3
Abbreviations and Descriptions of Subtests

SUBTEST	ABBREVIATION	DESCRIPTION
Block Design	BD	While viewing a constructed model or a picture in a Stimulus Book, the child uses red-and-white blocks to re-create the design within a specified time limit.
Similarities	SI	The child is presented two words that represent common objects or concepts and describes how they are similar.
Digit Span	DS	For Digit Span Forward, the child repeats numbers in the same order as presented aloud by the examiner. For Digit Span Backward, the child repeats numbers in the reverse order of that presented aloud by the examiner.
Picture Concepts	PCn	The child is presented with two or three rows of pictures and chooses one picture from each row to form a group with a common characteristic.
Coding	CD	The child copies symbols that are paired with simple geometric shapes or numbers. Using a key, the child draws each symbol in its corresponding shape or box within a specified amount of time.
Vocabulary	VC	For Picture Items, the child names pictures that are displayed in the Stimulus Book. For Verbal Items, the child gives definitions for words that the examiner reads aloud.
Letter-Number	LN	The examiner reads aloud a sequence of numbers and letters and the child is asked to recite the numbers in ascending order and the letters in alphabetical order.
Matrix Reasoning	MR	The child looks at an incomplete matrix and selects the missing portion from five response options.
Comprehension	CO	The child answers questions based on his or her understanding of general principles of social situations.
Symbol Search	SS	The child scans a search group and indicates whether the target symbol(s) match(es) any of the symbols in the search group within a specified time limit.
Picture Completion	PCm	The child views a picture and then points to or names the important part missing within a specified time limit.
Cancellation	CA	The child scans both a random and a structured arrangement of pictures and marks target pictures within a specified time limit.
Information	IN	The child answers questions that address a broad range of general knowledge topics.
Arithmetic	AR	The child mentally solves a series of orally presented arithmetic problems within a specified time limit.
Word Reasoning	WR	The child identifies the common concept being described in a series of clues.

Source: Wechsler, D. (2003a). *Wechsler Intelligence Scale for Children—Fourth Edition*, p. 2–3.

TABLE 7.4
Subtests and Composite Indexes*

VCI	PRI	PSI	VMI
Similarities	Block Design	Coding	Digit Span
Vocabulary	Picture Concepts	Symbol Search	Letter-Number Sequencing
Comprehension	Matrix Reasoning	*Cancellation*	*Arithmetic*
Information	*Picture Completion*		
Word Reasoning			

* Subtests not italicized are used to determine Full-Scale IQ.

Composite scores are useful in identifying learning disabilities.

The tests are also reliable and valid. For example, the WISC-IV internal consistency for the full scale is .97. Individual subtest reliabilities tend to average in the .80s (Wechsler, 2003b). The WISC-IV technical manual has 51 pages dedicated to providing evidence of validity, including evidence based on test content, internal structure, factor analysis, and relationships with numerous other variables (Wechsler, 2003b). As you can see, the WISC-IV, as well as its first cousins the WPPSI-III and WAIS-III, offers a comprehensive picture of the cognitive function of the individual. Such a test is useful in determining such things as mental retardation, giftedness, learning problems, and other related cognitive deficiencies.

Kaufman Assessment Battery for Children

KABC-II Measures cognitive ability for ages 3 to 18; provides choice of theoretical model of intelligence

The Kaufman Assessment Battery for Children, Second Edition (KABC-II) is an individually administered test of cognitive ability for children between the ages of 3 and 18. Depending on the age range, test times can vary from 25 to 70 minutes. Subtests and scoring allow for a choice between two theoretical models, one of which is Cattell's model of fluid and crystallized intelligence. However, both methods examine visual processing, fluid reasoning, and short-term and long-term memory. Scores are age-based and have a mean of 100 and an SD of 15, but also can be provided as a percentile rank or age equivalent (AGS Publishing, 2004b).

The norm group for the KABC-II was based on a sample of 3,025 that was stratified against the U.S. population for gender, race, SES, religion, and special education status. Reliability estimates are quite sound, ranging from .87 to .95 for composite score means. Subtest reliabilities are generally in the .80s range. Additional psychometric data such as validity is available in the manual.

The Role of Helpers in the Assessment of Intelligence

The assessment of intelligence takes advanced training, which is generally given in school psychology programs and many doctoral programs in counseling and clinical psychology. Although other helpers, such as learning disabilities

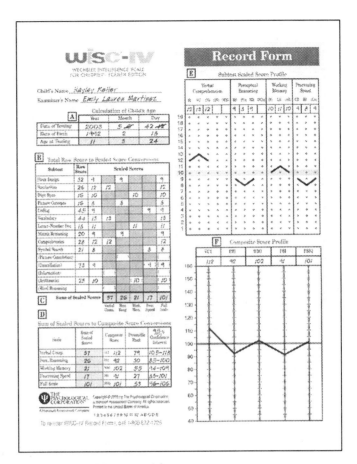

Figure 7.5 WISC-IV record form

Source: Wechsler, D. (2003a). *Wechsler Intelligence Scale for Children—
Fourth Edition*, p. 46. Copyright © 2003 by Harcourt Assessment, Inc.
Reproduced with permission. All rights reserved.

specialists, licensed clinical social workers, and licensed professional counselors, may have also obtained such training, many graduate programs in special education, counseling, and social work do not automatically offer these courses.

When a helper does have this training, he or she can provide a wide range of services to individuals, including the assessment of intelligence to help determine learning problems, mental retardation, giftedness, potential for learning, and possible neurological impairment. For those helpers who do not have the training to give an intellectual assessment, it is still imperative that they have sufficient knowledge of these kinds of tests so that they will know when to refer clients who might need such an assessment and be able to participate in the development of treatment plans for their clients who have had intellectual assessment.

Final Thoughts on Intelligence Testing

Intelligence testing can be used in a variety of ways, and if one is not careful, can be abused. Abuses over the years have been many, including the miscalculation of intelligence of minorities, over-classification of individuals who are learning disabled, "proof" of racial differences of ability, and a means of differentiating social classes. However, the astute examiner knows that the assessment of intelligence is complex and that intelligence, as measured by intelligence tests, is based on a number of factors including the environment, genetics, and biology. Thus, any conclusions about an individual should be made within the context of knowing the whole person as well as the complex societal issues that are involved. Determination of an individual's "IQ" should always have some degree of tentativeness.

Summary

We began this chapter by defining individual intelligence testing and noting that such tests are aptitude tests that measure a range of intellectual ability and offer a broad assessment of one's cognitive capabilities. We pointed out that intelligence tests are used in a variety of ways, such as assisting in determining giftedness, mental retardation, and learning disabilities; helping to understand changes in brain function resulting from accidents, dementia, the aging process, abuse, and disease processes; as part of the admissions process for some private schools; and as part of a personality assessment to help understand the whole person.

We next offered a brief introduction of models of intelligence, including Spearman's Two-Factor Approach, Thurstone's Multifactor Approach, Vernon's Hierarchical Model of Intelligence, Guilford's Multifactor/Multi-Dimensional Model, Cattell's Fluid and Crystal Intelligence, Piaget's Cognitive Development Theory, and Gardner's Theory of Multiple Intelligences. A summary of these models was presented in Table 7.1.

We discussed three major intelligence tests: the Stanford-Binet, Fifth Edition, the Wechsler tests (focusing on the WISC-IV), and the Kaufman Assessment Battery for Children. Relative to the Stanford-Binet, we noted that the test measures cognitive functioning of individuals from age 2 through 90. We also pointed out that it assesses verbal and nonverbal intelligence across five factors: fluid reasoning, knowledge, quantitative reasoning, visual-spatial processing, and working memory. We noted that it uses a vocabulary routing test to help determine the basal age of the examinee, or the point where testing is started, and that ceiling ages are used to determine when the testing should be completed. This test has been one of the most popular tests of intellectual functioning and continues to be widely used today.

Next, we discussed the Wechsler tests, particularly the WISC-IV. We pointed out that the WISC-IV is a downward extension of the WAIS-III and the WPPSI-III is a downward extension of the WISC-IV. We identified 15 subtests that can be assessed when administering the WISC-IV, although only ten are used in determining the examinee's Full-Scale IQ. Subtests are specific to four Composite Score Indexes which include Verbal Comprehension Index (VCI), Perceptual Reasoning Index (PRI), Working Memory Index (WMI), and Processing Speed Index (PSI). These indexes are important in determining possible learning problems. The Wechsler tests are probably the most widely used tests of mental ability and are used to assess mental retardation, giftedness, learning problems, and general cognitive functioning.

The last intelligence test we examined was the Kaufman Assessment Battery for Children, Second Edition (KABC-II), which measures cognitive ability of children from ages 3 to 18 and specifically focuses on visual processing, fluid reasoning, and short-term and long-term memory. We pointed out that the test can be scored based on a couple of models of intelligences, including Cattell's model of fluid and crystallized intelligence.

As the chapter neared its conclusion, we noted that only some helpers are given the advanced training needed for the assessment of intellectual ability. For those helpers who do not have such training, we pointed out the reasons it is still imperative that they have the basic knowledge of these kinds of tests.

Finally, we noted that over the years intelligence testing has been abused by miscalculating the intelligence of minorities, over-classifying individuals with learning disabilities, "proving" racial differences of ability, and differentiating social classes. We suggested that the astute examiner know that the assessment of intelligence is complex, is based on the environment, genetics, and biology, and that conclusions should be tentative and done within the context of knowing the whole person.

Chapter Review

1. Discuss some of the many ways that intelligence tests are used.

2. Highlight the major points of the following theories of intelligence:
   a. Spearman's Two-Factor Approach
   b. Thurstone's Multifactor Approach
   c. Vernon's Hierarchical Model of Intelligence
   d. Guilford's Multifactor/Multi-Dimensional Model
   e. Cattell's Fluid and Crystal Intelligence
   f. Piaget's Cognitive Development Theory
   g. Gardner's Theory of Multiple Intelligences

3. Why is Gardner's Theory of Multiple Intelligences revolutionary as compared to the more traditional models of intelligence?

4. Describe the concepts of basal level and ceiling level. How are these levels used in the Stanford-Binet?

5. Explain the differences between the WAIS-III, WISC-IV, and WPPSI-III.

6. Discuss the purposes of the Composite Indexes on the Wechsler tests of intelligence.

7. Although there are many similarities between the Stanford-Binet and the Wechsler tests of intelligence (e.g., both measure global intelligence, both compare nonverbal and verbal intelligence), some major differences exist. Discuss these differences and the strengths and weaknesses of both tests.

8. Discuss the role of helpers in the administration and interpretation of tests of intelligence.

Career and Occupational Assessment:
Interest Inventories,
Multiple Aptitude,
and Special Aptitude Tests

A friend of mine was struggling with whether or not to continue working toward his doctoral degree in psychology. He already had a master's degree, had worked a while in the field of mental health, and had begun his first semester toward his Ph.D. Every day he would come home from school and have panic attacks. He simply was not sure that this was the career path he wanted to take. He decided to take a Strong Interest Inventory, and his concerns were reinforced when the test revealed that he viewed learning more as a means to an end than as something to embrace. His personality orientation toward the world of work also did not quite fit those of most psychologists. He decided to quit his Ph.D. program and become a ski instructor. Later, he went into investment banking, and today he's a very successful insurance broker —and much happier. What a switch!

When I was 35 and making a paltry salary as an assistant professor, I thought, "If I joined the Reserves, I could make some extra money pretty easily." So I went down to the local recruiting center, where they told me, "First, you need to take this test." It was the Armed Services Vocational Aptitude Test Battery (the ASVAB). I knew about it because I had taught a brief overview of it in my testing class. It measured general cognitive ability as well as specific vocational aptitudes. I said, "Sure."

A couple of weeks later, a recruiter called and said, "We want you." I had scored high on all the scales and moderately high on mechanical aptitude. I pondered joining the Reserves but then called him back and said, "Thanks, but I think I'll pass." Despite my ability, I decided I didn't quite have the interest or inclination to be in the military. (Ed Neukrug)

This chapter is about tests that can help an individual make a decision about his or her academic or vocational path. Whether it's an interest inventory such as the one my friend took, or a multiple aptitude test such as the one I took, these instruments can be critical in helping an individual choose an occupation or a career. Thus, in this chapter we will examine tests that are used in occupational and career counseling, including interest inventories, which are a type of personality assessment, and special aptitude and multiple aptitude tests, which help an individual determine what he or she is good at. We will also examine some of the various roles helpers play in career and occupational assessment and conclude with some final thoughts about this important domain.

Defining Career and Occupational Assessment

Career and occupational assessment can take place at any point in an individual's life, but it is often most critical at transition points such as when an adolescent moves into high school and begins to ponder an occupation or a career, when a young adult finds a job or goes on to college, when an adult decides to crystallize his or her career choices, when a middle-aged adult makes a career shift, or when an older adult considers shifting out of his or her career. Although talking with a counselor can make these transitions smoother, tests provide a vital adjunct to this counseling process. Three kinds of tests are sometimes used in the vocational counseling process: interest inventories, multiple aptitude tests, and special aptitude tests.

In Chapter 1 interest inventories were defined as a type of personality assessment, similar to objective personality tests that are discussed in this chapter, but generally classified separately because of their popularity and very specific focus (see Figure 1.2). Our definition from Chapter 1 noted that interest inventories are used to determine a person's likes and dislikes as well as his or her personality orientation toward the world of work, and are almost exclusively used in the career counseling process. In contrast, we noted in Chapter 1 that multiple aptitude tests measure a number of homogeneous abilities and are used to predict the likelihood of success in any of a number of vocations, while special aptitude tests usually measure one homogenous area of ability and are used to predict success in a specific vocational area. Interest inventories, which focus on likes and dislikes, and special and multiple aptitude tests, which focus on ability, complement each other and are sometimes given together. In this chapter we will explore interest inventories, take a look at multiple aptitude tests, and conclude by discussing special aptitude tests.

Interest Inventories

Interest inventories Determine likes and dislikes from a career perspective; good at predicting job satisfaction

With an estimated 3,000,000 interest inventories administered each year, interest inventories have been particularly successful as an adjunct to the career counseling process and have become big business in the world of assessment (Hansen, 1995; Zytowski, 1994). This is probably partially due to the fact that interest inventories are fairly good at predicting job satisfaction based on occupational fit (Jagger, Neukrug, & McAuliffe, 1992; Ton & Hansen, 2001). For instance, if a person takes an interest inventory and chooses a job that seems to match his or her personality type, then that person is more likely to be satisfied in that occupation than a person whose personality type does not match his or her job. It should be noted, however, that interest in an area does not necessarily correlate with ability in that same area. For example, you might want to be a rock star, but if you lack certain musical abilities, your career may be short-lived.

Three of the most common interest inventories we will examine include the Strong Vocational Interest Inventory (CPP, 2002), the Self-Directed Search (SDS) (Holland, 1994), and the Career Occupational Preference System Interest Inventory (COPS) (EdITS, n.d.).

Strong Interest Inventory®*

One of the most commonly used career inventories is the "Strong." First developed in 1927 and published as the Strong Vocational Interest Blank (Strong, 1926), its latest version is called the Strong Interest Inventory (SII)®. The 317-item SII® is given to people aged 16 or older, takes 35 to 40 minutes to administer, and can be administered individually or in a group setting (Kelly, 2003). The SII® test report offers five different types of interpretive scales or indexes in the following areas:

- General Occupational Themes
- Basic Interest Scales
- Occupational Scales
- Personal Style Scales
- Total Response Index

General Occupational Themes

Strong—General Occupational Themes Uses Holland's theory of personality type (RIASEC)

The most commonly used score on the Strong is the one found on the General Occupational Themes, which offers a three-letter code based on Holland's hexagon model (see Figure 8.1). Holland defines six personality types: Realistic, Investigative, Artistic, Social, Enterprising, and Conventional. These classifications are further explained in Box 8.1. The SII® identifies the test-taker's top three Holland codes and places them in hierarchical order.

On the hexagon, codes adjacent to one another share more elements in common than nonadjacent ones. For example, a typical counselor or social worker

*Strong Interest Inventory is a registered trademark of CPP, Inc.

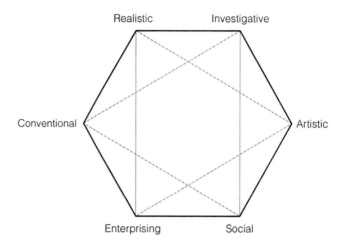

Figure 8.1 Holland's hexagon model of personality types

will have a Holland code of SAE, codes that are on adjacent corners of the hexagon and share many common elements. In contrast, people in the Artistic realm tend to have little interest in jobs or tasks in the Conventional category (located on the opposite side of the hexagon), such as accounting or bookkeeping.

Basic Interest Scales

Strong—Basic Interest Scales Identify broad areas of interest

The Basic Interest Scales identify the respondent's interest in 25 broad areas, such as science, math, music, teaching, law, and so on. The individual is shown his or her top five interest areas and can also view the 25 interest areas together with the corresponding Holland Codes (see Figure 8.2). Using T scores, individuals can compare themselves to the average scores of men (the dark bar), women (the light bar), or to a combined group of men and women (the number listed to the right of the bar). The higher the T score (remember that 50 is the mean and 10 is the standard deviation), the more interest a person will have in a particular area as compared with others.

Occupational Scales

Strong— Occupational Scales Compares interests to those of others with the same job

These scales provided the original basis for the 1927 Strong and allow an individual to compare his or her interests to the interests of individuals of the same sex who are satisfied in their jobs. Thus, respondents can compare how they scored on the Strong to the scores of individuals in 211 commonly held jobs who also took the Strong. The Strong lists the 10 occupations to which the respondent is most similar (see Figure 8.2), and then separately lists the T scores of the client as compared to all 211 occupations (not shown in the figure). The higher the T score, the more similar are one's interests to those of satisfied people in the stated job.

BOX 8.1
Holland's Personality and Work Types

Realistic: Realistic persons like to work with equipment, machines, or tools, often prefer to work outdoors, and are good at manipulating concrete physical objects. These individuals prefer to avoid social situations, artistic endeavors, or abstract tasks. Occupational settings in which you might find realistic individuals include filling stations, farms, machine shops, construction sites, and power plants.

Investigative: Investigative persons like to think abstractly, solve problems, and investigate. These individuals feel comfortable with the pursuit of knowledge and enjoy manipulating ideas and symbols. Investigative individuals prefer to avoid social situations and see themselves as introverted. Some settings in which you might find investigative individuals include research laboratories, hospitals, universities, and government-sponsored research agencies.

Artistic: Artistic individuals like to express themselves creatively, usually through artistic forms such as drama, art, music, and writing. They prefer unstructured activities in which they can use their imagination and express their creativity. Some settings in which you might find artistic individuals include the theater, concert halls, libraries, art or music studios, dance studios, orchestras, photography studios, newspapers, and restaurants.

Social: Social people are nurturers, helpers, and caregivers who have a high degree of concern for others. They are introspective and insightful and prefer work environments in which they can use their intuitive and caregiving skills. Some settings in which you might find social people include government social service agencies, counseling offices, churches, schools, mental hospitals, recreational centers, personnel offices, and hospitals.

Enterprising: Enterprising individuals are self-confident, adventurous, bold, and enjoy working with other people. They have good persuasive skills and prefer positions of leadership. They tend to dominate conversations and enjoy work environments in which they can satisfy their need for recognition, power, and expression. Some settings in which you might find enterprising individuals include life insurance agencies, advertising agencies, political offices, real estate offices, new and used car lots, sales offices, and management positions.

Conventional: Individuals of the Conventional orientation are stable, controlled, conservative, and cooperative. They prefer working on concrete tasks and like to follow instructions. They value the business world, clerical tasks, and tend to be good at computational skills. Some settings in which you might find conventional people include banks, business offices, accounting firms, and medical records departments.

Strong—Personal Style Scales
Assesses work style, learning environment, leadership style, and risk taking

Personal Style Scales

These scales gives an estimate as to how comfortable the test-taker is in certain activities, including work style (alone or with people), learning environment (practical vs. academic), leadership style (taking charge vs. letting others take charge), and risk taking/adventure (risk taker vs. non risk taker). T scores are used to compare individuals to men, women, or a combined group.

Figure 8.2 Strong Interest Inventory profile sheet

Source: Modified and reproduced by special permission of the Publisher, CPP, Inc., Mountain View, CA 94043 from the Strong Interest Inventory® instrument. © 1933, 1938, 1945, 1946, 1966, 1968, 1974, 1981, 1985, 1994 by CPP, Inc. Further reproduction is prohibited without the Publisher's written consent. Strong Interest Inventory is a registered trademark of CPP, Inc.

Total Response Index

The Total Response Index is a percentage breakdown of the client's responses across all of the interest areas measured by the Strong (e.g., school subjects, leisure activities, and so on). The Strong offers the total percentages of responses that were "like," "indifferent," and "dislike" in each of the interest areas. This information is helpful if you suspect a response set—that is, an area in which an individual's responses are all "likes," "indifferents," or "dislikes." In addition, a very large percentage of indifferent or dislike scores can sometimes indicate depression or apathy.

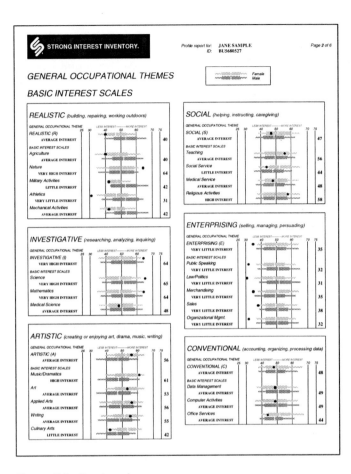

Figure 8.2 *Continued*

The Strong can be scored in a number of ways. The test booklet can be mailed to the testing center, on-site scoring software can be purchased and used, or the assessment can be administered over the Internet to produce immediate scoring reports. Norm data were updated in 1992 and 1993 based on the responses of more than 55,000 people in 50 different occupations (Kelly, 2003). Separate norms were created for men and women to account for occupational gender differences. Reliability coefficient alphas for the General Occupational Themes (Holland codes) were between .90 and .94. The Basic Interest Scales had alphas between .74 and .92 with a median of .87. The Occupational Scales had test-retest reliability estimates that ranged from .66 to .96. The four Personal Style Scales had coefficient alphas that ranged from .78 to .91 (Kelly, 2003). The test developers went to great lengths to produce evidence of concurrent validity for the General Occupational Themes, Basic Interest Scales, Occupational Scales, and Personal Style Scales. One method employed was comparing people's scores with the codes corresponding to their current occupations. The highest degree of fit was found for auto mechanics and carpenters, while child care providers and public relations directors had the lowest. Kelly (2003) contends that more work needs to be done to show evidence of predictive validity for the SII. Although ethnic minorities were underrepresented in the norm data, it appears there is sufficient validity to use the SII with minority groups (Kelly, 2003).

Self-Directed Search

SDS
This is a self-administered, scored, and interpreted test that was created by Holland and uses his personality types

The Self-Directed Search (SDS) was created by John Holland and is based on the Holland hexagon shown in Figure 8.1. As the name of the instrument suggests, the SDS can be self-administered, self-scored, and self-interpreted, although it is suggested that a counselor guide a client in his or her exploration. Although the instrument is based primarily on interests, it also includes self-estimates of competencies and ability. Once the instrument is scored and the client obtains his or her 3-letter Holland code, he or she can cross-reference the code with the Occupations Finder, which classifies more than 1,300 occupations by Holland type, or with a book entitled the *Dictionary of Holland Occupational Codes* (Gottfredson & Holland, 1996), which lists more than 12,000 occupational codes.

The SDS is available in four forms. Form R (Regular), is designed for high school students, college students, and adults; Form E (Easy-to-Read) is written at the fourth-grade level and can be used with students or adults who have limited reading ability; Form CE (Career Explorer) is for middle school and junior high students; and Form CP (Career Planning) is designed for professional-level employees (Brown, 2001). The SDS can be administered by hard copy booklet, computer software, or on the World Wide Web at www.self-directed-search.com (PAR, 2001).

Scoring for the test is done by simply adding the raw scores of each of the six types of personality, with the three highest scores, from highest to lowest, providing the individual's "Holland Code." Norm data for form R were based on 2,602 people between the ages of 17 and 65 from 25 different states. Internal reliability coefficients ranged from .90 to .94 for the combined scales (Brown, 2001). Form E was normed against 719 people from ages 15 to 72 with slightly higher reliability coefficients. Form CP was administered to only 101 working people aged 19 to 61, most of whom had been to college, and had a slightly lower reliability summary scale ranging between .87 and .93 (Brown, 2001). Validity of the SDS has been shown by calculating the most recent version of the Self-Directed Search with an earlier one, with summary scales correlating greater than .94. In fact, half of individuals had the same 3-letter Holland code for both, and two-thirds had the same first two Holland codes (Brown, 2001). Research on the Holland codes has consistently shown moderate to high validity with job satisfaction (Jagger, Neukrug, & McAuliffe, 1992; Ton & Hansen, 2001).

TABLE 8.1
COPSystem Assessments and Administration Times

MEASUREMENT	ACRONYM	FULL NAME	ADMINISTRATION TIME
Interests	COPS	Career Occupational Preference System Interest Inventory	20 to 30 min
Abilities	CAPS	Career Ability Placement Survey	50 min
Work values	COPES	Career Orientation Placement and Evaluation Survey	30 to 40 min

COPSystem

COPSystem
Three instruments that measure interests, abilities, and values

The COPSystem is a career measurement package that contains three instruments that can be used individually or together to aid in making career decisions. The three instruments measure interests, abilities, and values (see Table 8.1).

The tests can be hand scored, mailed to EdITS for machine scoring, or scored with on-site scoring software purchased from the publisher.

Career Occupational Preference System Interest Inventory (COPS)

COPS
Assesses interests along career clusters

The COPS is designed for individuals from seventh grade to adult and consists of 168 items which are based on high school and college curricula as well as sources of occupational information. Scores on the instrument are related to a unique career cluster model that is used to guide the individual to a number of career areas (see Figure 8.3). Although the publisher suggests the instrument can be used for a wide age group, norms are based on high school or college samples (EdITS, n.d.).

Career Ability Placement Survey (CAPS)

CAPS
Measures abilities in the work environment that relate to career clusters

The CAPS test measures abilities across eight different dimensions that relate to the career clusters (outer circle of Figure 8.3). The test allows individuals to identify which career fields are best suited to their abilities or identify careers for which more training may be required. The instrument is designed for middle school students through adults. Norm data are available for eighth- through twelfth-graders and for college students. Each of the eight subtests takes five minutes to administer, and the total test time is about 50 minutes. Hand scoring requires an additional 15 to 20 minutes.

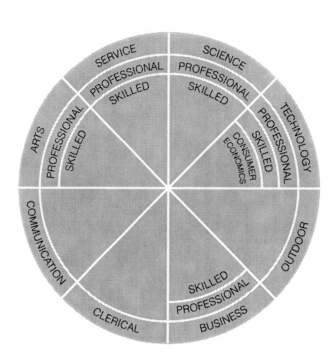

Figure 8.3 COPS career clusters

Source: COPSystem Examiner's Manual. Copyright © 1995 EdITS Publishing, San Diego, CA. Reprinted by permission.

Career Orientation Placement and Evaluation Survey (COPES)

COPES
Values in job
selection related
to career
clusters

COPES is an assessment of values that are important in occupational selection and job satisfaction. Scales are based on eight dichotomous poles (Table 8.2), which then are keyed to the career clusters in Figure 8.3 to assist in using values in choosing a career.

As with the CAPS and COPS, although this instrument is designed for middle school students through adults, norm data are available only from high school and college students.

Other Common Interest Inventories

Today, dozens of interest inventories are available for client use. However, a few stand out as being especially popular. For instance, The Campbell Interest and Skill Survey (CISS) is a self-report instrument measuring both interests and skills for a variety of occupations. It is intended for people 15 years or older, and is primarily for college-bound students or college-educated adults (NCS Pearson,

TABLE 8.2
The COPES Scales

Investigative	vs.	Accepting
Practical	vs.	Carefree
Independence	vs.	Conformity
Leadership	vs.	Supportive
Orderliness	vs.	Flexibility
Recognition	vs.	Privacy
Aesthetic	vs.	Realistic
Social	vs.	Reserved

2005a). SIGI PLUS is a computer-based (stand-alone, networked, or online) career self-assessment program primarily for high school and college students. It also provides up-to-date career information such as educational requirements, income, job satisfaction, and so on (Valpar, 2005). The Career Assessment Inventory – Enhanced Version is another instrument for career development and guidance for individuals 15 years and older. It also uses the familiar Holland codes (RIASEC) (NCS Pearson, 2005b). Clearly, experts in career and occupational assessment have many good tests from which to choose.

Multiple Aptitude Testing

Multiple aptitude tests Measure abilities and predict success in several fields

Multiple aptitude tests, as the name implies, measure several abilities at one time and are used to predict how an individual might perform in many different types of jobs. For example, the Armed Services Vocational Aptitude Battery (ASVAB), which will be discussed in greater detail, measures auto and shop knowledge, mechanical comprehension, general science, electronics knowledge, and so on. This type of information helps military administrators with placement decisions and is useful for those who are considering entering the armed services or who want to get a better idea of the skills they possess. Obviously, someone who has high mechanical aptitude and enjoys that type of work might be better suited to repairing jet aircraft or tank engines than working as a desk clerk.

Factor Analysis and Multiple Aptitude Testing

Factor analysis Helps developers determine differences and similarities between subtests

As you may recall from Chapter 3, test developers use factor analysis in demonstrating evidence of construct validity for their tests. This common statistical technique allows researchers to analyze large data sets to determine patterns and calculate which variables have a high degree of commonality. Using this process allows multiple aptitude test developers to assess the differences and similarities in the many abilities they are attempting to measure. For example, if you wanted to create a multiple aptitude test that assessed a variety of sports abilities, you could develop a number of tests, such as a softball throw, a 100-meter dash, a long jump, a 5-km run, a baseball throwing accuracy test, and a 50-meter swim. After giving the tests to your norm group and applying factor analysis to your data, you may find that the softball throw and the baseball accuracy test have so much overlap that you decide to remove one of them from your instrument or combine the two subtests into one. Two commonly used multiple aptitude tests that use factor analysis to show the purity of their component parts include the Armed Services Vocational Aptitude Battery and the Differential Aptitude Test.

Armed Services Vocational Aptitude Battery

ASVAB
Measures many abilities required for military and civilian jobs

The Armed Services Vocational Aptitude Battery (ASVAB) is the most widely used multiple aptitude test in the world (ASVAB, 2004). Originally developed in 1968, it has gone through many improvements since that time. The battery consists of eight "power tests," a term used to describe a test that has generous time limits (in contrast to a "speed test" such as a one-minute typing test). The tests include General Science, Arithmetic Reasoning, Word Knowledge, Paragraph Comprehension, Mathematics Knowledge, Electronics Information, Auto and Shop Information, and Mechanical Comprehension. The test consists of a total of 200 items and takes 170 minutes to administer. Scores for each of the eight tests, as well as three career exploration (composite) scores, are provided to the examinee. Combinations of the eight tests are used to form three composite scores in the areas of verbal skills, math skills, and science and technical skills. These three areas tend to be important for success in a number of jobs and contrast with the one general score that is given in many individual intelligence tests. The composite scores can be associated with job classifications in the U.S. Department of Labor's Occupational Information Network (O*NET). Although the ASVAB began as a test strictly for the military, over the years it has been altered and is now useful for both civilian and military occupations. The eight subtests and three composite scores are reported as T scores (mean of 50, SD of 10) as well as percentile ranks. Box 8.2 provides sample items that might appear on the exam.

ASVAB scores were normed against a 12,000-person sample called the Profile of American Youth in 1980. The sample was stratified against the 1979 U.S. Census results for gender and race. Reliability estimates for the ASVAB composite scores range from .87 to .92. Individual subtest reliabilities range from .66 to .88 (ASVAB, 2004). Content validity and content construction focused on knowledge required to perform specific jobs rather than the entire content domain. For example, instead of testing the complete domain of math, the math domain is geared toward knowledge and skills needed in the typical work environment. Numerous validity studies show correlations that range from a moderate .36 to an impressive .77 for predicting success in military occupations. Regarding construct validity, one study found a .79 correlation between ASVAB and ACT scores (Nicewander as cited by ASVAB, 2004). Another study found correlations ranging from .70 to .86 with the California Achievement Test (Streicher & Friedman as cited by ASVAB, 2004).

BOX 8.2
Sample ASVAB Questions

General Science
1. An eclipse of the sun throws the shadow of the
A. moon on the sun.
B. moon on the earth.
C. earth on the sun.
D. earth on the moon.

2. Substances that hasten chemical reaction time without themselves undergoing change are called
A. buffers.
B. colloids.
C. reducers.
D. catalysts.

Word Knowledge
3. The wind is variable today.
A. mild
B. steady
C. shifting
D. chilling

Math Knowledge
4. If 50 percent of X = 66, then X =
A. 33
B. 66
C. 99
D. 132

5. What is the area of this square?
A. 1 square foot
B. 5 square feet
C. 10 square feet
D. 25 square feet

Electronics Information
6. Which of the following has the least resistance?
A. wood
B. iron
C. rubber
D. silver

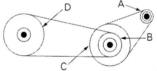

7. In this circuit diagram, the resistance is 100 ohms, and the current is 0.1 amperes. The voltage is
A. 5 volts.
B. 10 volts.
C. 100 volts.
D. 1,000 volts.

Automotive and Shop Information
8. A car uses too much oil when which of the following parts are worn?
A. pistons
B. piston rings
C. main bearings
D. connecting rods

9. A chisel is used for
A. prying.
B. cutting.
C. twisting.
D. grinding.

Mechanical Comprehension

10. In this arrangement of pulleys, which pulley turns fastest?
A. A   B. B   C. C   D. D

Solutions

1. B	2. D	3. C	4. D	5. D
6. D	7. B	8. B	9. B	10. A

Source: Adapted from ASVAB (Armed Services Vocational Aptitude Battery). (2004). The ASVAB career exploration program counselor manual. Retrieved June 7, 2004, from http://www.asvabprogram.com/downloads/asvab_counselor_manual.pdf

According to the manager of the ASVAB Career Exploration Program, the ASVAB is going through major revisions in an attempt to focus less on what students "can and can't do" and more on a "holistic" approach (J. Styers, personal communication, January 31, 2005). The first pending change is a new inventory, to be used with the current abilities test, with the proposed name of the "FYI Interest Inventory." This interest inventory will contain 90 items, can be self-scored or taken and scored online, and will indicate the test-taker's Holland type. Research sampling shows promising validity and reliability.

Differential Aptitude Tests

DAT
Measures
abilities and
interests to assist
with career
decision making

The Differential Aptitude Tests (DAT), Fifth Edition, is a long-standing series of tests for students in grades 7 through 12 that measures "students' ability to learn or to succeed in a number of different areas" (Hattrup & Schmitt, 1995, p. 301). Often administered and interpreted by school counselors, the DAT takes approximately 1½ to 2½ hours to complete, depending on whether the full or abbreviated version is used. The DAT has eight separate tests that measure verbal reasoning, numerical reasoning, abstract reasoning, perceptual speed and accuracy, mechanical reasoning, space relations, spelling, and language usage. The DAT also includes a Career Interest Inventory (CII) to determine what the student is good at as well as what careers might be of interest to him or her. It is easy to see how both sets of these scores can be useful to a school counselor when assisting a student in determining a possible occupation or college major. Raw scores are converted to percentiles and stanines.

Internal consistency reliability measures for the DAT are high, ranging between .80 and .95 for the different tests. Regarding construct validity, correlations with the DAT and several other major aptitude tests (ACT, ASVAB, SAT, and the California Achievement Test) range between .68 and .85 (Hattrup & Schmitt, 1995). Although correlations with DAT scores and high school grades were sound, no data have been provided regarding predictive validity in job performance. A healthy norm sample of approximately 170,000 students proportionately represented by geography, gender, socioeconomic status, ethnicities, and other factors was used for the Fifth Edition.

DAT PCA
Often used by
employers to
assess ability

An alternative version of the DAT for adults is called the Differential Aptitude Battery for Personnel and Career Assessment (DAT PCA). The DAT PCA measures ability and aptitude across eight different areas, similar to the DAT, and is often used for hiring purposes. It allows employers to determine one's current ability and aptitude for learning new skills during training. Like the DAT, the DAT PCA uses percentiles and stanines. Reliability estimates are sound, ranging between .88 and .94 (Wilson & Wing, 1995). The norm sample consisted of twelfth-grade students, which is a bit of a leap from the adult population for which the test is intended. Predictive validity correlations comparing DAT PCA scores with grades, job supervisors' ratings, and job performance fell in the .1 to .4 range (Wilson & Wing, 1995).

Special Aptitude Testing Defined

Special aptitude tests Designed to predict success in a vocational area

As noted earlier, special aptitude tests measure a homogenous area of ability and are generally used to predict success in a specific vocational area of interest. Thus, they are frequently used as a screening process to assess one's ability to perform a certain job or to master a new skill at work. Hiring and training employees is an expensive operation for any size of company, so you can imagine how useful these tests might be. Similarly, specialized vocational training in areas such as art, music, plumbing, and mechanics all require aptitudes that not everyone possesses. Hence, educational institutions frequently rely on special aptitude testing during the admission process.

The tests we will briefly examine in this section include the Clerical Test Battery, the Minnesota Clerical Assessment Battery, the U.S. Postal Service's 470 Battery Examination, the Federal Clerical Exam, the SkillsProfiler Series Mechanical Aptitude Test, the Technical Test Battery, the Wiesen Test of Mechanical Aptitude, the Arco Mechanical Aptitude and Spatial Relations Tests, the Bennett Test of Mechanical Comprehension, the Music Aptitude Profile, the Iowa Test of Music Literacy, the Group Test of Musical Ability, and the Advanced Measures of Music Audiation.

Clerical Aptitude Tests

Clerical aptitude tests Used for screening applicants for clerical jobs

Several tests are available to measure one's aptitude at performing clerical tasks. The Clerical Test Battery (CTB2), published by Psytech, measures clerical skill across a range of abilities, including verbal reasoning, numerical ability, clerical checking, spelling, typing, and filing. The CTB2 takes only 27 minutes to administer, and it can be completed with paper and pencil or on a personal computer. Reliability estimates for the subtests are sound and fall between .81 and .90. Reasonable evidence of validity is provided in the test manual. A similar type of clerical test is the Minnesota Clerical Assessment Battery, which measures traits such as typing, proofreading, filing, business vocabulary, business math, and clerical knowledge. Reliability estimates for the subtests are acceptable; however, Fitzpatrick (2001) questioned whether the publisher had provided adequate evidence of validity.

More than 500,000 people each year take the U.S. Postal Service's 470 Battery Examination (Learning Express, 2001). This test is required for most entry-level positions in the U.S. Postal Service such as clerk, mail handler, carrier, mark-up clerk, mail processor, flat sorter, and distribution clerk. The "470" measures aptitudes such as address checking, memory of addresses, number series, and capacity to follow oral directions. Similarly, those applying for civil service jobs are often required to take the Federal Clerical Exam published by the U.S. Office of Personnel Management. This 120-question test is completed in 100 minutes, and a passing score of 75 is required for most jobs, although the score may be higher for more competitive positions.

Mechanical Aptitude Tests

Mechanical aptitude tests Measure ability to learn mechanical principles and manipulate mechanical objects

Have you ever known people who could look at almost any mechanical-related problem (stalled car, leak underneath the sink, malfunctioning household appliance) and fix it? Obviously there is some learned information (crystallized intelligence) involved, but some people just seem to have a knack for it (fluid intelligence). Mechanical aptitude is generally considered the ability to learn physical and mechanical principles and manipulate mechanical objects. Put another way, it is the ability to understand how mechanical things work. Some people seem to have it, and some don't. (The authors of this book are in the second category.)

Many mechanical aptitude tests are available today, and small manufacturing companies, governmental agencies, and technical institutes frequently use them when they want to measure this ability before hiring or training someone. Benchmark Testware publishes a SkillsProfiler Series that includes mechanical aptitude tests in the areas of machine operator, shop apprentice, automotive mechanic, and industrial electrician. Benchmark Testware has a unique philosophy that mechanical aptitude can best be measured by using test questions related to household plumbing and carpentry rather than more abstract questions about pulleys and levers (Benchmark Testware, 1998). Some of the validity studies performed on the SkillsProfiler tests show remarkably high levels of predictive validity with job performance as rated by supervisors.

Psytech Corporation publishes a mechanical aptitude test called the Technical Test Battery (TTB2). This instrument measures three areas of ability, including mechanical reasoning, spatial reasoning, and visual acuity. The TTB2 has reasonable reliability and validity (Psytech, n.d.). Other common mechanical ability tests include the Wiesen Test of Mechanical Aptitude, the Arco Mechanical Aptitude and Spatial Relations Tests, Fifth Edition, and the Bennett Test of Mechanical Comprehension.

Artistic Aptitude Tests

Artistic aptitude tests Frequently used for art school admissions

Rating artistic ability is not an easy task, and although some tests have been developed (see Figure 8.4), they have not been widely used and have questionable reliability and validity (e.g., Meir Art Test, Graves Design Judgment Test). To demonstrate artistic ability, professional art schools require applicants to submit a portfolio. One of the drawbacks to this process is that a faculty member must usually subjectively score each portfolio, which can cause problems with reliability. One way to improve reliability is to have two or more individuals (raters) practice rating items similar to the ones they will eventually rate. Generally, as the parameters of what they are rating become more clearly defined (e.g., form, appeal, use of color, and so on), their ratings should increasingly be similar. Once they reach a high degree of agreement in their ratings, they are ready to rate the students' pieces (interrater reliability will be discussed in more detail in Chapter 10).

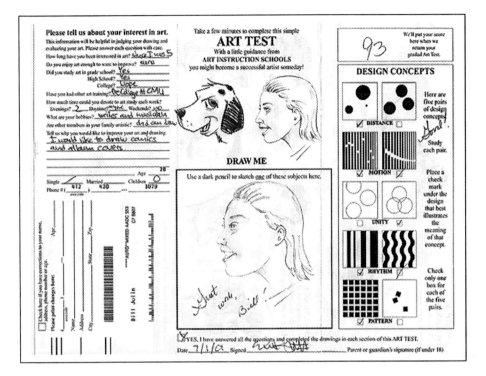

Figure 8.4 Commonly seen art test graphics from local art schools

For some art schools, individuals are asked to draw or copy pictures, such as the one above, and are told professionals will judge them. Unfortunately, this judging is not valid or reliable, and often the test is just a mechanism to attract students to their schools. Professional art schools are more likely to ask individuals to provide complex portfolios that are judged by a number of individuals.

Source: Bill Julin, "The results of my art test," *New Yinzer,* August 14, 2002. Available at www.newyinzer.com <file://www.newyinzer.com>. Reprinted by permission.

Musical Aptitude Tests

Musical aptitude tests Assess knowledge of music

One of the challenges of measuring musical aptitude is to be able to distinguish between one's ability to learn a distinct knowledge base, such as musical theory, history, and rhythm and cadence, and one's ability to actually play an instrument. Although several tests attempt to distinguish the ability to learn information from the ability to perform, they do so with some difficulty.

The Music Aptitude Profile, which is designed for students in grades 4 through 12, involves having the student listen to two musical excerpts and then answer a series of questions pertaining to the music. Traits that are measured include the student's ability to assess harmony, tone, melody, tempo, balance, and style. Unfortunately, test administration is lengthy, running 2½ hours. Split-half reliability coefficients were .90 for composite scores. Although evidence of validity appears fair, when comparing this test with what is defined as musical intelligence by Gardner (see Chapter 7), there is some question as to whether it actually conforms to Gardner's understanding of this trait (Cohen, 1995).

Another music test designed to measure students' "audiation," or the process of thinking about music in one's mind without it actually being there, is the Iowa Test of Music Literacy (Revised). Although it may be classified as an achievement test, it can also be used to determine a student's aptitude for music training. In this test the examinee not only listens to music, but is also required to read sheet music and compare what he or she is reading with what is being played (Radocy, 1998). Still other musical aptitude tests include the Group Test of Musical Ability and the Advanced Measures of Music Audiation.

The Role of Helpers in Occupational and Career Assessment

A wide range of helpers provide occupational and career assessment. For instance, middle school counselors administer interest inventories to help students begin to examine their occupational likes and dislikes. High school counselors and college counselors provide such inventories to help students begin to think about occupational choices and to help them make tentative choices about their college major. High school counselors can also be found orchestrating the administration of multiple aptitude tests and helping students interpret those tests to identify possible vocational strengths. Similarly, private practice clinicians can be found giving interest inventories and aptitude tests to help their clients examine what they are good at and to identify which occupational areas might best fit their personalities. Today, the administration of career and occupational assessment has become big business, and we can even find businesses that specifically focus upon such assessments.

These tests generally do not require advanced training to administer and are used by a wide range of helpers. However, all individuals who do administer such instruments should obtain the basic training necessary to be able to administer such instruments accurately and interpret the results wisely.

Final Thoughts Concerning Occupational and Career Assessment

The tests discussed in this chapter can be fundamental in helping an individual make important decisions regarding occupational and career choices. However, as with all testing, occupational and career assessment should not be done in a vacuum. Understanding the complexities of why one has interests and even abilities and why one ultimately chooses a particular occupation or career can be related to a myriad of reasons including psychodynamic issues (e.g., parental influences), social pressures (e.g., racism, sexism, peer pressure), environmental concerns (e.g, the economy), and family issues (e.g., sibling order). As colleges and universities have increasingly moved toward "career management centers," as opposed to career counseling centers, these issues have become paramount. Choosing a career or occupation should never be based solely on taking a test.

Summary

We began this chapter by highlighting the fact that career and occupational assessment can occur at any point in an individual's life but is often most critical at transitional points. We noted that interest inventories, multiple aptitude tests, and special aptitude tests are often used to assist an individual during these transitions, but that these tests are best used within a counseling context. We defined interest inventories as personality tests that measure likes and dislikes as well as one's personality orientation toward the world of work; multiple aptitude tests as tests that measure a number of homogeneous areas of ability and are used to predict likelihood of success in any of a number of vocational areas; and special aptitude tests as tests that usually measure one homogenous area of ability and are used to predict success in a specific vocational area. We first looked at interest inventories, then examined multiple aptitude tests and special aptitude tests.

The first interest inventory we examined was the Strong, one of the oldest career interest inventories. Its newest version focuses on five areas. The General Occupational Theme uses a Holland code to match personality type with occupations. The Basic Interest Scales also use the Holland code, this time to show how closely an individual's personality aligns with 25 broad interest areas. The Occupational Scales allow an individual to compare his or her interests to the interests of same-sex individuals from 211 occupations. The Personality Style Scales give estimates as to the test-taker's work style (alone or with people), learning environment (practical vs. academic), leadership style (taking charge vs. letting others take charge), and risk taking/adventure orientation (risk taker vs. non risk taker). Finally, the Total Response Index allows the examiner to see how the client responded to the test overall and can be important in identifying response set problems and the possibility of apathy or depression.

The Self-Directed Search (SDS), which was created by John Holland, also uses the Holland Codes and provides a personality orientation based on the client's self-estimates of interests, competencies, and ability. This easy-to-use instrument comes in a number of forms depending on the age and professional level of the client and can be cross-referenced with occupations having a Holland code similar to the client's code.

The next interest inventory we examined was the COPSystem, which is a career measurement package that contains three instruments. The Career Occupational Preference System Interest Inventory (COPS) measures interests, the Career Ability Placement Survey (CAPS) measures ability, and the Career Orientation Placement and Evaluation Survey (COPES) measures values. The scores on these tests can be cross-referenced with a number of career clusters that define occupations in key areas. We ended this section by discussing a few other common interest inventories such as CISS and SIGI PLUS.

In the next part of the chapter we took a look at two Multiple Aptitude Tests: the Armed Services Vocational Aptitude Battery (ASVAB) and the Differential Aptitude Test (DAT). We pointed out that these assessments often use factor analysis to assure that their individual tests they offer are unique and share little in common with one another.

The ASVAB, which is the most widely used multiple aptitude test, consists of eight power tests in the areas of General Science, Arithmetic Reasoning, Word Knowledge, Paragraph Comprehension, Mathematics Knowledge, Electronics Information, Auto and Shop Information, and Mechanical Comprehension. Scores for each of the eight tests, as well as three career exploration (composite) scores, are provided to the examinee. The composite scores can be associated with job occupations in the U.S. Department of Labor's Occupational Information Network (O*NET).

The Differential Aptitude Test (DAT) is for students in grades 7 through 12 and consists of eight separate tests that measure verbal reasoning, numerical reasoning, abstract reasoning, perceptual speed and accuracy, mechanical reasoning, space relations, spelling, and language usage. An alternative version of the DAT for adults called the Differential Aptitude Battery for Personnel and Career Assessment (DAT PCA) is also available and allows employers to determine an individual's current ability and aptitude for learning new skills during training.

In the last part of the chapter we reviewed a number of different kinds of special aptitude tests that are frequently used as a screening process to assess one's ability to perform a certain job or to master a new skill at work. We briefly examined special aptitude tests in the areas of clerical ability, mechanical ability, music ability, and artistic ability.

As the chapter neared its conclusion, we noted that a wide variety of helpers offer career and occupational assessment. Although advanced training is not needed to administer and interpret such instruments, these helpers must obtain the skills needed to be able to administer these tests accurately and interpret the results wisely.

The chapter concluded with a discussion of how occupational and career assessment should not be done in a vacuum. We pointed out that there are frequently a myriad of reasons why a person chooses an occupation or a career, including psychodynamic issues, social pressures, environmental concerns, and family issues. We concluded that choosing an occupation or a career should never be the result of taking a test and that counseling, in addition to assessment, should often be used.

Chapter Review

1. Distinguish between interest inventories, multiple aptitude tests, and special aptitude tests.

2. On the Strong Interest Inventory, there are five different types of interpretive scales or indexes. Describe each of them:
    a. General Occupational Themes
    b. Basic Interest Scales
    c. Occupational Scales
    d. Personal Style Scales
    e. The Total Response Index

3. The Self-Directed Search uses the Holland code to assist in identifying possible personality fit with occupations. Describe how it does this.

4. Describe some possible advantages of the COPSystem over the Strong and the Self-Directed Search.

5. Discuss why factor analysis is important to the development of a good multiple aptitude test.

6. Compare and contrast the different subtests of the ASVAB and the DAT. Which test would you prefer to take?

7. Describe the advantage of a multiple aptitude test, like the DAT, having an interest inventory attached to it.

8. Identify three or four special aptitude tests and discuss why they might be used in lieu of a multiple aptitude test.

9. What might be some disadvantages of special aptitude tests that measure vague constructs like music and art?

10. Discuss the role of the helper in the selection, administration, and interpretation of career and occupational assessment instruments. What kind of training do you think is necessary for an examiner in this area of assessment?

CHAPTER 9

Clinical Assessment: Objective and Projective Personality Tests

Several years ago I was asked to assess a client who had been diagnosed with a multiple personality disorder. At our first meeting, she told me that she had 254 personalities. I was fascinated. However, I was not testing her for the disorder, as she was in treatment, accepted her disorder, and was working hard on integrating her personalities. However, she had been denied Social Security disability compensation, and I had been asked to assess her ability to work. Thus, I needed to carefully choose the tests that I would use to assess her. When I had finished administering the tests, I concluded that she was not able to work at that time, but in a year she might be able to do so. She was not happy with my conclusion.

One of my former students was doing her dissertation on the relationship between self-actualizing values and the number of years one had meditated. She went to an Ashram and obtained permission from dozens of meditators to participate in her study. Using a test to measure self-actualizing values, she tested the meditators and correlated the test results with the number of years individuals had been meditating. She was quite surprised to find no relationship and subsequently came up to me and said, "There must be something wrong with this study, because I know there is a relationship!" I suggested that there was nothing wrong with her study and that not finding a relationship did not mean that meditation wasn't worthwhile, and indeed, it had already been found to be related to many attributes such as reduced stress levels. She ended up a bit dejected, but with a broader understanding of the limitations of objective tests.

I once was asked to do a broad personality assessment for a high school student some teachers were concerned about. I conducted a clinical interview and gave him some objective and projective tests and was somewhat surprised when a number of the projective tests clearly had a theme of destruction. I duly noted this in my report and warned the school about what I had found. Shortly afterward, he was arrested for property destruction! (Ed Neukrug)

This chapter is about clinical assessment, which often includes a clinical interview, objective testing, and/or projective testing. As you can see from the examples above, such assessments have a wide variety of applications and can be an important tool for the clinician or researcher. In this chapter we will define clinical assessment and examine some of the major objective and projective tests used in the clinical assessment process.

Defining Clinical Assessment

Clinical assessment is the process of assessing clients through multiple methods, including the clinical interview (see Chapter 12), the administration of informal assessment techniques (Chapter 10), and the administration of objective and projective tests. This process is used to gather information from clients for the following purposes:

1. To help clients gain greater insight,
2. To aid in case conceptualization and mental health diagnostic formulations,
3. To assist in making decisions concerning the use of psychotropic medications,
4. To assist in treatment planning,
5. To assist in court decisions (e.g., custody decisions; testing a defendant in a child molestation case),
6. To assist in job placement decisions (e.g., candidates for high-security jobs),
7. To aid in diagnostic decisions for health-related problems (e.g., Alzheimer's),
8. To identify individuals at risk (e.g., students at risk for suicide or students with low self-esteem).

In the rest of this chapter we will look at a number of objective and projective tests used in the clinical assessment process.

Objective Personality Testing

As discussed in Chapter 1, objective personality testing is a type of personality assessment that uses paper-and-pencil tests, often in multiple-choice or true/false formats, to assess various aspects of personality. Each objective personality test

TABLE 9.1
Objective Personality Tests and Their General Use

TEST NAME	GENERAL USE
Minnesota Multiphasic Personality Inventory (MMPI-2)	Psychopathology and Axis I disorders
Millon Clinical Multiaxial Inventory (MCM-III)	Personality disorders (Axis II) and symptomatology
Beck Depression Inventory II (BDI-II)	Presence and severity of depression
Myers-Briggs Type Indicator (MBTI)®	Personality types based on Jung's theory of personality (non-clinical population)
California Psychological Inventory (CPI)™	General personality characteristics (non-clinical population)
Coopersmith's Self-Esteem Inventory (SEI)	Level of self-esteem

Objective personality tests Paper-and-pencil tests to assess various aspects of personality

measures different aspects of an individual's personality based on the specific constructs defined by the test developer. For example, the Minnesota Multiphasic Personality Inventory (MMPI) measures psychopathology and is used to assist in diagnosis of emotional disorders. The Myers-Briggs Type Indicator (MBTI)® measures personality based on a construct created by Carl Jung of how people perceive their world and make judgments about it, and Coopersmith's Self-Esteem Inventory (SEI) measures self-esteem based on one's perception of self. Although these three tests measure very different aspects of personality, they all can be useful in building a picture of a client and his or her world. Let's take a look at some of the more common objective personality tests and explore how they are used.

Common Objective Personality Tests

Objective personality tests assess various aspects of personality and may increase client insight, identify pathology, and assist in treatment planning; however, how they do this can vary dramatically. In this section we will highlight six objective personality tests, each of which has a slightly different emphasis (see Table 9.1). In addition, some other popular objective tests will be briefly noted at the end of this section of the chapter.

Minnesota Multiphasic Personality Inventory – 2

MMPI-2 Assists in identifying psychopathology; takes skill to interpret

The most widely used diagnostic personality test is the Minnesota Multiphasic Personality Inventory (MMPI). The test was developed by Hathaway and McKinley in 1942, and the latest edition, the MMPI-2, was introduced in 1989 (Butcher, Dahlstrom, Graham, Tellegen, & Kaemmer, 1989). Since the MMPI-2 requires an eighth-grade reading level (Butcher et al., 1989), a version specific to

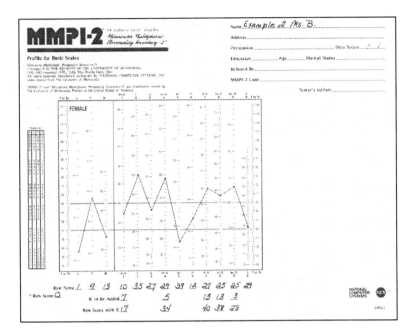

Figure 9.1 MMPI-2 profile form for basic scales

Based on the clinical interview of Mr. A, above, and his MMPI-2 profile, he has a diagnostic impression of dysthymia with hypochondriacal features.

Source: From Butcher et al. (1989). *Manual for administration and scoring: MMPI-2.* Copyright © by The Regents of the University of Minnesota 1942, 1943 (renewed 1970), 1989. This profile is Form 1989. All rights reserved. Reprinted by permission of University of Minnesota Press.

Three of six validity scales are particularly important for interpretation, and ten basic (clinical) scales are helpful in diagnosis.

adolescents was later released in 1992 as the MMPI-A. Both versions can be administered individually or in groups and require approximately 90 minutes for test-takers to complete the 567 items by hand. A computerized version is somewhat faster (Groth-Marnat, 2003). Although administration and scoring of the MMPI-2 is relatively straightforward, interpretation of the test is not. The manual states, "Interpreting it demands a high level of psychometric, clinical, personological, and professional sophistication as well as a strong commitment to the ethical principles of test usage" (Butcher et al., 1989, p. 11). To be qualified to adminster the test, examiners must have taken a minimum of a graduate level course in psychological testing and a graduate level course in psychopathology.

The MMPI-2 provides six validity scales, ten basic (clinical) scales, and fifteen content scales. However, the most commonly used scales are three of the validity scales and the ten basic scales (see Figure 9.1 and Table 9.2).

In interpreting the MMPI, it is important to understand the meaning of each scale. For example, a high L (Lie) score does not necessarily indicate compulsive lying but does indicate that the client is having trouble acknowledging his or her faults and that the entire test results are suspect and may have been "spoiled" (Butcher et al., 1989, p. 23). The Basic or Clinical Scales are particularly useful

TABLE 9.2
Most Commonly Used Scales of the MMPI–2

ABBREVIATION AND SCALE NUMBER	NAME	BRIEF DESCRIPTION
Validity Scales		
L	Lie	Lacks ability to admit minor faults or character flaws; does not necessarily indicate "lying," but that test scores may have been "spoiled."
F	Infrequency	Reflects random scoring which may indicate unwillingness to cooperate, poor reading skills, or "faking bad" to gain special attention.
K	Correction	Tendency to "slant" or "spin" answers to minimize appearance of poor emotional control or personal ineffectiveness.
Basic (Clinical) Scales		
Hs – 1	Hypochondriasis	Excessive concern regarding health with little or no organic basis, and rejecting reassurance of no physical problem.
D – 2	Depression	Depression and/or a depressive episode with feelings of discouragement, pessimism, and hopelessness.
Hy – 3	Conversion Hysteria	Conversion disorders where a sensory or motor problem has no organic basis; denial and lack of social anxiety often accompany symptoms.
Pd – 4	Psychopathic deviant	Frequent hostility toward authority, law, or social convention, with no basis in cultural deprivation, subnormal intelligence, or other disorders.
Mf – 5	Masculinity-femininity	Gender-role confusion and attempting to control homoerotic feelings; also emotions, interests, hobbies differing from one's gender group.
Pa – 6	Paranoia	Paranoia marked by interpersonal sensitivities and tendency to misinterpret intentions and motives of others.
Pt – 7	Psychasthenia	Obsessive-compulsive concerns (excessive worries and compulsive rituals) as well as generalized anxiety and distress.
Sc – 8	Schizophrenia	Wide range of strange beliefs, unusual experiences, and special sensitivities; often accompanied by social or emotional alienation.
Ma – 9	Hypomania	Displaying symptoms found in a manic episode such as hyperactivity, flight of ideas, euphoria, or emotional excitability.
Si – 0	Social introversion	High scores indicate increasing levels of social shyness and desire for solitude; low scores indicate the opposite (social participation).

in diagnosis and treatment planning, and patterns of responses by clients are often used in making decisions about clients as opposed to examining an individual score on any one scale. Since hundreds of patterns can arise from ten scales, computerized scoring is helpful in quickly finding a diagnosis, interpreting client issues, and treatment planning. The MMPI-2 defines "clinical significance" as a T score of 65 or greater, whereas the older MMPI established clinical significance as a T score of 70 or higher.

The Content Scales, which are not as frequently used, identify 15 specific traits such as anxiety, fears, anger, cynicism, and low self-esteem, and are useful in creating a more detailed perspective of the client as well as identifying other considerations for counseling.

As compared to the original MMPI, the MMPI-2 has 82 rewritten items. However, these items are so "psychometrically equivalent" to the original test that they have a .98 correlation; hence, the clinical scales are virtually unchanged (Graham, 2000, p. 189). To renorm the MMPI-2 against the non-clinical population, it was restandardized against a sample that included 2600 people living in seven states and was fairly representative of the 1980 U.S. Census; however, both Hispanic and Asian-Americans were slightly underrepresented in the sample (Butcher et al., 1989). Test-retest reliabilities for the basic scales range between .67 and .92 for normal males and .58 and .91 for a similar sample of women. Internal consistency estimates using the Cronbach alpha for the basic scales ranged between .34 and .87. The only evidence of validity provided in the MMPI-2 manual is discriminant validity. As you may recall, discriminant validity is the ability of the instrument to differentiate between different constructs. For example, MMPI-2 scores in depression should be minimally related to scores in hypochondriasis or conversion hysteria. However, the intercorrelations between scales were found to be quite high, primarily because many of the scales share test items (Groth-Marnat, 2003).

Millon Clinical Multiaxial Inventory, Third Edition

MCMI
Used to assess personality disorders (Axis II) and clinical symptomatology

The Millon Clinical Multiaxial Inventory (MCMI) has become the second most used objective personality test (Camara, Nathan, & Puente, 2000). The latest version of this test is designed to assess DSM-IV-TR personality disorders and clinical symptomatology (NCS Pearson, 2004). The MCMI-III, which is generally called the "Millon" (Mill-*on*), focuses on DSM-IV-TR Axis II disorders in contrast to the MMPI's focus on Axis I disorders (Groth-Marnat, 2003). The Millon has 175 true/false items, is written at an eighth-grade reading level, and is designed for individuals 18 years or older. Hence, there is also an adolescent version for ages 13 to 19 called the Millon Adolescent Clinical Inventory or MACI (NCS Pearson, 2005c).

The MCMI-III is much quicker to administer than the MMPI, requiring only 25 minutes (NCS Pearson, 2004). It can be taken via paper-and-pencil or on a computer. Scoring the Millon can be accomplished by using computer software, hand scoring, optical scan scoring, or a mail-in scoring service. The Millon has six different major scales: Clinical Personality Pattern Scales, Severe Personality Pathology Scales, Clinical Syndrome Scales, Severe Clinical Syndrome Scales,

TABLE 9.3
The Millon Clinical Multiaxial Inventory-III Scales

MAJOR SCALES	SUB-SCALE	NAME
Clinical Personality Pattern Scales		
	Scale 1	Schizoid
	Scale 2A	Avoidant
	Scale 2B	Depressive
	Scale 3	Dependent
	Scale 4	Histrionic
	Scale 5	Narcissistic
	Scale 6A	Antisocial
	Scale 6B	Aggressive/Sadistic
	Scale 7	Compulsive
	Scale 8A	Passive-Aggressive
	Scale 8B	Self-Defeating
Severe Personality Pathology Scales		
	Scale S	Schizotypal
	Scale C	Borderline
	Scale P	Paranoid
Clinical Syndrome Scales		
	Scale A	Anxiety
	Scale H	Somatoform
	Scale N	Bipolar: Manic
	Scale D	Dysthymia
	Scale B	Alcohol Dependence
	Scale T	Drug Dependence
	Scale R	Post-Traumatic Stress Disorder
Severe Clinical Syndrome Scales		
	Scale SS	Thought Disorder
	Scale CC	Major Depression
	Scale PP	Delusional Disorder
Modifying Indices		
	Scale X	Disclosure
	Scale Y	Desirability
	Scale Z	Debasement
Validity Index		
	V	Validity

Modifying Indices, and a Validity Index. The sub-scales to these major scales can be seen in Table 9.3.

The Millon uses a unique scoring method called the Base Rate (BR) that converts a raw score to a more meaningful standardized score based primarily on the psychiatric population. To do this, the publishers change the actual median for a non-psychiatric, or normal person, by setting it at 35, while the actual median for the psychiatric population is also changed and set at 60. A BR of 75 indicates that some of the features of that characteristic are present, while a BR of 85 indicates that the trait is clearly present (Groth-Marnat, 2003).

The norms for the interpretive report came from a clinical sampling of 998 people with a wide variety of diagnoses (NCS Pearson, 2004). There is also an additional norm group that can be used for a special Corrections Report that is based on 1,676 incarcerated inmates. The Corrections Report provides information that may be of value when doing a forensic evaluation, such as probable need for mental health services, probable need for anger management services, escape risk, suicidal tendencies, and so on (NCS Pearson, 2004).

Reliability coefficient alphas ranged from .67 to .90 for the scales and were predominately in the .80s (Millon as cited in Groth-Marnat, 2003). With regard to evidence of validity based on other variables (convergent validity), the MCMI-2 scales have been correlated with several other scales and measures such as the MMPI and the BDI. In general, most of the correlations were healthy and expected. One surprise was a low correlation (.29) between the MCMI-III Paranoid scale and the MMPI-2 Paranoia scale. Other studies using the MCMI-2 have demonstrated moderate to high predictive validity for the instrument with DSM-IV-TR diagnoses.

Beck Depression Inventory-II

BDI-II
Quick and easy method to assess depression

Originally introduced in 1961 by Aaron Beck and his colleagues, the Beck Depression Inventory (BDI) was designed to measure severity of depression (Beck, Steer, & Brown, 2003). The newer version, the BDI-II, was released in 1996, and today the inventory is ranked among the ten most frequently used psychological assessment instruments (Camara et al., 2000).

The BDI-II, which takes only 10 minutes to complete, asks clients to rate 21 questions on a scale from 0 to 3 based on depressive symptoms during the preceding two weeks. Scores are obtained by adding up the total points from the series of answers and are interpreted based on the scales listed in Table 9.4.

When giving the BDI-II, special attention should be directed to questions 2 (hopelessness), and 9 (suicidal ideation), as scores of 2 or higher may indicate a higher risk of suicide (Beck et al., 2003). The BDI-II is quite useful in identifying

TABLE 9.4
Interpreting Beck Depression Inventory Scores

SCORE	LEVEL OF DEPRESSION
0 to 13	No or minimal depression
14 to 19	Mild depression
20 to 28	Moderate depression
29 to 63 (maximum)	Severe depression
Below 4	Possible faking good

and assessing the severity of symptoms of depression; however, as with all tests, it should not be used as a sole criterion for making a diagnosis. Due to its ease of administration, the instrument is also useful as a means of measuring client progress by having the client take the instrument on an ongoing basis (Beck, 1995).

The norm group for the BDI-II included 500 outpatients who had been diagnosed with depression using the DSM-III-R or the DSM-IV. Another smaller sample of 120 Canadian college students was used as a normal comparative group (Beck et al., 2003). Using coefficient alpha, reliability was found to be .92 for outpatients and .93 for college students. As compared to the BDI, the content and criterion validity were increased in the BDI-II by having it more closely conform to the DSM-IV diagnosis criteria. In a study of convergent validity, a correlation of .93 was found for depressed outpatient clients who took both the BDI and BDI-II, and obtained means for the tests were 18.92 and 21.88, respectively (Beck et al., 2003). As was found in this study, scores on the BDI-II are generally about 3 points higher than those on the BDI. Finally, having clients with other disorders take the instrument, and finding scores that were not as high as those of clients with depression, showed discriminant validity.

Myers-Briggs Type Indicator®*

MBTI
Popular method to assess normal personality; based on Carl Jung's psychological types

More than two million people each year take the Myers-Briggs Type Indicator (MBTI)® test, making it the most widely used personality assessment for normal functioning (Quenk, 2000). Although the MBTI® instrument has enjoyed tremendous success and been used in a variety of settings, there has also been a "gap" between scientists' and practitioners' regard for the instrument, which the latest versions have attempted to mend (Mastrangelo, 2001). The MBTI® instrument is based on the original work of Carl Jung (1921/1964) and his book *Psychological Types*. Through observation, Jung noted that people have basic characteristics along a diametrically opposed continuum regarding several factors, including extroversion or introversion, sensing or intuiting, thinking or feeling.

After reading Jung's book, Katharine Briggs and her daughter Isabel Briggs Myers became fascinated with Jung's typology of people. They ultimately added a fourth dimension to Jung's factors, which they called judging versus perceiving (Fleenor, 2001; Quenk, 2000). Believing this typology could help people with career selection and better understanding of self and others, they created an instrument that eventually became known as the Myers-Briggs Type Indicator®. In 1975 the instrument was sold to CPP, Inc., who continue to update and publish it.

Today the MBTI® instrument is used in a wide variety of settings: in therapists' offices to assist clients to develop a deeper understanding of self; in marriage and family counseling sessions and workshops to help clients examine

---

* Myers-Briggs Type Indicator is a trademark or registered trademark of the Myers-Briggs Type Indicator Trust in the United States and other countries.

EXTRAVERSION (E) ---------------------------- INTROVERSION (I)
Energy directed   Energy directed inward
outward to people and   to ideas and concepts
objects

SENSING (S) -------------------------------- INTUITION (N)
Perception comes   Perception comes
mainly from the five   mainly from observing
senses   patterns and hunches

THINKING (T) ------------------------------- FEELING (F)
Decisions are based on   Decisions are based on
logic, fact, and   personal and social
rationality   values

JUDGING (J) -------------------------------- PERCEIVING (P)
Makes decision quickly   Makes decisions based
based on T or F; likes   on S or N; likes
organization, planning,   spontaneity, flexibility,
schedules   and diversions

Figure 9.2 The four MBTI® dichotomies

differences and similarities of personality types in families; in business and industry to help employees understand why individuals respond the way that they do; and in career counseling to help individuals find careers that match their personality types.

The four dimensions of the MBTI® instrument can be seen in Figure 9.2, and assessment results indicate preferences respondents favor across these four dichotomies. For example, social workers, counselors, and psychologists are often INFP, INFJ, and ENFJ types, while police officers are often ISTJ or ESTJ types. Although some use the MBTI® as a career selection tool, the manual states that it should not be used as a screening tool for hiring employees (Mastrangelo, 2001).

The latest versions of the MBTI® instrument are forms M and Q. Form M was released in 1998 and contains 93 items with improved accuracy using Item Response Theory (IRT). Form M only takes 15 to 25 minutes to administer, is written at a seventh-grade reading level, and is geared toward individuals 14 and older. It can be hand scored, computer scored, or mailed to the publisher for scoring. A computer-generated profile sheet for form M can be seen in Figure 9.3. Form Q was released in 2001 and has 144 items, takes 25 to 35 minutes to administer, and is for adults 18 and older. Form Q also uses IRT and the same norm group that form M uses (CPP, 2002). The norm group for forms M and Q was a national randomized sample of 3,200 adults. Coefficient alphas for form M

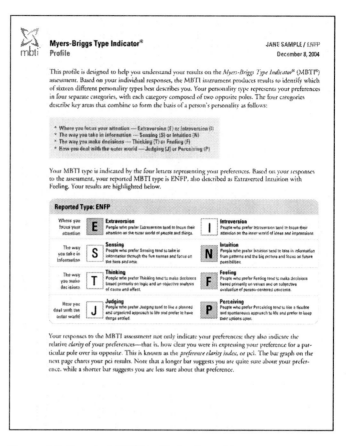

Figure 9.3 Sample MBTI® Profile for Form M

Source: Modified and reproduced by special permission of the Publisher, CPP, Inc., Mountain View, CA 94043 from Myers-Briggs Type Indicator® Form M by Katharine C. Briggs, Isabel Briggs Myers. Copyright 1998 by Peter B. Myers and Katharine D. Myers. All rights reserved. Further reproduction is prohibited without the Publisher's written consent. Myers-Briggs Type Indicator, MBTI, Myers-Briggs, and Introduction to Type are trademarks or registered trademarks of the Myers-Briggs Type Indicator Trust in the United States and other countries.

are generally .90 or higher for each dichotomous scale (CPP, 2002). However, another study in the manual using test-retest reliability across all four dichotomies had only 65% of the participants receiving the same score after only four weeks (Mastrangelo, 2001). The MBTI® manual reports several studies providing some evidence of validity. Evidence is sound for the four separate scales, but it is lacking for the synergistic combination of the four scales (Mastrangelo, 2001). Another study showing evidence of validity found that 90% of the people taking the test agreed with the results on a self-report best fit. Further evidence of validity was found by comparing MBTI® results with the California Psychological Inventory discussed in the next section.

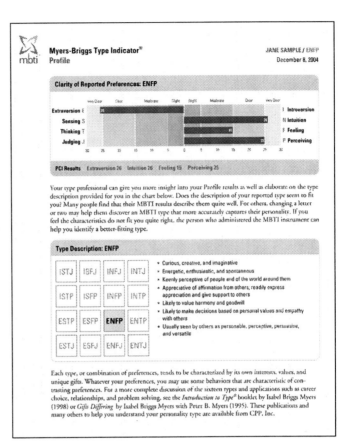

Figure 9.3 Continued

California Psychological Inventory (CPI)™*

CPI
Measures basic
personality traits
of "normal"
clients

The California Psychological Inventory™, Form 434 (CPI 434), is a version of a personality inventory that was developed more than 50 years ago. Used to describe basic personality characteristics, the CPI™ is generally given to non-psychopathological or normal clients to further client insight and has been used extensively as a research instrument. As the name implies, it has 434 items. The CPI™ can be given individually or in a group setting, is geared toward individuals aged 13 years or older, and takes approximately 45 to 60 minutes to complete. Although it can be used for a wide age group, almost two-thirds of its 6000-person norm group were high school or undergraduate students (Atkinson, 2003). A shorter version of the instrument, the CPI™ 260, is well suited for business use.

---

* California Psychological Inventory is a trademark of CPP, Inc.

20 folk scales and 3 vector scales are useful in personality assessment.

The CPI™ 434 results contain three categories of scales: 20 Folk Scales, three Vector Scales, and 13 Special Purpose scales. Further details of the Folk Scales and Vector Scales can be seen in Table 9.5.

The 13 Special Scales are available only through CPP's computer scoring report. The Special Scales tend to be career and business related and have scales such as managerial potential, work orientation, creative temperament, leadership potential, amicability, law enforcement orientation, and so forth.

Raw scores on the Folk Scales are converted to T scores (M = 50, SD = 10) (see sample profile in Figure 9.4). However, some scales use a 60 or higher as a "high" score while other scales might not be considered "high" until they reach a T of 70. Using the manual can facilitate interpretation of the scores. Although the test views high scores as indicative of positive mental health (except for the femininity/masculinity scale), in practice some individuals would favor a low score on the same quality for which others might favor a high score (e.g., "dominance").

Using internal consistency, mean reliability estimates for the CPI were found to be .76 while test-retest reliability had a mean estimate of .68 (Hattrup, 2003). Although the CPI™ is a frequently used instrument, evidence of validity has been criticized due to the fact that some of the separate scales do not discriminate clearly from one another, with correlations among some scales registering as high as .82 (Hattrup, 2003). This is likely the result of the test developer simply choosing the 20 Folk Scales based on what was interesting to him, as opposed to any sound theoretical construct. Despite this limitation, many of the scales still hold quite a bit of interest for clinicians working with clients.

Coopersmith's Self-Esteem Inventory

Coopersmith's SEI
Assesses self-esteem of children in relation to general self, peers, parents, and school

Coopersmith's Self-Esteem Inventory (SEI) is designed to measure self-esteem of children aged 8 through 15 (Coopersmith, 1989). The inventory measures how children regard themselves in relation to four areas: general self (24 items), self in relation to peers (8 items), self in relation to parents (8 items), and self in relation to school (8 items). A total score is obtained by multiplying by 2 the total number of positive self-esteem items chosen by the child. Generally, a total self-esteem score is obtained first, and with individuals showing evidence of low self-esteem, the examiner can go back to the four subscores and determine if one or more areas are particularly low. A lie scale that comprises eight of the items is scored separately, and the authors vaguely state that a "high" lie score can indicate defensiveness. A short form of the test is also available. This form uses 25 of the items and in this case, only a total score is obtained. This form can be used with children and an adapted version of this form has also been used with adults.

Although the manual shows some impressive reliability data, such as internal consistency reliability that ranges from .87 to .90 for grades 4 through 8, the information is based on some rather dated studies that go back to the early 1970s (Coopersmith, 1989). Similarly, although evidence of construct, concurrent, and predictive validity is given in the manual, the studies are rather dated and some of the studies show meager validity data.

TABLE 9.5
The CPI™ Form 434 Scales

ABBREVIATION	NAME	BRIEF DESCRIPTION
Folk Scales		
Do	Dominance	Leadership ability
Cs	Capacity for status	Characteristics such as ambition and self-confidence that are required for social status
Sy	Sociability	Desire for or avoidance of social situations
Sp	Social presence	Assertiveness and self-assurance
Sa	Self-acceptance	Feelings of self-worth and emotional security
In	Independence	Need for autonomy at work and in relationships
Em	Empathy	Ability to perceive the inner world of another person
Re	Responsibility	Dependability, trustworthiness, and rational sense of duty to society's needs
So	Socialization	Social maturity and automatic adherence to social norms
Sc	Self-control	Self-direction and control of behavior versus impulsiveness and pleasure seeking
Gi	Good impression	Mainly a validity scale to determine if a person is "faking good"
Cm	Communality	Validity scale to detect random answering
Wb	Well-being	Level of adjustment and psychological distress; also "faking bad"
To	Tolerance	Designed to assess how accepting and non-judgmental one is
Ac	Achievement via conformance	Orientation to achievement and the preference for a structured environment to achieve
Ai	Achievement via independence	Used to predict success in college based on presence of self-motivation
Ie	Intellectual efficiency	Ability to effectively use resources, think clearly, and make plans
Py	Psychological-mindedness	Insight into others' behaviors; also interest in scholarly research
Fx	Flexibility	Ability to adapt and change thinking/behaviors; high scores may indicate emotional volatility
F/M	Femininity/Masculinity	Consistency of beliefs, values, and occupations with traditional gender roles
Vector Scales		
Vector 1	Externality-internality	Extroversion versus introversion, as well as confidence and self-assurance
Vector 2	Norm-favoring versus norm questioning	Preference for following societal norms and social conformity
Vector 3	Self-realization	Measures one's level of self-understanding or self-realization

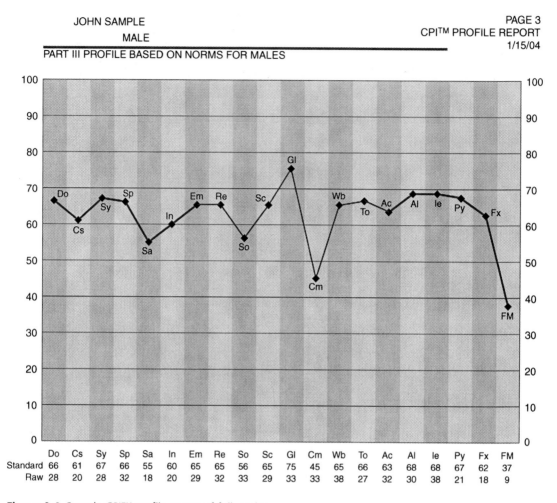

PART III PROFILE BASED ON NORMS FOR MALES

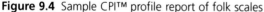

	Do	Cs	Sy	Sp	Sa	In	Em	Re	So	Sc	Gl	Cm	Wb	To	Ac	Al	Ie	Py	Fx	FM
Standard	66	61	67	66	55	60	65	65	56	65	75	45	65	66	63	68	68	67	62	37
Raw	28	20	28	32	18	20	29	32	33	29	33	33	38	27	32	30	38	21	18	9

Figure 9.4 Sample CPI™ profile report of folk scales

On a positive note, the authors gave the instrument to students in a number of different settings, and thus have broad ethnic comparisons. As a result of differential total scores that are an apparent function of ethnicity, they do not offer one score that is representative of high self-esteem, and instead they leave interpretation of the student's self-esteem score up to the test administrator. They do note that self-esteem should be viewed in broad categories (e.g., low, medium, and high), rather than just one number. Generally speaking, mean scores ranged from the mid-50s to the mid-70s for most of the studies, and the range of standard deviations was between approximately 12 and 20. Finally, due to the dated nature of the instrument, some of the questions may seem a little odd or unclear to some students. Thus, the test is best given one-on-one to assure that students understand the items. This has implications, of course, for group testing, which is desired by some school counselors and others who work with children. Thus, professionals who are interested in examining the self-esteem of children may also want to examine other similar measures, such as the Piers-Harris Children's Self-Concept Scale, the Tennessee Self-Concept Scale, the Multidimensional Self-Esteem Inventory (MSEI), and the Culture-Free Self-Esteem Inventory.

Other Common Objective Personality Tests

Numerous other objective personality tests are available, but we have room to describe just a few of these personality instruments here. The 16 PF Fifth Edition primarily measures 16 different personality factors identified by Raymond Cattell. It also assesses five global factors, three validity scales and has options for vocational scores (Holland type), criterion scores (such as emotionality, sociability, and creativity), and a couple's compatibility score. The instrument is for ages 16 and older, takes less than 50 minutes to administer, and can be taken online or with paper and pencil (NCS Pearson, 2005d). The Taylor-Johnson Temperament Analysis 2002 Edition assesses personality variables that affect social, family, marital, work, and other environments. It is used in counseling emotionally normal adolescents and adults as individuals, couples, families, or in vocational situations (Axford & Boyle, 2005). Both the 16 PF and the Taylor-Johnson Temperament Analysis can be used for relationship assessment; however, other instruments have been created specifically to appraise marriages or partnerships. For instance, the Marital Satisfaction Inventory – Revised (MSI-R) is an instrument to assess the severity and nature of the conflict in a relationship or partnership. The inventory takes only 25 minutes to administer, is inexpensive, and has respectable validity and reliability, making it a nice tool for therapists doing relationship counseling (Bernt & Frank, 2001).

Projective Testing

Projective tests Responses to stimuli are used to interpret personality factors

In Chapter 1, projective personality testing was defined as a type of personality assessment in which a client is presented a stimulus to which to respond, and subsequently, personality factors are interpreted based on the client's responses. We noted that such testing is often used to identify psychopathology and to assist in treatment planning.

When interpretations about client responses are made, they are often based on normative data. However, because clients are responding in an open-ended manner to vague stimuli, the number and kind of responses are innumerable, and the validity of many of these tests is often called into question. Despite this limitation, projective tests can be quite helpful as one additional tool in the clinical assessment process. Dozens of projective tests exist, and we will explore some of the more prevalent ones.

Common Projective Tests

The most popular projective tests include the Thematic Apperception Test (TAT), the Rorschach Inkblot Test, the Bender Visual-Motor Gestalt Test, Second Edition, the House-Tree-Person, the Kinetic House-Tree-Person Test, the Sentence Completion Series, and the EPS Sentence Completion. The following discussion offers a brief overview of these instruments.

The Thematic Apperception Test and Related Instruments

TAT
Clients create a story based on cards with vague pictures; TAT is based on Murray's need-press personality theory.

The Thematic Apperception Test (TAT) was developed by Henry Murray and his colleagues in 1938 and consists of a series of 31 cards with vague pictures on them, although only 8 to 12 cards are generally used during an assessment depending on the age and gender of the client as well as the client's presenting issues. Showing the cards one at a time, the examiner asks the client to create and describe a story that has a beginning, middle, and end. The storytelling process allows great access to the client's inner world and shows how that world is affected by the client's needs and by environmental forces, known as press.

The ambiguous pictures on the cards are more structured than inkblot tests such as the Rorschach; consequently, the TAT tends to draw out from the client issues related more to current life situations than deep-seated personality structures (Groth-Marnat, 2003) (see Figure 9.5). The TAT is based on Murray's need-press personality theory, which states that people are driven by their internal desires, such as attitudes, values, goals, etc. (needs), or by external stimuli (press) from the environment. Therefore, individuals are constantly struggling to balance these two opposing forces (Groth-Marnat, 2003).

The TAT has been extensively researched; however, it still lacks a level of standardization that most objective personality tests have achieved (Groth-Marnat, 2003). There is no universally agreed upon scoring and interpretation method, although most clinicians use a qualitative process of interpreting responses. Hence there is considerable controversy over reliability and validity of the instrument. When scoring systems have been used in a controlled setting, interscorer reliability has been as high as .82 (Pennebaker & King, 1999); however, if responses were interpreted by clinicians outside of a laboratory setting, this figure would likely drop (Groth-Marnat, 2003). Studies to show evidence of validity have been difficult to perform due to the nature of this projective test, but some argue that objective studies of validity are not as important for this test as for other types of instruments (Karon, 2000). For instance, some suggest that the rich narrative detail developed through the TAT gives the therapist a unique window into the client's psyche. Indeed, the value of the TAT seems to be supported by its widespread use, as it is the sixth most frequently used test by clinical psychologists (Camara et al., 2000) (see Table in Section Three Introduction).

Due to the age of the cards, and the fact that the human figures in the cards are almost exclusively white, many of the cards may seem biased and dated at first glance. Attempts to counter some of the TAT's problems include Southern

Figure 9.5 TAT Figure 12F

Source: Pearson Assessments. 2004. Thematic Apperception Test. Available from http://www.pearsonassessments.com. Reprinted by permission of Pearson Assessments.

Mississippi's TAT (SM-TAT), and the Apperceptive Personality Test (APT). The APT has only eight cards with multicultural pictures and an objective scoring method. Although the SM-TAT and APT are probably superior instruments (more modern, more rigorous methodology, and greater validity), the long tradition of the TAT will probably prevent its replacement (Groth-Marnat, 2003).

In addition to the TAT, the Children's Apperception Test (CAT), designed for children ages 3 to 10, has been developed. This instrument has only 10 cards (because of children's shorter attention spans), and the pictures depict animals rather than humans (because it was thought that children could relate more easily to animals). In addition, a later version of the CAT, the CAT-H, was made that depicts humans. Despite the development of these instruments, the TAT is still frequently used with children, probably due to its familiarity among clinicians.

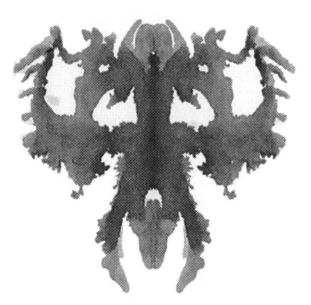

Figure 9.6 Inkblot similar to those on the Rorschach

Source: www.albinoblacksheep.com (2005). Inkblot test. Retrieved on January 29, 2005, from http://www.albinoblacksheep.com/flash/inkblot.php

Rorschach Inkblot Test

Rorschach Inkblot Test Clients are asked to identify what they see in 10 inkblots; the unconscious mind "projects" itself onto the image.

Herman Rorschach developed his famous inkblot test in 1921 by splattering ink onto pieces of paper and folding them in half to form a symmetrical image (see Figure 9.6). After much experimentation, he chose 10 cards to create the Rorschach Inkblot Test that is still used today. When giving the Rorschach, clinicians show clients cards, one at a time, and ask them to talk about what they see on the card. A follow-up inquiry with clients addresses issues of what they actually saw, how they saw it, and where on the card it was seen. Ultimately, the clinician wants to see exactly what the client saw on the card.

Rorschach, a student of Carl Jung, believed the ambiguous shapes of the inkblots allowed the test-taker to project his or her unconscious mind onto these images. By 1959 the Rorschach had become the most frequently used instrument in clinical practice (Sundberg, 1961), and it continues to be the most frequently used projective personality test (Camara et al., 2000). Although it has had tremendous popularity, it has also been closely scrutinized and criticized. By 1955, more than 3,000 journal articles had been written about it (Exner, 1974), and a recent ERIC and PsychInfo database search shows more than 8500 articles in which the Rorschach is cited. The greatest difficulty with the Rorschach has been providing

BOX 9.1
Rorschach Use in Clinical Practice

Card IV of the Rorschach is known by some as the "father card" because it shows what some see as a hefty, overbearing figure with a large penis. When I was giving the Rorschach to a 17-year-old female high school student, I obtained what is sometimes called a "shock response." I showed her this card and although she had made fairly normal responses to the other cards, when seeing this card she said to me, rather emphatically, "I see nothing there." Upon inquiry later, I again asked her to give me a response to that card, at which point she firmly put the card face down and said, "I told you I didn't see anything there." When all testing was complete, I looked at the young woman and asked, "Were you molested?" at which point she broke down and started to sob…. This was the beginning of counseling for this young woman who had never shared this secret before.

—*Ed Neukrug*

adequate validity. Another challenge of the Rorschach test is that it requires extensive training and practice to use. However, the authors of the current text believe this instrument still has merit and can be a useful tool in the assessment process (see Box 9.1).

Exner's scoring system examines location, determinants, and content.

One of the most popular scoring systems for the Rorschach was developed by Exner (1974). This system uses three components: location, determinants, and content. *Location* is the portion of the blot to which the response occurred, and the examinee's responses are broken down into categories such as the whole blot (w), common details (D), unusual details (Dd), and white space details (S). *Determinants* are used to describe the manner in which the examinee understood what he or she saw, and these are broken down into (1) form ("that looks just like a bat"), (2) color (e.g., "it's blood, because it's red") (3) shading ("it looks like smoke because it's grayish-white"). Finally *content* is scored based on 22 categories such as whole human, human detail, animal, art, blood, clouds, fire, household items, sex, and so on. Specific content can hold meaning; for instance, a goat can be an indication of a person being obstinate, or a number of animal responses by an adult could be an indication of immature psychosexual development (children tend to include lots of animals in their responses). Once all of the data have been recorded, a fairly complex series of calculations are used to create numerical ratios, percentages, and derivations with which to interpret the results. Scoring systems such as Exner's are very complex and are important ways of managing the large amount of interpretive material the client is presenting.

Bender Visual-Motor Gestalt Test, Second Edition

Lauretta Bender originally published the Bender Visual-Motor Gestalt Test in 1938. After several revisions, it is now called the Bender Gestalt II. It is a brief

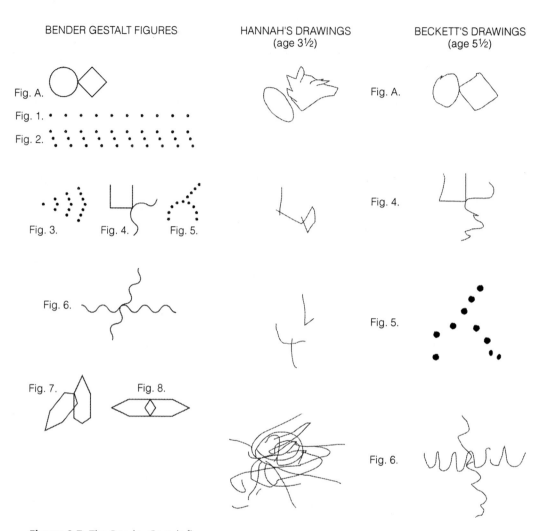

Figure 9.7 The Bender Gestalt figures

Above are reproductions of four of nine figures of the Bender Visual Motor Gestalt from two children who are developmentally on target. When Hannah couldn't reproduce Figure 6, she became very frustrated. Look at how much easier it is for the older child, Beckett, to reproduce the figures.

Bender
Gestalt II
Assists in identifying developmental, psychological, or neurological deficits

test that takes only 5 to 10 minutes to administer and measures an individual's developmental level and psychological functioning, and can be used to assess neurological deficits after a traumatic brain injury. The test asks children aged 4 to 7 and individuals 8 to 85+ to draw the nine figures shown in Figure 9.7. Children 4 to 7 have four additional figures to replicate, and individuals 8 to 85+ have three additional figures to copy.

The latest version of the instrument, the Bender Gestalt II, had a norm group of 4000 individuals who were representative of the 2000 U.S. Census (Riverside Publishing, 2004d). This version uses a new, global, 5-point scoring system. A score of 0 represents no resemblance or scribbling, and a score of 4 represents a nearly perfect drawing (Brannigan, Decker, & Madsen, 2004). This version provides standard scores, T scores, and percentile ranks. As you might suspect, the test can examine psychomotor development of children by comparing a child's response to mean responses of children belonging to the child's age group; personality factors such as compulsivity in completing the drawing accurately (graduate students!); and neurological impairment, such as might be evidenced when an individual cannot accurately place the diamond in drawing 8 (see Figure 9.7).

Individuals are asked to replicate Bender Gestalt figures.

Accurately interpreting a number of these factors takes advanced training and should not be attempted without such a background. The original version of the Bender Gestalt showed some evidence that it was measuring the factors it purported to measure, and reliability data showed test-retest reliability at .84 while interrater reliability was shown to be in the low to mid .90s (Naglieri, Obrzut, & Boliek, 1992). The newest version of the test shows even more promise at measuring the educational and psychological constructs it is designed to measure, and the test should continue to evidence high reliability estimates (Brannigan, Decker, & Madsen, 2004).

House-Tree-Person and Other Drawing Tests

Drawing tests Quick, simple, and effective projective tests

It's not quite clear when the use of drawing tests began, but over the last 50 years they have become some of the most popular, simple, and effective projective devices. By asking clients to draw simple pictures, one can gain tremendous insight into a client's life and perhaps unconscious undertow.

Buck introduced the original House-Tree-Person (H-T-P) drawing test in 1948 (Burns, 1987). He simply asked clients to draw a house, a tree, and a person on three separate pieces of paper. The Kinetic House-Tree-Person Drawing Test is slightly different in that the client is asked to draw all the figures "with some kind of action" on one sheet of paper (8½" × 11") presented horizontally (Burns, 1987, p. 5). Burns (1987) believes the tree is the universal metaphor for human development as seen in religion, myth, poetry, art, and sacred literature:

> *In drawing a tree, the drawer reflects his or her individual transformation process. In creating a person, the drawer reflects the self or ego functions interacting with the tree to create a larger metaphor. The house reflects the physical aspects of the drama.* (p. 3)

Numerous books and materials describe how to specifically interpret the H-T-P and K-H-T-P drawings. Table 9.6 provides examples of a few interpretive suggestions (Buck, 1987).

Other drawing tests exist, such as the Draw-A-Man, Draw-A-Woman, or the Kinetic Family Drawing, which asks the individual to draw his or her family doing something together. These tests all try to tap into unconscious aspects of the individual's self by focusing on slightly different content. Drawing tests do

TABLE 9.6
Sample of Suggested K-H-T-P Interpretations (Buck, 1987)

CHARACTERISTIC	INTERPRETATION
General	
Unusually large drawings	Aggressive tendencies; grandiose tendencies; possible hyper or manic conditions
Unusually small drawings	Feelings of inferiority, ineffectiveness or inadequacy; withdrawal tendencies; feelings of insecurity
Very short, circular, sketch strokes	Anxiety, uncertainty, depression, and timidity
House	
Large chimney	Concerns about power, psychological warmth, or sexual masculinity
Very small door	Reluctant accessibility; shyness
Absence of windows	Suggests withdrawal and possible paranoid tendencies
Tree	
Broken or cut-off branches	Feelings of trauma
Upward pointed branches	Reaching for opportunities in the environment
Slender trunk	Precarious adjustment or hold on life
Person	
Unusually large head	Overvaluation of intelligence; dissatisfaction with body; preoccupation with headaches
Hair emphasis on head, chest, or beard	Virility striving; sexual preoccupation
Wide stance	Aggressive defiance and/or insecurity

not require artistic prowess on the part of the client, are quickly administered, and can often produce important interpretive material for the clinician.

Sentence Completion Tests

Sentence completion tests Can reveal unconscious issues, but validity and reliability information is unavailable

"This book is....." Completing a sentence has been used as a projective device since Galton and Jung (see Chapter 1), and although you are not likely to see a sentence stem asking about a specific book, you *are* likely to see sentence stems that ask you to describe your relationship with your mother, father, spouse, lover, friends, and so on. Two of the more common sentence completion tests are the Sentence Completion Series and the EPS Sentence Completion Technique. In addition, clinicians will sometimes create their own sentence completion tests that can be used when giving a personality battery.

The Sentence Completion Series is a "semi-projective" series of tests for gathering personality and psychodiagnostic information from adolescents and adults. The series contains eight forms with 50 sentence stems per form. Individual forms address specific issues such as family, marriage, work, aging, and so on. An interpretive manual makes suggestions on how to examine the general tone; however, there is no objective scoring methodology. Hence, there is also no reliability, validity, or norm data. It is certainly a useful instrument, but its greatest weakness is the lack of any psychometric data (Moreland & Werner, 2001).

The EPS Sentence Completion Technique, published by Psychological Assessment Resources, is specifically designed for working with clients who are mildly mentally retarded or of borderline intelligence. The publisher defines this range as an IQ between 55 and 83. The instrument contains 40 sentence stems that can be used to elicit responses in one of nine problem themes such as interpersonal relationships, work and school, sexuality, residential living, and so on. An individual can give the test without graduate training in testing; however, interpretation requires graduate level schooling. As with the previous instrument, there is no objective scoring method, norm data, nor validity and reliability information (Peterson & Reinehr, 1998).

Although questions about the validity and reliability of sentence completion tests remain, it is clear that these instruments can provide a quick method of obtaining a client's feelings and unconscious thoughts about important issues in the client's life.

The Role of Helpers in Clinical Assessment

Because clinical assessment can add one more piece of knowledge about a client, it should always be considered as an additional tool to use. Therefore, all helpers can, and perhaps should, be involved in some aspects of clinical assessment. For instance, an elementary school counselor might consider using a self-esteem inventory when working with young children to help identify students who are struggling with self-esteem issues, while a high school counselor might want to use any of a wide range of objective personality measures to help identify concerns and aid in setting goals for students. College counselors, agency clinicians, social workers, and private practice professionals all might use a wide range of clinical assessment tools as part of their repertoire to help identify issues and devise strategies for problem solving. Clinicians should reflect on what kinds of clinical assessment tools would benefit their clients at their particular setting and whether they have sufficient training to give such assessments (e.g., projective tests generally require advanced training).

Final Thoughts on Clinical Assessment

The clinical assessment process assists helpers in making decisions that often will affect clients' lives in critical ways. Such decisions can result in persons being labeled, institutionalized, incarcerated, stigmatized, placed on medication, losing or gaining a job, being granted or denied access to their children, and more. Test givers should remember the impact that their decisions will have on clients and monitor the quality of the tests they use, their level of competence to administer tests, and their ability to make accurate interpretations of client material. Acting in any other fashion is practicing incompetence.

Summary

We began this chapter by noting that clinical assessment examines the client through multiple methods, including the clinical interview, the administration of informal assessment techniques, and the administration of objective and projective tests. This process is used (1) as an adjunct to counseling, (2) for case conceptualization and diagnostic formulations, (3) to determine psychotropic medications, (4) for treatment planning, (5) for court decisions, (6) for job placement, (7) to aid in the diagnosis of health-related problem (e.g., Alzheimer's), and (8) to screen for people at risk (e.g., those who might commit suicide).

In the next part of the chapter we examined a number of widely used objective personality tests. First we looked at the MMPI-2 which provides a number of scales, of which the most commonly used are the three validity scales (lie, infrequency, and correction) and the ten basic (clinical) scales: hypochondriasis, depression, conversion hysteria, psychopathic deviant, masculinity-femininity, paranoia, psychasthenia, schizophrenia, hypomania, and social introversion.

In contrast to the MMPI-2, which assesses mostly Axis I disorders, we noted that the Millon assesses DSM-IV-TR Axis II disorders and clinical symptomatology. This test offers six major scales including Clinical Personality Pattern Scales, Severe Personality Pathology Scales, Clinical Syndrome Scales, Severe Clinical Syndrome Scales, Modifying Indices, and a Validity Index. The Millon sets a Base Rate (BR) to determine responses that indicate a trait's presence.

The Beck Depression Inventory-II (BDI-II), another very popular objective test, asks 21 questions related to depression, and can be quickly answered and scored. The test is valuable for assessing depression or suicidal ideation, and it can be used on an ongoing basis for the evaluation of positive changes in counseling.

The Myers-Briggs Type Indicator (MBTI)®, which measures normal personality functioning, is based on Jung's six psychological types as well as two additional types identified by the test's creators, Katharine Briggs and Isabel Briggs Myers. The four opposing personality dichotomies are as follows:

- extroverted (E) versus introverted (I),
- sensing (S) versus intuiting (N),
- thinking (T) versus feeling (F),
- judging (J) versus perceiving (P).

Some evidence shows that combinations of the four dichotomies may indicate certain global personality traits.

The California Psychological Inventory (CPI)™ is generally used with non-psychopathological clients and contains 20 Folk Scales, three Vector Scales, and 13 Special Purpose scales. Although intercorrelations are high among some scales, the CPI™ continues to be of interest to many clinicians who are working with normally functioning clients.

Coopersmith's Self-Esteem Inventory (SEI), another objective test we examined, assesses how children, aged 8 through 15, regard themselves in relation to four areas: general self, self in relation to peers, self in relation to parents, and self in relation to school. Although the manual shows some impressive validity and reliability data, most of the data are based on studies that go back to the early 1970s. We went on to discuss some other common objective personality tests and relationship inventories.

In the last part of the chapter we examined projective tests that are often used to identify psychopathology and to assist in treatment planning. The first projective test we examined was the Thematic Apperception Test (TAT). Developed by Henry Murray in 1938, the TAT consists of 31 cards with vague pictures on them. Showing select cards, the examiner asks the client to tell a story that has a beginning, middle, and end. Client responses are interpreted based on Murray's need-press personality theory, which states that people are driven by their internal desires (needs) or by the external stimuli (press) from their environment. Because some view the TAT pictures as being dated and culturally biased, updated versions of the test have been developed. However, many clinicians continue to prefer the original TAT.

The Rorschach was the next projective test we examined. Developed in 1921 by Herman Rorschach, the examiner asks the client to reveal everything he or she sees on each of 10 inkblots. Interpretation of responses assumes that the client is projecting onto the inkblot his or her unconscious thoughts. One of the most well known scoring systems for the Rorschach, which was developed by Exner, looks at location, or portion of the blot where the response occurred; determinants, or the manner in which the examinee understood what he or she saw; and content, or what the examinee actually saw.

The Bender Visual-Motor Gestalt Test was originally published in 1938 by Lauretta Bender. Now called the Bender Gestalt II, it is a brief test that asks a client to copy a number of figures. Interpretation of client drawings reveals information about the client's developmental level and psychological functioning, as well as neurological deficits after a traumatic brain injury.

As the chapter continued, we looked at a number of drawing tests, including the House-Tree-Person, the Kinetic House-Tree-Person, Draw-A-Man, Draw-A-Woman, and Kinetic Family Drawing. We pointed out that these drawings symbolize issues and developmental changes in a person's life and that interpretation of such drawings takes a well-trained clinician who understands the multiple meanings of objects.

Sentence completion tests were the final type of projective test we examined in the chapter. We noted that such tests offer stems to which the client can respond. We pointed out that such sentence completion tests provide a quick method of accessing a client's feelings and unconscious thoughts about important issues in his or her life.

As the chapter neared its conclusion, we highlighted the fact that clinicians in all settings should consider when it might be appropriate to use a clinical assessment tool. Such tools can add to the clinician's understanding of the client and can aid in treatment planning. We concluded by noting that the clinical assessment process results in making decisions for clients that often will affect their lives in critical ways and that test givers should remember the impact these decisions will have on clients.

Chapter Review

1. Describe some of the uses of clinical assessment.

2. Distinguish between objective and projective testing and compare and contrast how each can be used in clinical assessment.

3. For each of the following tests, describe its main purpose, the kinds of scales that are used in test interpretation, and the population for which it is geared.
   a. Minnesota Multiphasic Personality Inventory (MMPI-2)
   b. Millon Clinical Multiaxial Inventory (MCMI-III)
   c. Beck Depression Inventory II (BDI-II)
   d. Myers-Briggs Type Indicator (MBTI)
   e. California Psychological Inventory (CPI)
   f. Coopersmith Self-Esteem Inventory (SEI)

4. For each of the following tests, briefly describe its main purpose, how it is given, the population for which it is geared, and how test results are interpreted.
   a. Thematic Apperception Test (TAT)
   b. Rorschach Inkblot Test
   c. Bender Visual-Motor Gestalt Test, Second Edition
   d. House-Tree-Person Test
   e. Kinetic House-Tree-Person Test
   f. Sentence Completion Series
   g. EPS Sentence Completion

5. Because many projective tests do not have the level of test worthiness of objective personality tests, some argue that their use should be curtailed. What are your thoughts on this subject?

6. Discuss the role of helpers in objective and projective testing.

Informal Assessment: Observation, Rating Scales, Classification Methods, and Records and Personal Documents

I was teaching a graduate course in testing, and because I knew that some students have trouble understanding basic test statistics, I went out of my way to make sure I was available for them. I gave them my home number and cell phone number, and I met with them individually if they wanted extra help. In addition, I offered two extra classes on the weekend for those who might need additional assistance in understanding some of the more difficult concepts. At the end of the semester, students had an opportunity to rate the class using a 6-point rating scale (1 is low, 6 is high). They rated seven aspects of the class, including such things as the amount they learned, how useful the information was, how helpful and sensitive the instructor was, and so forth. After this particular course was finished, I looked at my ratings, which had a mean of about 5.3. Not bad, I thought to myself. However, to my chagrin, I noticed that the rating for "helpfulness" was only 4.8, the lowest of all the items. I reflected on why this was so, and I couldn't come up with an answer. I must admit it bothered me, especially since I had gone out of my way to offer additional help. The next semester I saw one of the students from the class and asked her about the low rating. She said, "Well, the class was at night (7:10 – 9:50 PM), and many of the students were upset that you went the whole time." I said, "Well, I was supposed to go the whole time." She said, "Yeah, I know, but a lot of them just wanted to get home." I suddenly realized that some of the

students may have given me a lower rating for doing what I was sup-
posed to be doing—teaching in the allotted time period. "What a drag,"
I said to myself. Well, I guess that's what happens when you deal with
the subjectivity of rating scales! (Ed Neukrug)

This chapter is about informal assessment procedures. Whether it is an end-of-semester evaluation of faculty or a dream journal of a client, informal assessment techniques can have a huge impact on a person. In this chapter we will start by defining informal assessment and then identify a number of different kinds of informal assessment techniques, including observation, rating scales, classification schemes, and records and personal documents. As the chapter continues, we will discuss the test worthiness of informal assessment. We will conclude the chapter with some final thoughts regarding informal assessment.

Defining Informal Assessment

Informal asessment procedures "Homegrown" methods developed to meet specific needs

By their very nature, informal assessment techniques are subjective and thus have a unique role in the assessment process. Whereas the kinds of assessment we have examined up to this point in the text were, for the most part, created and produced in association with national publishing companies and used nationally, the types of assessments in this chapter are "homegrown"—that is, developed by individuals who have specific assessment needs. Because they are homegrown, the amount of time, money, and expertise put into their development is generally much less than it is for those nationally developed instruments. Thus, reliability, validity, and cross-cultural issues are generally not formally addressed and often are lacking. Despite this obvious drawback, such instruments can supply valuable information when assessing an individual.

Although informal assessment procedures lack test worthiness, they have distinct advantages.

Although informal assessment techniques are generally not as test worthy as formal assessment procedures, they have some advantages over formal assessment techniques:

1. The addition of an informal assessment technique to the total assessment process increases our ability to better understand the whole person.
2. Informal assessment procedures can be designed to assess the exact attribute we are attempting to measure, whereas formal assessment techniques provide a wide net of assessment—sometimes so wide that we do not gain enough information about the specific attribute being examined.
3. Informal assessment procedures can often be developed or gathered in a rather short amount of time, providing important information in a timely fashion.
4. Many informal assessment procedures are nonintrusive; that is, you are not directly gathering information from the client (e.g., a student's cumulative record file at school). Thus, they provide a nonthreatening mechanism for gathering information about the individual.

5. Informal assessment techniques generally are free or low-cost procedures.

6. Informal assessment procedures tend to be easy to administer and relatively easy to interpret.

Types of Informal Assessment

Dozens of informal assessment techniques can enhance our understanding of the whole person. In fact, because informal assessment techniques are, by their nature, informal, a creative examiner can often come up with unique types of techniques never before used. However, several types of informal assessment techniques are frequently used, including observation, rating scales, classification schemes, and records and personal documents.

Observation

Observation
Conducted by professionals, significant others, or clients themselves

Observation can be an important assessment tool that provides one additional mechanism of understanding the individual being assessed. Observation can be done by professionals who wish to observe the individual (e.g., school counselors observing students in the classroom), by significant others who have the opportunity to observe the individual in natural settings (e.g., parents observing a child at home), and even by oneself, such as when a client is asked to observe specific targeted behaviors he or she is working on changing (e.g., eating habits). Often, when observing an individual, the observer conducts an event or a time sample.

Event sampling
Observing a targeted behavior with no regard to time

Event sampling is the viewing and assessment of a targeted behavior without regard for time. Often, in evaluating the targeted behavior, general comments are made about the behavior or a rating scale is used to evaluate the behavior. For instance, the school counselor who is interested in observing the "acting-out" behavior of a student could view the child for an entire school day and note when the acting-out behavior is exhibited. Of course, "acting out" would have to be clearly defined.

Time sampling
Observing behaviors during a set amount of time

In contrast to event sampling, with time sampling a specific amount of time is set aside for the observation. For instance, it would be inconvenient for a school counselor to spend a whole day observing the behaviors of one student, but the counselor might choose three 15-minute periods during the day in which to view the student's behavior. Ideally, this time sample would give the counselor a snapshot of the student's overall behavior, including any acting-out behavior.

Event and time sampling
Observing a targeted behavior for a set amount of time

For the sake of convenience, time and event sampling often are combined. In the example given of observing the acting-out behaviors of a student, it would make sense for the counselor to pick three 15-minute segments of time (time sample) in which to observe the acting-out behaviors (event sample) of the student. Scheduling the observation times would free up the counselor to do other important tasks during the day. (See Box 10.1.)

BOX 10.1
Disruptive Observation of a Third-Grade Class

While working in New Hampshire, I was once asked to "debrief" a third-grade class which had just finished a trial period in which a young boy, who was paraplegic and severely mentally retarded, had been mainstreamed into their classroom. During this trial period, a stream of observers from a local university had visited the classroom. The observers would sit in the back and take notes about the interactions between the students. This information was to be used at a later date to decide whether it was beneficial to all involved to mainstream the student with the disability.

When I met with the students, they clearly had adapted well to the presence of this young boy who was disabled. Although the students seemed to have difficulty forming deep relationships with him, his presence seemed in no way to detract from their studies or from their other relationships in the classroom. However, almost without exception, the students noted that the constant stream of observers interfering with their daily schedule had been quite annoying. Perhaps if a limited time sample had been used, the students would not have reacted so strongly.

—Ed Neukrug

Another example of combining time and event sampling is when an instructor, who is teaching counseling skills, decides to randomly observe targeted responses from three 5-minute segments of clinical interviews from each of a dozen students who handed in one-hour tapes of themselves counseling clients. If the instructor were to carefully listen to the whole hour of each student's tape and stop and start the tape every time a certain response is made (e.g., attempt at empathy), it would likely take him or her dozens of hours to listen to all of the tapes.

EXERCISE 10.1 **Application of Observational Techniques**

In small groups, devise ways that you might be able to use observational techniques. Try to incorporate the use of event sampling and time sampling in your examples. Share your answers in class.

Rating Scales

Rating scales
Subjective quantification of an attribute or characteristic

Halo effect
Overall impression of client causes inaccurate rating

A rating scale is an instrument used by an individual to evaluate or assess attributes or characteristics being presented to the rater. By their very nature, rating scales are subjective because the evaluation or assessment is based on the rater's "inner judgment" and thus can be filled with biases. Thus, the potential for error in ratings is great and although rating scales are easily developed and quick to administer, they should be used carefully.

Although a number of sources of error exist for rating scales, two of the most frequently cited are the *halo effect* and *generosity error* (Aiken, 1996). The halo effect occurs when a positive overall impression of an individual clouds the rating of that person in one select area, and generosity error occurs when the individual doing the rating identifies with the person being rated and thus rates the

Generosity error
Identification
with client
causes inaccurate rating

individual inaccurately. An example of the halo effect is the supervisor who mistakenly rates an outstanding supervisee high on being punctual, despite the fact that the supervisee consistently comes to work late. The supervisor's overall favorable impression has caused an error in the rating of this one attribute. An example of generosity error is the student who ranks a fellow student high on exhibiting effective empathic responses because the first student identifies with the anxiety the second student feels about being under the microscope.

Despite some of the potential problems with rating scales, they are easily created and can be completed rather quickly, so they offer a convenient mechanism for assessing individuals. Commonly used rating scales include numerical scales, graphic scales, semantic differential scales, and rank-order scales.

Numerical Scales

Numerical scale
Statement or
question followed by a
number line

Numerical scales generally provide a written statement or question that can be rated from high to low on a number line. An example is shown below:

Rate the effectiveness of your supervisor:

1	2	3	4	5	6	7	8
Low							High

Numerical scales are also commonly used during therapy as a way to prioritize issues or assess progress. When I (Charles Fawcett) am counseling, I frequently use numerical scales to assess progress. For example, I might say, "When you first came in eight weeks ago, you said that on a scale of 1 to 10 your depression was an 8. Using that same scale, where do you think you are, on average, this week?" Another common form of numerical scale is called the Subjective Units of Disturbance scale, or SUD (Wolpe, 1991). The SUD scale is frequently used in desensitization therapies such as Behavior Therapy, Eye Movement Desensitization and Reprocessing (EMDR) and Thought Field Therapy (TFT) (Wolpe, 1991; Shapiro, 2001; Callahan & Callahan, 2003). As the desensitization treatment is progressing, the therapist frequently asks the client his or her SUD based on a scale of 0 to 10 to determine treatment effectiveness. When I am using SUD scales with TFT, I attempt to get the client's SUD to a 2 or below before moving on to another issue.

Graphic-Type Scales (Likert-Type Scales)

Likert scale
Statement followed by words
reflecting a continuum of
behaviors or
feelings

Graphic-type scales generally have a statement followed by words that reflect a continuum from favorable to unfavorable regarding the quality being measured. A number line may or may not be associated with the words. An example is shown below.

Rate how much you liked your supervisor:

1	2	3	4	5
Not at all	Somewhat	Moderately So	Very Much	Extremely

An example of a graphic-type scale used during counseling can be seen in EMDR protocol, where clients are asked to rate their belief of a new positive cognition on a scale from 1 (completely untrue) to 7 (completely true). Called the Validity Of Cognition (VOC) scale (Wilson, Becker, & Tinker, 1995; Shapiro, 2001), this graphic-type scale is a good example how informal scales can be quickly adopted into psychotherapy practice.

Semantic Differential Scales

Semantic differential scale
Number line with opposite traits at each end

Semantic differential scales provide a statement followed by one or more pairs of words that reflect opposing traits. A number line may or may not be associated with the dichotomous pairs of words. Below is a semantic differential scale with a number line.

Place an "X" on the line to represent how much of each quality you possess.

sadness ———————————————— happiness
    1   2   3   4   5   6   7   8

introverted ———————————————— extroverted
    1   2   3   4   5   6   7   8

anxious ———————————————— calm
    1   2   3   4   5   6   7   8

As you can see from the above example, a Semantic Differential Scale can easily be created if you were interested in quickly assessing the behaviors and/or affect of a client. Such a scale can be helpful in assessing clients' needs and setting treatment goals. Of course, such scales can have broad educational and psychological applications.

Rank-Order Scales

Rank order
A method for clients to order their preferences

Rank-order scales provide a series of statements which the respondent can rank order based on his or her preferences. For instance, the following rank-order scale could be used as part of a larger instrument to determine preference for counseling style.

Rank Order Your Preference for Doing Counseling

For the following statements, place a 1 next to the item that you most prefer, a 2 next to the item you second most prefer, and so on down to a 5 next to the item you prefer least.

_____ I prefer listening to clients and then reflecting back what I hear from them in order to facilitate client self-growth.

_____ I prefer advising clients and suggesting mechanisms for change.

_____ I prefer interpreting client behaviors in the hope that they will **gain** insight into themselves.

_____ I prefer helping clients identify which behaviors they would like to change.

_____ I prefer helping clients identify which thoughts are causing problematic behaviors and helping them to develop new ways of thinking about the world.

EXERCISE 10.2 **Application of Rating Scales**

In small groups, devise ways that you might be able to use rating scales. Try to incorporate the use of the different types of rating scales discussed in the chapter. Share your answers in class.

Classification Systems

Classification systems
Provide information regarding presence or absence of attribute or characteristic

In contrast with rating scales that tend to assess a quantity of an attribute or characteristic, classification systems provide information about whether an individual has, or does not have, certain attributes or characteristics. Three common classification inventories include behavior and feeling word checklists, sociometric instruments, and situational tests.

Behavior and Feeling Word Checklists

Behavior/feeling word checklists
Allow clients to quickly evaluate their actions or emotions

Behavior and feeling word checklists allow an individual to identify those words that best describe his or her feeling state or the kinds of behaviors he or she might exhibit. Such a list can quickly help an individual or an examiner identify issues a client might need to work on. Box 10.2 is a behavior checklist that could be used to help identify abusive behaviors. This is followed by a feeling word list that could help an examiner understand a client or assist the client to achieve greater self-understanding (Box 10.3).

Sociometric Instruments

Sociometric instruments
Used to assess the social dynamics of a group

Sociometric instruments make it possible to assess the relative position of an individual within a group. This type of instrument is often used when one wants to determine the dynamics of individuals within a group, organization, or institution. For instance, if I were interested in knowing how well a group of preschool students liked one another, I could ask each of them to privately tell me the name of the individual who was their best friend. Then I might ask them to tell me the name of their second-best friend. I could then map this ranking. Figure 10.1 shows such a mapping. Here, you can see that Emma is particularly well-liked, while Jamiah is a "social isolate."

Situational Tests

Another type of tool sometimes used to classify individuals is a situational test. This kind of assessment uses contrived, but natural, situations to examine how a

---

BOX 10.2
Behavior Checklist of Abusive Behaviors

Check those behaviors you have exhibited toward your partner and your partner has exhibited toward you

	Exhibited by You to Your Partner	Exhibited by Partner to You
1. Hitting	____	____
2. Pulling hair	____	____
3. Throwing objects	____	____
4. Burning	____	____
5. Pinching	____	____
6. Choking	____	____
7. Slapping	____	____
8. Biting	____	____
9. Tying up	____	____
10. Hitting walls or other inanimate objects	____	____
11. Throwing objects with intent to break them	____	____
12. Restraining or preventing from leaving	____	____

Situational tests
Role-play to determine how individuals might act

person is likely to respond in real-life situations. For instance, when applying to doctoral programs, I (Ed Neukrug) was asked to role-play a counselor with one of the faculty members in the doctoral program. He role-played the same client with every potential student, and the faculty were then able to assess my clinical skills and compare them to those of other potential students in this contrived yet realistic role-play. Today, situational tests are frequently used in business and industry to determine whether an employee has the skills to be promoted.

EXERCISE 10.3 **Application of Classification Systems**

In small groups, devise ways to use classification systems. Try to incorporate the use of the various types of classification systems discussed in the chapter. Share your answers in class.

Records and personal documents
Sheds light on beliefs, values, and behaviors of the client

Records and Personal Documents

Records and personal documents can help the examiner understand the beliefs, values, and behaviors of the person being assessed. Such records and personal documents can be obtained directly from the individual, from individuals close to the person (e.g., parents, loved ones), and from just about any institution with which the client has interacted, such as educational institutions, mental health

BOX 10.3
Feeling Word List

Circle the feeling words that best describe you.

Abandoned	Angry	Aggressive	Arrogant
Apprehensive	Awful	Argumentative	Ashamed
Anxious	Aggravated	Bored	Bitter
Blind	Broken-hearted	Burdened	Betrayed
Concerned	Confused	Criticized	Cut-Off
Claustrophobic	Difficult	Defensive	Distressed
Depressed	Doubtful	Dirty	Deceived
Disappointed	Disloyal	Discontented	Drained
Discouraged	Disgusted	Disrespected	Embarrassed
Exasperated	Envious	Empty	Egotistical
Fearful	Forced	Failure	Forlorn
Forsaken	Futile	Frigid	Frustrated
Grieving	Guilty	Hateful	Haughty
Helpless	Hopeless	Humiliated	Hurt
Hurried	Impatient	Insecure	Incapable
Impossible	Irresponsible	Irritated	Intolerant
Inadequate	Longing	Imposed upon	Indecisive
Jealous	Lost	Lonely	Left out
Lying	Miserable	Let Down	Misunderstood
Mean	Obligated	Nauseated	Neglected
Nervous	Punished	Oppressed	Overwhelmed
Paranoid	Pressured	Powerless	Pained
Pitiful	Repulsive	Provoked	Panicked
Rejected	Selfish	Resentful	Restless
Restricted	Sorrowful	Shameful	Shattered
Sour	Shocked	Stubborn	Stuck-up
Suppressed	Stupid	Smug	Sad
Shy	Spiteful	Scared	Skeptical
Stifled	Troubled	Terrified	Tormented
Teased	Unaccepted	Troubling	Thoughtless
Traumatized	Uneasy	Undesirable	Unneeded
Unfriendly	Unhelpful	Unfulfilled	Unpleasant
Unhappy	Unworthy	Unsuccessful	Unwanted
Used	Unloved	Useless	Unsociable
Unconcerned	Vindictive	Unreliable	Upset
Victimized	Wrong	Wasted	Worthless
Weary		Wounded	

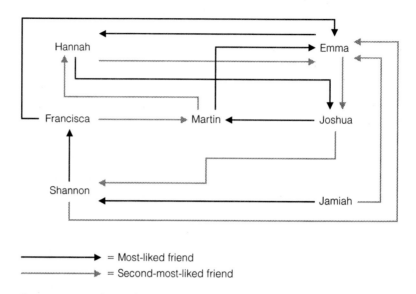

= Most-liked friend

= Second-most-liked friend

Figure 10.1 Sociometric mapping of a preschool class

agencies, and clients' places of employment. Some of the more common records and personal documents include biographical inventories, cumulative records, anecdotal information, autobiographies, journals and diaries, and genograms.

Biographical Inventories

Biographical inventories
Provides detailed picture of client's life

Biographical inventories provide a detailed picture of the individual from birth. They can be the result of an involved, structured interview that is conducted by the examiner, or they can be created by having the client complete a checklist or respond to a series of questions. Biographical inventories will often cover the same kinds of items that are found in a structured interview (see Chapter 12 for a description of the structured interview). The following kinds of information are often gathered in a biographical inventory:

- Demographic information
  - age
  - sex
  - ethnicity
  - address
  - date of birth
  - e-mail address
  - phone number(s) (home and cell)
- Presenting problem
  - nature of problem
  - duration of problem

- severity of problem
- previous treatment of problem
- Family of origin
  - names and basic descriptions of primary caregivers in family of origin
  - names and basic descriptions of siblings in family of origin
  - names and basic descriptions of significant others involved with family of origin
  - placement in family of origin
  - quality of relationships in family of origin
  - traumatic events in family of origin
- Current family
  - nature of relationship with current domestic partner
  - length of relationship with current domestic partner
  - names, ages, and basic descriptions of children, step-children, and foster children
  - names and basic descriptions of significant others involved with current family
  - quality of relationships in current family
  - traumatic events in current family
- Educational history
  - highest degree attained by each parent and college major, if any
  - highest degree attained by each spouse and college major, if any
  - highest or current educational level of children
- Vocational background
  - detailed work history from adolescence
  - detailed work history of spouse/significant other
  - work history of parents
  - current salary of primary family members
  - assessment of current job satisfaction of client and spouse or significant other
- Financial history
  - economic status/social class of family of origin
  - current economic status/social class
  - history of any financial hardships
- History of counseling and mental illness
  - detailed counseling/psychiatric history
  - detailed counseling/psychiatric history of significant other
  - detailed counseling/psychiatric history of children
  - history of mental illness in family of origin and extended family
  - use of psychotropic medication in current family and family of origin
- Medical history
  - significant medical problems
  - significant medical problems of significant other
  - significant medical problems of children, stepchildren, foster children
  - significant medical problems in family of origin

- current status of medical problems in immediate family
- current use of medication: give names and dosages

■ Substance use and abuse history
  - Cigarette smoking
    ____ None   Number of years: _____
    Number of cigarettes per day: _____
  - Alcohol use
    ____ None   ____ Occasional   ____ Regular   ____ Heavy   ___ Binge
    Number of years: ____
  - Illegal drugs
    Type of drug(s) (Respond multiple times if more than one drug)
    Usage: ____ None ____ Occasional   ____ Regular   ____ Heavy
    Number of years: _____
  - Prescription drug abuse
    Type of drug(s) (Respond multiple times if more than one drug)
    ____ None   ____ Occasional   ____ Regular   ____ Binge
    Number of years: _____

■ History of legal issues
  - Nature of legal issue
  - Effect on self
  - Effect on others

■ Check if changes have occurred in any of the following over the last six months:
    ____ Weight   ____ Appetite
    ____ Sleep patterns ____ Interest in sex
    ____ Sexual activity ____ General level of activity
  Explain any items checked:

■ Sexual orientation
    ____ Heterosexual
    ____ Bisexual
    ____ Homosexual
    ____ Unclear

■ History of aggressive behaviors
  - Nature of past acting-out behaviors:
  - Current violent ideation:
  - Likelihood of acting out:

■ History of self-injurious behaviors
  - Nature of past behaviors:
  - Current ideation (suicide or other):
  - Likelihood of injuring self:

■ Affective and mental state (Check all that apply)
    ____ Depressed   ____ Anxious   ____ Euphoric
    ____ Tearful   ____ Sad   ____ Irritable
    ____ Angry   ____ Passive   ____ Apathetic
    ____ Delusions   ____ Hallucinations ____ Emotional lability
    ____ Panicky   ____ Compulsions   ____ Obsessive thoughts

____ Phobic   ____ Passive   ____ Fearful
____ Low self-esteem   ____ Guilt   ____ Memory problems
Explain any items checked (note intensity and duration):

Cumulative Records

Cumulative records
Collected documentation from a school, employer, or mental health agency

Almost assuredly, a cumulative record of significant behaviors we have exhibited has been kept on most of us. For instance, cumulative records are commonplace in schools, where information about a child's test scores, grades, behavioral problems, family issues, relationships with others, and other matters are stored. Also, most workplaces maintain some kind of cumulative record on each employee. These records can add vital information to our understanding of the whole person and can generally be accessed with a written request form signed by the client.

Anecdotal Information

Anecdotal information
Subjective comments or notes in client's records regarding usual patterns or atypical behaviors

Anecdotal information can sometimes be found in an individual's cumulative record and generally includes behaviors of an individual that are consistent (e.g., Jonathan is always punctual) or inconsistent (Samantha, who generally gets along with her co-workers, had an altercation with one today). Anecdotal information can give us insight about the usual manner in which a person behaves or about inconsistent or rarely seen behaviors that may offer glimpses into the inner world of the client.

Autobiography

Autobiography
Asking client to write his or her life story

In contrast to biographical inventories that help us collect in-depth and comprehensive information about a person, asking an individual to write an autobiography allows an examiner to gain subjective historical information that for some reason stands out in an individual's life. In some ways, the information highlighted by an individual in his or her autobiography is a type of projective test in that the individual unconsciously chooses certain information to include—information that has affected the development of the individual's sense of self. For creative and insightful individuals, writing an autobiography can be an enjoyable process that can reveal much about the self-awareness of the client.

Journals and Diaries

Journals and diaries
Having clients log their daily thoughts, actions, or dreams

Some individuals enjoy and benefit from keeping an ongoing journal or diary. For instance, dream journals can provide valuable insight into self by revealing unconscious drives and desires and by uncovering patterns that indicate issues in a client's life. Clients can often learn how to "get in touch with their dreams" simply by keeping a dream journal next to their beds and writing down their memories of dreams as soon as they awake. In fact, it has been shown that individuals can be taught how to remember their dreams in this fashion (Ullman & Zimmerman, 1979; Hill, 2004). Similarly, diaries can help to uncover the inner world of the client and identify important patterns of behavior. By examining themes found in journals and diaries, helpers and clients may focus more

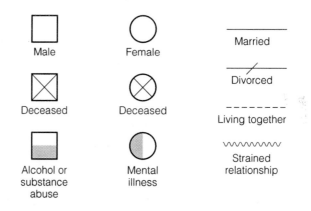

Figure 10.2 Common genogram symbols

attention on behaviors that may have seemed insignificant. Journals and diaries can add an important "inside" perspective to our understanding of the total person.

Genogram
Map of client's family relationships and relevant history

Genograms

A popular and informative assessment tool is the genogram. It can also serve as a focal point or discussion aid during treatment. The genogram is a map of an individual's family tree that may include the family history of illnesses, mental disorders, substance use, expectations, relationships, cultural issues, and other concerns for counseling. Usually the therapist draws the genogram while asking the client questions; however, drawing or completing the genogram can be given as homework. There are numerous symbols and items that can be included on the genogram. Figure 10.2 displays a few of the common or basic symbols. Of course you are always welcome to add more of your own.

Dates or ages are useful on the genogram. Some prefer adding the year born, and if applicable, the year deceased, near each individual's name. Another method is to include the age of the individual inside his box or her circle. Similarly, the year married or the cumulative years married can be placed above the marriage relationship line. As noted in Figure 10.3, special symbols identifying substance use or mental illness can be helpful in tracking family genetics, highlighting stressors caused by abuse or illness, and generating discussion with the client. Creating the genogram to at least the level of the client's grandparents is important to fully capture these trends in the family. In Figure 10.3, you can see an abbreviated version of a genogram for Joe Smith.

EXERCISE 10.4 **Application of Records and Personal Documents**

In small groups, devise ways to use records and personal documents. Try to incorporate the various types of records and personal documents discussed in the chapter. Share your answers in class.

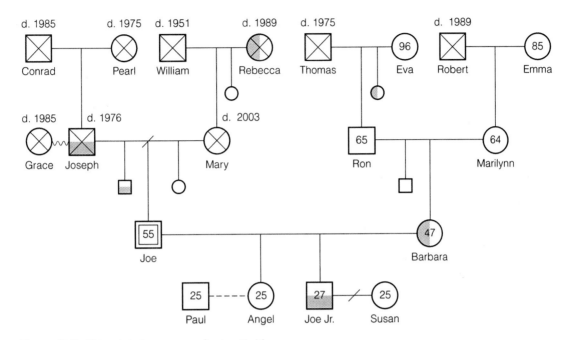

Figure 10.3 Abbreviated genogram for Joe Smith

Test Worthiness of Informal Assessment

As already noted earlier in this chapter, informal assessment techniques tend to be less valid, reliable, and cross-culturally sensitive than formal assessment techniques, although they do tend to be quite practical. But let's take a look at what we mean when we talk about these attributes within the context of informal assessment techniques.

Validity

Validity of informal techniques
Based on clearly defining a set of behaviors

Validity of informal assessment techniques has to do with how well the examiner is defining that which is being assessed. For instance, if I am concerned about the acting-out behavior of a middle school child, I need to clearly define the behavior identified as "acting out," and I need to be specific on where acting-out behaviors are being exhibited. For example, does acting out include only inappropriate behaviors in the classroom, or does it also include inappropriate behaviors in the hallway, on the playground, on field trips, and at home? Also, exactly which "inappropriate" behaviors are we talking about? Does acting out include pushing, interrupting, making inappropriate nonverbal gestures, or withdrawing in class? The more clearly one is able to identify the kinds of behaviors and the place the behaviors are exhibited, the easier it will be to collect information about that domain, and consequently, the more valid will be the assessment. Thus, when referring to informal assessment techniques, we are generally not involved in assessing validity in the traditional ways, but more concerned about how clearly we are defining the domain being measured (see Exercise 10.5).

EXERCISE 10.5 **Validity of Informal Assessment Techniques**

In small groups, consider the various kinds of informal assessment techniques listed below and demonstrate how you might show evidence that the information being assessed is valid.

Observation

Rating scales
- numerical scales
- graphic scales
- semantic differential scales
- rank-order scales

Classification systems
- behavior and feeling word checklists
- sociometric instruments
- situational tests

Records and personal documents
- biographical data inventories
- anecdotal records
- cumulative records
- autobiographies
- personal journals (e.g., dream journals and diaries)

Reliability

Reliability of informal techniques Based on interrater reliability, which is agreement or consistency among two or more evaluators

With informal assessment, the better we define the behavior being assessed, the more reliable our data collection will be. Thus, with informal assessment there is an intimate relationship between validity and reliability. Ideally, when conducting informal assessment, two individuals who are highly trained in understanding the meaning of the data being collected should collect and categorize the data. Practically, this is rarely done. For instance, it would be nearly impossible to have two trained individuals log the dreams of an individual unless that individual was in a controlled setting, like a sleep clinic. Or, consider the earlier example of the acting-out middle school student. In this case, it would be ideal if two individuals observed the child at the same time and knew exactly what acting-out behaviors they were looking for and in which context to look for them (the classroom, playground, home, etc.). Subsequent to observing the child, they could crosscheck their observations and see if they had collected similar information. If this were possible, when comparing such accuracy statistically, we would be examining the interrater reliability of the observers.

For instance, when I (Ed Neukrug) was in college, I and a friend worked with a psychology professor who was examining how quickly thirsty mice could learn that a drop of water was on a receptacle on the black side of a box. The box had removable sides, one of which was black and the other was white. By randomly moving the sides, but always keeping the water in the receptacle on the black side, the learning curve of thirsty mice could be assessed. My friend and I would place a mouse in the middle of the box and separately rate whether or not the mouse went to the correct side (the black side) and took a drink. However, to increase our validity, and consequently the reliability of our ratings, we had to be clear about what was considered a learned behavior by the mice. For instance, was walking over to the black side and venturing toward the water

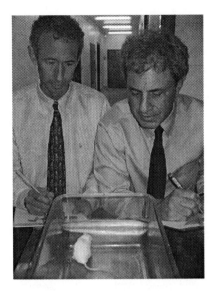

As Ed and Charlie observe the mouse, they hope that they attain high interrater reliability. But in reality, the mouse is the one observing them.

receptacle, but not touching it, considered a learned response? What if the mouse walked over and looked into the receptacle but did not drink? And what if the mouse walked over to the receptacle, looked in, stuck its tongue out and touched the water, but didn't appear to swallow? Did the mouse exhibit the learned response in this case? A "correct" response had to be clearly defined for us, and the more clearly it was defined, the more similar would be our ratings. In fact, in this case, good interrater reliability was said to have been obtained when the correlation between our ratings reached .80 or higher.

In another example of interrater reliability, I had two graduate students learn how to rate the empathic responses of dozens of individuals who had responded to a role-play client on an audiotape. These two graduate students were taught how to rate empathy on a five-point scale using increments of .5, from a low of .5 to a high of 5.0. Thus, I had to be clear on what was meant by empathy and how to determine whether a response deserved a .5, 1, 1.5, 2, 2.5, 3, 3.5, 4, 4.5, or 5 rating. In both cases, it took weeks to train the two raters in their understanding of empathy and the use of the scale to the point where they had an interrater reliability of .80. Based on this example, it is easy to see why the attainment of interrater reliability in the use of informal assessment techniques is rarely achieved.

Cross-Cultural Fairness

Cross-cultural fairness
Possibility of bias must be recognized and addressed

The nature of informal assessment procedures makes them particularly vulnerable to cultural bias. This can happen in two ways. First, as a result of unconscious or conscious bias, an examiner, observer, or rater may misinterpret the verbal or nonverbal behaviors of a minority client. Second, the examiner, observer, or rater may simply be ignorant about the verbal or nonverbal behaviors of a particular minority group. For instance, an example of unconscious bias affecting one's observation might be an examiner who is asked to observe the behaviors of an Asian student and mistakenly assumes a particular student is bright because Asians as a group tend to do better academically than other ethnic groups. An example of ignorance is when the same observer falsely assumes the student has psychological issues because the Asian student does not readily express feelings. In actuality, in many Asian countries nonexpression of certain feelings is considered a worthy attribute (Robinson & Howard-Hamilton, 2000).

Despite the fact that informal assessment techniques are easily affected by bias, they still can add much to the assessment of an individual. Because they are uniquely geared toward the particular behavior of an individual, one can pick and choose exactly which behaviors to observe. This can enhance our understanding of the individual. Thus, informal assessment can be a mixed bag when it comes to cross-cultural fairness, and results need to be examined carefully.

Practicality

Practicality
Informal procedures are inexpensive, easy to administer, and easy to interpret

The practical nature of informal assessments makes them particularly useful. Such assessments are generally low-cost or cost-free, can be created or obtained in a short amount of time, are relatively easy to administer, and with the exception of possible cultural bias, are fairly easy to interpret. Thus, when completing a broad assessment of an individual, informal assessments should often be considered as one additional method of assessment.

Final Thoughts on Informal Assessment

Although informal assessment techniques sometimes have questionable reliability, validity, and may not always be cross-culturally fair, they provide additional tools for understanding clients. Thus, when making important decisions about a person, these techniques should generally not be used alone but can be an important addition to a broader assessment battery. When using informal assessment techniques, keep in mind the potential impact of the decisions one is making about a client.

Summary

This chapter offered an overview of informal assessment. We noted that by their very nature, informal assessment techniques are subjective and are developed by individuals who have specific assessment needs. We pointed out that because they are "homegrown," the amount of time, money, and expertise put into their development is generally much less than for nationally developed instruments. Thus, reliability, validity, and cross-cultural issues are generally not formally addressed, and data often are lacking. These techniques do, however, have the following advantages: (1) they offer an additional assessment mechanism, (2) they can provide a highly specific assessment measure, (3) they can be developed in a short amount of time, (4) they are nonintrusive, (5) they are free or low-cost, and (6) they are easy to administer and interpret.

The first informal assessment technique we discussed was observation. Two types of observation highlighted were event sampling, which is the viewing and assessment of a targeted behavior without regard for time, and time sampling, which takes place when a specific amount of time is set aside for the observation. Sometimes time sampling and event sampling are combined.

Next, we examined rating scales, which are used to assess a quantity of an attribute being presented to the rater. We noted that such scales are subjective and can be filled with bias and errors, including the halo effect and generosity error. Some common types of rating scales included numerical scales, graphic scales, semantic differential scales, and rank-order scales. We noted that in contrast to rating scales, classification systems provide information about whether an individual has, or does not have, certain attributes or characteristics. Three common classification systems are behavior and feeling word checklists, sociometric instruments, and situational tests.

The last kind of informal assessment techniques we examined were records and personal documents. These assessment tools can help the examiner understand the beliefs, values, and behaviors of the person being assessed and can be obtained from numerous sources including the client, individuals close to the client, institutions, and agencies. Some of the more common records and personal documents include biographical inventories, cumulative records, anecdotal information, autobiographies, journals and diaries, and genograms.

We noted that informal assessment techniques tend to be less valid, reliable, and cross-culturally sensitive than formal assessment techniques, although they are also quite practical. We pointed out that the validity of informal assessment techniques has to do with how well the examiner is defining what is being assessed. We also stressed that the better we define the behavior being assessed (the more valid our definition is), the more reliable will be our data collection. Ideally, informal assessment techniques should be administered by a minimum of two individuals, and the interrater reliability of these two individuals should be at least .80.

Relative to cross-cultural issues, we noted that the examiner may misinterpret the verbal or nonverbal behaviors of a member of a minority group as a result of unconscious or conscious bias. Second, the observer, rater, or respondent may simply be ignorant about the verbal or nonverbal behaviors of a particular minority group. Despite problems with bias, informal procedures are often useful because they are uniquely geared toward the particular behavior of an individual.

Finally, we pointed out that informal assessment techniques are practical in that they are generally low-cost or cost-free, can be created or obtained in a short amount of time, are relatively easy to administer, and are fairly easy to interpret. We stressed that when used wisely, informal assessment techniques provide additional mechanisms for understanding the person.

Chapter Review

1. Define informal assessment procedures and describe some of the ways that they can be used.

2. Describe the two types of observation and give some examples of how you might use observation in a clinical setting.

3. Describe and give examples of the following types of rating scales: numerical scales, graphic scales, semantic differential scales, and rank-order scales.

4. Many sources of error exist in the application of rating scales. Discuss how the halo effect and generosity error can deleteriously affect the rating of individuals.

5. For each of the following types of classification systems, give an example of how it can be used in a clinical setting: behavior and feeling word checklists, sociometric instruments, situational tests.

6. Many types of records and personal documents can be useful in the assessment process. For each of the ones listed below, describe how you might use it in a clinical setting:
   a. biographical inventory
   b. cumulative records
   c. anecdotal information
   d. autobiography
   e. journals and diaries
   f. genogram

7. Discuss how validity is determined with regard to informal assessment procedures.

8. Discuss interrater reliability and its importance to the informal assessment process.

9. Discuss the strengths and weaknesses of informal assessment procedures relative to cross-cultural issues.

10. Because informal assessment procedures can be easily and quickly developed and administered, they are practical to use. However, this very fact means that they often are not developed in a manner that yields good reliability or validity. Discuss the strengths and weaknesses of this aspect of informal assessment procedures.

Diagnosis and Writing
the Assessment Report

In the last section of the text we will examine how to make a diagnosis (Chapter 11), which is a type of an assessment of an individual, and then look at the process of writing a comprehensive test report, which partly involves the use of diagnosis (Chapter 12).

In Chapter 11 we begin by discussing the importance of making a diagnosis and describing the *Diagnostic and Statistical Manual, Fourth Edition–Text Revision (DSM-IV-TR)*. We offer a brief history of the DSM-IV-TR and go on to discuss the five axes of DSM-IV-TR that are used in making a diagnosis, including: Axis I: "Clinical Disorders and Other Conditions That May Be a Focus of Clinical Attention," Axis II: "Personality Disorders and Mental Retardation," Axis III: "General Medical Conditions," Axis IV: "Psychosocial and Environmental Problems," and Axis V: "Global Assessment of Functioning." We offer some examples of how a five-axes diagnosis is made and present some case studies for practice. We conclude the chapter with a discussion of the importance of diagnosis in the total assessment process.

Chapter 12 is the last chapter in the text. In this chapter we note that the assessment report is the "deliverable" or "end product" of the assessment process, and suggest that its purpose is to synthesize an assortment of assessment techniques so that one gains a deeper understanding of the examinee. We then go on to discuss three methods of collecting data for the report: conducting the clinical interview, choosing appropriate assessment procedures, and conducting an environmental assessment.

We first discuss the importance of conducting a clinical interview and offer guidelines for conducting an effective interview. We then distinguish among three kinds of interviews that can be used to gather information: structured, unstructured, and semi-structured interviews. We next examine the process of selecting an appropriate assessment technique, often based on the interview with the client. We discuss the importance of considering the breadth and depth of the chosen instruments and note that the clinician will often choose from a broad array of instruments, such as the ones we have examined in this text. Next, we consider the information that can be obtained by conducting an environmental assessment, in which the clinician collects information from a client's home, school, or workplace through observation or self-reports.

In the rest of Chapter 12 we suggest ways of writing effective test reports and delineate topics that must be covered to create a thorough assessment of a client. As you read through this chapter, we offer an example of a fictitious client and show how each section of the assessment report would be written. The complete assessment report can be found in Appendix E of the text.

CHAPTER 11

Diagnosis in the Assessment Process

It was 1975, and part of my job as an outpatient therapist at a mental health center entailed answering the crisis counseling phones every ninth night. I would sleep at the center and answer a very loud phone that would ring periodically throughout the night, usually with a person in crisis on the other end. Every once in a while, a former client of the center would call in and start to read aloud from his case notes, which he had stolen from the center. Parts of these notes were a description of his diagnosis from what was then the second edition of the Diagnostic and Statistical Manual (DSM-II). In a sometimes angry, sometimes funny tone, he would read these clinical terms that were supposed to be describing him. I could understand his frustration when reading these notes over the phone, as in some ways, the diagnosis seemed removed from the person—a label. "Was this really describing the person, and how was it helpful to him?" I would often wonder.
(Ed Neukrug)

An important aspect of the clinical assessment and appraisal process is skillful diagnosis. Today, the use of diagnosis permeates the mental health professions, and although there continues to be some question as to its helpfulness, it is clear that making diagnoses and using them in treatment planning has become an integral part of what all mental health professionals do. Thus, in this chapter we will examine the use of diagnosis.

We will start the chapter by discussing the importance of making a diagnosis and then describe the *Diagnostic and Statistical Manual, Fourth Edition—Text Revision* (DSM-IV-TR). We will offer a brief history of the DSM-IV-TR and discuss its five axes that are used in making a diagnosis. We will also show how a five-axes diagnosis is made and present some case studies for you to practice on. We will conclude the chapter with a discussion of the importance of diagnosis in the total assessment process.

The Importance of a Diagnosis

- John is in fifth grade and has been assessed as having a conduct disorder and attention deficit disorder with hyperactivity (ADHD). John's mother has a panic disorder and is taking antianxiety medication. Her father is bipolar and taking lithium. Jill is John's school counselor. John's individualized educational plan (IEP) states that he should see Jill for individual counseling and for group counseling. Jill must also periodically consult with John's mother and father.

- Tamara has just started college. After breaking up with her boyfriend, she became severely depressed and unable to concentrate on her schoolwork; her grades have dropped from As to Cs. She comes to the college counseling center and sobs during most of her first session with her counselor. She admits having always struggled with depression but states that "This is worse than ever; I need to get better if I am going to stay in school. Can you give me any medication to help me so I won't have to drop out?"

- Benjamin goes daily to the day treatment center at the local mental health center. He seems fairly coherent and generally in good spirits. He has been hospitalized for schizophrenia on numerous occasions and now takes Haldol and Cogentin to relieve his symptoms. He admits to Jordana, one of his counselors, that when he doesn't take his medication he believes that computers have consciousness and are conspiring through the World Wide Web to take over the world. His insurance company pays for his treatment. He will not receive treatment unless Jordana specifies a diagnosis on the insurance form.

There are many reasons to diagnose.

With evidence that a large percentage of Americans have or will experience an emotional disorder (Hersen & Van Hasselt, 2001), it is clear that regardless of where you are employed, you will be working with clients who have serious emotional problems. These individuals have been labeled as displaying abnormal behavior or having an emotional disorder and have been given or are in need of a diagnosis for treatment purposes and/or for legal reasons (Fong, 1995; Hinkle, 1994a, 1994b; Hohenshil, 1994). Recognizing the pervasiveness of mental health problems, and acknowledging that all mental health professionals will be working with individuals with mild to severe problems, most of today's training programs include instruction on diagnosis (Hinkle, 1994a, b; Hohenshil, 1993a, 1993b; 1994; Neukrug & Schwitzer, 2006; Schwitzer, 1996). Diagnosis is an important skill for helping professionals, for the following reasons:

1. Federal and state laws (e.g., PL94-142, Individuals with Disabilities Education Improvement Act: IDEIA) now require that students with severe emotional disorders be serviced in the schools. Thus, school counselors, school psychologists, and other school-based mental health professionals will likely deal with students who have severe emotional problems. The use of diagnosis helps to identify the specific mental

disorder with which a student may be struggling and can be useful in deciding treatment strategies.

2. Today, a mental disorder diagnosis has become mandatory if medical insurance is to reimburse for treatment. In addition, insurance companies will monitor progress as a function of the kind of diagnosis made.

3. With the pervasive use of a diagnostic classification system such as DSM-IV-TR, clinicians must become familiar with the nomenclature if they are to effectively communicate with one another.

4. With increasing evidence that many mental health disorders are influenced, if not determined, by biological factors (e.g., genetics, environmental factors such as lead paint, etc.), a definitive diagnosis that points to a biological influence can be critical for the proper treatment of an individual.

5. Diagnosis has become one additional and critical aspect of the total assessment process and can be helpful in case conceptualization and in treatment planning.

It has become clear that knowledge of diagnosis is necessary for every mental health professional. Clearly, the most well known diagnostic classification system is DSM-IV-TR. But how does this classification system work?

What Is DSM-IV-TR?

DSM-IV-TR
Accepted diagnostic classification system for mental disorders

Derived from the Greek words *dia* (apart) and *gnosis* (to perceive or to know), the term *diagnosis* refers to the process of making an assessment of an individual from an outside, or objective, viewpoint (Segal & Coolidge, 2001). Although attempts have been made to classify mental disorders since the turn of the century, it was not until 1952 that the American Psychiatric Association published the first comprehensive diagnostic system, called the *Diagnostic and Statistical Manual* (DSM-I). Although DSM-I had many critics and was indeed a crude effort at a diagnostic system, it did represent the first modern-day attempt to classify mental disorders. DSM-I was revised numerous times over the years to its current edition, the DSM-IV-TR. This version, which is a distant cousin from the original DSM-I, offers explicit ways of determining a diagnosis and presents a five-part multiaxial diagnostic system (APA, 2000; Hinkle, 1994b). Although the DSM-IV-TR has its critics, it has become the most widespread and accepted diagnostic classification system of emotional disorders in the world (Seligman, 1999; Wakefield, 1992).

The DSM-IV-TR offers five axes to assist in diagnosis and treatment of mental disorders. Although many clinicians do not use all five axes, a good number will find two or more of the axes useful. Axis I describes "Clinical Disorders and Other Conditions That May Be a Focus of Clinical Attention," Axis II delineates "Personality Disorders and Mental Retardation," Axis III explains "General Medical Conditions," Axis IV describes "Psychosocial and Environmental Problems," and Axis V offers a "Global Assessment of Functioning."

The use of the five axes underscores one of the most important purposes of the DSM-IV-TR classification system: to *describe* and *communicate* with other professionals who are familiar with the system in an effort to enhance agreement and improve the sharing of information among clinicians about the client picture they are observing (Neukrug & Schwitzer, 2006). In addition, a diagnosis can help a clinician determine the primary focus of counseling. For example, a focus on a mood problem might be dealt with differently from a focus on somatic complaints, or a focus on an adjustment problem is dealt with differently from a focus on problems related to long-term life patterns, such as a personality disorder. Determining the focus can assist the clinician when deciding which interventions might be most useful. Although all five axes can be helpful in determining the kind of intervention, the first two axes focus specifically on the kind of disorder involved and are generally most important in determining treatment plans.

Axes I and II: The Mental Disorders[1]

The first two axes of DSM-IV-TR offer a wealth of information on specific mental disorders. Such information helps clinicians determine which specific disorder a client might be struggling with. The following very brief overview defines the mental disorders included in Axis I and II, highlights cross-cultural issues related to the diagnosis of mental disorders, and summarizes hundreds of pages of information from Axis I and Axis II of DSM-IV-TR. For an in-depth review of the disorders, please see DSM-IV-TR (APA, 2000).

Understanding the Mental Disorders

Each item includes features, subtypes, patterns, and differentiation from similar disorders.

Each mental disorder covered in DSM-IV-TR describes (1) the disorder's main features; (2) subtypes and variations in client presentations; (3) the typical pattern, course, or progression of symptoms; and (4) how to differentiate the disorder from other, similar ones. The DSM-IV-TR also provides findings about predisposing factors, complications, and associated medical and counseling problems when they are known, and it does not hypothesize about etiology of a disorder when information is not known. DSM-IV-TR diagnoses are intended to be theory-neutral descriptions of behavior, thoughts, mood, physiology, functioning, and distress. Thus, using DSM-IV-TR categories and descriptors allows clinicians to describe clients and communicate with mental health colleagues while being able to apply their own theoretical orientation to the treatment planning process (Jongsma & Peterson, 1999; Seligman, 2004).

One misperception beginning clinicians sometimes have is that using clinical diagnoses, like those of the DSM-IV-TR, means that one must view all client concerns and interests from a very clinical, psychopathological viewpoint. In reality, the DSM-IV-TR system is used to share information about a very small

---

[1] Parts of this section are paraphrased from DSM-IV-TR (APA, 2000).

subset of human behavior or experience—those conditions that meet the "mental disorder" definition. In fact, from a diagnostic standpoint, the vast majority of human behavior does not meet the definition of "mental disorder" and instead is "functional," "normal," and "ordered," rather than "dysfunctional," "abnormal," or "disordered." Thus, each DSM-IV-TR mental disorder is constructed to be a distinct pattern of difficulty that is currently causing the client distress, significant impairment in some area of day-to-day functioning, or increased risk of disability (APA, 2000; Schwitzer & Everett, 1997). It should also be remembered that many of those individuals who meet the definition of having a mental disorder live a rather normal life in many, if not most, ways.

Cultural Issues and the Mental Disorders

Culturally appropriate responses are not diagnosable. Client experiences that are considered to be expected reactions or culturally appropriate responses to life events are not diagnosable as mental disorders, even when they cause distress or dysfunction in the client's life. For example, while counseling may focus on the grief process following the loss of a loved one, a diagnosis of major depression usually is not made even when the person experiences major depression criteria such as extreme sadness, insomnia, or poor concentration during the first two months following the loss. Even significant disruptions in mood and functioning are accepted as culturally appropriate during the grief process.

Similarly, client concerns that are considered to be expected, or culturally appropriate, phase of life developmental experiences are not diagnosed as mental disorders regardless of distress or dysfunction they may cause in life. For example, identity confusion in adolescence, which is often associated with distress about long-term life goals, relationships, and values, is viewed as a normal, expected experience and therefore not diagnosed as a mental disorder.

The DSM-IV-TR was constructed with much greater attention to issues of age, gender, socioeconomic status, and culture than were past editions. For example, age differences in symptoms often appear in DSM-IV-TR, such as the notation that major depression is associated with increased withdrawal in children, oversleeping in adolescents, and cognitive problems such as memory loss in older adults.

Relevant gender-specific information about prevalence and symptoms is provided in DSM-IV-TR. For example, the clinician is alerted that bipolar disorders are equally common among men and women, unlike major depression, which is diagnosed more commonly among women, or obsessive-compulsive disorder, which is diagnosed more commonly among men. Similarly, differences in prevalence according to socioeconomic status are described for some diagnoses.

The DSM-IV-TR notes that clinicians tend to overdiagnose or misdiagnose certain disorders as a function of culture or age. For example, counselors are alerted that schizophrenia is sometimes diagnosed instead of bipolar disorder in non-White cultural groups and younger clients. Other cultural differences also are highlighted, such as the fact that clients from diverse backgrounds present depression in varying ways. For instance, somatic complaints, such as headaches among Latinos and fatigue and weakness among Asians, are symptoms that could be representative of depression more frequently in these cultural groups than in others. In addition, the DSM-IV-TR includes an appendix of culture-specific client experiences not included elsewhere. For example, *nervios* is included as a common type of stress disorder among Latinos, and includes symptoms of emotional distress, nervousness, tearfulness, and bodily complaints. Also consider the term *koro*, which is defined as follows in the DSM-IV-TR:

> *A term, probably of Malaysian origin, that refers to an episode of sudden and intense anxiety that the penis (or in females, the vulva and nipples) will recede into the body and possibly cause death. . . . (APA, 2000, p. 900)*

Axis I Disorders: Clinical Disorders and Other Conditions That May Be a Focus of Clinical Attention

Axis I disorders are considered treatable and often temporary.

This axis includes all disorders except those classified as personality disorders or as mental retardation (Axis II disorders). Generally, Axis I disorders are considered treatable in some fashion, and are often reimbursable by insurance companies as a function of mental health or related services. These disorders are described below.

Disorders Usually First Diagnosed in Infancy, Childhood, or Adolescence

The disorders in this section are generally found in childhood; however, at times individuals are not diagnosed with the disorder until they are adults. Particularly important for school counselors, the disorders include learning disorders, motor skills disorders, communication disorders, pervasive developmental disorders, attention-deficit and disruptive behavior disorders, feeding and eating disorders of infancy or early childhood, tic disorders, elimination disorders, and other disorders of infancy, childhood, or adolescence.

Delirium, Dementia, Amnestic, and Other Cognitive Disorders

Delirium, dementia, and amnestic disorders are all cognitive disorders that represent a significant change from past cognitive functioning of the client. All of these disorders are caused by a medical condition or a substance (e.g., drug abuse, medication, or allergic reaction).

Mental Disorders Due to a General Medical Condition

This diagnosis is made when a mental disorder is found to be the result of a medical condition and include personality changes and mental disorders not otherwise specified. Other disorders that may at times be the result of a medical condition are listed under the following specific diagnostic categories: delirium, dementia, amnestic disorder, psychotic disorder, mood disorder, anxiety disorder, sexual dysfunction, and sleep disorder.

Substance-Related Disorders

A substance-related disorder is a direct result of the use of a drug or alcohol, the effects of medication, or exposure to a toxin. These substances include alcohol, amphetamine, caffeine, cannabis, cocaine, hallucinogens, inhalants, nicotine, opioids, phencyclidine (PCP), sedatives, and hypnotics.

Schizophrenia and Other Psychotic Disorders

All disorders classified in this section share one thing in common: psychotic symptomatology is the most distinguishing feature. The disorders include schizophrenia, schizophreniform disorder, schizoaffective disorder, delusional disorder, brief psychotic disorder, shared psychotic disorder, psychotic disorder due to a general medical condition, substance-induced psychotic disorder, and psychotic disorder not otherwise specified.

Mood Disorders

The disorders in this category include mood disturbances of the depressive, manic, or hypomanic type. The mood disorders are divided into five broad categories: depressive disorders, bipolar disorders, mood disorder due to a general medical condition, substance-induced mood disorder, and mood disorder not otherwise specified.

Anxiety Disorders

There are many types of anxiety disorders, each with its own discrete characteristics. They include panic attack, agoraphobia, panic disorder with or without agoraphobia, agoraphobia without history of panic disorder, specific phobia, obsessive-compulsive disorder, posttraumatic stress disorder, acute stress disorder, generalized anxiety disorder, anxiety disorder due to a general medical condition, substance-induced anxiety disorder, and anxiety disorder not otherwise specified.

Somatoform Disorders

Somatoform disorders are characterized by symptoms that would suggest a physical cause. However, no such cause can be found, and there is strong evidence that links the symptoms to psychological causes. Somatoform disorders include somatization disorder, undifferentiated somatoform disorder, conversion disorder, pain disorder, hypochondriasis, body dysmorphic disorder, and somatoform disorder not otherwise specified.

Factitious Disorders

As opposed to somatoform disorders, which describe individuals who believe that their physical symptoms have a physiological etiology, factitious disorders describe individuals who intentionally feign physical or psychological symptoms in order to assume the sick role. Two subtypes include factitious disorder with predominantly psychological signs and symptoms and factitious disorder with predominantly physical signs and symptoms.

Dissociative Disorders

Dissociative disorders occur when there is a disruption of consciousness, memory, identity, or perception of the environment. Dissociative disorders include dissociative amnesia, dissociative fugue, dissociative identity disorder (formerly called multiple personality disorder), depersonalization disorder, and dissociative disorder not otherwise specified.

Sexual and Gender Identity Disorders

This section includes disorders that focus on sexual problems or identity issues related to sexual issues. They include sexual dysfunctions, paraphilias, gender identity disorders, and sexual disorder not otherwise specified.

Eating Disorders

These disorders focus on severe problems with the amount of food intake by the individual that can potentially cause serious health problems or death. They include anorexia nervosa, bulimia nervosa, and eating disorder not otherwise specified.

Sleep Disorders

These disorders have to do with severe sleep-related problems and are broken down into four subcategories: primary sleep disorders, sleep disorder related to another mental condition, sleep disorder due to a general medical condition, and substance-induced sleep disorder.

Impulse Control Disorders Not Elsewhere Classified

Impulse control disorders are highlighted by the individual's inability to stop himself or herself from exhibiting certain behaviors. They include intermittent explosive disorder, kleptomania, pyromania, pathological gambling, trichotillomania, and impulse-control disorder not otherwise specified.

Adjustment Disorders

Probably the most common disorders clinicians see in private practice, adjustment disorders are highlighted by emotional or behavioral symptoms that arise in response to psychosocial stressors. The subtypes of this diagnosis include adjustment disorders with depressed mood, with anxiety, with mixed anxiety and depressed mood, with disturbance of conduct, with mixed disturbance of emotions and conduct, and unspecified adjustment disorder.

After the class has become familiar with the disorders included in Axis I, your instructor may ask a student to role-play an Axis I diagnosis. Using the criteria listed in the DSM-IV-TR, try to identify the diagnosis (you may also want to use the decision tree located in DSM-IV-TR to guide you). You may want to role-play a series of Axis I diagnoses.

Axis II Disorders: Personality Disorders and Mental Retardation

Axis II disorders tend to be lifelong and resistant to treatment.

Axis II diagnoses tend to be long-term disorders in which treatment almost always has little or no effect on changing the presenting symptoms of the individual. The two kinds of Axis II disorders are mental retardation and personality disorders.

Mental Retardation

Characterized by intellectual functioning significantly below average (below the second percentile) as well as problems with adaptive skills, mental retardation can have many different etiologies. There are four categories of mental retardation: mild mental retardation (IQ of 50-55 to approximately 70), moderate mental retardation (IQ of 35-40 to 50-55), severe mental retardation (IQ of 20-25 to 35-40), and profound mental retardation (IQ below 20 or 25).

Personality Disorders

Individuals with a personality disorder show deeply ingrained, inflexible, and enduring patterns of relating to the world that lead to distress and impairment in functioning. Such an individual may have difficulty understanding self and others, may be labile, have difficulty in relationships, and have problems with impulse control. Personality disorders are generally first recognized in adolescence or early adulthood and often remain throughout one's lifetime. There are three clusters of personality disorders, with each cluster representing a general way of relating to the world.

Cluster A includes paranoid, schizoid, and schizotypal personality disorders. Individuals with these disorders all exhibit characteristics that may be considered odd or eccentric by others.

Cluster B disorders include the antisocial, borderline, histrionic, and narcissistic personality disorders. Individuals suffering from these disorders are generally dramatic, emotional, overly sensitive, and erratic.

Cluster C includes the avoidant, dependent, and obsessive-compulsive personality disorders. Common characteristics found within this cluster are anxious and fearful traits.

EXERCISE 11.2 **Diagnosing Axis II Disorders**

After the class has become familiar with the disorders included in Axis II, your instructor may ask a student to role-play one of the personality disorders.

Using the criteria listed in the DSM-IV-TR, try to identify the diagnosis. You may want to role-play a few of the personality disorders.

Axis III: General Medical Conditions

Axis III lists medical conditions that cause disorders or may affect treatment.

Axis III provides the clinician the opportunity to report relevant medical conditions of the client. If the medical condition is clearly related to the cause or worsening of a mental disorder, then a medical condition is noted on Axis I and listed on Axis III. If the medical condition is not a cause of the mental disorder but will affect overall treatment of the individual, then it is listed only on Axis III. An example of an Axis III medical condition that could be a cause of an Axis I diagnosis would be the development of hypothyroidism that causes an anxiety disorder. In this case, on Axis I the anxiety disorder due to a general medical condition is noted, and on Axis III the specific medical condition is listed. The International Classification of Diseases, ninth revision (ICD-9-CM), an abbreviated form of which is found in the DSM-IV-TR, is used to code the Axis III medical condition. Axis I uses the DSM-IV-TR classification and includes a reference to the medical condition.

Axis I: Anxiety Disorders Due to a General Medical Condition (293.84)

Axis III: Hypothyroidism, acquired (244.9)

On the other hand, if an individual has a sleep disorder and subsequently develops acute prostatitis (infection of the prostate) that worsens, but did not cause, the sleep disorder, the diagnosis would be written as

Axis I: Narcolepsy (347)

Axis III: Prostatitis (618.9)

If there is no Axis III diagnosis, then "Axis III: None" is included in the diagnosis.

EXERCISE 11.3 **Diagnosing Medical Conditions**

Your instructor may ask one or more of the role-play clients from Exercise 11.1 or 11.2 to role-play a medical condition listed in DSM-IV-TR. Identify the medical condition in DSM-IV-TR and write out the Axis I,

Axis II, and Axis III diagnoses. Make sure that the medical condition is listed twice if it causes the Axis I or Axis II diagnosis.

Axis IV: Psychosocial and Environmental Problems

Axis IV lists psychosocial and environmental factors affecting the client.

Axis IV includes psychosocial or environmental problems that affect the diagnosis, treatment, and prognosis of mental disorders listed on Axes I and II. Generally, such problems will be listed only on Axis IV, but in those cases where it is believed that such stressors may be a prime cause of the mental disorder, a reference should be made to them on Axis I or II. General categories of psychosocial and environmental problems include problems with one's primary support group, problems related to the social environment, educational problems, occupational problems, housing problems, economic problems, problems with access to health care services, and problems related to interaction with the legal system/crime. An example of an Axis IV diagnosis is

Axis IV: Job Loss.

EXERCISE 11.4 Diagnosing Psychosocial and Environmental Problems

Your instructor may ask the role-play client(s) from Exercise 11.3 to continue to role-play, or start a new role-play, but this time portray psychosocial and/or environmental problems. Identify the condition in DSM-IV-TR and write out the Axis I, Axis II, Axis III, and Axis IV diagnoses. Make sure that the psychosocial and environmental problem is listed twice if it is a cause of the Axis I or Axis II diagnosis.

Axis V: Global Assessment of Functioning (GAF)

Axis V-GAF Numerical scale (0–100) indicating the clients' overall functioning

Axis V is a scale used by the clinician to assess the client's overall functioning and is based on an assessment of the client's psychological, social, and occupational functioning. The GAF scale ranges from very severe dysfunction to superior functioning, and a score of 0 means there is inadequate information to make a judgment (see Table 11.1). In giving a GAF rating, the clinician can report current functioning, the highest functioning within the past year, or any other relevant GAF ratings based on the uniqueness of the situation.

EXERCISE 11.5 Using the GAF Scale

Your instructor may have the class continue the role play(s) from Exercise 11.4, or start a role-play of a new client. Determine a GAF score for the client based on this role-play. You may need to probe with the client to make an accurate assessment of the score. Have each student in the class do this exercise independently, and then compare your scores with one another.

Making a Diagnosis

The DSM-IV-TR offers decision trees to assist the clinician in differential diagnosis. Thus, if one is considering two or more diagnoses that share similar symptoms, the decision tree walks the clinician through a series of steps designed to

TABLE 11.1
Global Assessment of Functioning Scale (GAF)

CODE*

100 I 91	Superior functioning in a wide range of activities, life's problems never seem to get out of hand, is sought out by others because of his or her many positive qualities. No symptoms.
90 I I 81	Absent or minimal symptoms (e.g., mild anxiety before an exam), good functioning in all areas, interested and involved in a wide range of activities, socially effective, generally satisfied with life, no more than everyday problems or concerns (e.g., an occasional argument with family members).
80 I I 71	If symptoms are present, they are transient and expectable reactions to psychosocial stressors (e.g., difficulty concentrating after family argument); no more than slight impairment in social, occupational, or school functioning (e.g., temporarily falling behind in schoolwork).
70 I I 61	Some mild symptoms (e.g., depressed mood and mild insomnia) OR some difficulty in social, occupational or school functioning (e.g., occasional truancy, or theft within the household), but generally functioning pretty well, has some meaningful inter- personal relationships.
60 I 51	Moderate symptoms (e.g., flat affect and circumstantial speech, occasional panic attacks) OR some difficulty in social, occupational, or school functioning (e.g., few friends, conflicts with peers or co-workers).
50 I 41	Serious symptoms (e.g., suicidal ideation, severe obsessional rituals, frequent shoplifting) OR any serious impairment in social occupational, or school functioning (e.g., no friends, unable to keep a job).
40 I I I 31	Some impairment in reality testing or communication (e.g., speech is at times illogical, obscure, or irrelevant) OR major impairment in several areas, such as work or school, family relations, judgment , thinking, or mood (e.g., depressed man avoids friends, neglects family, and is unable to work; child frequently beats up younger children, is defiant at home, and is failing at school).
30 I I 21	Behavior is considerably influenced by delusions or hallucinations OR serious impairment in communication or judgment (e.g., sometimes incoherent, acts grossly inappropriately, suicidal preoccupation) OR inability to function in almost all areas (e.g., stays in bed all day; no job, home, or friends).
20 I I 11	Some danger of hurting self or others (e.g., suicide attempts without clear expectation of death: frequently violent; manic excitement) OR occasionally fails to maintain minimal personal hygiene (e.g., smears feces) OR gross impairment in communication (e.g., largely incoherent or mute).
10 I 1 0	Persistent danger of severely hurting self or others (e.g., recurrent violence) OR persistent inability to maintain minimal personal hygiene OR serious suicidal act with clear expectation of death. Inadequate information

* Note: Use intermediate codes when appropriate, e.g., 45, 68, 72.
Source: Used with permission from the *Diagnostic and Statistical Manual of Mental Disorders,* Fourth Edition, Text Revision, p. 34. Copyright 2000. American Psychiatric Association.

EXERCISE 11.6 **Using the Five Axes of DSM-IV-TR**

Examine the cases that follow, and using this chapter as well as the DSM-IV-TR as your guide, describe each client on the five axes of DSM-IV-TR. The answers can be found at the end of the chapter.

JOSHUA

Joshua is a 10-year-old only child. His parents, Marie, who is 27, and Billy, who is 28, have been married for six years and have commented on what a difficult child Joshua has been since birth. They state that he always had a difficult time in school and could not read until he was in fourth grade. His reading scores have been particularly low, and his teacher has suggested having him tested for a possible reading learning disability. No obvious physical problems have been found to cause his deficiency in reading.

In addition to his reading problems, Joshua seems to cry easily and often "has a fit" when he has to leave home to go to school. He is plagued by nightmares, often revolving around issues of being alone or separated from his parents. He often has stomachaches and has been known to vomit at school on numerous occasions. Joshua's reading problems and his anxiety have interfered with his ability to build friendships, and he has no close friends and few peers he relates to at school. His parents, who are college educated, are worried that their son will not make it through high school, and they are concerned about his social relationships.

TRINA

Trina is a 53-year-old separated female with no children. She presents with moderate depression and states she has had fleeting thoughts of suicide. However, she remarks that she would never kill herself—"that would be just damn stupid." When you inquire about her depression, she notes that her husband just "got up and left me!" Trina goes on to say that her husband left her about two months ago, and she has been feeling depressed ever since. She reports having no past history of depression.

Trina is morbidly obese, weighing about 320 lbs at 5'4" tall. She states, "I have always been fat, and

that's why my husband married me—he loves fat ladies—well, he used to." She states that her life is worthless, and she is worried that she will never find anyone else who will love her like her husband did. She states that her life revolved around her husband because she would be his "cook, errand girl, friend, and everything else." She goes on to note that she has never felt this way before. Although she reports having a few friends, she states that they can hardly fill the hole she has had in her heart since her husband left. Trina has a high school education and has worked intermittently in the food industry. She currently is employed on a part-time basis and states, "At least I don't think about him when I'm at work." She notes that she is relieved that she is in counseling and hopes that she can build a new life, even without him.

HENRY

Henry is 75 years old and currently lives in a group home for the mentally ill. Until he was in his early 30s, he was married and raising two children. However, when he was about 34 he began to have delusional thoughts, thinking that he had been somehow picked to be the next Czar of the Soviet Empire. At that time, he would often go to the Russian consulate and walk in front of the building carrying a sign that said, "Your Czar is here, I have arrived." A couple of times he tried to run into the consulate, was arrested, and landed in jail overnight. Since his early 30s he has had little or no contact with his children and has alternated between living on the streets, being in state hospitals, and living in group homes. His wife divorced him about forty years ago and he has not heard from her since. Although medication seems to have settled down his delusional thoughts, he has never been the same as he was before he became delusional. For years he has not been able to hold a job and has had no social outlets. He has a flat affect and is often incoherent. Despite his limitations, he seems to be able to function on a minimal level in group homes or on the streets.

When making a diagnosis, list all five axes when possible or appropriate.

assist in choosing the most appropriate diagnosis. Making an appropriate diagnosis is critically important because the diagnosis will affect treatment planning and choices of psychotropic medication. It is possible for a client to have more than one Axis I and Axis II diagnosis, and in those cases the additional diagnoses should be reported. A typical multiaxial assessment may look something like the following:

Axis I	309.0	Adjustment Disorder with Depressed Mood
Axis II	301.82	Avoidant Personality Disorder
Axis III		No Diagnosis
Axis IV		Divorce
Axis V		GAF = 60 (current); 75 (highest in past year)

As you become more familiar with DSM-IV-TR, the process of making a diagnosis will become easier and you will see how helpful such a diagnosis can be in treatment planning. Exercise 11.6 gives you an opportunity to use DSM-IV-TR in making a diagnosis.

Final Thoughts on DSM-IV-TR in the Assessment Process

Diagnosis adds clarity to the assessment process.

DSM-IV-TR is one additional piece of the total assessment process. Along with the clinical interview, the use of tests, and informal assessment procedures, it can provide a broad understanding of the client and can be a critical piece in the treatment planning process. Consider what it might be like to establish a treatment plan if only one test were used. Then, consider what it would be like if two tests were used, then two tests and an informal assessment procedure, then two tests, an informal assessment procedure, and a clinical interview, and finally, two tests, an informal assessment procedure, a clinical interview, and a diagnosis. Clearly, the more "pieces of evidence" we can gather, the clearer our snapshot of our client becomes and this, in turn, yields better treatment planning.

Summary

We began this chapter by discussing the importance of a diagnosis and noting that no matter where you work, you will be faced with individuals who have a mental disorder. Specifically, we noted that diagnostic skills are important because there are federal laws pertaining to the schools and the labeling of children, diagnosis is required for insurance reimbursement, having a common system for diagnosis allows us to communicate effectively with colleagues, there is evidence of biological determinants of many mental disorders, and accurate diagnosis is an essential part of the total assessment process.

In the next part of the chapter we gave a brief history of the *Diagnostic and Statistical Manual* and then discussed the five axes of DSM-IV-TR. We noted that

Axis I describes "Clinical Disorders and Other Conditions That May Be a Focus of Clinical Attention," Axis II delineates "Personality Disorders and Mental Retardation," Axis III explains "General Medical Conditions," Axis IV describes "Psychosocial and Environmental Problems," and Axis V offers a "Global Assessment of Functioning."

Looking at Axes I and II, we noted that the section on each mental disorder describes the disorder's main features, subtypes and variations in client presentations, the progression of symptoms, and how to differentiate disorders. We also noted that the DSM-IV-TR provides findings about predisposing factors, complications, and associated medical and counseling problems and does not hypothesize about etiology when information is unknown. We pointed out that DSM-IV-TR diagnoses are intended to be theory-neutral descriptions of disorders, thus allowing clinicians to apply their own theoretical orientation to the treatment planning process. From a diagnostic standpoint, we noted that the vast majority of human behavior does not meet the definition of "mental disorder."

From a cultural perspective, we noted that expected, culturally appropriate behavior or predictable developmental experiences are not diagnosed as mental disorders. We highlighted the fact that the DSM-IV-TR was constructed with much greater attention to issues of age, gender, socioeconomic status, and culture than were past editions. We also noted that the DSM-IV-TR mentions that clinicians sometimes overdiagnose or misdiagnose certain disorders in clients of a specific culture or age. We noted that the DSM-IV-TR includes an appendix of culture-specific client experiences not included elsewhere.

Next we offered a brief overview of the Axis I and Axis II disorders and then went on to describe Axis III Disorders: General Medical Conditions. We noted that when a medical condition is found to somehow cause or be related to an Axis I or Axis II condition, it should be listed on that axis as well as on Axis III. This, we noted, is similar to how one would list the psychosocial stressors in Axis IV. Finally, we presented the General Assessment of Functioning scale and noted how it is used to rate the client's level of functioning on Axis V. We gave examples of how to make a diagnosis using the five axes and offered some case studies as practice.

The chapter concluded with a discussion about the importance of a diagnosis in the total process of assessing a client. We noted that the more "pieces of evidence" we can gather (e.g., tests, informal assessment, clinical interviews, and a diagnosis), the clearer our snapshot of our client becomes and the better our treatment planning will be.

Chapter Review

1. Explain why diagnosis is important in the following settings:
   a. schools
   b. mental health agencies
   c. private practice
   d. hospital settings

2. Describe the ways in which diagnosis can be abused.

3. Make an argument for the usefulness of diagnosis.

4. List and describe each of the five axes of DSM-IV-TR and show how it is used.

5. Describe how each mental disorder is explained in DSM-IV-TR (Axis I and Axis II disorders).

6. Relative to the mental disorders, describe how DSM-IV-TR addresses cross-cultural issues.

7. Give examples of how Axis III and Axis IV disorders may or may not be listed on two axes.

8. Describe each of the individuals listed in Exercise 11.6 on the five axes of DSM-IV-TR. If you have already completed Exercise 11.6 or would like additional practice in making diagnoses, use case vignettes from readings or case examples from your classes.

ANSWERS TO EXERCISE 11.6: **Using the Five Axes of DSM-IV-TR**

JOSHUA

Axis I:	315.00	Rule Out Reading Disorder
	309.21	Separation Anxiety Disorder
Axis II:	None	
Axis III:	Stomachaches	
Axis IV:	Problems relating to peers at school	

Axis V: GAF = 61 (Current)

TRINA

| Axis I: | 309.0 | Adjustment Disorder with Depression, Acute |
| Axis II: | None | |

Axis III: 278.00   Obesity

Axis IV: Separation from husband

Axis V: GAF = 55 (Current) (75 over past year)

HENRY

Axis I:	295.60	Schizophrenia, Residual Type
Axis II:	None	
Axis III:	None	
Axis IV:	Severe psychosocial problems: Intermittent homelessness Problems forming friendships	

Axis V: GAF = 23 (Over past year)

The Assessment Report Process: The Interview, Assessment Techniques, Environmental Assessment, and the Report

"Increasing numbers of people are writing and reading increasing numbers of mental health records for increasing number of purposes, and that trend is likely to continue" (Reynolds, Mair, & Fischer, 1995, p. 1).

When I began working with clients in the early 1970s, I was dutiful about writing down my case notes on lined paper. Soon it was the mid-70s, and I got a job as an outpatient therapist at a mental health center. I was compulsive about conducting thorough clinical interviews, and religious about dictating my case notes, my intake summaries, and my quarterly summaries. My dictations were carefully typed out by secretaries and placed in client folders. Ten years later, I was in private practice. I was still compulsive about conducting a thorough interview and about writing up my case notes—again on lined paper. But soon an innovation arrived I hadn't expected—the computer. I started doing my notes on the computer—that was a relief for me, although not everyone felt the same way. Soon after my discovery of the computer, the HMOs and PPOs multiplied and an increasing number of laws were passed that had to do with case note confidentiality, the rights of insurance companies, and the rights of clients. The paperwork was beginning to drive me nutty! Soon, computer programs were devised to help write case reports and Internet connections to the insurance companies to streamline billing became a reality, but it happened a little too late for me. I'm out of here. No more private practice for me—too much paperwork! (Ed Neukrug)

As you can see from the above quote and vignette, the process of gathering information about clients and writing reports that will affect them has become increasingly complex. In this chapter we will examine this process. First, we will discuss the purpose of the assessment report and then identify three aspects critical to the process of gathering information for the report, including conducting the interview, choosing appropriate assessment techniques, and conducting an environmental assessment. Finally, we will suggest ways to write effective test reports and we will supply an example of such a report.

Purpose of the Assessment Report

Assessment report
Written summary, synthesis, and recommendations from the assessment

The assessment report is the "deliverable" or "end product" of the assessment process. Its purpose is to synthesize an assortment of assessment techniques so that a deeper understanding of the examinee is made and recommended courses of action are offered (Appelbaum, 1990; Ownby, 1997). Such courses of action can vary dramatically, based on the reason the individual is being assessed. For instance, reports have been used for the following purposes:

1. To provide insight to clients for therapy.
2. To suggest treatment options in counseling.
3. To help determine which psychotropic medications to use.
4. To suggest educational services for students with special needs (e.g., for students who are mentally retarded, learning disabled, or gifted).
5. To offer direction when providing vocational rehabilitation services.
6. To assist the courts in making difficult decisions (e.g., custody decisions, sanity defenses, determination of guilt or innocence).

Complex decisions regarding clients' lives are often based on the assessment report. Thus, synthesizing the information gathered and placing it in the report is a craft, and proficiency at it is only accomplished after one has considerable training and practice administering assessment techniques and writing reports. This chapter will explore three ways to gather information for the assessment report and provide a model for writing such a report.

Gathering Information for the Report: Garbage In, Garbage Out

Gathering information for the report is as important as writing the report, because your report will reflect the methods you used to obtain your information. If you choose inappropriate instruments or conduct a poor interview, your report will be filled with error and bias. In gathering information for your report, you should take into account the breadth and depth of your assessment procedures.

Breadth
Covering all important or relevant issues

The breadth of the assessment has to do with casting a wide enough net to assure that the examiner has done all that is necessary to adequately assess what he or she is looking for. Breadth should be based upon the purpose for which the individual is being assessed. For instance, if a middle school student came to see a school counselor to examine career possibilities, the counselor would likely conduct an interview focused on vocational interests and offer a broad-based career interest inventory to gather information from the student about his or her general interests. However, if an adult came in as a result of depression, anxiety, and general discontent in life, a very broad assessment might be called for to help establish a diagnosis and determine treatment goals. In this case, it would not be unusual to conduct a clinical interview, administer a number of objective and projective tests, and perhaps interview others to assess the client's relationships at home and at work.

Depth
Extent and seriousness of a concern

The depth of the assessment has to do with assuring that one is using techniques that reflect the intensity of the issue(s) being examined. As with breadth, depth is also dependent on the purpose for which the client is being assessed. For instance, conducting an in-depth clinical interview and offering a rather complex interest inventory that helps the middle school student determine a career would be too involved—too much depth. On the other hand, offering a personality inventory like the Myers-Briggs for the individual suffering from depression, anxiety, and discontentment in life would not be enough depth. In the latter case, it might be appropriate to conduct an involved clinical interview that attempts to assess underlying factors, to administer complex instruments that yield possible diagnoses and underlying pathology (e.g., the MMPI-2), and possibly to interview others who know the client.

In considering breadth and depth, clinicians should take into account the type of interview being conducted, the kinds of assessment instruments that should be used, and whether or not an environmental assessment is called for.

Conducting the Clinical Interview

Clinical interview
Critical to the assessment process; can be structured, unstructured, or semi-structured

The clinical interview accomplishes a number of tasks not possible through the use of other assessment techniques, including the following:

1. Setting a tone for the types of information that will be covered during the assessment process.
2. Allowing the client to become desensitized to information that can be very intimate and personal.
3. Allowing the examiner to assess the nonverbal signals of the client while he or she is talking about sensitive information, thus giving the examiner a sense of items it might be important to focus upon.
4. Allowing the examiner to learn firsthand the problem areas of the client and place them in perspective.
5. Giving the client and examiner the opportunity to study each other's personality style to assure that they can work together.

Prior to and during the interview, Drummond (2004) suggests a number of factors to consider in order to adequately assess one's client. For instance, he suggests that the examiner do the following things:

1. Know why the client is being interviewed. The breadth and depth of the interview will vary as a function of the reason for the interview.
2. Establish trust and rapport.
3. Provide an environment that is comfortable and assures confidentiality.
4. Focus on verbal and nonverbal cues in an effort to gather all of what the person is communicating to you.
5. Keep the goals of the interview clear so that you can accomplish your assessment while allowing the client the freedom to take the interview where he or she needs to take it.

With these points in mind, examiners need to determine whether to use a structured, unstructured, or semi-structured interview when gathering information from the client. Of course, the amount of information needed should be considered carefully and could affect the kind of interview one conducts. The following discussion examines the differences among these types of interviews.

The Structured Interview

Structured interview Uses pre-established questions to assess broad range of behaviors

In a structured interview, the interviewer asks the examinee to respond to pre-established items. This is often done verbally, although sometimes clients are asked to respond to written items. A structured interview can provide the following benefits:

- offers broad enough areas of content to cover topics a practitioner may otherwise have missed (assures breadth of coverage),
- increases the reliability of results by ensuring that all prescribed items will be covered (Crippa, Sanches, Hallak, Loureiro, & Zuardi, 2001),
- helps the examiner focus on specific items that may otherwise be missed or difficult to cover during an unstructured interview,

On the negative side, structured interviews can have the following drawbacks:

- the examiner may miss an important piece of information due to the fact that items on the structured interview are pre-determined,
- clients may experience the interview as dehumanizing,
- clients may misinterpret items or examiners may misinterpret client responses, because clients (e.g., minority clients) may be unfamiliar with items and follow-up to questions is less likely with a structured interview (Roth, Van Iddekinge, Huffcutt, Eidson, & Bobko, 2002).
- this type of interview does not always allow for depth of information to be covered because the interviewer is more concerned with gathering all the information than going into detail about a potentially sensitive area.

The Unstructured Interview

Unstructured interview
Examiner asks questions based on client responses

In an unstructured interview the examiner does not have a pre-established list of items or questions to which the client can respond; instead, client responses to examiner inquiries will set the direction for follow-up questioning. The unstructured interview offers the following advantages:

1. Creates an atmosphere that is more conducive to building rapport.
2. Allows the client to feel as if he or she is directing the interview, thus allowing the client to discuss items that he or she deems important.
3. Offers the potential for greater depth of information because the clinician can focus upon a potentially sensitive area and possibly uncover underlying issues that the client might otherwise avoid revealing.

On the other hand, the unstructured interview may have the following disadvantages:

1. Not allowing for breadth of coverage as the interviewer might miss information because he or she is "caught up" in the client's story instead of following a prescribed set of questions.
2. One may end up spending more time on some items than one might like.

The Semi-Structured Interview

Semi-structured interview
Allows flow between structured and unstructured approaches

The semi-structured interview uses prescribed items, which allows the examiner to obtain the necessary information within a relatively short amount of time. However, this kind of interview also gives leeway to the examiner should the client need to "drift" during the interview process. Allowing the client to discuss potentially emotion-filled topics can be cathartic, open up new issues of importance, and be an important tool in the rapport-building process. The skilled examiner can easily flow back and forth between structured and unstructured approaches. If time is not an issue, a semi-structured interview can provide the breadth and depth needed when interviewing clients.

Computer-Driven Assessment

Computer-driven assessment
Provides wide range of coverage and can result in sophisticated report

Whether you are conducting a structured, unstructured, or semi-structured interview, a number of computer programs can be of assistance. For instance, one such program (Schinka, 2003) has the interviewer or the client complete 120 items that divulge information about a wide range of personal issues, and the user receives a computer-generated report that describes the client's presenting problems, legal issues, current living situation, tentative diagnosis, emotional state, treatment recommendations, mental status, health and habits, disposition, and behavioral/physical descriptions. Computer-assisted questioning is as reliable or more reliable than structured interviews and can provide an accurate diagnosis at a minimal cost (Greist, 1998; Richman, Kiesler, Weisb, & Drasgow, 1999; Sturges, 1998). The case reports that are generated by such computer-driven programs

---

BOX 12.1
Proper Assessment of a Client

As mentioned in Chapter 9, I once was asked to write an assessment report for a client who had been denied disability insurance despite the fact that she had been diagnosed as having a multiple personality disorder. Aware of her disorder, and having worked hard to integrate her various personalities in therapy, she was, however, quite depressed and at times would dissociate. Because the task at hand was to assess the client's ability to work rather than to affirm her diagnosis, it was important to choose instruments that would address the assessment question: Could this client effectively hold down employment?

—Ed Neukrug

---

have become so sophisticated that most well-trained clinicians cannot tell them apart from reports written by seasoned professionals. Thus, the examiner can integrate the information gathered from the computer-generated report into his or her own report.

Choosing an Appropriate Assessment Instrument

After the interview, clinicians can consider the purpose of their assessment as well as the breadth and depth of the information needed. Then clinicians can choose from a broad array of assessment instruments, such as those we examined in this text, including assessment of educational ability (Chapter 6), assessment of intelligence (Chapter 7), career and occupational assessment (Chapter 8), clinical assessment (Chapter 9), and informal assessment (Chapter 10).

It is important that clinicians carefully reflect on which are the most appropriate instruments to use. In fact, it is unethical to assess an individual using instruments that are not related to the purpose of the assessment being undertaken (see ACA, 1995; APA, 2002) (see Box 12.1).

Conducting an Environmental Assessment

Environmental assessment
Naturalistic and systems-oriented approach to assessment that involves collecting information about clients from their home, work, or school

An often neglected but valuable source of information is an individual's environment. Often called environmental assessment, this kind of assessment includes collecting information from a client's home, school, or workplace through observation or self-reports. This form of appraisal is more systems oriented and naturalistic than most of the other types and is so critical that Axis IV of DSM-IV-TR is dedicated to understanding how the environment influences a person's well-being and diagnosis. Environmental assessments can widen the net of assessment and thus provide additional breadth and depth to the assessment process. Such assessment can be eye-opening because even when clients do not intentionally mislead their therapists, they will often present a distorted view based on their own inaccurate perceptions or hide information because of embarrassment or shame. Observing their environments is one way to fill in the missing details.

BOX 12.2
A Home Visit

"There is a story about Milton Erickson, an unusually clever and insightful therapist, being asked to make a house call on a reclusive woman who never spoke to anyone and seldom left her house. Dr. Erickson spent less than an hour with the lady and found out she was depressed, felt unneeded and lonely, and was so shy she arrived at church late and left early so she wouldn't have to interact with anyone. He observed she had several African violets in her modest home. So, as he left, he gave her this prescription: 'Start growing more flowers, ask the priest to notify you of every birth, wedding, and death in the parish, and send a flower on every occasion.' She did . . . and it changed her life. Many years later, Dr. Erickson read a newspaper account of several hundred people attending the funeral of the 'African Violet Lady.'"

—*Tucker-Ladd, 2000*

Visiting a client's home, classroom, or workplace can yield a plethora of information that could otherwise evade even the most seasoned therapist. For instance, imagine if after administering your assessment procedures and conducting your interview you were to visit your client's home and find that he had old magazines stacked to the ceiling. Or consider the 10-year-old little angel in your office who dramatically changes her demeanor when around other girls the same age. Or imagine your surprise at meeting your client's wife and discovering that she is kind, considerate, and attractive, unlike the raving, angry, and pathetic spouse that he had portrayed her to be.

Home visits are almost always profitable, and it is not unusual to discover important information about your client that you would rarely ascertain in therapy (Yalom, 2002) (see Box 12.2). Additionally, discussing the home visit with the client beforehand can generate productive conversations. For instance, you might notice that as you discuss an upcoming visit your client suddenly becomes anxious due to some reason not yet discussed with the clinician. This anxiety can then be processed and explored during the session. Another benefit is the fact that the home visit can be construed by the client as an affirmation of your level of caring and commitment (Yalom, 2002). This can do wonders in building rapport and trust. Visits to the workplace can also generate useful information; however, caution must be exercised in order to maintain the client's confidentiality.

Finally, school and classroom visits are often useful in making assessments for children and adolescents. The school visit also allows the helping professional to assess other environmental factors such as lighting, seat position, room layout, and distracting noises that may be related to a student's underperformance. Understanding a child's social interactions can often be achieved only by observing the student in the classroom or on the playground. School counselors or school psychologists may also be asked to assess the environment of their school.

EXERCISE 12.1 **Self-Reflection Exercise**

If you were in therapy and your therapist came to visit your home or work environment, would he or she learn something about you that you had not self-disclosed? In small groups discuss why you might "neglect" to tell your therapist certain things about your home or work environment and how useful an environmental assessment would be in revealing the "true" you.

Although environmental assessment can often be done by simple observation, numerous instruments are available to assist in this process. A few are listed below.

- *Comprehensive Assessment of School Environments Information Management System (CASE-IMS).* This instrument is used to assess the entire school environment and climate. It uses self-report surveys of students, parents, teachers, and the principal. The data from the assessment indicates the school's strengths and weaknesses as normed against other schools (Manduchi & Yazak, 2001).
- *Behavior Rating Inventory of Executive Function.* This observational assessment is for home and school use (by the child's teacher(s) and guardian) for children aged 5 to 18 to determine impairment to executive functions as a result of learning disabilities, developmental disorders, attention disorders, depression, medical conditions, and so on. The instrument appears to have reasonable validity and reliability (Fitzpatrick & Schraw, 2003).
- *Emotional or Behavior Disorder Scale.* This instrument is designed for use in the home or school environment to identify behavioral or emotional problems through observation of children aged 5 to 21. Although it is brief and easy to use, its validity and reliability have come into question (Harrison & Lee, 1988)

Writing the Report

Know the laws, and remember that clients will often have access to the written report.

After you have conducted a thorough assessment of your client, you will be ready to write your report. Reports are scrutinized today more than ever before because they are the mechanism used by the interviewer to communicate his or her assessment to others and are often used by funding agencies and supervisors when evaluating a clinician's work. Thus, when writing a report, the interviewer needs to make the report clear, concise, and easy to understand. It is also important to keep the reader in mind and not try to dazzle the reader with one's brilliance, overuse psychological jargon, or use a patronizing tone (Armstrong, 1980; Harvey, 1997; Reynolds et al., 1995; Weddig, 1984; Wiener & Kohler, 1986).

As a result of laws passed over the years, such as the Family Educational Rights and Privacy Act of 1974, the Freedom of Information Act, and the Health Insurance Portability and Accountability Act (HIPAA) (see Chapter 2), clients will generally have access to their records if they choose to review them. Keeping this in mind, try to write the report so that a client or parent can understand it. Harvey (1997) offers the following suggestions to make a report more readable:

*Keep report
readable—
attend to
writing style.*

1. Shorten sentence lengths.
2. Minimize the number of difficult words.
3. Reduce the use of jargon.
4. Reduce the use of acronyms.
5. Omit passive verbs.
6. Increase the use of subheadings.

Other points you might consider when writing the report include the following (Drummond, 2004; Ownby, 1997; Mertens, 1976; Schwartz and Wilkinson, 1987):

1. Describe behaviors that are representative of client issues.
2. Be non-judgmental.
3. Only label when it is necessary and valuable to do so for the client's well being.
4. Don't be afraid to take a stand if you feel strongly that the information warrants it (e.g., the information leads you to believe a client is in danger of harming self).
5. Point out both strengths and weaknesses of your client.

The actual format of the report will vary from setting to setting. For example, a large mental health clinic may specify a preferred or required format for its therapists. Similarly, a social worker in private practice may be driven to a particular format by insurance provider requirements, while a school counselor may have to use an established format required by his or her guidance supervisor.

Although report formats can vary dramatically, often they will include the following sections: (1) demographic information, (2) presenting problem or reason for referral, (3) family background, (4) significant medical/counseling history, (5) substance use and abuse, (6) educational and vocational history, (7) other pertinent information, (8) mental status, (9) assessment results, (10) diagnosis, (11) summary and conclusions, and (12) recommendations. Now we will look at each of these areas in more detail.

Demographic Information

In this section we find basic information about the client, including such items as the client's name, address, phone number, e-mail address, date of birth, age, sex, ethnicity, and date of interview. Also, it is in this section that the name of the interviewer is placed. Often, this information is included at the top of the report. The following is an example of the demographic information gathered from a fictitious client, Mr. Unclear.

Name: Eduardo (Ed) Unclear   D.O.B.: 1/8/1956
Address: 223 Confused Lane   Age: 48
        Coconut Creek, Florida   Sex: Male

Phone: 954-969-8096
E-mail: junclear@hotmail.net
Name of Interviewer: May I. Assessu

Ethnicity: Hispanic
Date of Interview: 2/22/2004

Presenting Problem or Reason for Referral

In this section, the person who referred the client is generally noted (e.g., self-referred, physician, counselor) and an explanation is given as to why the individual has come for counseling and/or why the examiner has been asked to do the assessment. For instance, here it might be explained that a social worker has been asked to do a court assessment of a child for a custody hearing; a school psychologist has been asked to assess a child who has been exhibiting severe behavioral problems at school, for a possible diagnosis of emotional disturbance; or a licensed clinician in private practice might suggest to a client an assessment to help sort out a diagnosis and to set treatment goals. Continuing with our example of Mr. Unclear, we might include the following information:

> *This 48-year-old married male was self-referred due to high levels of stress. The client stated that he has felt "anxious" for the past two years and intermittently depressed for the past seven or eight years. He states that he is discontented with his marriage and confused about his future. An assessment was conducted to assist in determining diagnosis and course of treatment.*

Family Background

The family background section of the report is an opportunity to give the reader an understanding of possible factors concerning the client's upbringing that may be related to his or her presenting problem. Trivial bits of information should be left out of this section, and opinions regarding this information should be saved for the summary and conclusions section of the report.

In this section it is often useful to mention where the individual grew up, sexes and ages of siblings, whether the client came from an intact family, who were the major caretakers, and significant others who may have had an impact on the client's life. The examiner may also want to relay important stories from childhood that have affected how the client defines himself or herself. For adults, one should also include such items as marital status, marital issues, ages and sexes of children, and significant others. Using our example, we might include the following information:

> *Mr. Unclear was raised in Miami, Florida. His parents were Cuban refugees, and Mr. Unclear notes that when he was 5 years old, his parents fled Cuba on a fishing boat with him and his two brothers, José, who is two years older, and Juan, who is two years younger. Mr. Unclear comes from an intact family. His father died approximately four years ago of a "heart disorder." He states that his parents were "loving but strict" and notes that his father was "in charge" of the family and would often "take a belt to me." However, he describes both parents as loving and caring and says that they "took care of all my needs." He reports that he and his brothers were always close and that both brothers currently live*

within 1 mile of his home. He states that his younger brother is married and has two children, and he describes his other brother as single and a "closeted homosexual." His father, he reports, was a bookkeeper and his mother a stay-at-home mom. He and his brothers went to Catholic school, and he states that he tended to be a good student and had the "normal" number of friends.

Mr. Unclear notes that when he was 20 he met his wife Carla in college. They married when he was 21 and quickly had two children, Carlita and Carmen, who are now 27 and 26. Both daughters are college-educated, work in professional jobs and are married. Carlita has two children aged 3 and 4, while Carmen has one child aged 5. He noted that both daughters and their families live close to him. He states that although his marriage was "good" for the first 20 years, in recent years he has found himself feeling unloved and depressed. He wonders if he should remain in the marriage.

Significant Medical/Counseling History

This section of the report delineates any significant medical history, especially any physical conditions that may be affecting the client's psychological state. In addition, any history of counseling should be noted in this section. Mr. Unclear's medical and counseling history is summarized below:

Mr. Unclear states that approximately four years ago he was in a serious car accident that subsequently left him with chronic back pain. Although he takes prescribed medication intermittently for the pain, he states that he mostly tries to "live without drugs." He noted that he often feels fatigued and has trouble sleeping, often sleeping only four hours a night. However, he reports that his medical exam has revealed no apparent medical reason for his fatigue and sleep difficulties. He notes no other significant medical history, although he reports that in the past two years he has had obsessive worry related to fears of dying of a heart attack.

Mr. Unclear notes that after the birth of his second child, his wife needed surgery to repair vaginal tears. He states that since that time she has complained of pain during sex, and their level of intimacy dropped significantly. He notes that he and his wife went to couples therapy for about two months approximately 15 years ago. He feels that counseling did not help, and he notes that it "particularly did nothing to help our sex life."

Substance Use and Abuse

This section reports the use and abuse of any legal or illegal substances that may be addictive or potentially harmful to the client. Thus, the interviewer should report the use or abuse of food, cigarettes, alcohol, prescription medication, and illegal drugs. In reference to Mr. Unclear, we include the following information:

Mr. Unclear states that he does not smoke cigarettes and occasionally smokes cigars ("I will never smoke a Cuban cigar," he notes). He describes himself as a moderate drinker and states that he has a couple of beers a day but does not tend to drink "hard liquor." He reports taking prescription medication "intermittently" for chronic back pain and he denies the use of illegal substances. He describes his eating habits as "normal."

Educational and Vocational History

This section describes the client's educational background and delineates his or her job path and career focus. For Mr. Unclear, we include the following information:

> *Mr. Unclear went to Catholic school in Miami, Florida, and reports that he excelled in math but always had difficulty with reading and spelling. After high school, he went on to college at Miami University, majoring in business administration. After graduating with his bachelor's degree, he obtained a job as an accountant at a major tobacco import company, where he worked for 17 years. During that time he began to work on his master's in business administration but stated he never finished his degree because it was "boring." Approximately eight years ago he changed jobs and obtained employment as an accountant at a local new car company. He states he changed jobs to "make more money."*
>
> *Mr. Unclear reports that relative to his accounting work, his "books were always perfect," although he went on to note that he was embarrassed by his inability to prepare a well-written report. He reports feeling dissatisfied with his career path and wanting to do something more meaningful with his life. However, he states that "I am probably too old to change careers now."*

Other Pertinent Information

This is a "catch-all" category that addresses any significant information that has not been noted elsewhere. Issues that might be addressed in this section could be related to sexual orientation, changes in sexual desires, or any sexual dysfunction; any current or past legal problems that may be affecting functioning; and any financial problems the client may be having. For Mr. Unclear we include the following information:

> *Mr. Unclear states that he is unhappy with his sex life and reports having limited intimacy with his wife. He denies having an extramarital affair but states "I would have one if I met the right person." He notes that he is "just making it" financially, and that it was difficult to support his two children through college. He denies any problems with the law.*

Mental Status

Mental status exam
Assesses appearance and behavior, emotional state, thought, and cognitive functioning

A mental status exam is an assessment of the client's appearance and behavior, emotional state, thought components, and cognitive functioning. This assessment is used to assist the interviewer in making a diagnosis and in treatment planning (Polanski & Hinkle, 2000; Aiken, 2003). A short synopsis of each of the four areas of the mental status exam follows.

Appearance and Behavior

This part of the mental status exam reports the client's observable appearance and behaviors during the clinical interview. Thus, often such items as manner of dress, hygiene, body posture, tics, significant nonverbal behaviors (eye contact or the lack thereof, wringing of hands, swaying), and manner of speech (e.g., stuttering, tone) are reported.

Emotional State

When assessing emotional state, the examiner describes the client's affect and mood. The affect is the client's current, prevailing feeling state (e.g., happy, sad, joyful, angry, depressed, etc.), and may also be reported as constricted or full, appropriate or inappropriate to content, labile, flat, blunted, exaggerated, and so forth. The client's mood, on the other hand, represents the long-term, underlying emotional well being of the client and is usually assessed through client self-report. Thus, a client may seem anxious and sad during the session (affect) and report that his or her mood has been depressed.

Thought Components

The manner in which a client thinks can reveal much about how he or she comes to understand and make meaning of the world. Thought components are generally broken down into the content and the process of thinking. Clinicians will often make statements about thought content by addressing whether the client has delusions, distortions of body image, hallucinations, obsessions, suicidal or homicidal ideation, and so forth. The kinds of thought processes often identified include circumstantiality, coherence, flight of ideas, logical thinking, intact as opposed to loose associations, organization, and tangentiality.

Cognition

Cognition includes a statement as to whether the client is oriented to time, place, and person (knows what time it is, where he or she is, and who he or she is); an assessment of the client's short- and long-term memory; an evaluation of the client's knowledge base and intellectual functioning; and a statement about the client's level of insight and ability to make judgments.

Although much more can be said about each of these four areas, generally, when incorporating a mental status into a report, all four areas are collapsed into a one- or two-paragraph statement about the client's presentation. Usually, a statement about the client's demeanor, orientation, affect, intellectual functioning, judgment, insight, and suicidal or homicidal ideation are included. However, other areas are generally reported only if they are deemed significant. A description of Mr. Unclear's mental status follows:

> Mr. Unclear was well groomed for the interview, wearing a tailored suit. He was able to maintain appropriate eye contact and was oriented to time, place, and person. During the interview he appeared anxious, often rubbing his hands together. He stated that he often felt fatigued and that he has difficulty sleeping, often sleeping only four hours a night. He described himself as feeling intermittently depressed over the past seven or eight years. He appeared to be above average intellectually and his memory was intact. His judgment and insight

---

EXERCISE 12.2 **Writing the Mental Status Report**

Your instructor may ask a student to role-play a client being interviewed. (It might also help if the student chose to reflect a diagnosis in DSM-IV-TR.) After the role-play is complete, all other students in class should write a mental status report. Share your reports with the instructor, and come up with one

mental status report for the class. Compare your own report to the final version produced in class. This type of role-play can be repeated in small groups if you would like to gain further practice writing mental status exams.

> *seemed good and he appeared motivated for treatment. He states that he sometimes has suicidal thoughts, but denies he has a plan or would ever kill himself. He notes, "This is against my religion." He denies homicidal ideation.*

Assessment Results

Assessment results
Provide results that will be understandable to all readers.

It is often helpful to begin this section with a simple list of the assessment procedures that were used. Next, the results of the assessment procedures are generally presented. When presenting test results, it is important to not just give out raw scores. Instead, offering converted or standardized test scores that the reader will understand is usually more helpful (e.g., percentiles, DIQs, etc.). It should be remembered that the client, parents, or some other non-professional may read these results, so it is important to state the results in language that is unbiased and understandable to the reader. An example might be, "Johnny scored a 300 on his SAT, which is 2 standard deviations below the mean and places him at the lower 2% of his peers in the twelfth grade."

The results of the assessment should be concise, yet cover all items that are clearly relevant to the presenting concerns or that clearly stand out as a result of the assessment. Results should be presented objectively, and interpretations should be kept to a minimum if used at all. In the summary and conclusions section, the examiner will have the opportunity to hypothesize about what is happening with the client. The following is an example of the assessment section of the report for Mr. Unclear.

> *Tests used: The Beck Depression Inventory; the Sentence Completion Test, the Kinetic Family Drawing (KFD), the MMPI-II, Rorschach Inkblot Test, the Strong Interest Inventory, Thematic Apperception Test, and the Wide Range Achievement Test (WRAT).*
>
> *Mr. Unclear obtained a BDI-II score of 24, which places him in the moderate range of depression, and his responses showed some evidence of possible suicidal ideation. The MMPI supports this finding, as it shows a man with moderate to severe depression and mild anxiety who is generally "discontented with the world" and feels a lack of intimacy in his life. It suggests assessing for possible suicidal ideation.*
>
> *The Rorschach and the TAT show an individual who is grounded in reality and open to testing, as was evidenced by his willingness to readily respond to initial inkblots and TAT cards, his ability to complete stories in the TAT, and the*

fact that many of his responses were "common" responses. Feelings of depression and hopelessness are evident in a number of responses, including not readily seeing color in many of the forms he saw on the "color cards" of the Rorschach and a number of pessimistic stories that generally had depressive endings to them on the TAT.

On the KFD, Mr. Unclear placed his father as an angel in the sky, and included his wife, mother, children, and grandchildren. His mother was standing next to him while his wife was off to the side with the grandchildren. He also placed himself in a chair and when talking about the picture stated, "I'm sitting because my back hurts." The picture showed the client and his family at his mother's house having a Sunday dinner while it rained outside. Rain could be indicative of depressive feelings. A cross was prominent in the background and was larger than most of the people in the picture, which is likely an indication of strong religious beliefs and could also indicate a need to be taken care of.

On the sentence completion test Mr. Unclear made a number of references to missing his father, such as "The thing I think most about is missing my father." He also referenced continual back pain. Finally, he noted discontent with his marriage, such as when he said, "Sex is nonexistent" on the sentence completion.

On the Strong, Mr. Unclear's two highest personality codes were Conventional and Enterprising, respectively. All the other codes were significantly lower. Individuals of the Conventional type are stable, controlled, conservative, sociable, and like to follow instructions. Enterprising individuals are self-confident, adventurous, sociable, have good persuasive skills, and prefer positions of leadership. Careers in business and industry where persuasive skills are important are good choices for these individuals.

On the WRAT, Mr. Unclear scored at the 86th percentile in math and at the 65th and 42nd percentile in reading and spelling, respectively. These results could indicate a possible learning disorder in spelling, although cross-cultural considerations should be taken into account due to the fact that Mr. Unclear was an immigrant to this country at a young age.

Diagnosis

This is the section where a clinical diagnosis is generally made using the criteria from the *Diagnostic and Statistical Manual* (DSM-IV-TR; APA, 2000) (see Chapter 11). The diagnosis is an outgrowth of the whole assessment process and is based on the integration of all of the knowledge gained (Seligman, 2004). As mentioned in Chapter 11, the DSM-IV-TR offers five axes of diagnosis:

Axis I: Clinical Disorders and Other Conditions That May Be a Focus of Clinical Attention. This includes all childhood and adult mental disorders with the exception of personality disorders and mental retardation. It also includes problem areas that are not considered mental disorders, called "other areas that may be a focus of clinical attention."

Axis II: Personality Disorders and Mental Retardation. This is reserved for recording two specific groups of diagnoses: Personality Disorders and Mental Retardation, both of which are long-standing, entrenched, rigid, typically lifelong conditions.

Axis III: General Medical Conditions. This axis provides a place to list medical problems and physical complaints (e.g., chronic pain, thyroid disorder) that might be associated with the client's counseling concerns.

Axis IV: Psychosocial and Environmental Problems. Axis IV provides a place to list external, social, relational, or environmental problems (e.g., poverty, recent divorce) that might be associated with the client's counseling concerns.

Axis V: Global Assessment of Functioning, or GAF Scale. This scale ranges from 1 to 100 and is used by the interviewer to estimate the client's overall functioning in everyday life. Higher numbers represent higher-level functioning.

A fully prepared, formal DSM-IV-TR diagnosis provides complete information about the client's experiences on all five axes. Using our example of Mr. Unclear, we might prepare the following five-axes diagnosis:

Axis I:	296.22	Major Depression, Single Episode, Moderate
	309.28	Rule Out Adjustment Disorder with Mixed Anxiety and Depressed Mood
Axis II:		No diagnosis
Axis III:		Chronic back pain
Axis IV:		Discontent with job
		Marital discontent
Axis V:		GAF = 45 (Over past year)

In this example, the diagnosis describes a client who is experiencing symptoms of a moderate episode of major depression, including ongoing feelings of depression, fatigue, and sleep problems (Axis I); shows no signs of any long-term personality disorder symptoms (Axis II); has difficulties with chronic back pain—a general medical condition (Axis III); is discontented with his career and marriage—psycho-social stressors (Axis IV); and has several "serious" symptoms such as periodic thoughts about suicide (Axis V).

Summary and Conclusions

Report summary should have no new information.

This section is the examiner's chance to pull together all of the information that has been gathered. Often, this is the only section of the report that is read by others, so it is important that it is accurate and does not leave out any main points. However, it should not be excessively long. Making it accurate, succinct, and relevant is the key to writing a good summary. One major error in writing summaries, we have found, is adding information that has not been included elsewhere. *The summary should have no new information.* Although inferences can be made in this section, they must be logical, sound, defendable, and based on facts that are mentioned in your report. We also generally recommend writing a paragraph or two about the strengths of the individual. All too often we have found that this is left out of reports. The following might be a summary and conclusions section based on the information we have gathered from Mr. Unclear:

> *Mr. Unclear is a 48-year-old married male who was self-referred due to feelings of depression, anxiety, and discontentment with his job and his marriage. Mr. Unclear fled from Cuba to Miami, Florida with his parents and two siblings when he was 5 years old. He describes his family as close, and he continues to live near his children, siblings, and mother. His father died approximately four years ago. During college he was married and he and his wife subsequently raised two girls who are now in their mid-20s and married.*

> *Mr. Unclear finished college with a degree in business and has been working as an accountant over the past 25 years. He reports feeling dissatisfied with his career path and wanting to do something more meaningful with his life. He also reports marital discord, which he attributes partly to medical problems his wife had after the birth of their second child. These problems, he states, resulted in diminishing sexual relations with his wife.*

> *Mr. Unclear was oriented during the session but appeared anxious and talked about feelings of depression. He noted that he often feels fatigued, has difficulty sleeping, and has fleeting thoughts of suicide, which he states he would not act upon. Recently, he has had obsessive worries about having a heart attack, although there is no medical reason to support his concerns. Chronic back pain due to a car accident a few years ago seems to exacerbate his current feelings of depression.*

> *Throughout testing there were consistent themes of depression, isolation, and hopelessness. This was evidenced by high scores on the BDI-II and the MMPI-II depression scale, as well as specific responses to the Rorschach, TAT cards, the KFD, and the sentence completion. Discontentment with his marriage, sadness about the loss of his father, and chronic pain were other issues that arose through testing. Testing also revealed a person who is in a field that is a good match for his personality. However, he might be more challenged if given a position with additional responsibilities and leadership skills. Such a change should probably not occur unless Mr. Unclear attains a handle on his depression. Finally, testing also shows a possible learning disability in spelling, although cross-cultural issues may have affected his score.*

> *On a positive note, testing and the clinical interview showed a man who was neatly dressed and open to meeting with this examiner. He has worked hard in his life and is proud of the family he has raised. He was grounded in reality, willing to engage interpersonally, and showed good judgment and insight. He seems to be aware of many of his most pressing concerns and showed some willingness to address them.*

Recommendations

This last section of the report should be based on all of the information gathered. It should make logical sense to the reader. Although some prefer writing this section in paragraph form, we prefer listing each recommendation, as we believe this format is clearer to the reader. The signature of the examiner generally follows this last section.

The following might be some recommendations for Mr. Unclear:

1. Counseling, 1 hour a week for depression, possible anxiety, marital discord, and career dissatisfaction.
2. Possible marital counseling with particular focus on sexual relations of the couple.
3. Referral to a physician/psychiatrist for medication, possibly anti-depressants.
4. Possible further assessment for learning problems.
5. Long-term consideration of a career move following alleviation of depressive feelings and addressing possible learning problems.
6. Possible orthopedic re-evaluation of back problems.

_____

Signature of the Examiner

Summarizing the Writing of an Assessment Report

As you can see, a great deal of information is gathered from the client, and much of it is included in the report. Although one could probably write a short novel about a client after gathering information from an in-depth interview, generally the skilled examiner will keep the report between two and five pages, single-spaced. Box 12.3 summarizes the major points that should be gathered through an assessment report, and in Appendix E you can see Mr. Unclear's report in its entirety.

Summary

In this chapter we examined the process of gathering information for the assessment report and described how to write the actual report. We began the chapter by noting that the assessment report is the end product of the assessment process, and suggested that its purpose is to synthesize an assortment of assessment techniques so that one gains a deeper understanding of the examinee. We stated that reports are often used to provide insight for clients in therapy, to suggest treatment options, to help determine psychotropic medications, to suggest educational services, to offer direction when providing vocational rehabilitation services, and to assist the courts in making difficult decisions.

BOX 12.3
Summary of Assessment Report

The following categories are generally assessed in a report.

DEMOGRAPHIC INFORMATION

Name:	D.O.B.:
Address:	Age:
Phone:	Sex:
Ethnicity:	E-mail address:
Date of interview:	Name of interviewer:

PRESENTING PROBLEM
OR REASON FOR REFERRAL

1. Who referred the client to the agency?
2. What is the main reason the client contacted the agency?
3. Reason for assessment

FAMILY BACKGROUND

1. Significant factors from family of origin
2. Significant factors from current family
3. Some specific issues that may be mentioned: where the individual grew up, sexes and ages of siblings, whether the client came from an intact family, who were the major caretakers, important stories from childhood, sexes and ages of current children, significant others, and marital concerns

SIGNIFICANT MEDICAL/
COUNSELING HISTORY

1. Significant medical history, particularly anything related to the client's assessment (e.g., psychiatric hospitalization, heart disease leading to depression)
2. Types and dates of previous counseling

SUBSTANCE USE AND ABUSE

1. Use or abuse of food, cigarettes, alcohol, prescription medication, and illegal drugs
2. Counseling related to use and abuse

EDUCATIONAL AND VOCATIONAL HISTORY

1. Educational history (e.g., level of education and possibly names of institutions)
2. Vocational history and career path (names and types of jobs)
3. Satisfaction with educational level and career path
4. Significant leisure activities

OTHER PERTINENT INFORMATION

1. Legal concerns and history of problems with the law
2. Issues related to sexuality (e.g., sexual orientation, sexual dysfunction)
3. Financial problems
4. Other concerns

THE MENTAL STATUS EXAM

1. Appearance and behavior (e.g., dress, hygiene, posture, tics, nonverbals, manner of speech)
2. Emotional state (e.g., affect and mood)
3. Thought components (e.g., content and process: delusions, distortions of body image, hallucinations, obsessions, suicidal or homicidal ideation, circumstantiality, coherence, flight of ideas, logical thinking, intact as opposed to loose associations, organization, and tangentiality)
4. Cognitive functioning (e.g., orientation to time, place, and person; short- and long-term memory; knowledge base and intellectual functioning; insight and judgments)

ASSESSMENT RESULTS

1. List assessment and test instruments used.
2. Summarize results.
3. Avoid raw scores and state results in unbiased manner.
4. Consider using standardized test scores and percentiles.

continued

BOX 12.3
Continued

DIAGNOSIS

1. DSM-IV-TR diagnoses (include other diagnoses, such as medical, rehabilitation, when important)
2. Usually note all five axes of DSM-IV-TR:
   - *Axis I: Clinical Disorders and Other Conditions That May Be a Focus of Clinical Attention*
   - *Axis II: Personality Disorders and Mental Retardation*
   - *Axis III: General Medical Conditions*
   - *Axis IV: Psychosocial and Environmental Problems*
   - *Axis V: Global Assessment of Functioning, or GAF Scale*

SUMMARY AND CONCLUSIONS

1. Integration of all previous information
2. Accurate, succinct, and relevant
3. No new information
4. Inferences that are logical, sound, defendable, and based on facts in the report
5. At least one paragraph that speaks to the client's strengths

RECOMMENDATIONS

1. Based on all the information gathered
2. Should make logical sense to reader
3. In paragraph form or as a listing
4. Usually followed by signature of examiner

As the chapter continued we discussed the importance of providing a wide enough net to appropriately address the breadth and depth needed for the particular assessment at hand. We then identified three critical ways of gathering information for the report, including conducting the interview, choosing appropriate assessment techniques, and conducting an environmental assessment.

We next noted that the clinical interview has a special place in the assessment process as it helps to set a tone, desensitizes the client to talking about personal information, affords the opportunity to assess client nonverbals, places a client's issues in perspective, and allows the client and examiner an opportunity to assure that they can work together. We then offered guidelines for how to conduct an interview, including knowing why the client is being interviewed, establishing trust and rapport, providing a comfortable and confidential environment, focusing on verbal and nonverbal cues, and keeping the goals of the interview in mind but allowing the client to discuss what he or she needs to discuss.

We went on to distinguish three types of interviews. We noted that a structured interview asks the examinee to respond to pre-established items or questions, whereas an unstructured interview is more open-ended. The semi-structured interview, we pointed out, uses prescribed items but also gives leeway to the examiner should the client need to "drift" during the interview process. We pointed out some strengths and weaknesses of each of these approaches, especially as they relate to gathering information that has breadth and depth. We also noted that computer-assisted assessment can often help in the information-gathering process and can be integrated into the examiner's assessment report.

We next examined the process of selecting an appropriate assessment technique, which often will be based on the interview with your client. We stressed the importance of considering the breadth and depth of information provided by the chosen instruments and noted that clinicians will often choose from a broad array of instruments, such as the ones examined in this text.

The environmental assessment was the last method of information gathering discussed in this chapter. This kind of assessment allows the clinician to cast a wider net and includes such things as collecting information from a client's home, school, or workplace through observation or self-reports, and we pointed out that one can often garner information from an environmental assessment that is not available through traditional assessment techniques or through a clinical interview.

As the chapter continued we went on to discuss how to write the actual assessment report. We noted that reports today are scrutinized more than ever before, and we stressed the importance of developing a writing style that is clear, concise, and easy to understand. We suggested using short sentences, minimizing the use of difficult words or acronyms, omitting passive verbs, using proper subheadings, describing behaviors, being non-judgmental, avoiding the use of labels when possible, taking a stand when necessary, and pointing out the strengths and weaknesses of the client.

In the last part of the chapter we examined the format of the report. We noted that the areas addressed when gathering information from a client often parallel the areas included in the actual report. They include (1) demographic information, (2) presenting problem or reason for the report, (3) family background, (4) significant medical/counseling history, (5) substance use and abuse, (6) vocational and educational history, (7) other pertinent background information, (8) mental status, (9) assessment or test results, (10) diagnosis, (11) summary and conclusions, and (12) recommendations. We discussed each area and offered a case example.

Chapter Review

1. Describe some purposes of the assessment report.

2. Describe what it means to choose an assessment instrument with "breadth and depth."

3. Explain the possible tasks that can be accomplished through the use of a clinical interview.

4. Compare and contrast structured, semi-structured, and unstructured interview techniques.

5. What place can computer-generated reports take in the assessment report process?

6. Explain and give examples of an environmental assessment.

7. What can an environmental assessment add to the understanding of the individual?

8. Explain the impact of laws such as the Family Educational Rights and Privacy Act of 1974, the Freedom of Information Act, and the Health Insurance Portability and Accountability Act (HIPAA) on the preparation of assessment reports.

9. Highlight some attributes that make an assessment report readable.

10. Make a list of the kinds of information generally obtained in an assessment report.

11. Describe the four components of a mental status exam. Interview a student in class and then write a one- or two-paragraph mental status exam.

12. Conduct an assessment of a client and use the categories listed in this chapter to write an assessment report.

Websites of Codes of Ethics of Select Mental Health Professional Associations

American Counseling Association (ACA)
  Main website: http://www.counselor.org
  Code of ethics: http://www.counseling.org/resources/ethics.htm

American Association of Marriage and Family Therapy (AAMFT)
  Main website: http://www.aamft.org
  Code of ethics: http://www.aamft.org/resources/LRMPlan/Ethics/
    ethicscode2001.asp

American Association of Pastoral Counselors (AAPC)
  Main website: http://www.aapc.org
  Code of ethics: http://www.aapc.org/ethics.htm

American Mental Health Counselors Association (AMHCA)
  Main website: http://www.amhca.org
  Code of ethics: http://www.amhca.org/code

American Psychiatric Association (APA)
  Main website: http://www.psych.org
  Code of ethics: http://www.psych.org/psych_pract/ethics/ppaethics.cfm

American Psychological Association (APA)
  Main website: http://www.apa.org
  Code of ethics: http://www.apa.org/ethics

American School Counselor Association (ASCA)
Main website: http://www.schoolcounselor.org
Code of ethics: http://www.schoolcounselor.org/content.asp?contentid=173

Certified Rehabilitation Counselors
Main website: http://www.crccertification.com
Code of ethics: http://www.crccertification.com/code.html

National Association of Social Workers (NASW)
Main website: http://www.naswdc.org
Code of ethics: http://www.socialworkers.org/pubs/code/code.asp

National Organization of Human Service Education (NOHSE)
Main website: http://www.nohse.org
Ethical standards of human service professionals: http://www.nohse.org/ethstand.html

Code of Fair Testing Practices in Education

Prepared by the Joint Committee on Testing Practices

The Code of Fair Testing Practices in Education (*Code*) is a guide for professionals in fulfilling their obligation to provide and use tests that are fair to all test takers regardless of age, gender, disability, race, ethnicity, national origin, religion, sexual orientation, linguistic background, or other personal characteristics. Fairness is a primary consideration in all aspects of testing. Careful standardization of tests and administration conditions helps to ensure that all test takers are given a comparable opportunity to demonstrate what they know and how they can perform in the area being tested. Every test taker should have the opportunity to prepare for the test and should be informed about the general nature and content of the test. Fairness also extends to the accurate reporting of individual and group test results. Fairness is not an isolated concept, but must be considered in all aspects of the testing process.

The *Code* applies broadly to testing in education (admissions, educational assessment, educational diagnosis, and student placement) regardless of the mode of presentation, so it is relevant to conventional paper-and-pencil tests, computer based tests, and performance tests. It is not designed to cover employment testing, licensure or certification testing, or other types of testing outside the field of education. The *Code* is directed primarily at professionally developed tests used in formally administered testing programs. Although the *Code* is not intended to cover tests made by teachers for use in their own classrooms, teachers are encouraged to use the guidelines to help improve their testing practices.

The *Code* addresses the roles of test developers and test users separately. Test developers are people and organizations that construct tests, as well as those

Source: Code of Fair Testing Practices in Education. (2004). Washington, DC: Joint Committee on Testing Practices.

that set policies for testing programs. Test users are people and agencies that select tests, administer tests, commission test development services, or make decisions on the basis of test scores. Test developer and test user roles may overlap, for example, when a state or local education agency commissions test development services, sets policies that control the test development process, and makes decisions on the basis of the test scores.

Many of the statements in the *Code* refer to the selection and use of existing tests. When a new test is developed, when an existing test is modified, or when the administration of a test is modified, the development process should be implemented so that the resulting tests are consistent with the *Code*.

The *Code* provides guidance separately for test developers and test users in four critical areas:

A. Developing and Selecting Appropriate Tests
B. Administering and Scoring Tests
C. Reporting and Interpreting Test Results
D. Informing Test Takers

The Code is intended to be consistent with the relevant parts of the Standards for Educational and Psychological Testing (American Educational Research Association [AERA], American Psychological Association [APA], and National Council on Measurement in Education [NCME], 1999). The Code is not meant to add new principles over and above those in the Standards or to change their meaning. Rather, the Code is intended to represent the spirit of selected portions of the Standards in a way that is relevant and meaningful to developers and users of tests, as well as to test takers and/or their parents or guardians. Organizations, institutions, and individual professionals that endorse the Code commit themselves to safeguarding the rights of test takers by following the principles listed. This Code may be adopted and promulgated by states, school districts, and organizations that develop and use tests as a sign of their commitment to fairness as a critical element of appropriate testing practice.

The Code has been prepared by the Joint Committee on Testing Practices, a cooperative effort among several professional organizations. The aim of the Joint Committee is to act, in the public interest, to advance the quality of testing practices. Members of the Joint Committee include the American Counseling Association (ACA), the American Educational Research Association (AERA), the American Psychological Association (APA), the American Speech-Language-Hearing Association (ASHA), the National Association of School Psychologists (NASP), the National Association of Test Directors (NATD), and the National Council on Measurement in Education (NCME).

A. Developing and Selecting Appropriate Tests

TEST DEVELOPERS	TEST USERS
Test developers should provide the information and supporting evidence that test users need to select appropriate tests.	Test users should select tests that meet the intended purpose and that are appropriate for the intended test takers.
A-1. Provide evidence of what the test measures, the recommended uses, the intended test takers, and the strengths and limitations of the test, including the level of precision of the test scores.	A-1. Define the purpose for testing, the content and skills to be tested, and the intended test takers. Select and use the most appropriate test based on a thorough review of available information.
A-2. Describe how the content and skills to be tested were selected and how the tests were developed.	A-2. Review and select tests based on the appropriateness of test content, skills tested, and content coverage for the intended purpose of testing.
A-3. Communicate information about a test's characteristics at a level of detail appropriate to the intended test users.	A-3. Review materials provided by test developers and select tests for which clear, accurate, and complete information is provided.
A-4. Provide guidance on the levels of skills, knowledge, and training necessary for appropriate review, selection, and administration of tests.	A-4. Select tests through a process that includes persons with appropriate knowledge, skills, and training.
A-5. Provide evidence that the technical quality, including reliability and validity, of the test meets its intended purposes.	A-5. Evaluate evidence of the technical quality of the test provided by the test developer and any independent reviewers.
A-6. Provide to qualified test users representative samples of test questions or practice tests, directions, answer sheets, manuals, and score reports.	A-6. Evaluate representative samples of test questions or practice tests, directions, answer sheets, manuals, and score reports before selecting a test.
A-7. Avoid potentially offensive content or language when developing test questions and related materials.	A-7. Evaluate procedures and materials used by test developers, as well as the resulting test, to ensure that potentially offensive content or language is avoided.
A-8. Make appropriately modified forms of tests or administration procedures available for test takers with disabilities who need special accommodations.	A-8. Select tests with appropriately modified forms or administration procedures for test takers with disabilities who need special accommodations.
A-9. Obtain and provide evidence on the performance of test takers of diverse subgroups, making significant efforts to obtain sample sizes that are adequate for subgroup analyses. Evaluate the evidence to ensure that differences in performance are related to the skills being assessed.	A-9. Evaluate the available evidence on the performance of test takers of diverse subgroups. Determine to the extent feasible which performance differences may have been caused by factors unrelated to the skills being assessed.

B. Administering and Scoring Tests

TEST DEVELOPERS	TEST USERS
Test developers should explain how to administer and score tests correctly and fairly.	Test users should administer and score tests correctly and fairly.
B-1. Provide clear descriptions of detailed procedures for administering tests in a standardized manner.	B-1. Follow established procedures for administering tests in a standardized manner.
B-2. Provide guidelines on reasonable procedures for assessing persons with disabilities who need special accommodations or those with diverse linguistic backgrounds.	B-2. Provide and document appropriate procedures for test takers with disabilities who need special accommodations or those with diverse linguistic backgrounds. Some accommodations may be required by law or regulation.
B-3. Provide information to test takers or test users on test question formats and procedures for answering test questions, including information on the use of any needed materials and equipment.	B-3. Provide test takers with an opportunity to become familiar with test question formats and any materials or equipment that may be used during testing.
B-4. Establish and implement procedures to ensure the security of testing materials during all phases of test development, administration, scoring, and reporting.	B-4. Protect the security of test materials, including respecting copyrights and eliminating opportunities for test takers to obtain scores by fraudulent means.
B-5. Provide procedures, materials and guidelines for scoring the tests, and for monitoring the accuracy of the scoring process. If scoring the test is the responsibility of the test developer, provide adequate training for scorers.	B-5. If test scoring is the responsibility of the test user, provide adequate training to scorers and ensure and monitor the accuracy of the scoring process.
B-6. Correct errors that affect the interpretation of the scores and communicate the corrected results promptly.	B-6. Correct errors that affect the interpretation of the scores and communicate the corrected results promptly.
B-7. Develop and implement procedures for ensuring the confidentiality of scores.	B-7. Develop and implement procedures for ensuring the confidentiality of scores.

C. Reporting and Interpreting Test Results

TEST DEVELOPERS	TEST USERS
Test developers should report test results accurately and provide information to help test users interpret test results correctly.	Test users should report and interpret test results accurately and clearly.
C-1. Provide information to support recommended interpretations of the results, including the nature of the content, norms or comparison groups, and other technical evidence. Advise test users of the benefits and limitations of test results and their interpretation. Warn against assigning greater precision than is warranted.	C-1. Interpret the meaning of the test results, taking into account the nature of the content, norms or comparison groups, other technical evidence, and benefits and limitations of test results.
C-2. Provide guidance regarding the interpretations of results for tests administered with modifications. Inform test users of potential problems in interpreting test results when tests or test administration procedures are modified.	C-2. Interpret test results from modified test or test administration procedures in view of the impact those modifications may have had on test results.
C-3. Specify appropriate uses of test results and warn test users of potential misuses.	C-3. Avoid using tests for purposes other than those recommended by the test developer unless there is evidence to support the intended use or interpretation.
C-4. When test developers set standards, provide the rationale, procedures, and evidence for setting performance standards or passing scores. Avoid using stigmatizing labels.	C-4. Review the procedures for setting performance standards or passing scores. Avoid using stigmatizing labels.
C-5. Encourage test users to base decisions about test takers on multiple sources of appropriate information, not on a single test score.	C-5. Avoid using a single test score as the sole determinant of decisions about test takers. Interpret test scores in conjunction with other information about individuals.
C-6. Provide information to enable test users to accurately interpret and report test results for groups of test takers, including information about who were and who were not included in the different groups being compared, and information about factors that might influence the interpretation of results.	C-6. State the intended interpretation and use of test results for groups of test takers. Avoid grouping test results for purposes not specifically recommended by the test developer unless evidence is obtained to support the intended use. Report procedures that were followed in determining who were and who were not included in the groups being compared and describe factors that might influence the interpretation of results.
C-7. Provide test results in a timely fashion and in a manner that is understood by the test taker.	C-7. Communicate test results in a timely fashion and in a manner that is understood by the test taker.
C-8. Provide guidance to test users about how to monitor the extent to which the test is fulfilling its intended purposes.	C-8. Develop and implement procedures for monitoring test use, including consistency with the intended purposes of the test.

D. Informing Test Takers

Under some circumstances, test developers have direct communication with the test takers and/or control of the tests, testing process, and test results. In other circumstances the test users have these responsibilities.

Test developers or test users should inform test takers about the nature of the test, test taker rights and responsibilities, the appropriate use of scores, and procedures for resolving challenges to scores.

D-1. Inform test takers in advance of the test administration about the coverage of the test, the types of question formats, the directions, and appropriate test-taking strategies. Make such information available to all test takers.

D-2. When a test is optional, provide test takers or their parents/guardians with information to help them judge whether a test should be taken—including indications of any consequences that may result from not taking the test (e.g., not being eligible to compete for a particular scholarship)—and whether there is an available alternative to the test.

D-3. Provide test takers or their parents/guardians with information about rights test takers may have to obtain copies of tests and completed answer sheets, to retake tests, to have tests rescored, or to have scores declared invalid.

D-4. Provide test takers or their parents/guardians with information about responsibilities test takers have, such as being aware of the intended purpose and uses of the test, performing at capacity, following directions, and not disclosing test items or interfering with other test takers.

D-5. Inform test takers or their parents/guardians how long scores will be kept on file and indicate to whom, under what circumstances, and in what manner test scores and related information will or will not be released. Protect test scores from unauthorized release and access.

D-6. Describe procedures for investigating and resolving circumstances that might result in canceling or withholding scores, such as failure to adhere to specified testing procedures.

D-7. Describe procedures that test takers, parents/guardians, and other interested parties may use to obtain more information about the test, register complaints, and have problems resolved.

Note: The membership of the Working Group that developed the Code of Fair Testing Practices in Education and of the Joint Committee on Testing Practices that guided the Working Group is as follows:

Peter Behuniak, PhD

Lloyd Bond, PhD

Gwyneth M. Boodoo, PhD

Wayne Camara, PhD

Ray Fenton, PhD

John J. Fremer, PhD (Co-Chair)

Sharon M. Goldsmith, PhD

Bert F. Green, PhD

William G. Harris, PhD

Janet E. Helms, PhD

Stephanie H. McConaughy, PhD

Julie P. Noble, PhD

Wayne M. Patience, PhD

Carole L. Perlman, PhD

Douglas K. Smith, PhD (deceased)

Janet E. Wall, EdD (Co-Chair)

Pat Nellor Wickwire, PhD

Mary Yakimowski, PhD

Lara Frumkin, PhD, of the APA served as staff liaison.

The Joint Committee intends that the Code be consistent with and supportive of existing codes of conduct and standards of other professional groups who use tests in educational contexts. Of particular note are the Responsibilities of Users of Standardized Tests (Association for Assessment in Counseling, 1989), APA Test User Qualifications (2000), ASHA Code of Ethics (2001), Ethical Principles of Psychologists and Code of Conduct (1992), NASP Professional Conduct Manual (2000), NCME Code of Professional Responsibility (1995), and Rights and Responsibilities of Test Takers: Guidelines and Expectations (Joint Committee on Testing Practices, 2000).

Supplemental Statistical Equations

Pearson Product-Moment Correlation

$$r = \frac{N\Sigma XY - (\Sigma X)(\Sigma Y)}{\sqrt{N\Sigma X^2 - (\Sigma X)^2}\sqrt{N\Sigma Y^2 - (\Sigma Y)^2}}$$

Where: N is the number of scores
X is the first set of test scores
Y is the second set of test scores

Kuder-Richardson

$$KR_{20} = \left[\frac{n}{n-1}\right]\left[\frac{SD^2 - \Sigma pq}{SD^2}\right]$$

Where: n is the number of items on the test
SD is the standard deviation
p is the proportion of correct items
q is the proportion of incorrect items

Coefficient Alpha

$$r = \left[\frac{n}{n-1}\right]\left[\frac{SD^2 - \Sigma SD_i^2}{SD^2}\right]$$

Where: n is the number of items on the test
SD is the standard deviation
ΣSD_i^2 is the sum of the variances of item scores

Standard Deviation – Alternative Formula

$$SD = \sqrt{\frac{\Sigma X^2}{N} - M^2}$$

Where: SD is the standard deviation

X are the test scores

N is the number of scores

M is the mean of the test scores

Converting Percentiles from z Scores

The look-up table below can be used to quickly convert a z score to an approximate percentile rank.

z SCORE	PERCENTILE	z SCORE	PERCENTILE	z SCORE	PERCENTILE
−6.0	0.0000001%	−1.1	13.57%	1.1	86.43%
−5.0	0.00003%	**−1.0**	**15.87%**	1.2	88.49%
−4.0	0.0032%	−0.9	18.41%	1.3	90.32%
−3.0	**0.13%**	−0.8	21.19%	1.4	91.92%
−2.9	0.19%	−0.7	24.20%	1.5	93.32%
−2.8	0.26%	−0.6	27.43%	1.6	94.52%
−2.7	0.35%	−0.5	30.85%	1.7	95.54%
−2.6	0.47%	−0.4	34.46%	1.8	96.41%
−2.5	0.62%	−0.3	38.21%	1.9	97.13%
−2.4	0.82%	−0.2	42.07%	**2.0**	**97.72%**
−2.3	1.07%	−0.1	46.02%	2.1	98.21%
−2.2	1.39%	**0.0**	**50.00%**	2.2	98.61%
−2.1	1.79%	0.1	53.98%	2.3	98.93%
−2.0	**2.28%**	0.2	57.93%	2.4	99.18%
−1.9	2.87%	0.3	61.79%	2.5	99.38%
−1.8	3.59%	0.4	65.54%	2.6	99.53%
−1.7	4.46%	0.5	69.15%	2.7	99.65%
−1.6	5.48%	0.6	72.57%	2.8	99.74%
−1.5	6.68%	0.7	75.80%	2.9	99.81%
−1.4	8.08%	0.8	78.81%	**3.0**	**99.87%**
−1.3	9.68%	0.9	81.59%	4.0	99.997%
−1.2	11.51%	**1.0**	**84.13%**	5.0	99.99997%

Due to the fact percentiles are not evenly spaced along the bell curve (by definition), you cannot interpolate between scores on the above table. Consequently, if a more precise percentile is needed that is not listed above, the formula for calculating percentiles can be used.

The formula used to convert a z score to a percentile rank is

$$f(z) = \frac{1}{\sqrt{2\pi}} e^{\frac{z^2}{2}}$$

where z is the given z score.

Assessment Report

Demographic Information

Name: Eduardo (Ed) Unclear

Address: 223 Confused Lane
            Coconut Creek, Florida

Phone: 954-969-8096

E-Mail: junclear@hotmail.net

Name of Interviewer: May I. Assessu

D.O.B.: 1/8/1956

Age: 48

Sex: Male

Ethnicity: Hispanic

Date of Interview: 2/22/2004

Presenting Problem or Reason for Referral

This 48-year-old married male was self-referred due to high levels of stress. The client stated that he has felt "anxious" for the past two years and intermittently depressed for the past seven or eight years. He states that he is discontented with his marriage and confused about his future. An assessment was conducted to assist in determining diagnosis and course of treatment.

Family Background

Mr. Unclear was raised in Miami, Florida. His parents were Cuban refugees, and Mr. Unclear notes that when he was 5 years old, his parents fled Cuba on a fishing boat with him and his two brothers, José, who is two years older, and Juan, who is two years younger. Mr. Unclear comes from an intact family. His father died approximately four years ago of a "heart disorder." He states that his parents were "loving but strict" and notes that his father was "in charge" of the family and would often "take a belt to me." However, he describes both parents as loving and caring and says that they "took care of all my needs." He reports that he and his brothers were always close and that both brothers currently live within 1 mile of his home. He states that his younger brother is married and has two children, and he describes his other brother as single and a "closeted homosexual." His father, he reports, was a bookkeeper and his mother a stay-at-home mom. He and his brothers went to Catholic school, and he states that he tended to be a good student and had the "normal" number of friends.

Mr. Unclear notes that when he was 20 he met his wife Carla in college. They married when he was 21 and quickly had two children, Carlita and Carmen, who are now 27 and 26. Both daughters are college-educated, work in professional jobs and are married. Carlita has two children aged 3 and 4, while Carmen has one child aged 5. He noted that both daughters and their families live close to him. He states that although his marriage was "good" for the first 20 years, in recent years he has found himself feeling unloved and depressed. He wonders if he should remain in the marriage.

Significant Medical/Counseling History

Mr. Unclear states that approximately four years ago he was in a serious car accident that subsequently left him with chronic back pain. Although he takes prescribed medication intermittently for the pain, he states that he mostly tries to "live without drugs." He noted that he often feels fatigued and has trouble sleeping, often sleeping only four hours a night. However, he reports that his medical exam has revealed no apparent medical reason for his fatigue and sleep difficulties. He notes no other significant medical history, although he reports that in the past two years he has had obsessive worry related to fears of dying of a heart attack.

Mr. Unclear notes that after the birth of his second child, his wife needed surgery to repair vaginal tears. He states that since that time she has complained of pain during sex, and their level of intimacy dropped significantly. He notes that he and his wife went to couples therapy for about two months approximately 15 years ago. He feels that counseling did not help, and he notes that it "particularly did nothing to help our sex life."

Substance Use and Abuse

Mr. Unclear states that he does not smoke cigarettes and occasionally smokes cigars ("I will never smoke a Cuban cigar," he notes). He describes himself as a moderate drinker and states that he has a couple of beers a day but does not tend to drink "hard liquor." He reports taking prescription medication "intermittently" for chronic back pain and he denies the use of illegal substances. He describes his eating habits as "normal."

Educational and Vocational History

Mr. Unclear went to Catholic school in Miami, Florida, and reports that he excelled in math but always had difficulty with reading and spelling. After high school, he went on to college at Miami University, majoring in business administration. After graduating with his bachelor's degree, he obtained a job as an accountant at a major tobacco import company, where he worked for 17 years. During that time he began to work on his master's in business administration but stated he never finished his degree because it was "boring." Approximately eight years ago he changed jobs and obtained employment as an accountant at a local new car company. He states he changed jobs to "make more money."

Mr. Unclear reports that relative to his accounting work, his "books were always perfect," although he went on to note that he was embarrassed by his inability to prepare a well-written report. He reports feeling dissatisfied with his career path and wanting to do something more meaningful with his life. However, he states that "I am probably too old to change careers now."

Other Pertinent Information

Mr. Unclear states that he is unhappy with his sex life and reports having limited intimacy with his wife. He denies having an extramarital affair but states "I would have one if I met the right person." He notes that he is "just making it" financially, and that it was difficult to support his two children through college. He denies any problems with the law.

The Mental Status Exam

Mr. Unclear was well groomed for the interview, wearing a tailored suit. He was able to maintain appropriate eye contact and was oriented to time, place, and person. During the interview he appeared anxious, often rubbing his hands together. He stated that he often felt fatigued and that he has difficulty sleeping, often sleeping only four hours a night. He described himself as feeling intermittently depressed over the past seven or eight years. He appeared to be above average intellectually and his memory was intact. His judgment and insight seemed good and he appeared motivated for treatment. He states that he sometimes has suicidal thoughts, but denies he has a plan or would ever kill himself. He notes, "This is against my religion." He denies homicidal ideation.

Assessment Results

Tests used: The Beck Depression Inventory; the Sentence Completion Test, the Kinetic Family Drawing (KFD), the MMPI-2, Rorschach Inkblot Test, the Strong Interest Inventory, Thematic Apperception Test, and the Wide Range Achievement Test (WRAT3).

Mr. Unclear obtained a BDI-II score of 24, which places him in the moderate range of depression, and his responses showed some evidence of possible suicidal ideation. The MMPI supports this finding, as it shows a man with moderate to severe depression and mild anxiety who is generally "discontented with the world" and feels a lack of intimacy in his life. It suggests assessing for possible suicidal ideation.

The Rorschach and the TAT show an individual who is grounded in reality and open to testing, as was evidenced by his willingness to readily respond to initial inkblots and TAT cards, his ability to complete stories in the TAT, and the fact that many of his responses were "common" responses. Feelings of depression and hopelessness are evident in a number of responses, including not readily seeing color in many of the forms he saw on the "color cards" of the Rorschach and a number of pessimistic stories that generally had depressive endings to them on the TAT.

On the KFD, Mr. Unclear placed his father as an angel in the sky, and included his wife, mother, children, and grandchildren. His mother was standing next to him while his wife was off to the side with the grandchildren. He also placed himself in a chair and when talking about the picture stated, "I'm sitting because my back hurts." The picture showed the client and his family at his mother's house having a Sunday dinner while it rained outside. Rain could be indicative of depressive feelings. A cross was prominent in the background and was larger than most of the people in the picture, which is likely an indication of strong religious beliefs and could also indicate a need to be taken care of.

On the sentence completion test Mr. Unclear made a number of references to missing his father, such as "The thing I think most about is *missing my father.*" He also referenced continual back pain. Finally, he noted discontent with his marriage, such as when he said, "Sex is *nonexistent*" on the sentence completion.

On the Strong, Mr. Unclear's two highest personality codes were Conventional and Enterprising, respectively. All the other codes were significantly lower. Individuals of the Conventional type are stable, controlled, conservative, sociable, and like to follow instructions. Enterprising individuals are self-confident, adventurous, sociable, have good persuasive skills, and prefer positions of leadership. Careers in business and industry where persuasive skills are important are good choices for these individuals.

On the WRAT, Mr. Unclear scored at the 86th percentile in math and at the 65th and 42nd percentile in reading and spelling, respectively. These results could indicate a possible learning disorder in spelling, although cross-cultural considerations should be taken into account due to the fact that Mr. Unclear was an immigrant to this country at a young age.

Diagnosis

Axis I: 296.22 Major Depression, Single Episode, Moderate
309.28 Rule Out Adjustment Disorder with Mixed Anxiety and Depressed Mood

Axis II: No diagnosis

Axis III: Chronic back pain

Axis IV: Discontent with job
Marital discontent

Axis V: GAF = 45 (Over past year)

Summary and Conclusions

Mr. Unclear is a 48-year-old married male who was self-referred due to feelings of depression, anxiety, and discontentment with his job and his marriage. Mr. Unclear fled from Cuba to Miami, Florida, with his parents and two siblings when he was 5 years old. He describes his family as close, and he continues to live near his children, siblings, and mother. His father died approximately four years ago. During college he was married and he and his wife subsequently raised two girls who are now in their mid-20s and married.

Mr. Unclear finished college with a degree in business and has been working as an accountant over the past 25 years. He reports feeling dissatisfied with his career path and wanting to do something more meaningful with his life. He also reports marital discord, which he attributes partly to medical problems his wife had after the birth of their second child. These problems, he states, resulted in diminishing sexual relations with his wife.

Mr. Unclear was oriented during the session but appeared anxious and talked about feelings of depression. He noted that he often feels fatigued, has difficulty sleeping, and has fleeting thoughts of suicide, which he states he would not act upon. Recently, he has had obsessive worries about having a heart attack, although there is no medical reason to support his concerns. Chronic back pain due to a car accident a few years ago seems to exacerbate his current feelings of depression.

Throughout testing there were consistent themes of depression, isolation, and hopelessness. This was evidenced by high scores on the BDI-II and the MMPI-II depression scale, as well as specific responses to the Rorschach, TAT cards, the KFD, and the sentence completion. Discontentment with his marriage, sadness about the loss of his father, and chronic pain were other issues that arose through testing. Testing also revealed a person who is in a field that is a good match for his personality. However, he might be more challenged if given a position with additional responsibilities and leadership skills. Such a change should probably not occur unless Mr. Unclear attains a handle on his depression. Finally, testing also shows a possible learning disability in spelling, although cross-cultural issues may have affected his score.

On a positive note, testing and the clinical interview showed a man who was neatly dressed and open to meeting with this examiner. He has worked hard in his life and is proud of the family he has raised. He was grounded in reality, willing to engage interpersonally, and showed good judgment and insight. He seems to be aware of many of his most pressing concerns and showed some willingness to address them.

Recommendations

Counseling, 1 hour a week for depression, possible anxiety, marital discord, and career dissatisfaction.

Possible marital counseling with particular focus on sexual relations of the couple.

Referral to a physician/psychiatrist for medication, possibly antidepressants.

Possible further assessment for learning problems.

Long-term consideration of a career move following alleviation of depressive feelings and addressing possible learning problems.

Possible orthopedic re-evaluation of back problems.

Sigmund Freud, MD

Signature of the Examiner

Glossary

ability test Test that measures what a person can do in the cognitive realm. Achievement and aptitude tests are types of ability tests.

achievement test A type of ability test that measures what one has learned. Types of achievement tests include survey battery tests, diagnostic tests, and readiness tests.

ACT score Created by converting a raw score to a standard score that generally uses a mean of 21 and a standard deviation of 5 for college-bound students. The mean score for all students, including those who are not college-bound, is 18.

age comparison scoring A type of standard score calculated by comparing an individual score to the average score of others who are the same age.

alternate, parallel, or equivalent forms reliability A method for determining reliability by creating two or more alternate, parallel, or equivalent forms of the same test. These alternate forms mimic one another yet are different enough to eliminate some of the problems found in test-retest reliability (e.g., looking up an answer). In this case, rather than giving the same test twice, the examiner gives the alternate form the second time.

Americans with Disabilities Act (PL 101-336) Law stating that to assure proper test administration, accommodations must be made for individuals with disabilities who are taking tests for employment and that testing must be shown to be relevant to the job in question.

anecdotal information Generally includes behaviors of an individual that are consistent or inconsistent; may assist in the assessment process.

aptitude test A type of ability test that measures what one is capable of doing. Types of aptitude tests include intelligence tests, cognitive ability tests, special aptitude tests, and multiple aptitude tests.

Army Alpha test An instrument created by Robert Yerkes, Lewis Terman, and others during World War I to screen recruits for the military. Generally considered the first modern group test.

assessment A broad array of evaluative procedures that yield information about a person. An assessment may consist of many procedures, including a clinical interview, personality tests, ability tests, observation, environmental assessment, and records and personal documents.

assessment report The "deliverable" or "end product" of the assessment process. Its purpose is to synthesize an assortment of assessment techniques so that a deeper understanding of the examinee is obtained and recommended courses of action can be offered.

Association for Assessment in Counseling and Education (AACE) A professional counselors' organization dedicated to the "creation, development, production, and use of assessment and diagnostic techniques."

autobiography Created by asking an individual to write subjective information that stands out in his or her life. In some ways, the information highlighted in an individual's autobiography is a type of projective test of his or her unconscious mind.

behavior or feeling word checklist A classification system that allows an individual to identify those words that best describe his or her feeling state or the kinds of behaviors he or she might exhibit.

Binet, Alfred Commissioned by the Ministry of Public Education in Paris in 1904 to develop an intelligence test to assist in the integration of "subnormal" children into the schools. His work led to the development of the first modern-day intelligence test.

biographical inventories Provides a detailed picture of the individual from birth. They can be obtained by conducting an involved, structured interview or by having the client answer a series of items on a checklist or respond to a series of questions.

Buckley Amendment (FERPA)   Also known as the Family Educational Rights and Privacy Act of 1974, this law affirms the right of all individuals to have access to their school records, including test records.

Carl Perkins Act (PL 98-524)   Passed in 1984, this law assures that adults or special groups in need of job training have access to vocational assessment, counseling, and placement. These groups include people who are economically and academically disadvantaged, who have physical disabilities, who are entering nontraditional occupations, who are incarcerated, and so on.

Cattell, James   One of the earliest psychologists to use statistical concepts to understand people. His main emphasis became testing mental functions, and he is known for coining the term "mental test."

Cattell, Raymond   Differentiated fluid (innate) intelligence from crystallized (learned) intelligence and attempted to remove cultural bias from intelligence testing.

Civil Rights Acts (1964 and Amendments)   Laws requiring that any test used for employment or promotion be shown to be suitable and valid for the job in question. If this is not done, alternative means of assessment must be provided. Differential test cutoffs are not allowed.

class interval   Grouping scores from a frequency distribution within a predetermined range in order to create a histogram or frequency polygon.

classification system   A mechanism whereby information is provided about whether an individual possesses certain attributes or characteristics (asking a person to check off those adjectives that seem to best describe him or her). Includes behavior and feeling word checklists, situational tests, and sociometric instruments. A type of informal assessment.

clinical assessment   The process of assessing the client through multiple methods, including the clinical interview, informal assessment techniques, and objective and projective tests.

clinical interview   A critical step in the assessment process. Interviews can be structured, unstructured, or semi-structured.

coefficient of determination (shared variance)   The underlying commonality that accounts for the relationship between two sets of variables. It is calculated by squaring the correlation coefficient.

cognitive abilities tests   Often based on what one has learned in school, these instruments measure a broad range of cognitive abilities and are useful in making predictions about the future (e.g., whether an individual is likely to succeed in college). A type of aptitude test.

competence in the use of tests   In accordance with most professional code of ethics, examiners are required to have adequate training and knowledge before using a test. Some test publishers have a tiered system to describe the levels of training required to administer their tests.

computer-driven assessment   Allowing a computer program to assist in the assessment process and preparation of reports. Some observers believe computer-assisted questioning is at least as reliable as structured interviews and can provide an accurate diagnosis at a low cost.

Conant, James Bryant   Harvard president who conceived the idea of the SAT (formerly Scholastic Aptitude Test), which was developed by the Educational Testing Service after World War II. Conant thought that such tests could identify the ability of individuals and ultimately help to equalize educational opportunities.

concurrent validity   Evidence that test scores are related to an external source that can be measured at around the same time the test is being given ("here and now" validity).

confidentiality   An ethical (not legal) obligation to protect the client's right to privacy. There are some instances in which confidentiality should be broken, such as when clients are in danger of harming themselves or someone else.

construct validity   Evidence that a test measures a specific concept or trait. Construct validity includes an analysis of a test through one or more of the following methods: experimental design, factor analysis, convergence with other instruments, and/or discrimination with other measures.

content validity   Evidence that the test developer adequately surveyed the domain (the field) the test is to cover, that test items match that domain, and that test items are accurately weighted for relative importance.

convergent validity   A method of demonstrating construct validity by correlating a test with some other well-known measure or instrument.

Corey, Corey, and Callanan's Ethical Decision-Making Model   Eight steps that a practitioner should go through when making complex ethical decisions: identifying the problem, identifying the potential issues involved, reviewing the relevant ethical guidelines, knowing relevant laws and regulations, obtaining consultation, considering possible and probable courses of action, listing the consequences of various decisions, and deciding on what appears to be the best course of action.

correlation coefficient   The relationship between two sets of scores. Correlation coefficients range from +1 to –1 and generally are reported in decimals of one-hundredths. A positive correlation shows a tendency for scores to be related in the same direction, while a negative correlation indicates an inverse relationship.

criterion referencing   A method of scoring in which test scores are compared to a predetermined value or a set criterion.

criterion-related validity   The relationship between a test and a standard (external source) to which the test should be related. The external standard may be in the here-and-now (concurrent validity) or a predictor of future criteria (predictive validity).

Cronbach's coefficient alpha   A method of measuring internal consistency by calculating test reliability using all the possible split-half combinations. This is done by correlating the scores for each item on the test with the total score on the test and finding the average correlation for all of the items.

cross-cultural sensitivity   Awareness of the potential biases of assessment procedures when selecting, administering, and interpreting such procedures, as well as acknowledging the potential effects of age, cultural background, disability, ethnicity, gender, religion, sexual orientation, and socioeconomic status on test administration and test interpretation.

cumulative records   File containing information about a client's test scores, grades, behavioral problems, family issues, relationships with others, and other matters. School and workplace records are examples of cumulative records that can add vital information to our understanding of clients.

derived score   Score obtained by comparing an individual's score to the norm group by converting his or her raw score to a percentile or standard score such as z score, T score, Deviation IQ, stanine, sten score, normal curve equivalent (NCE), college or graduate school entrance exam score (e.g., SAT, GRE, and ACT), or publisher-type score, or by using developmental norms such as age comparison and grade equivalent.

developmental norms   Direct comparison of an individual's score to the average scores of others at the same age or grade level. Examples include age comparison and grade equivalent scoring.

Deviation IQ   Standard score with a mean of 100 and a standard deviation of 15. As the name implies, these scores are generally used in intelligence testing.

Diagnostic and Statistical Manual, Fourth Edition – Text Revision (DSM-IV-TR)   A comprehensive system published by the American Psychiatric Association that provides five axes to assist mental health professionals in diagnosing and treating mental disorders.

diagnostic test   Test that assesses problem areas of learning. Often used to assess learning disabilities. Generally classified as a type of achievement test.

discriminant validity   A method of demonstrating construct validity by correlating a test with other dissimilar instruments to ensure lack of a relationship.

Division 5 of the American Psychological Association   A professional organization for psychologists that promotes "research and practical application of psychological assessment, evaluation, measurement, and statistics."

environmental assessment   A naturalistic and systems approach to assessment in which practitioners collect information about clients from their home, work, or school environments.

Esquirol, Jean   Used language to identify different levels of intelligence while working in the

French mental asylums; his work led to the concept of verbal intelligence.

ethical code   Professional guidelines for appropriate behavior and guidance on how to respond under certain conditions. Each professional group has its own ethical code, including guidelines for counselors, psychologists, social workers, marriage and family therapists, psychiatrists, human service professionals, and others.

event and time sampling   Observing a targeted behavior for a set amount of time.

event sampling   Noting a specific behavior with no regard to time.

experimental design validity   Using experimentation to show that a test measures a specific concept or construct.

face validity   Superficial observation that a test appears to cover the correct content or domain. This is not an actual form of validity since the appearance of test items may or may not accurately reflect the domain.

factor analysis   This common statistical technique allows researchers to analyze large data sets to determine patterns and calculate which variables have a high degree of commonality. Therefore it is a method of demonstrating construct validity by statistically examining the relationship between subscales and the larger construct. It is also frequently used in multiple aptitude tests to help developers determine differences and similarities between subtests.

FERPA   Family Educational Rights and Privacy Act of 1974 (also known as the Buckley Amendment), which affirms the right of all individuals to gain access to their school records, including test records.

Freedom of Information Act   This law assures the right of individuals to access their federal records, including test records. Most states have similar laws that assure access to state records.

frequency distribution   A method of understanding test scores by ordering a set of scores from high to low and listing the corresponding frequency of each score across from it.

frequency polygon   A method of converting a frequency distribution of scores into a line graph. After combining scores by class interval, the class intervals are placed along the x-axis and the frequency of scores along the y-axis.

Galton, Sir Francis   Examined relationship of sensorimotor responses to intelligence. He hypothesized that individuals who had a quicker reaction time and stronger grip strength were superior intellectually.

Gardner, Howard   Vehemently opposed current constructs of intelligence measurement and developed his own theory of multiple intelligences asserting that there are eight or nine intelligences: verbal-linguistic, mathematical-logical, musical, visual-spatial, bodily-kinesthetic, interpersonal, intrapersonal, naturalist, and existential intelligence.

generosity error   Error that occurs when an individual rates another person inaccurately because he or she identifies with the person being rated.

genogram   A map of an individual's family tree that may include the family history of illnesses, mental disorders, substance use, expectations, relationships, cultural issues, and other concerns relevant to counseling. Special symbols may be used to assist in creating this map.

grade equivalent scoring   A type of standard score calculated by comparing an individual's score to the average score of others at the same grade level.

Guilford, J. P.   Developed a multifactor/multidimensional model of intelligence based on 180 factors. His three-dimensional model can be represented as a cube and involves three kinds of cognitive ability: operation, content, and product.

halo effect   Error that occurs when the overall impression of an individual clouds the rating of that person in one or more select areas.

Health Insurance Portability and Accountability Act (HIPAA)   Ensures the privacy of client records, including testing records, and the sharing of such information. In general, HIPAA restricts the amount of information that can be shared without client consent and allows clients to have access to their records, except for process notes used in counseling.

histogram   A method of converting a frequency distribution of scores into a bar graph. After combining scores by class interval, the class intervals are placed along the x-axis and the frequency of scores along the y-axis.

Individualized Education Plan (IEP)   PL94-142 states that children who are identified as having a learning disability will be provided a school team that will create an Individualized Education Plan to assist the student with his or her learning problem(s).

Individuals with Disabilities Education Improvement Act (IDEIA) (Expansion of PL 94-142)   This legislative act assures the right of students to be tested, at the school system's expense, if they are suspected of having a disability that interferes with learning. These students must be given accommodations for their disability and taught within the "least restrictive environment," which often is a regular classroom.

informal assessment instruments   Assessment instruments that are often developed by the user and are specific to the testing situation. All of these instruments can be used to assess broad areas of ability and personality attributes in a variety of settings. Types of informal assessment instruments include observation, rating scales, classification systems, and records and personal documents.

informed consent   Principle that individuals being assessed should give their permission for the assessment after they are given information concerning such items as the nature and purposes of the assessment, fees, involvement by others in the assessment process (e.g., teachers, therapists), and the limits of confidentiality.

intelligence quotient   Concept developed by Lewis Terman, who divided chronological age by mental age and multiplied the quotient by 100 to derive a score that he called "IQ."

intelligence test, individual   Test that measures a broad range of intellectual ability and can provide a broad assessment of one's cognitive capabilities. Often used to identify mental retardation, giftedness, learning disabilities, and general cognitive functioning. A type of aptitude test.

interest inventories   Tests that measure likes and dislikes as well as one's personality orientation toward the world of work. Generally used in career counseling. A type of personality test.

internal consistency   A method of determining reliability of an instrument by looking within the test itself, or not going "outside of the test" to determine a reliability estimate as is done with test-retest or parallel forms reliability. Some types of internal consistency reliability include split-half (or

odd-even), Cronbach's Coefficient Alpha, and Kuder-Richardson.

interquartile range   Provides the range of the middle 50% of scores around the median. Because it eliminates the top and bottom quartiles, the interquartile range is most useful with skewed curves because it offers a more representative picture of where a large percentage of the scores fall.

interval scale   A scale of measurement in which there are equal distances between measurements but no absolute zero reference point.

invasion of privacy   All tests invade one's privacy, but concerns about invasion of privacy are lessened if the client has given informed consent, has the ability to accept or refuse testing, and knows the limits of confidentiality.

Jaffee v. Redmond   In this case, the Supreme Court upheld the right of a licensed social worker to keep her case records confidential. Describing the social worker as a "therapist" and "psychotherapist," the ruling will likely protect all licensed therapists in federal courts and may affect all licensed therapists who have privileged communication.

journals and diaries   Can provide valuable insight into self, or to a clinician, by revealing unconscious drives and desires and by uncovering patterns that highlight issues in a client's life.

Jung, Carl   Developed a list of 100 words (word association) to which subjects were asked to respond as quickly as possible. Depending on the response and the answer time, Jung believed he could identify mental illness. He also created the personality type construct that is used in the Myers-Briggs Type Inventory.

Kitchener's moral ethical-decision making model   Kitchener developed a model for making ethical decisions based on five moral principles: autonomy, beneficence, nonmaleficence, justice, and fidelity.

Kraeplin, Emil   Developed a crude word association test to study schizophrenia in the 1880s.

Kuder-Richardson   A method of calculating internal consistency by using all the possible split-half combinations. This is done by correlating the scores for each item on the test with the total score on the test and finding the average correlation for all of the items.

Likert scale A graphic-type rating scale that has a statement followed by words that reflect a continuum that range from favorable to unfavorable regarding the quality being measured. A number line may or may not be associated with the words.

mean A measure of central tendency that is calculated by adding all of the scores and dividing by the total number of scores. It is the arithmetic average of the scores.

measures of central tendency Indicators of what is occurring in the midrange or "center" of a group of scores. Three measures of central tendency are the mean, median, and mode.

measures of variability Indicators of how much scores vary in a distribution. Three types of measures of variability are the range, interquartile range, and the standard deviation.

median A measure of central tendency which is the middle score, or the score for which 50% of scores fall above and 50% fall below. In a skewed curve or skewed distribution of test scores, the median is generally the most accurate measure of central tendency since it is not affected by unusually high or low scores.

***Mental Measurements Yearbook* by Buros** A sourcebook of reviews of more than 2000 different tests, instruments, or screening devices. Most large universities carry these editions in hardbound copy and more recently, online.

mental status exam A portion of the assessment and written report that addresses the client's appearance and behavior, emotional state, thought components, and cognitive functioning.

Miner, J. B. Developed one of first group interest inventories in 1922 to assist large groups of high school students in selecting an occupation.

mode A measure of central tendency which is the score that occurs more often than any other.

multiple aptitude tests Tests that measure many aspects of ability. Often useful in determining the likelihood of success in a number of vocations. A type of aptitude test.

Murray, Henry Developed the Thematic Apperception Test (TAT), which asks a subject to view a number of standard pictures and create a story to explain the situation as he or she best understands it. This test is based on his needs-press theory.

negatively skewed curve A set of test scores where the majority fall at the upper or positive end. It is said to be a negatively skewed curve or distribution because a few "negative" or low-end scores have stretched or skewed the curve to the left.

No Child Left Behind (NCLB) Act A federal act that requires all states to have a plan in place to show how, by the year 2014, all students will have obtained proficiency in reading/language arts and math. The act has caused many states to develop standards of learning whose purpose is to assess all students and ensure they are meeting the minimum standards.

nominal scale A scale of measurement in which numbers are arbitrarily assigned to represent different categories or variables. The only math that can be applied to these numbers is calculation of the mode.

norm referencing A method of scoring in which test scores are compared to a group of other scores called the norm group.

normal curve A bell-shaped curve showing the usual frequency distribution of values of measured human traits and other natural phenomena.

normal curve equivalents (NCE) scores Frequently used in the educational community, this is a form of standard scoring that has 99 equal units along a bell-shaped curve, with a mean of 50 and a standard deviation of 21.06.

numerical scale A form of rating in which a statement or question is followed by a choice of numbers arranged from high to low along a number line.

objective personality testing Paper-and-pencil tests, often in multiple-choice or true/false formats, that assess various aspects of personality. Often used to increase client insight, to identify psychopathology, and to assist in treatment planning. A type of personality test.

observation Observing behaviors of an individual in order to develop a deeper understanding of one or more specific behaviors. (e.g., observing a student's acting-out behavior in class or assessing a client's ability to perform eye-hand coordination tasks to determine potential vocational placements). A type of informal assessment.

ordinal scale A scale of measurement in which the magnitude or rank order is implied; however, the distance between measurements is unknown.

Parsons, Frank Leader of the vocational counseling movement.

percentiles A method of comparing raw scores to a norm group by calculating the percentage of people falling below an obtained score, with ranges from 1 to 99, and 50 being the mean.

personality testing Tests in the affective realm used to assess habits, temperament, likes and dislikes, character, and similar behaviors. Types of personality tests include interest inventories, objective personality tests, and projective personality tests.

Piaget, Jean Approached intelligence from a developmental perspective by observing how children's cognitions were shaped as they grew. He identified four stages of cognitive development: sensorimotor, preoperational, concrete operational, and formal operational. He also believed that cognitive development is adaptive, and he devised the concepts of assimilation and accommodation.

positively skewed curve A set of test scores in which the majority fall at the lower or negative end. It is said to be a positively skewed curve or distribution because a few "positive" or high-end scores have stretched or skewed the curve to the right.

practicality of test selection When selecting a test, one of the cornerstones of test worthiness is practicality. Practical concerns include time, cost, format, readability, and ease of administration, scoring, and interpretation.

predictive validity Evidence that test scores are able to predict a future criterion or standard.

privileged communication The legal right to maintain privacy of a conversation. The privilege belongs to the client, and only the client can waive that privilege.

projective personality tests Tests that present a stimulus to which individuals can respond. Personality factors are interpreted based on the individual's response. Often used to identify psychopathology and to assist in treatment planning. A type of personality test.

proper diagnosis Due to the delicate nature of diagnoses, ethical codes stress that professionals should be particularly careful when deciding which assessment techniques to use in forming a diagnosis for a mental disorder.

publisher-type scores Created by test developers who generate their own unique standard score that employs a mean and standard deviation of the publisher's choice.

quincunx Also known as Galton's board, it is a board with protruding pins or nails whereupon balls dropped will fall along the bell or normal curve.

range The simplest measure of variability is the range, which is calculated by subtracting the lowest score from the highest score and adding 1.

rank order A rating scale providing a series of statements that the respondent is asked to place from highest to lowest based on his or her preferences.

rating scales Scales developed to assess any of a number of attributes of the examinee. Can be rated by the examinee or someone who knows the examinee well (for example, students rating a faculty member's teaching ability or a teacher rating a student's ability to make empathic responses). A type of informal assessment.

ratio scale A scale of measurement that has a meaningful zero point and equal intervals and thus can be manipulated by all mathematical principles.

raw score An untreated score before manipulation or processing to make it a standard score, as must be done for all norm-referenced tests. Raw scores alone tell us little, if anything, about how a person has done on a test. We must take an individual's raw score and do something to it to give it meaning.

readiness tests Tests that measure one's readiness for moving ahead in school. Often used to assess readiness to enter kindergarten or first grade. A type of achievement test.

records and personal documents Assessing behaviors, values and beliefs of an individual by examining such items as diaries, personal journals, genograms, or school records. A type of informal assessment.

release of test data Test data should be released to others only if the client has signed a release form. The release of such data is generally granted only to individuals who can adequately interpret the test data, and professionals should assure that those who receive such data do not misuse the information.

reliability   The degree to which test scores are free from errors of measurement, also, the capacity of an instrument to provide consistent results.

Rorschach, Herman   A student of Carl Jung, he created the Rorschach Inkblot test by splattering ink onto sheets of paper and folding them in half. He believed the interpretation of an individual's reactions to these forms could tell volumes about the individual's unconscious life.

SAT/GRE-type scores   Standard score that generally has a standard deviation of 100 and a mean of 500 for each section of the exam. However, since the scores are reported based on the norms for the last three years of examinees, the mean and standard deviation will vary slightly each year.

scales of measurement   Ways of defining the attributes of numbers and how they can be manipulated. The four types of measurement scales are nominal, ordinal, interval, and ratio.

scatterplot   A graph of two sets of test scores used to visually display the relationship or correlation. If the dots are plotted closer together, the correlation is moving toward a positive or negative one. If the dots are spread out or completely random, the correlation is closer to zero.

Section 504 of the Rehabilitation Act   This act applies to all federally funded programs receiving financial assistance and was established to prevent discrimination based on disability.

semantic differential   A rating scale that provides a statement followed by one or more pairs of words that reflect opposing traits. A number line may or may not be associated with the dichotomous pairs of words.

semi-structured interview   Uses prescribed items and thereby allows the examiner to obtain the necessary information within a relatively short amount of time. However, this kind of interview also gives leeway to the examiner should the client need to "drift" during the interview process.

Sequin, Edouard   Worked with mentally retarded persons and developed the form board to increase his patients' motor control and sensory discrimination. This was the forerunner to performance IQ.

single aptitude tests   See *special aptitude tests.*

situational tests   Used to examine how an individual is likely to respond in a contrived but natural situation. An example of this type of procedure is when a potential doctoral student counsels a role-play client. A type of informal assessment.

skewed curve   A set of test scores that do not fall along the normal curve.

sociometric instruments   A classification system that identifies the relative position of an individual within a group. This type of instrument is often used when one wants to determine the dynamics of individuals within a group, organization, or institution. A type of informal assessment.

Spearman, Charles Edward   Believed in a two-factor approach to intelligence that included a general factor (*g*) and a specific factor (*s*), both of which he considered important in understanding intelligence.

Spearman-Brown formula   A mathematical formula that can be used with split-half or odd-even reliability estimates to increase the accuracy, which is impaired because of the shortening (splitting in half) of the test.

special aptitude tests   Tests that measure one aspect of ability. Often useful in determining the likelihood of success in a vocation (e.g., a mechanical aptitude test to determine success as a mechanic). A type of aptitude test.

split-half or odd-even reliability   This method of internal consistency reliability splits the test in half and correlates the scores of one half of the test with the other half. Hence, it requires only one form and one administration of the test.

standard deviation   A measure of variability that describes how scores vary around the mean. In all normal curves the percentage of scores between standard deviation units are the same; hence, the standard deviation combined with the mean can tell us a great deal about a set of test scores.

standard error of measurement   The range of scores where we would expect a person's score to fall if he or she took the instrument over and over again—in other words, where a "true" score might lie. It is calculated by taking the square root of 1 minus the reliability and multiplying that number by the standard deviation.

standard scores   Scores derived by converting an individual's raw score to a new score that has a new mean and new standard deviation. Standard scores are generally used to make test results easier for the examinee to interpret.

stanines Derived from the term "standard nines," this is a standardized score frequently used in schools. Often used with achievement tests, stanines have a mean of 5 and a standard deviation of 2, and range from 1 to 9.

sten scores Derived from the name "standard ten," a standard score that is commonly used on personality inventories and questionnaires. Stens have a mean of 5.5 and a standard deviation of 2.

Strong, Edward Led a team of researchers in the 1920s to develop the Strong Vocational Interest Blank. The test is now known as the Strong Interest Inventory and is still one of the most popular interest inventories ever created.

structured interview An interview in which the examinee is asked to respond to a set of pre-established items. This is often done verbally, although sometimes clients can respond to written items.

survey battery tests Paper-and-pencil tests, usually given in school settings, that measure broad content areas. Often used to assess progress in school. A type of achievement test.

t **score** A type of standard score that can be easily converted from a z score. T scores have a mean of 50 and a standard deviation of 10 and are generally used with personality tests.

Terman, Lewis Professor at Stanford University who analyzed the Binet and Simon scale and made a number of revisions to create the Stanford-Binet intelligence test that is still used today. Terman was the first to incorporate in his test the ratio of chronological age and mental age, calling it the "intelligence quotient" or "IQ."

test administration Tests should be administered appropriately as defined by the way they were established and standardized. Alterations to this process should be noted and interpretations of test data adjusted if conditions were not ideal.

test scoring and interpretation The process of examining tests and making judgments about test data. Professionals should reflect on how issues of test worthiness, including the reliability, validity, cross-cultural fairness, and practicality of the test, might affect the results.

test security Professionals have the responsibility to make reasonable efforts to assure the integrity of test content and the security of the test itself. Professionals should not duplicate tests or change test material without the permission of the publisher.

test worthiness Determined by an objective analysis of a test in four critical areas: (1) *validity:* whether or not it measures what it is supposed to measure; (2) *reliability:* whether or not the score an individual receives on a test is an accurate measure of his or her true score; (3) *cross-cultural fairness:* whether or not the score the individual obtains is a true reflection of the individual and not a reflection of cultural bias inherent in the test, and (4) *practicality:* whether or not it makes sense to use a test in a particular situation.

test-retest reliability Giving the test twice to the same group of people, and then correlating the scores of the first test with those of the second test to determine the reliability of the instrument.

tests A subset of assessment techniques that yield scores based on the gathering of collected data.

Thorndike, Edward Believed that tests could be given in a format that was more reliable than the previous methods. His work culminated with the development of the Stanford Achievement Test in 1923.

Thurstone, Louis Developed a multifactor approach or model of intelligence that included seven primary factors: verbal meaning, number ability, word fluency, perception speed, spatial ability, reasoning, and memory.

time sampling A form of observation in which a number of behaviors are noted during a set duration of time.

unstructured interview Interview in which the examiner does not have a pre-established list of items or questions to which the client can respond; instead, client responses to examiner inquiries establish the direction for follow-up questioning.

validity The degree to which all of the accumulated evidence supports the intended interpretation of test scores for the intended purpose. Validity is a unitary concept that attempts to answer the question, How well does a test measure what it's supposed to measure?

Vernon, Philip Believed that subcomponents of intelligence could be added in a hierarchical manner to get a score for a cumulative (g) factor. Many of today's intelligence tests continue to use this concept.

Woodworth's Personal Data Sheet   An instrument with 116 items developed to screen World War I recruits for their susceptibility to mental health problems. It is considered the precursor of all modern-day personality inventories.

Wundt, Wilhelm   Developed one of the first psychological laboratories. He also set out to create "a new domain of science" that he called physiologi-

cal psychology, which later became known as psychology.

Yerkes, Robert   President of the American Psychological Association during World War I, he chaired a special committee designed to screen new recruits. The committee developed the Army Alpha test.

z score   The most fundamental standard score, which is created by converting an individual's raw score to a new score that has a mean of 0 and a standard deviation of 1.

References

Achievement Tech. (2002). Effectiveness report: South Plainfield schools' quest to leave no child behind. Retrieved on September 26, 2004, from http://www.achievementtech.com/pdf/SouthPlainField.pdf

ACT, Inc. (1997). *ACT Assessment technical manual*. Iowa City, IA: Author.

ACT, Inc. (2004a). ACT information for life transitions. Retrieved on April 26, 2004, from http://www.act.org

ACT, Inc. (2004b). National distributions of "percent at or below" for ACT test scores, ACT-tested high school graduates of 2001, 2002, and 2003. Retrieved on April 26, 2004, from http://www.act.org/aap/pdf/norms.pdf

ACT, Inc. (2004c). Facts about the ACT assessment. Retrieved on June 6, 2004, from http://www.act.org/news/aapfacts.html

AGS Publishing. (2004a). PIAT-R/NU: Peabody Individual Achievement Test-Revised-Normative Update. AGS publishing: A comprehensive resource. Retrieved on February 9, 2005, from http://www.agsnet.com/group.asp?nGroupInfoID=a29060

AGS Publishing. (2004b). *KABC-II: Kaufman Assessment Battery for Children, Second Edition*. Retrieved June 5, 2004, from http://www.agsnet.com/group.asp?nGroupInfoID=a21000

Aiken, L. R. (1996) *Rating scales and checklists*. New York: Wiley.

Aiken, L. R. (2003). Psychological testing and assessment (11th ed.). Boston: Allyn and Bacon.

American Counseling Association (ACA). (1995). *Code of ethics and standards of practice* (Rev. ed.). Alexandria, VA: Author.

American Counseling Association (ACA). (2003). Standards for qualifications of test users. Retrieved October 10, 2004, from http://aac.ncat.edu/documents/Standards%20for%20Qualifications%20of%20Test%20Users.DOC

American Educational Research Association, American Psychological Association, and National Council on Measurement in Education (AERA, APA, & NCME) (1999). *Standards for educational and psychological testing*. Washington, DC: AERA.

American Psychiatric Association. (2000). *Diagnostic and statistical manual of mental disorders* (4th ed., text revision). Washington, DC: Author.

American Psychological Association. (1954). *Technical recommendations for psychological tests and diagnostic techniques*. Washington, DC: Author.

American Psychological Association. (2000). Guidelines for principles and accreditation of programs in professional psychology. Retrieved on April 14, 2005, from http://www.apa.org/ed/gp2000.html

American Psychological Association. (2002). Ethics code of psychologists. Retrieved November 22, 2002, from http://apa.org/ethics

American Psychological Association. (2003). *Ethical principles of psychologists and code of conduct*. Retrieved June 15, 2003, from http://www.apa.org/ethics

Anastasi, A. (1985). Mental measurement: Some emerging trends. In J. V. Mitchell, Jr. (Ed.), *The Ninth Mental Measurements Yearbook* (pp. xxiii–xxix). Lincoln, NE: University of Nebraska Press.

APA Practice Organization (2002). Getting ready for HIPAA: What you need to know now: A primer for psychologists. Washington, DC: Author.

Appelbaum, S. (1990). The relationship between assessment and psychotherapy. *Journal of Personality Assessment, 54,* 791–801.

Armed Services Vocational Aptitude Battery (ASVAB). (2004). The ASVAB career exploration program counselor manual. Retrieved June 7, 2004, from http://www.asvabprogram.com/downloads/asvab_counselor_manual.pdf

Armstrong, J. S. (1980). Unintelligible management research and academic prestige. *Interfaces, 10*(2), 80–86.

Association for Assessment in Counseling and Education (AACE). (2003). Responsibilities of users of standardized tests (RUST). Retrieved October 10, 2004, from http://aac.ncat.edu/Resources/documents/RUST2003%20v11%20Final.pdf

Association for Assessment in Counseling and Education (AACE). (2004a). Welcome to the AACE Website. Retrieved October 10, 2004, from http://aac.ncat.edu/

Association for Assessment in Counseling and Education (AACE). (2004b). Documents and links: Key documents in assessment and testing. Retrieved October 11, 2004, from http://aac.ncat.edu/resources.html.

Atkinson, M. (2003). Review of the California Psychological Inventory™ Third Edition. In B. S. Plake, J. C. Imapara, and R. A. Spies (Eds.), *The Fifteenth Mental Measurements Yearbook* (pp. 159–161). Lincoln, NE: Buros Institute of Mental Measurements.

Axford, S., & Boyle, G. (2005). Review of the Taylor-Johnson Temperament Analysis 2002 Edition. *The Sixteenth Mental Measurements Yearbook*. Retrieved on February 9, 2005, from http://gateway.ut.ovid.com/gw1/ovidweb.cgi

Baker, S. R., Robinson, J. E., Danner, M. J. E., & Neukrug, E. (2001). Community social disorganization theory applied to adolescent academic achievement (Report No. UD034167). (ERIC Document Reproduction Service No. ED453301).

Bartram, D. (2001). American Psychological Association (APA) test user qualifications task force. Retrieved February 21, 2004, from http://www.intestcom.org/APA_Test_Use_ Task_Force.htm

Beck, A. T., Steer, R. A., & Brown, G. K. (2003). *BDI-II manual.* San Antonio, TX: Psychological Corporation.

Beck, A. T., Steer, R. A., & Brown, G. K. (2004). *Beck depression inventory, II.* San Antonio, TX: Harcourt Assessment.

Beck, J. (1995). *Cognitive therapy: Basics and beyond.* New York: Guilford Press.

Beck, M. (1995). Review of the Kindergarten Readiness Test. In J. C. Conoley and J. C. Impara (Eds.), *The Twelfth Mental Measurements Yearbook* (pp. 538–540). Lincoln, NE: Buros Institute of Mental Measurements.

Benchmark Testware. (1998). Pre-employment aptitude testing: Mechanical aptitude. Retrieved on June 12, 2004, from http://www.aptitude-testing.com/

Benes, K. (1992). Review of the Peabody Individual Achievement Test – Revised. In J. J. Kramer and J. C. Conoley (Eds.), *The Eleventh Mental Measurements Yearbook* (pp. 649–652). Lincoln, NE: Buros Institute of Mental Measurements.

Bernt, F., & Frank, M. L. (2001). Review of the Marital Satisfaction Inventory – Revised. In B. S. Plake and J. C. Impara (Eds.), *The Fourteenth Mental Measurements Yearbook* (pp. 710–714). Lincoln, NE: Buros Institute of Mental Measurements.

Bond, L. (1990). Understanding the black/white student gap on measures of quantitative reasoning. In F. C. Serafica, A. I. Schwebel, R. K. Russes, P. D. Issac, & L. B. Myers (Eds.), *Mental health of ethnic minorities* (pp. 89–107). New York: Praeger.

Bradley, R. W. (1994a). Tests and counseling: How did we ever become partners? *Measurement and Evaluation in Counseling, 26*(4), 224–226.

Bradley, R. W. (1994b). The marriage between tests and counseling redux: Still a failure after 20 years? *Measurement and Evaluation in Counseling, 26*(4), 224–226.

Bradley, R., & Waters, E. (1985). Review of the Gesell Readiness Test. In J. V. Mitchell, Jr. (Ed.), *The Ninth Mental Measurements Yearbook* (pp. 609–611). Lincoln, NE: Buros Institute of Mental Measurements.

Brannigan, G., Decker, S., & Madsen, D. (2004). Innovative features of the Bender-Gestalt II and expanded guidelines for the use of the global scoring system. *Assessment Service Bulletin Number 1*. Retrieved on July 15, 2004, from http://www.riverpub.com/products/clinical/bg/9-95644_BenderII_ASB1.pdf

Bridgeman, B., & Morgan, R. (1996). Success in college for students with discrepancies between performance on multiple-choice and essay tests. *Journal of Educational Psychology, 88,* 333–340.

Brookhart, S., & Cross, L. (1998). Review of the Iowa Tests of Basic Skills Forms K, L, and M. In J. C. Impara and B. S. Plake (Eds.), *The Thirteenth Mental Measurements Yearbook* (pp. 536–546). Lincoln, NE: Buros Institute of Mental Measurements.

Brown, M. (2001). Review of the Self-Directed Search Fourth Edition Forms R, E, and CP. In B. S. Plake and J. C. Impara (Eds.), *The Fourteenth Mental Measurements Yearbook* (pp. 1105–1107). Lincoln, NE: Buros Institute of Mental Measurements.

Brown, W. (1910). Some experimental results in the correlation of mental abilities. *British Journal of Psychology, 3,* 296–322.

Bryson, B. (2003). *A short history of nearly everything.* New York: Broadway Books.

Buck, R. (1987). *Kinetic-House-Tree-Person drawings (K-H-T-P): An interpretative manual.* New York: Brunner/Mazel.

Butcher, J., Dahlstrom, W., Graham, J., Tellegen, A., & Kaemmer, B. (1989). *Manual for administration and scoring: MMPI-2.* Minneapolis: University of Minnesota Press.

Callahan, R., & Callahan, J. (2003). ATFT certified algorithm level TFT training manual. (Available from Callahan Techniques, Ltd., PO Box 1220, La Quinta, CA, 92253.)

Camara, W., Nathan, J., & Puente, A. (2000). Psychological test usage: Implications in professional psychology. *Professional Psychology: Research and Practice, 31,* 141–154.

Cattell, R. (1971). *Abilities: Their structure, growth, and action.* Boston: Houghton Mifflin.

Cattell, R. (1979). Are culture-fair intelligence tests possible and necessary? *Journal of Research and Development in Education, 12,* 3–13.

Cattell, R. (1980). The heritability of fluid, gf, and crystallized, gc, intelligence, estimated by a least squares use of the MAVA method. *British Journal of Educational Psychology, 50,* 253–265.

Claiborn, C. (1991). The Buros tradition and the counseling profession. *Journal of Counseling and Development, 69,* 456–457.

Cohen, A. (1995). Review of the Musical Aptitude Profile 1988 Revision. In J. C. Conoley and J. C. Impara (Eds.), *The Twelfth Mental Measurements Yearbook* (pp. 663–666). Lincoln, NE: Buros Institute of Mental Measurements.

Cohen, J., & Swerdlik, M. (1999). *Psychological testing and assessment: An introduction to tests and measurement* (4th ed.). Mountain View, CA: Mayfield.

Cole, D., Truglio, R., & Peeke, L. (1997). Relation between symptoms of anxiety and depression in children: A multitrait–multimethod–multigroup assessment. *Journal of Consulting and Clinical Psychology, 65,* 110–119.

College Board. (2004). SAT I as a predictor of college grades. Retrieved June 6, 2004, from http://www.collegeboard.com/ prod_downloads/about/news_info/cbsenior/ yr2002/pdf/eleven.pdf

Consulting Psychologists Press (CPP). (2002). Comparing the MBTI Form G and Form M. Retrieved on September 5, 2004, from http://www.cpp.com/products/mbti/ FormM_vs_FormG.pdf

Coopersmith, S. (1989). *Self-Esteem Inventory.* Palo Alto, CA: Consulting Psychologists Press.

Corey, G., Corey, M., & Callanan, P. (2003). *Issues and ethics in the helping professions* (6th ed.). Pacific Grove, CA: Brooks/Cole.

Council for Accreditation of Counseling and Related Educational Programs (CACREP). (2001). 2001 standards. Retrieved on April 20, 2005, from http://www.cacrep.org/2001Standards.html

Cowdery, K. (1926). Measurement of professional attitudes: Differences between lawyers, physicians and engineers. *Journal of Personnel Research, 5,* 131–141.

Crippa, J., Sanches, R., Hallak, J., Loureiro, S., & Zuardi, A. (2001). A structured interview guide increases Brief Psychiatric Rating Scale reliability in raters with low clinical experience. *Acta Psychiatrica Scandinavica, 103,* 465–470.

Crocker, L., & Schmitt, A. (1987). Improving multiple-choice and open-ended analytical questions. *The Journal of Experimental Education, 55,* 201–205.

Cronbach, L. (1951). Coefficient alpha and the internal structure of tests. *Psychometrika, 16,* 297–334.

Cross, L. (2001). Review of the Peabody Individual Achievement Test – Revised 1998 Normative Update. In B. S. Plake and J. C. Impara (Eds.), *The Fourteenth Mental Measurements Yearbook* (pp. 904–906). Lincoln, NE: Buros Institute of Mental Measurements.

Division 5 (2004). APA divisions: Evaluation, measurement, and statistics. Retrieved October 10, 2004, from http://www.apa.org/about/division/div5.html

Doyle, K. (1974). Theory and practice of ability testing in ancient Greece. *Journal of the History of Behavioral Sciences, 10,* 202–212.

Drummond, R. J. (2004). *Appraisal procedures for counselors and helping professionals* (5th ed.). Upper Saddle River, NJ: Pearson.

DuBois, P. (1970). *A history of psychological testing.* Boston: Allyn and Bacon.

EdITS. (n.d.). COPS: Career Occupational Preference System Interest Inventory. Interest inventory assessment for career exploration and counseling. Retrieved on July 25, 2004, from http://www.edits.net/cops.html

Educational Testing Service (ETS). (2003–2004). *Graduate Record Exams, 2003–2004: Guide to the use of scores.* Princeton, NJ: Author.

Educational Testing Service (ETS). (2004–2005). GRE 2004–2005: Guide to the use of scores. Retrieved on June 6, 2004, from http://ftp.ets.org/pub/gre/994994.pdf

Esquirol, J. (1838). *Des maladies mentales considerees sous les rapports medical, hygienique, et medico-legal.* Paris: Bailliere.

Exner, J. (1974). The Rorschach: A comprehensive system. New York: Wiley.

Fairtest. (n.d.). Challenge to Gesell as kindergarten placement exam. Fairtest: The national center for fair and open testing. Retrieved on April 25, 2004, from http://www.fairtest.org/examarts/fall88/GESELL.html

Federal Register, 42(163), 42474-42518. (1977). Regulation implementing Education for All Handicapped Children Act of 1975 (PL94-142).

Fitzpatrick, C., & Schraw, G. (2003). Review of the Behavior Rating Inventory of Executive Function. In B. S. Plake, J. C. Imapara, and R. A. Spies (Eds.), *The Fifteenth Mental Measurements Yearbook* (pp. 112–117). Lincoln, NE: Buros Institute of Mental Measurements.

Fitzpatrick, R. (2001). Review of the Minnesota Clerical Assessment Battery. In B. S. Plake and J. C. Impara (Eds), *The Fourteenth Mental Mea-

surements Yearbook* (pp. 769-771). Lincoln, NE: Buros Institute of Mental Measurements.

Fleenor, J. (2001). Review of the Myers-Briggs Type Indicator Form M. In B. S. Plake and J. C. Impara (Eds.), *The Fourteenth Mental Measurements Yearbook* (pp. 816–818). Lincoln, NE: Buros Institute of Mental Measurements.

Flugel, J. (1941). *A hundred years of psychology: 1833–1933.* Andover, Hants: Chapel Rivers.

Fong, M. L. (1995). Assessment and DSM-IV diagnosis of personality disorders: A primer for counselors. *Journal of Counseling Development, 73,* 635–639.

Frontline. (1999). *The secrets of the SATs.* Retrieved November 21, 2003, from http://www.pbs.org/wgbh/pages/frontline/shows/sats/etc/script.html

Galton, F. (1879). Psychometric facts. *Nineteenth Century, 5,* 425–433.

Gardner, H. (1983). *Frames of mind.* New York: Basic Books.

Gardner, H. (1996). *MI: Intelligence, understanding and the mind* [motion picture]. (Available from Media Into the Classroom, 10573 W. Pico Blvd. #162, Los Angeles, CA 90064.)

Gardner, H. (1999). *Intelligence reframed: Multiple intelligence for the 21st century.* New York: Basic Books.

Gardner, H. (2003). Multiple intelligences after twenty years. Paper presented at the American Educational Research Association. Chicago: April 21, 2003. Retrieved on June 16, 2004, from http://pzweb.harvard.edu/PIs/HG_MI_after_20_years.pdf

Geisinger, K. (1994). Psychometric issues in testing students with disabilities. *Applied Measurement in Education, 7,* 121–140.

Geisinger, K. (2000). Psychological testing at the end of the millennium: A brief historical review. *Professional Psychology, Research, and Practice, 31,* 117–119.

Gesell Institute of Human Development. (2000–2002). The Gesell Institute of Human Development. Retrieved, June 9, 2004, from http://www.gesellinstitute.org

Gillham, N. (2001). *A life of Sir Francis Galton: From African exploration to the birth of eugenics.* New York: Oxford University Press.

Glosoff, H. L., Herlihy, B., & Spense, B. E. (2000). Privileged communication in the counselor-client relationship. *Journal of Counseling and Development, 78*(4), 454–462.

Goldman, L. (1994). The marriage between tests and counseling redux: Summary of the 1972 article. *Measurement and Evaluation in Counseling and Development, 26*(4), 214–216.

Goodwin, L. (2002a). Changing conceptions of measurement validity: An update on the new standards. *Journal of Nursing Education, 41,* 100–106.

Goodwin, L. (2002b). The meaning of validity. *Journal of Pediatric Gastroenterology and Nutrition, 35,* 6–7.

Goodwin, L., & Goodwin, W. (1999). Measurement myths and misconceptions. *Psychology Quarterly, 14,* 408–427.

Gottfredson, G. D., & Holland, J. (1996). Dictionary of Holland occupational codes (3rd ed.). Lutz, FL: Psychological Assessment Resources.

Gould, S. J. (1996). The mismeasure of man (Rev. and expanded). New York: Norton.

Graham, J. (2000). *MMPI-2: Assessing personality and psychopathology* (3rd ed.). New York: Oxford University Press.

Grant, J., & Davis, L. (1997). Selection and use of content experts for instrument development. *Research in Nursing & Health, 20,* 269–274.

Greist, J. (1998). Computer-based assessment of patients. *Journal of Clinical Psychopharmacology, 18,* 359–361.

Gronlund, N., & Linn, R. (1990). *Measurement and evaluation in teaching.* New York: Macmillan.

Groth-Marnat, G. (2003). *Handbook of psychological assessment* (4th ed.). Hoboken, NJ: Wiley.

Guilford, J. (1967). *The nature of human intelligence.* New York: McGraw-Hill.

Guilford, J. (1988). Some changes in the structure of the intellect model. *Educational and Psychological Measurement, 48,* 1–4.

Halperin, J., & McKay, K. (1998). Psychological testing for child and adolescent psychiatrists: A review of the past 10 years. *Journal of the American Academy of Child and Adolescent Psychiatry, 37,* 575–583.

Haney, W. (1981). Validity, vaudeville, and values: A short history of social concerns over standardized testing. *American Psychologist, 36,* 1021–1033.

Hansen, J. C. (1995). Interest assessment (Report No. EDO-CG-95-13). Greensboro, NC: ERIC Clearinghouse on Counseling and Student Services. (ERIC Document Reproduction Service No. ED 389-961.)

Harcourt Assessment. (2002). *OLSAT 8 technical manual.* San Antonio, TX: Author.

Harcourt Assessment. (2004a). *Stanford Achievement Test Series, Tenth Edition: Technical data report.* San Antonio, TX: Author.

Harcourt Assessment. (2004b). OLSAT 8 machine-scoreable test packs. Retrieved on October 7, 2004, from http://harcourtassessment.com/haiweb/Cultures/en-US/Products/Product+Detail.htm?CS_ProductID=015-8611-56X&CS_Category=SEducationalAssessment&CS_Catalog=TPC-USCatalog

Harcourt Assessment. (2004c). *Miller Analogies Test technical manual: Guide to interpretation.* San Antonio, TX: Author.

Harcourt Assessment. (2005a). Wechsler Individual Achievement Test®—Second Edition (WIAT®–II). Retrieved on February 9, 2005, from http://harcourtassessment.com/haiweb/Cultures/en-US/Products/Product+Detail.htm?CS_ProductID=015-8983-262&CS_Category=AchievementBasicSkills&CS_Catalog=TPC-USCatalog

Harcourt Assessment. (2005b). The Miller Analogies Test. Retrieved on February 9, 2005, from http://harcourtassessment.com/haiweb/Cultures/en-US/dotCom/milleranalogies/MillerAnalogies.com.htm

Harrington, T. F. (1995). Assessment of abilities (Report No. EDO-CG-95-12). Greensboro, NC: ERIC Clearinghouse on Counseling and Student Services (ERIC Document Reproduction Service No. ED 389-960).

Harrison, P., & Lee, S. (1988). Review of the Emotional or Behavior Disorder Scale. In J. C. Impara and B. S. Plake (Eds.), *The Thirteenth Mental Measurements Yearbook* (pp. 413–417). Lincoln, NE: Buros Institute of Mental Measurements.

Hartman, N., McDaniel, M., & Whetzel, D. (2004). Racial and ethnic difference in performance. In J. Wall & G. Watz (Eds.), *Measuring up: Assessment issues for teachers, counselors, and admin-*

istrators (pp. 99–115). Greensboro, NC: CAPS Press.

Harvey, V. (1997). Improving readability of psychological reports. *Professional Psychology: Research and Practice, 28,* 271–274.

Harwell, M., & Lukin, L. (2005). Review of the Metropolitan Achievement Tests Eighth Edition. *The Sixteenth Mental Measurements Yearbook.* Retrieved on November 14, 2004, from http://gateway.ut.ovid.com/gw1/ovidweb.cgi

Hattrup, K. (2003). Review of the California Psychological Inventory™ Third Edition. In B. S. Plake, J. C. Imapara, and R. A Spies (Eds.), *The Fifteenth Mental Measurements Yearbook* (pp. 161–163). Lincoln, NE: Buros Institute of Mental Measurements.

Hattrup, K., & Schmitt, N. (1995). Review of the Differential Aptitude Test, Fifth Edition. In J. C. Conoley and J. C. Impara (Eds.), *The Twelfth Mental Measurements Yearbook* (pp. 301–305). Lincoln, NE: Buros Institute of Mental Measurements.

Hersen, M., & Van Hasselt, V. B. (2001). (Eds.). *Advanced abnormal psychology* (2nd ed.). New York: Plenum Press.

Hewitt, M., & Homan, S. (1991). Readability. In R. A. Thompson (Ed.), *Classroom reading instruction* (pp. 305–318). Dubuque, IA: Kendall/Hunt.

Hill, C. E. (Ed.). (2004). *Dream work in therapy: Facilitating exploration, insight, and action.* Washington, DC: American Psychological Association.

Hinkle, S. (1994a). *Psychodiagnosis for counselors: The DSM-IV* (Report No. MF01/PC01). Greensboro, NC: ERIC Clearinghouse on Counseling and Student Services (ERIC Document Reproduction Service No. ED 366-890).

Hinkle, S. (1994b). The DSM-IV: Prognosis and implications for mental health counselors. *Journal of Mental Health Counseling, 16*(2), 174–183.

Hohenshil, T. H. (1993a). Teaching the DSM-III-R in counselor education. *Counselor Education and Supervision, 32,* 267–275.

Hohenshil, T. H. (1993b). Assessment and diagnosis. *Journal of Counseling and Development, 72,* 7.

Hohenshil, T. H. (1994). DSM-IV: What's new? *Journal of Counseling & Development, 73,* 105–107.

Holland, J. L. (1994). *The self-directed search* (rev. ed.). Odessa, FL: Psychological Assessment Resources.

Homan, S., & Hewitt, M. (1983). *Cross-validation of the new Homan-Hewitt Readability Formula.* Paper presented at the Annual Meeting of the National Council on Measurement in Education, Montreal, Canada.

Homan, S., Hewitt, M., & Linder, J. (1994). The development and validation of a formula for measuring single-sentence test item readability. *Journal of Educational Measurement, 31,* 349–358.

House, J., & Johnson, S. (1993a). Predictive validity of the Graduate Record Examination Advanced Psychology Test for graduate grades. *Psychology Reports, 73*(1), 184–186.

House, J., & Johnson, S. (1993b). Graduate Record Examination scores and academic background variables as predictors of graduate degree completion. *Educational and Psychological Measurement, 53,* 551–556.

Jaffee v. Redmond, 518 U.S. 1 (U.S. Supreme Ct., 1996).

Jagger, L., Neukrug, E., & McAuliffe, G. (1992). Congruence between personality traits and chosen occupation as a predictor of job satisfaction for people with disabilities. *Rehabilitation Counseling Bulletin, 36,* 53–60.

Joint Committee on Testing Practices (JCTP). (2002). Code of fair testing practices in education. Washington, DC: American Psychological Association.

Jongsma, A. E., Jr., & Peterson, L. M. (1999). *The complete adult psychotherapy treatment planner* (2nd ed.). New York: Wiley.

Juhnke, G. A. (1995). Mental health counseling assessment: Broadening one's understanding of the client and the client's presenting concerns. (Report No. EDO-CG-95-3). Greensboro, NC: ERIC Clearinghouse on Counseling and Student Services (ERIC Document Reproduction Service No. ED388883).

Jung, C. (1964). *Psychological types* (Trans. H. G. Baynes). London, England: Pantheon. (Original work published in 1921.)

Jung, C., & Riklin, F. (1904). Untersuchungen über assoziationen gesunder. *Journal für Psychologie uünd Neurologie, 3,* 55–83.

Kamphaus, R. (2001). Review of the Metropolitan Readiness Test Sixth Edition. In B. S. Plake and J. C. Impara (Eds.), *The Fourteenth Mental Measurements Yearbook* (pp. 747–749). Lincoln, NE: Buros Institute of Mental Measurements.

Kaplan, R. M., & Saccuzzo, D. P. (2001). *Psychological testing: Principles, applications, and issues* (5th ed.). Pacific Grove: Brooks/Cole.

Karon, B. (2000). The clinical interpretation of the Thematic Apperception Test, Rorschach, and other clinical data: A reexamination of statistical versus clinical prediction. *Professional Psychology: Research and Practice, 31,* 230–233.

Kelly, K. (2003). Review of the Strong Interest Inventory. In B. S. Plake, J. C. Impara and R. A Spies (Eds), *The Fifteenth Mental Measurements Yearbook* (pp. 893–897). Lincoln, NE: Buros Institute of Mental Measurements.

Kim, J., & Suen, H. K. (2000). The Relationship between Early Assessment of Children and Later Achievement: A Validity Generalization Study. Paper presented at the annual meeting of the American Educational Research Association, New Orleans, LA.

Kingsbury, G. (2001). Review of the KeyMath Revised: A diagnostic inventory of essential mathematics [1998 normative update]. In B. S. Plake and J. C. Impara (Eds.), *The Fourteenth Mental Measurements Yearbook* (pp. 638–640). Lincoln, NE: Buros Institute of Mental Measurements.

Kitchener, K. S. (1984). Intuition, critical evaluation and ethical principles: The foundation for ethical decisions in counseling psychology. *The Counseling Psychologist, 12*(3), 43–45.

Kitchener, K. S. (1986). Teaching applied ethics in counselor education: An integration of psychological processes and philosophical analysis. *Journal of Counseling and Development, 64*(5), 306–311.

Knapp, T., & Brown, J. (1995). Ten measurement commandments that often should be broken. *Research in Nursing & Health, 18,* 465–469.

Koenig, J., & Wiley, A. (1996). The validity of the Medical College Admission Test for predicting performance in the first two years of medical school. *Academic Medicine, 71,* S83–S85.

Law School Admissions Council (LSAC). (2004a). Test score accuracy: Reliability and standard error of measurement. Retrieved June 6, 2004, from http://www.lsac.org/LSAC.asp?url=/additional-info/lsat-scores-as-predictors.asp

Law School Admissions Council (LSAC). (2004b). LSAT scores as a predictor to law school performance. Retrieved June 6, 2004, from http://www.lsac.org/LSAC.asp?url=/additional-info/lsat-scores-as-predictors.asp

Learning Express. (2001). Postal worker exam (2nd ed.). Retrieved June 12, 2004, from http://www.learnatest.com/shop/BookDetail.cfm?coreID=1576853314&type=B&seqNum=0&mbc=POST&sbc=POSTAL

Lohman, D., & Hagen, E. (2002). *CogAT form 6 research handbook.* Itasca, IL: Riverside Publishing.

Mabry, L. (1995). Review of the Wide Range Achievement Test 3. In J. C. Conoley and J. C. Impara (Eds.), *The Twelfth Mental Measurements Yearbook* (pp. 1106–1110). Lincoln, NE: Buros Institute of Mental Measurements.

Mabry, L., & Stoner, G. (1995). Review of the Metropolitan Readiness Tests, Fifth Edition. In J. C. Conoley and J. C. Impara (Eds.), *The Twelfth Mental Measurements Yearbook* (pp. 612–614). Lincoln, NE: Buros Institute of Mental Measurements.

Manduchi, J., & Yazak, D. (2001). Review of the Comprehensive Assessment of School Environments Information Management System. In B. S. Plake and J. C. Impara (Eds.), *The Fourteenth Mental Measurements Yearbook* (pp. 306–308). Lincoln, NE: Buros Institute of Mental Measurements.

Markwardt, F. C. (1989). Peabody Individual Achievement Test – Revised. Circle Pines, MN: AGS Publishing.

Mastrangelo, P. (2001). Review of the Myers-Briggs Type Indicator Form M. In B. S. Plake and J. C. Impara (Eds.), *The Fourteenth Mental Measurements Yearbook* (pp. 818–819). Lincoln, NE: Buros Institute of Mental Measurements.

McAuliffe, G., Eriksen, K., & Associates. (2000). *Preparing counselors and therapists: Creating constructivist and developmental programs.* Virginia Beach, VA: The Donning Company.

Medical College Admissions Test (MCAT). (2003). Characteristics of examinees and summary data.

Combined April/August 2003 MCAT. Retrieved June 6, 2004, from http://www.aamc.org/students/mcat/examineedata/pubs.htm

Mertens, D. (1976). Expectations of teachers-in-training: The influence of a student's sex and a behavioral vs. descriptive approach in a biased psychological report. *Journal of School Psychology, 14,* 223–229.

Meyer, G. J.,Finn, S. E., Eyde, L. D., Kay, G. G., Moreland, K. L., Dies, R. R., et al. (2001). Psychological testing and psychological assessment: A review of evidence and issues. *American Psychologist, 56,* 128–165.

Miner, J. (1922). An aid to the analysis of vocational interest. *Journal of Educational Research, 5,* 311–323.

Minton, H. (1988). *Lewis M. Terman: Pioneer in psychological testing.* New York: New York University Press.

Moreland, K., & Werner, P. (2001). Review of the Sentence Completion Series. In B. S. Plake and J. C. Impara (Eds.), *The Fourteenth Mental Measurements Yearbook* (pp. 1109–1110). Lincoln, NE: Buros Institute of Mental Measurements.

Naglieri, J., Obrzut, J. E., & Boliek, C. (1992). Review of the Bender Gestalt Test. In J. J. Kramer and J. C. Conoley (Eds.), *The Eleventh Mental Measurements Yearbook* (pp. 101–106). Lincoln, NE: Buros Institute of Mental Measurements.

NCS Pearson. (2004). MCMI-III: Millon Clinical Multiaxial Inventory-III. Retrieved on September 2, 2004, from http://www.pearsonassessments.com/tests/mcmi_3.htm

NCS Pearson. (2005a). CISS: Campbell Interest and Skill Survey. Retrieved on February 10, 2005, from http://www.pearsonassessments.com/tests/ciss.htm

NCS Pearson. (2005b). Career Assessment Inventory – The Enhanced Version. Retrieved on February 10, 2005, from http://www.pearsonassessments.com/tests/cai_e.htm

NCS Pearson. (2005c). MACI: Millon Adolescent Clinical Inventory. Retrieved on February 10, 2005, from http://www.pearsonassessments.com/tests/maci.htm

NCS Pearson. (2005d). 16PF Fifth Edition. Retrieved on February 9, 2005, from http://www.pearsonassessments.com/tests/sixtpf_5.htm

National Association of School Psychologists (NASP). (2000). Standards for training and field placement programs in school psychology. Retrieved on April 14, 2005, from http://nasponline.org/certification/FinalStandards.pdf

National Education Association (NEA). (2002–2004). "No Child Left Behind" Act/ESEA. Retrieved on May 21, 2004, from http://www.nea.org/esea/

Neisser, U., Boodoo, G., Bouchard, T., Boykin, A. W., Brody, N., Ceci, S. J., et al. (1996). Intelligence: Knowns and unknowns. *American Psychologist, 51*(2), 77–101.

Neukrug, E., Lovell, C., & Parker, R. (1996). Employing ethical codes and decision-making models: A developmental process. *Counseling and Values, 40,* 98–106.

Neukrug, E., & Schwitzer, A. (2006). Skills and tools for today's counselors and psychotherapists: From natural helping to professional counseling. Pacific Grove, CA: Brooks/Cole.

Novak, C. (2001). Review of the Metropolitan Readiness Test, Sixth Edition. In B. S. Plake and J. C. Impara (Eds.), *The Fourteenth Mental Measurements Yearbook* (pp. 747–749). Lincoln, NE: Buros Institute of Mental Measurements.

Ownby, R. (1997). Psychological reports: A guide to report writing in professional psychology (3rd ed.). New York: Wiley.

Parsons, F. (1909). *Choosing a vocation.* Boston: Houghton Mifflin.

Parsons, F. (1989). *Choosing a vocation.* Garrett Park, MD: Garrett Park. (Reprint of 1909 version.)

Pennebaker, J., & King, L. (1999). Linguistic styles: Language use as an individual difference. *Journal of Personality and Social Psychology, 77,* 1296–1312.

Peterson, C., & Reinehr, R. (1998). Review of the EPS Sentence Completion Technique. In J. C. Impara and B. S. Plake (Eds.), *The Thirteenth Mental Measurements Yearbook* (pp. 423–426). Lincoln, NE: Buros Institute of Mental Measurements.

Piaget, J. (1950). *The psychology of intelligence* (M. Piercy & D. Berlyne, Trans.). London: Routledge & Kegan Paul Ltd.

Plake, B., & Conoley, J. (1995). *Using Buros Institute of Mental Measurements materials in counseling and therapy.* Greensboro, NC: ERIC Clearinghouse on Counseling and Student Services (ERIC Document Reproduction Service No. ED 391 987).

Plake, B., Conoley, J., Kramer, J., & Murphy, L. (1991). The Buros Institute of Mental Measurements: Comment to the tradition of excellence. *Journal of Counseling and Development, 69,* 449–455.

Polanski, P. J., & Hinkle, J. S. (2000). The mental status examination: Its use by professional counselors. *Journal of Counseling and Development, 78,* 357–364.

Powers, D. (1988). Incidence, correlates, and possible causes of test anxiety in graduate admission testing. *Advances in Personality Assessment, 7,* 49–75.

Psychological Assessment Resources, Inc. (PAR). (2001). Welcome to the Self-Directed Search by John L. Holland. Retrieved on July 25, 2004, from http://www.self-directed-search.com/index.html

Psytech. (n.d.). The technical test battery: the technical manual. Retrieved on June 12, 2004, from http://www.psytech.co.uk/downloads/manuals/ttbman.pdf

Quenk, N. (2000). *Essentials of Myers-Briggs Type Indicator assessment.* New York: Wiley.

Radocy, R. (1998). Review of the Iowa Test of Music Literacy Revised. In J. C. Impara and B. S. Plake (Eds.), *The Thirteenth Mental Measurements Yearbook* (pp. 552–555). Lincoln, NE: Buros Institute of Mental Measurements.

Remley, R. P., Herlihy, B., & Herlihy, S. B. (1997). The U.S. Supreme Court decision in *Jaffe v. Redmond*: Implications for counselors. *Journal of Counseling and Development, 75,* 213–218.

Reynolds, J. F., Mair, D. C., & Fischer, P. C. (1995). *Writing and reading mental health records: Issues and analysis* (2nd ed.). Mahwah, NJ: Erlbaum Associates.

Richman, W., Kiesler, S., Weisb, S., & Drasgow, F. (1999). A meta-analytic study of social desirability distortion in computer-administered questionnaires, traditional questionnaires, and interviews. *Journal of Applied Psychology, 84,* 754–775.

Riverside Publishing. (2004a). Stanford-Binet Intelligence Scales, Fifth Edition. Retrieved on April 21, 2004, from http://www.riverpub.com/products/clinical/sbis5/features.html

Riverside Publishing. (2004b). Woodcock-Johnson III (WJ III) Complete Battery overview. Retrieved on February 9, 2005, from http://www.riverpub.com/products/clinical/wj3/complete.html

Riverside Publishing. (2004c). The Cognitive Abilities Test (CogAT), Form 6. Retrieved June 5, 2004, from http://www.riverpub.com/products/group/cogat6/overview.html

Riverside Publishing. (2004d). Bender Visual-Motor Gestalt Test, Second Edition: Technical qualities. Retrieved on July 15, 2004, from http://www.riverpub.com/products/clinical/bg/technical.html.

Roback, A. (1961). *History of psychology and psychiatry.* New York: Philosophical Library.

Robinson, T., & Howard-Hamilton, M. (2000). *The convergence of race, ethnicity, and gender: Multiple identities in counseling.* Upper Saddle River, NJ: Prentice-Hall.

Rogers, B. (1992). Review of the Peabody Individual Achievement Test – Revised. In J. J. Kramer and J. C. Conoley (Eds.), *The Eleventh Mental Measurements Yearbook* (pp. 652–654). Lincoln, NE: Buros Institute of Mental Measurements.

Rogers, B. (2001). Review of the Wechsler Adult Intelligence Scale, Third Edition. In B. S. Plake and J. C. Impara (Eds.), *The Fourteenth Mental Measurement Yearbook* (pp. 1336–1340). Lincoln, NE: Buros Institute of Mental Measurements.

Roid, G. (2003). *Stanford-Binet intelligence scales, fifth edition, technical manual.* Itasca, IL: Riverside Publishing.

Rorschach, H. (1942). *Psychodiagnostics.* (P. V. Lamkau, Trans.). Bern, Switzerland: Verlag Hans Huber.

Roth, P., Bevier, C., Bobko, P., Switzer, F., & Tyler, P. (2001). Ethnic group differences in cognitive ability in employment and educational settings: A meta-analysis. *Personnel Psychology, 54,* 297–330.

Roth, P., Van Iddekinge, C., Huffcutt, A., Eidson, C., & Bobko, P. (2002). Corrections for range restriction in structured interview ethnic group differences: The values may be larger than researchers thought. *Journal of Applied Psychology, 87,* 369–376.

Rowley, G. (1976). The reliability of observational measures. *American Educational Research Journal, 13,* 51–59.

Salkind, N. J. (2004). Statistics for people who (think they) hate statistics (2nd ed.). Thousand Oaks, CA: Sage Publications.

Schinka, J. A. (2003). *Mental status checklist–adult.* Lutz, FL: Psychological Assessment Resources.

Schwartz, N., & Wilkinson, W. (1987). Perceptual influence of psychoeducational reports. *Psychology in the Schools, 24,* 127–135.

Schwitzer, A. M. (1996). Using the inverted pyramid heuristic in counselor education and supervision. *Counselor Education and Supervision, 35,* 258–267.

Schwitzer, A. M., & Everett, A. (1997). Reintroducing the *DSM-IV:* Responses to ten counselor reservations about diagnosis. *The Virginia Counselors Journal, 25,* 54–64.

Segal, D. L., & Coolidge, F. L. (2001). Diagnosis and classification. In M. Hersen & V. B. Van Hasselt (Eds.), *Advanced abnormal psychology* (2nd ed.) (pp. 5–22). New York: Kluwer Academic/ Plenum Publishers

Seligman, L. (1999). Twenty years of diagnosis and the DSM. *Journal of Mental Health Counseling, 21,* 229–239.

Seligman, L. (2004). *Diagnosis and treatment planning in counseling* (3rd ed.). New York: Plenum.

Shapiro, F. (2001). *Eye movement desensitization and reprocessing: Basic principles, protocols and procedures* (2nd ed.). New York: Guilford Press.

Southwest Educational Development Laboratory (SEDL). (2000). Kindergarten Readiness Test. Retrieved on November 14, 2004, from http://www.sedl.org/cgi-bin/mysql/rad.cgi?searchid=57

Spearman, C. (1910). Correlation calculated from faulty data. *British Journal of Psychology, 3,* 271–295.

Spearman, C. (1970). *The abilities of man.* New York: AMS Press. (Original work published in 1932.)

Strong, E. (1926). An interest test for personnel managers. *Journal of Personnel Research, 5,* 194–203.

Sturges, J. (1998). Practical use of technology in professional practice. *Professional Psychology: Research and Practice, 29,* 183–188.

Sundberg, N. (1961). The practice of psychological testing in clinical services in the United States. *American Psychologist, 16,* 79–83.

Sutton, R., & Knight, C. (1995). Review of the Kindergarten Readiness Test. In J. C. Conoley and J. C. Impara (Eds.), *The Twelfth Mental Measurements Yearbook* (pp. 538–541). Lincoln, NE: Buros Institute of Mental Measurements.

Swenson, L. (1997). *Psychology and law for the helping professions* (2nd ed.). Pacific Grove, CA: Brooks/Cole.

Tapping into multiple intelligences (n.d.). *What is the theory of multiple intelligences (M. I.)?* Retrieved June 16, 2004, from http://www.thirteen.org/edonline/concept2class/month1/

Thompson, R. (1999). Reliability generalization: An important meta-analytic method, because it is incorrect to say, "The test is unreliable." Paper presented at the Annual Meeting of the Southwest Educational Research Association, San Antonio, TX.

Thorndike, R. (1997). *Measurement and evaluation in psychology and education* (6th ed.). Upper Saddle River, NJ: Simon & Schuster.

Thorndike, R., & Lohman, D. (1990). *A century of ability testing.* Chicago: Riverside.

Thurstone, L. (1938). *Primary mental abilities.* Chicago: University of Chicago Press.

Ton, M., & Hansen, J. (2001). Using a person-environment fit framework to predict satisfaction and motivation in work and marital roles. *Journal of Career Assessment, 9*(4), 315–331.

Tucker-Ladd, C. (2000). Psychological self-help. *Mental Health Net.* Retrieved February 7, 2005, from http://mentalhelp.net/psyhelp/chap2/chap2k.htm

Ullman, M., & Zimmerman, N. (1979). *Working with dreams.* New York: Delacorte Press.

U.S. Census Bureau. (n.d.). U.S. and world population clocks. Retrieved April 3, 2004, from www.census.gov/main/www/popclock.html

U.S. Department of Education. (n.d.a). *Overview of the No Child Left Behind Act of 2001.* Retrieved

February 22, 2004, from http://www.ed.gov/nclb/overview/intro/index.html

U.S. Department of Education. (n.d.b). *Stronger accountability: Questions and answers on No Child Left Behind.* Retrieved on April 21, 2004, from http://www.ed.gov/nclb/accountability/schools/accountability.html

U.S. Department of Health and Human Services. (n.d.). *Prohibited discriminatory acts.* Retrieved October 12, 2004, from http://www.os.dhhs.gov/ocr/504.html

U.S. Department of Health and Human Services. (2003). *HIPAA.* Retrieved August 7, 2003, from the http://www.hhs.gov/ocr/hipaa/

Vacc, N. A. (1982). A conceptual framework for continuous assessment of clients. *Measurement and Evaluation in Guidance, 15*(1), 40–47.

Valpar. (2005). SIGI PLUS: Educational and Career Planning Software. Retrieved on February 10, 2005, from http://www.valparint.com/

Vernon, P. (1961). *The structure of human abilities* (2nd ed.). London: Methuen.

Wakefield, J. C. (1992). The concept of mental disorder: On the boundary between biological facts and social values. *American Psychologist, 47,* 373–388.

Walsh, W. B., & Betz, N. (2001). Test and assessment (4th ed.). Upper Saddle River, NJ: Prentice Hall.

Ward, A. (1995). Review of the Wide Range Achievement Test III. In J. C. Conoley and J. C. Impara (Eds.), *The Twelfth Mental Measurements Yearbook* (pp. 1110–1111). Lincoln, NE: Buros Institute of Mental Measurements.

Watkins, C. E., Jr., & Campbell, V. L. (1990). Testing and assessment in counseling psychology: Contemporary developments and issues. *The Counseling Psychologist, 18*(2), 189–197.

Watson, R. (1968). *The great psychologists from Aristotle to Freud.* Philadelphia: Lippincott.

Wechsler, D. (2003a). WISC-IV administration and scoring. San Antonio, TX: Harcourt Assessment.

Wechsler, D. (2003b). WISC-IV technical and interpretive manual. San Antonio, TX: Harcourt Assessment.

Weddig, R. (1984). Parental interpretation of psychoeducational reports. *Psychology in the Schools, 21,* 477–481.

Wiener, J., & Kohler, S. (1986). Parents' comprehension of psychological reports. *Psychology in the Schools, 23,* 265–269.

Wilkinson, G. S. (1993).The Wide Range Achievement Test—III. Wilmington, DE: Jastak.

Wilson, S., Becker, L., & Tinker, R. (1995). Eye movement desensitization and reprocessing (EMDR) treatment for psychologically traumatized individuals. *Journal of Consulting and Clinical Psychology, 63,* 928–937.

Wilson, V., & Wing, H. (1995). Review of the Differential Aptitude Test for Personnel and Career Assessment. In J. C. Conoley and J. C. Impara (Eds.), *The Twelfth Mental Measurements Yearbook* (pp. 305–309). Lincoln, NE: Buros Institute of Mental Measurements.

Wollack, J. (2001). Review of the KeyMath Revised: A diagnostic inventory of essential mathematics [1998 normative update]. In B. S. Plake and J. C. Impara (Eds.), *The Fourteenth Mental Measurements Yearbook* (pp. 640–641). Lincoln, NE: Buros Institute of Mental Measurements.

Wolpe, J. (1991). *The practice of behavior therapy* (4th ed.). New York: Pergamon Press.

Yalom, I. (2002). *The gift of therapy: An open letter to a new generation of therapists and their patients.* New York: HarperCollins.

Zuckerman, E. (2003). *The paper office: Forms, guidelines, and resources to make your practice work ethically, legally, and profitably* (3rd ed.). New York: Guilford Press.

Zusne, L. (1984). *Biographical dictionary of psychology.* Westport, CT: Greenwood.

Zytowski, D. G. (1994). Tests and counseling: We are still married and living in discriminant analysis. *Measurement and Evaluation in Guidance, 15,* 15–21.

Index